Violence in Schools
Cross-National and Cross-Cultural Perspectives

Edited by

Florence L. Denmark
Pace University
New York, New York

Herbert H. Krauss
Pace University
New York, New York

Robert W. Wesner
Psychological Dimensions, Inc.
New York, New York

Elizabeth Midlarsky
Columbia University
New York, New York

and

Uwe P. Gielen
St. Francis College
Brooklyn, New York

 Springer

Library of Congress Cataloging-in-Publication Data

Violence in schools : cross-national and cross-cultural perspectives / edited by
    Florence L. Denmark ... [et al.].
        p. cm.
    Includes bibliographical references and index.
    ISBN 0-387-23199-4
    1. School violence—Cross-cultural studies.   I. Denmark, Florence.

LB3013.3.V586 2005
371.7'82—dc22   2004063215

A C.I.P. Catalogue record for this book is available
from the Library of Congress.

ISBN-10: 0-387-23199-4   Printed on acid-free paper.
ISBN-13: 9-780-387-23199-0

Printed in the United States of America.

9 8 7 6 5 4 3 2 1   (TB/IBT)

springeronline.com

To all of the professionals concerned with understanding,
preventing, and reducing school violence

Foreword

Laura Barbanel

Violence in Schools: Cross-National and Cross-Cultural Perspectives is an important and timely book. Over the past decade, youth violence, particularly violence in the schools, has become a serious national and international concern. The social response has often been to focus on harsher sentences and greater discipline. But getting tough with juvenile offenders by trying them as adults, thought to reduce the likelihood that they will commit more crimes, does not necessarily work. Youths transferred to adult criminal court have, in fact, significantly higher rates of subsequent felonies than those who remain in juvenile courts. Rather than treating school violence as a police matter only, we need to think of it as a public health matter. The U.S. Surgeon-General released a report on Youth Violence (2001) redefining this issue as a public health issue. From a health point of view, we know that although antibiotics are an important contribution to public health, inoculation is even more important. Clearly, in the area of school violence it is important for us to formulate strategies for prevention.

When we think of school violence we usually think of those incidents that are covered in the media. School murders by students are the most notorious and are attended to by the media in a way that rivets public attention. It alarms parents and educators and gets the general public concerned. In fact, violence among children and youth is one of those things that many adults think of as symptomatic of the decay of society. Are our schools more violent than they were in the past? Is this symptomatic of an increasingly violent society? A variety of statistical surveys have been done, most pointing to the fact that school violence as a whole has decreased. The Surgeon General's report indicates that the risk of school violence has not changed substantially over the last two decades.

What has increased is the perception by parents and children that their schools are not safe, and that they are at risk for nonviolent victimization. Bullying and fights are the things that children fear the most about their schools. This goes along with an increased perception that the adults in their environment don't care and cannot or will not do anything to protect them. Despite the dramatic incidents that have occurred, children are actually less likely to become victims of crime in their schools than in their homes or neighborhoods. But the perception is otherwise.

WHAT IS SCHOOL VIOLENCE?

Although most of us think of mass murder as the key descriptor of school violence, school violence is about a range of things from bullying to aggravated assault, from suicide to homicide. *Suicide* is a form of violent behavior, and a significant number of mass murderers have contemplated suicide before thinking about murder. If we understand suicide as involving the lessening of inhibition around aggression, then we can see the importance of suicide and suicidal gestures as important risk factors for other kinds of violence. *Nonfatal victimization* and *fights* are the types of violent behavior that students complain about the most. The Center for Disease Control (CDC) (1999) reported that nearly 15% of students polled state that they have been in one or more physical fights in the last 12 months. Males are more likely to report a fight on school property than females (2 to 1 ratio) and students in lower grades (ninth grade and below) are more likely to be in a fight on school property than students in higher grades. *Assaults against teachers* are a form of school violence that needs serious attention. *Bullying*, which has become a serious concern as of late, has been variously defined, at times including relatively benign forms of social interactions and elsewhere considering more serious forms which threaten bodily harm. It would appear that painting all types of teasing with the same tar brush might be counterproductive.

This book, composed of a collection of chapters from experts from all over the world, attempts to explore many of the questions that come up in this field. The editors, Florence L. Denmark, Herbert H. Krauss, Robert W. Wesner, Elizabeth Midlarsky, and Uwe P. Gielen are all well known in their respective fields. The assembly of authors from various countries makes it clear that the issues are not unique to the United States, but is on the international stage as well. The book explores the history of violence, ways of coping with it in schools, and, most important, ways of preventing it.

CAUSES

There are many explanations offered for school violence. Most of these explanations are speculative, but also instructive. In thinking about the teen years, where the greatest number of violent incidents are reported, we know that the following characteristics are associated with these years: impulsivity, searching for a place for oneself; idealism and extremism; highly developed fantasy; and violence as a compensatory mechanism. Add to these features the stage-specific dynamics, the exposure to violence in the family and the community, drug or alcohol use, the availability of firearms, prejudice based on difference, and the inability to resolve conflict in any way other than physical and the resulting mix is lethal.

PREVENTION

There are programs all over the United States that are set up with violence prevention in mind. The Surgeon General's report contains a list of model programs, but we do not hear about these programs in the media because violence prevention is not newsworthy. In many such programs, the students feel supported and understand that the "grown-ups" need to be told when there is a concern that another student is at risk for becoming violent. These students have learned that there are some principles that are more important than not "tattling" and, therefore, with this understanding, they have averted dangerous situations. New York State has a "Save Schools" program where teachers and pupil personnel workers are required to have two hours of instruction in "violence prevention."

What characterizes a good program? Successful programs are collaborative and systemic—that is, the whole school, perhaps the whole district, must be involved in the program. It is valuable if a classroom teacher institutes a conflict resolution course. These children will benefit and grow with the shared experience. If it is not something that fits in with the entire school program—if it is not systemic—then it will not serve the purpose that we wish it to, that is, the prevention of violence in the school.

WHO SHOULD BE INCLUDED IN THE PROGRAM?

All of the members of the school community must be included in the plan: students, teachers, administrators, pupil personnel workers, other staff in the school, the school board, security professionals, and community groups. For a program to be successful, all of the people who are involved must feel some kind of ownership. Policies and procedures cannot be developed by the administrators and then dictated. Students need to feel that they belong to a community that cares, even as parents need to feel that their input is valued.

Parents frequently feel that the schools are not the least bit interested in their input and that they are frequently the last to know about what is going on in their childrens' lives. Staff has to feel safe in the school and administrators must enforce the rules that impact on the safety of their staff. Teachers must be helped to learn how to manage their classrooms to make the climate of the classroom safe. Important in any program is finding the positive incentives, that is, reward and recognition for positive behavior.

School violence is complex and requires a complex and multi-faceted approach. There are many programs and pathways available. Most important, the school should not simply choose any program but also collaborate on developing a program. It is important for there to be an open dialogue in this development. And finally, it is critical that we believe that our efforts can be successful. Each of the authors in this book deals with a part of this complex whole. Putting all of the pieces presented herein together makes a gestalt that moves our understanding along as well as our belief that we can be successful.

References

Department of Health and Human Services. (2001). *Youth violence: A report of the Surgeon General*. Washington, D.C.: U.S. Government Printing Office.

Center for Disease Control and Prevention (1999). *Ten great public health achievements-United States, 1900–1999*. Morbidity and Mortality Weekly Report, 48, 241–243.

Acknowledgments

We wish to acknowledge the valuable contributions made by the following individuals. We are extremely grateful to Melissa Laracuenta, who co-authored "What Can We Do About School Violence?" and helped with the organization of this volume. We also wish to thank James Pride, who gave considerable assistance in compiling this volume. We thank the Springer editor, Judy Jones, who stayed on top of this project.

We also wish to acknowledge the following institutions: the New York Academy of Sciences, which supported us in coming together to present a workshop on this topic; the International Organization for the Study of Group Tensions, which cosponsored the workshop; and the Psychology Department at Pace University for its additional sponsorship of the conference and its provision of resources used in the preparation of this volume.

Contents

Chapter 1

Violence in the Schools
An Introduction

THE EDITORS

Violence has occurred in schools throughout recorded history (Aries, 1962). Although the rate of violent crime involving youth, whether in or outside of the schools is not currently "spinning out of control," it is, and ought to be, of great concern. Over the course of the twentieth century, the nature of student "problem behavior" has changed from small irritations to serious and increasingly dangerous actions. Thus, while in the 1940s, teachers reported the most important school problems to be excessive noise, littering, and gum chewing, by the 1980s, these problems had been displaced by rape, robbery, and substance abuse. By the 1990s, substantial numbers of both teachers and students reported being afraid to go to school (Lexington Herald Leader, 1993).

Indeed, graphic images of young people sprawled bleeding on school playgrounds or crowding into hospital emergency rooms clutching their gunshot wounds have shaken deeply held beliefs about the meaning and significance of childhood and adolescence. In contrast to the mistaken impressions that youth is typically a period of protected innocence, children and adolescents are more frequently victims of crime than any other age group in the United States (Rennison, 1999). Moreover, in contrast to violence in the earlier part of the twentieth century, today's violence is more apt to be lethal and more likely to occur in places once thought to be safe, including schools (Elliott, Hamburt, & Williams, 1998). In addition to inhibiting development and learning, and either directly or indirectly

1

increasing feelings of anxiety and vulnerability in those subjected to it, violence begets further violence as victims become bullies, and worse (Baldry, 2003; Haynie et al., 2001).

Setting aside for the moment the question of whether the rates of violence against children and the incidence and prevalence of psychopathology in that sub-population have actually been on the upswing, it is clear that they are intolerably high. No one seems to doubt that we and our children have been and continue to be submerged in a sea of economic insecurity, class distinctions, and invidious ethnic, sub-cultural and gender discrimination which compromise the life chances of those who experience them (e.g., Hochshild, 2003; Ostrove & Cole, 2003; Teitz & Chapple, 1998). It has been argued that we and our children live in an era in which family life has deteriorated (Parkman, 1995) and in which we are bombarded with images of interpersonal conflict and violence. Of the latter, our children receive a double dose via the media and through video-games (Anderson & Bushman, 2001; Anderson & Bushman, 2002; Bushman & Anderson, 2001).

The milieu in which our children currently reside is certainly not bereft of its positive elements. Nevertheless, even if we grant that certain features of our children's lives have improved in recent decades, it is clear that other features, including many that are critical for children's well-being, have gotten significantly worse. So much have conditions deteriorated that Garbarino (1995), for one, believes our children are living in a *socially toxic environment*. By coining and applying that phrase he means "that the social context of children, the social world in which they live, has become poisonous to their development" (Garbarino, 1995, p. 3). To continue his metaphor, as the water we fish and the seas and the soil we farm become dangerously polluted, so, too, has our social environment become increasingly unwholesome. To Garbarino,

> The social equivalents of lead and smoke in the air, PCBs in the water, and pesticides in the food chain include violence, poverty and other economic pressures, depression, trauma, despair, nastiness, and alienation. These forces contaminate children and youth [and the rest of us] and are the elements of social toxicity. (Garbarino, 1995, p. 4)

Predictably, the children whose developmental paths are most likely to be deformed and compromised by these pollutants are those who have been most extensively exposed to them.

> As the social environment becomes more toxic, it is the most vulnerable children who show the effects first, those who have accumulated the most developmental risk factors. These risk factors include being a single parent, poverty, racism, drug addiction or alcoholism, trauma from violence, and emotional problems that impair parenting. ... [I]t is not the presence of any one or even two of these risk factors but their accumulation that developmentally disables children. Such

> accumulation overwhelms the child – particularly when it occurs without a
> parallel accumulation of opportunity factors. Once overwhelmed, children are
> likely to fall prey to the socially toxic influences that surround them. (Garbarino,
> 1995, p. 4)

Evidence from a variety of sources indicates that the social environment that we have constructed for our children, especially our male children, is noisome and that its toxicity, if anything, has increased. Margolin
and Gordis (2000) report, for example, that in some inner city neighborhoods approximately one-third of pre-teenage and teenage children have
been directly victimized by community violence, and all have been exposed to it. Of the two sexes, results of numerous studies indicate consistently that males are more likely than females to be involved in physical
aggression at school, both as perpetrators and as victims (Cornell & Loper,
1998; Furlong, Morrison, Chung, Bates, & Morrison, 1997). According to
the Centers for Disease Control and Prevention (1994$_a$) between 1985 and
1991, homicide among 15 to 19 year-old males increased one-and-a-half
times and was the second leading cause of death for this group. The increase in the rate of homicide for 15 to 19 year-old African American males
was even greater (Jenkins & Bell, 1992). This finding expectedly follows the
precept that what befalls non-African Americans has a magnified impact
on African American males, a group whose homicide rate was already ten
times that of whites and for whom homicide was already the leading cause
of death (Centers for Disease Control, 1994b). In fact, in regard to its rate
of youth homicide (11.0 per 100,000 for those between the ages of 10 and
29), the United States more closely resembles a developing country or one
in social upheaval (e.g., Ecuador, 15.9; Mexico, 15.3; Philippines, 12.2; Russian Federation, 18.0) than a stable Euro-system democracy (Canada, 1.7;
United Kingdom, 0.9; Denmark, 1.5; Germany, 0.8; France, 0.6; Australia,
1.6) (Krug, Dahlberg, Mercy, Zwi, & Lazano, 2002).

Garbarino (1995) cites the significant increase in the presence and intensity of emotional and behavioral problems experienced by American
children between 1974 and 1989 and the concomitant increase in the relative proportion of children judged as needing psychotherapy as found in
surveys conducted by Achenbach and Howell (1995), and he uses Achenbach's Child Behavior checklist (CBCL) as further support for the view
that the social environment in which children are raised has deteriorated.
While in 1976 about 10 percent of the children surveyed were judged to be
in need of psychological intervention (psychotherapy), by 1989 that proportion had risen to approximately 18 percent. The survey results further
indicate that in contrast to responses by children in 1976, children in 1989
were more likely to experience negative emotions (e.g., anxiety, sadness,
and distress) more frequently and intensely, and they reported liking school
less.

To a substantial degree, our schools are safe havens in contrast to our neighborhoods. Nonetheless they are not immune to many of the viruses that beset our culture. Schools participate in our culture wars, our sexism, racism, and classism (Achenbach & Howell, 1003; Cole & Omari, 2003; Hochschild, 2003; Ostrove & Cole, 2003; Teitz & Chapple, 1998). Because of its importance and the central role it plays in our society, some of our most well-meaning, best educated, most civic-minded, and brightest citizens are drawn to service in the educational establishment. However, as in the case of any institution of power that controls and dispenses influence, money, and jobs, our schools also attract men and women of lesser talents and meaner intentions. Thus, just as violence by pupils may reflect the results of the toxic environment in which children are raised, a further contribution to the problem of school violence may come from the inept and even cruel behavior by certain teachers in our schools (Turner, 2002).

If we focus only on physical violence, all evidence points to our schools as being among the safest places for children (Vossekuil, Reddy, Fein, Borum & Modzeleski, 2000). Less than one percent of violent deaths of children (either murder or suicide) occur on or around school property (Mulvey & Caufman, 2001). Furthermore, the rate of violence within our schools or during school activities has declined between 1993 and 2000 (Vossekuil et al., 2000), and the rate of criminal victimization taking place in schools remained constant between 1989 and 1995 (Snyder & Sickmund, 1999). However, that this is the case ought not to be taken to mean our schools are violence-free. The U.S. Department of Education (1997) estimated from the survey responses given by public school principals that during the period 1996 to 1997 approximately 4000 sexual batteries or rapes, 7000 robberies, and 11,000 attacks involving weapons took place during school sponsored events. There is every reason to assume that these figures greatly underestimate the scope of the problem. Were these figures not enough to set in motion a national public outcry about violence in our schools, the murders that have occurred at schools in Jefferson County (Columbine), Colorado; Jonesboro, Arkansas; West Paducah, Kentucky; and elsewhere have surely sufficed to do so. As Mulvey and Cauffman (2001, p. 797), suggest,

> As Joseph Stalin, of all people, noted in another time, "A single death is a tragedy, a million deaths is a statistic"... Unfortunately, there now may have been enough tragedies to precipitate action.

It should be noted that the school shootings that took place in the latter part of the 1990s and those which have occurred more recently had precursors. Excluding gang related and drug related incidents, the U.S. Secret Service in partnership with the U.S. Department of Education have identified 37 similar incidents involving 41 current or recent students who intentionally attacked, primarily with firearms, other students or school personnel in the period extending from 1974 to October 2000 (Vossekuil, et al., 2000). These incidents took place in 26 states. In over half of these cases at least one school administrator, faculty or staff member was targeted. At least one person was murdered in two-thirds of these incidents.

The recent spate of murderous assaults on our schools has set in motion a reaction that is both intense and broad-based. Elements at every level of our society from the Executive Branch of our national government to local Parent Teacher Associations have been sensitized to the issues raised by violence in our schools and have been energized to take steps to deal effectively with them. As Mulrey and Cauffman (2001, p. 797) point out,

> This concern, moreover, has gone beyond simple statements and speculations. A heightened awareness of the potential tragedy of a school-related violent incident has prompted school administrators, law enforcement professionals, and mental health professionals to put into place methods for identifying and intervening proactively with potentially violent students and situations. Many communities have seen curriculum changes, the adoption of "safe school" policies, new weapons-reporting requirements, and increased efforts to refer problem students to mental health professionals. For example, several years ago, New York City spent over 28 million dollars on metal detectors... and numerous school districts have implemented mandatory school uniform policies to cut down on gang identification... After the shooting at Columbine, the principal distributed a memorandum requesting students to report on other students whom they deemed to be demonstrating maladaptive behavior (e.g., dressing oddly, being loners...). *Currently, professionals seem open to trying just about anything to combat the perceived dangers of school violence.* (emphasis ours)

As part of the effort to inform all interested parties about what is known about violence in schools, how its occurrence might be reduced, and the techniques through which its consequences might be ameliorated, three of the Editors of this volume, Florence L. Denmark and Herbert H. Krauss of Pace University and Robert W. Wesner, a scientific publisher, brought together a group of experts to present a workshop on this topic at the New York Academy of Sciences to concerned academics, practitioners, school administrators, teachers, and parents. This workshop was hosted by the Academy and co-sponsored by Pace University and the International Organization for the Study of Group Tensions. The success that greeted the workshop stimulated our interest in producing a book that would address the subject more comprehensively and with greater attention to detail. To better achieve that end, two well-known scholars, Elizabeth Midlarsky of Teachers College, Columbia University and Uwe P. Gielen of St. Francis College were recruited to join in creating and producing the proposed volume.

The Editors were not brought together by happenstance. Each is a recognized authority in his or her field. Each believes that no one is more vulnerable to violence and its consequences than are children (e.g., Margolin & Gordis, 2002). Those of us who are entrusted with the care and protection of these children while they are in the school milieu must be cognizant of every threat to their safety and their well being. Furthermore the Editors all share similar beliefs and attitudes about what this proposed volume must do:

- It must recognize that violence is a global problem (e.g. Krug et al., 2002). Consequently our efforts to deal with it must be informed by an international perspective.
- It must take a broad view of what violence is and what produces it. Violence is much more than physical assault. It is also intentional neglect and abusive behavior of a variety of stripes, including racism, sexism, and cultural discrimination and suppression. While the potential for violent action may be rooted in our biology, it is absolutely clear that most often violence is a cognitive act that is influenced primarily by the social world into which we are born, in which we develop, and which constitutes our present sense of experienced reality (e.g., UNESCO, 1989, cited in Silverberg & Gray, 1992).
- It must take into account the history of the phenomenon. School violence is not a problem that is new, or that has been limited to a particular ethnic group, locale, or historical period. An understanding of the history may be a means for understanding and ultimately ameliorating the current state of affairs (Prothrow-Stith & Quaday, 1996; Volokh & Snell, 1998).
- It must, in acknowledging the shortcomings of the moment, not be overpowered by them. We have had too much success in taking rational, intentional action to improve our condition to warrant a lapse into a posture of defeatism. Racism is not vanquished but its direct impact is greatly diminished. The same might be said for sexism, and many of the other "isms" that blight our lives. Furthermore, many other societies have succeeded in finding more harmonious ways of living together. If nothing else, we can learn from them. Surely every attempt to improve our lot brings unintended consequences. These are nothing more than additional challenges that can be overcome provided we do not become infected with a "This is the best of all possible worlds" quietism that is all too often associated with specious arguments of either biological or economic determinism.
- It must be up to date and speak with legitimate authority yet be accessible in style and substance to its intended audience: scholars, school administrators, teachers, and staff; practitioners of the helping professions; and educated lay people.

Readers will, of course, come to their own opinions as to how well the Editors succeeded in producing a book that achieved the desired ends.

The book that you are about to peruse is organized into sections flowing from general information regarding school violence to specific descriptions of it in the United States and in countries worldwide. A general description of violence in our society is presented by Herbert H. Krauss in "Conceptualizing Violence", while Elizabeth Midlarsky, and Helen Marie Klein review historical facts regarding school violence in "A History of Violence in the Schools". School violence is described in terms of various internal and external factors in: "Warning Signs: School Violence Prevention" by June F. Chisholm and Alfred W. Ward, "Developmental Aspects of School Violence: A Contextualist Approach" by Roseanne L. Flores, and "Gender and Ethnicity Issues in School Violence" by Darlene C. DeFour. Another example of how violence is exhibited in schools is included in "Sexual Violence in the Schools" by Beatrice J. Krauss, Herbert H. Krauss, Joanne O'Day, and Kevin Rente . While the first half of this volume generally focuses on the United States, the next section describes school violence in countries across the world. Violence in Japan ("Bulling and *Ijime* in Japanese Schools: A Sociocultural Perspective" by Takashi Naito and Uwe P. Gielen), the Philippines ("A Perspective on Child Abuse in the Philippines: Looking at Institutional Factors" by Richard Velayo), in Arabic countries ("Manifestations of Violence in Arab Schools and Procedures for Reducing It" by Ramadan A. Ahmed), and in Australia ("Violence in Schools-Australia" by Judith E. Papházy) are presented by authors who are experts regarding these issues in their respective countries. Strategies and intervention techniques to prevent violence are discussed by Daniel A. Krauss in "Predicting School Violence" and Maram Hallak, Kathryn Quina, and Charles Collyer in "Preventing Violence in Schools: Lessons from King and Gandhi". Finally, in the concluding chapter, Florence L. Denmark and Melissa Laracuenta summarize and make concluding statements regarding the state of school violence as it is today and goals for the prevention of it in the future.

REFERENCES

Aries, P. (1962). *Centuries of childhood*. New York: Alfred A. Knopf.

Achenbach, T. & Howell, C. (1993). Are American children's problems getting worse? A 13 year comparison. *Journal of the American Academy of Child and Adolescent Psychiatry, 32*, 1145–1154.

Anderson, C.A. & Bushman, B.J. (2001). Effects of violent video games on aggressive behavioral, aggressive cognition, aggressive affect, physiological arousal, and prosocial behavior: A meta-analytic review of the scientific literature. *Psychological Science, 12*, 353–359.

Anderson, C.A. & Bushman, B.J. (2002). Media violence and the american public revisited. *American Psychologist, 57,* 448–450.

Baldry, A.C. (2003). Bullying in schools and exposure to domestic violence. *Child Abuse and Neglect, 27(7),* 713–732.

Bushman, B.J. & Anderson, C.A. (2001). Media violence and the american public: Scientific facts versus media misinformation. *American Psychologist, 56,* 477–489.

Center for Disease Control and Prevention. (1994$_a$). Homicide among 15–19 year old males: United states 1963–1991. *Morbidity and Mortality Weekly Report, 43,* 725–727.

Center for Disease Control and Prevention. (1994$_b$). Annual summary of births, deaths, marriages, divorces, and deaths: United States, 1993. *Morbidity and Mortality Weekly Report, 42* (13).

Cole, E.R. & Omari, S.R. (2003). Race, class and the dilemmas of upward mobility for African Americans, *Journal of Social Issues, 59,* 785–802.

Cornell, D.G. & Loper, A.B. (1998). Assessment of violence and other high-risk behaviors with a school survey. *School Psychology Review, 27(2),* 317–330.

Elliott, D., Hamburg, B., & Williams, K. (1998). Violence in American schools: An overview. In D. Elliott, B. Hamburg, & K. Williams, Eds. *Violence in American schools* (pp. 3–28). Cambridge: Cambridge University Press.

Furlong, M., Morrison, G., Chung, A., Bates, M., & Morrison, R. (1997). School violence. In G. Bear (Ed.), *Children's needs.* Arlington, VA: National Association of School Psychologists.

Garbarino, J. (1995). Growing up in a socially toxic environment: Life for children and families in the 1990's. In G.B. Melton (Ed.) *The Individual, the Family, and Social Good: Personal Fulfillment in Times of Change.* Nebraska Symposium on Motivation, 42, Lincoln, Nebraska: University of Nebraska Press, 1–20.

Haynie, D., Nansel, T., Eitel, P., Crump, A., Saylor, K., Yu, K., & Simons-Morton, B. (2001). Bullies, victims, and bully/victims. *Journal of Early Adolescence, 21(1),* 29–49.

Hochschild, J.L. (2003). Social class in public schools. *Journal of Social Issues, 59,* 821–840.

Jenkins, J.C., & Bell, C.C. (1992). Adolescent violence: Can it be curbed? *Adolescent Medicine: State of the Art Reviews, 1,* 71–86.

Krug, E.G., Dahlberg, L.L., Mercy, J.A., Zwi, A.B., & Lazano, R. (2002). *World Report on Violence and Health.* Geneva: World Health Organization.

Lexington Herald-Leader (1993). Armed for School. Lexington, KS: Lexington-Herald Leader.

Margolin, G. & Gordis, E.B. (2002). The effects of family and community violence on children. *Annual Review of Psychology, 51,* 445–479.

Mulvey, E.P. & Cauffman, E. (2001) The inherent limits of predicting school violence. *American Psychologist, 56,* 797–802.

Osofsky, J.D. (1997). Children and youth violence: An overview of the issues. In J.D. Osofsky (Ed.) *Children in a Violent Society.* New York: Guilford, pp. 3–8.

Ostrove, J.M. & Cole, E.R. (2003). Privileging class: Toward a critical psychology of Social class in the context of education. *Journal of Social Issues, 59,* 677–692.

Parkman, A.M. (1995). The deterioration of the family: A law and economics perspective. In G.B. Melton (Ed.) *The Individual, the Family and Social Good: Personal Fulfillment in Times of Change.* Nebraska Symposium on Motivation, 42, 21–52. Lincoln, Nebraska: University of Nebraska Press.

Prothrow-Stith, D. & Quaday, S. (1996). Communities, schools, and violence. In A.M. Hoffman (Ed.), *Schools, violence, and society* (pp. 153–161). Westport, CT: Praeger.

Rennison, C.M. (1999). *Criminal victimization 1998.* Washington, DC: US Department of Justice.

Snyder, H. & Sickmund, M. (1999). *Juvenile offenders and victims: 1999 national report.* Washington, D.C: Office of Juvenile Justice and Delinquency Prevention.

Teitz, M.B. & Chapple, K. (1998). The causes of inner city poverty: Eight hypotheses in search of reality. *Cityscape: A Journal of Policy Development and Research, 3,* 33–70.

Turner, S. (2002). *Something to cry about: An argument against corporal punishment of children in Canada.* Waterloo, Ontario, Canada: Wilfred Laurier University Press.

UNESCO (1989). The Seville Statement (1986) drafted at the 6ᵗʰ International Colloquim on Brain and Aggression. Adopted at UNESCO's general conference session. Paris 17 October to 16 November 1989. Cited in J. Silverberg & J.P. Gray (Eds.) (1992). *Aggression in humans and other primates.* New York: Oxford. Appendix 295–297.

U.S. Department of Education. (1997). *Principal/school disciplinary survey on school violence. Fast response survey system, 63,* Washington, D.C: National Center of Educational Statistics.

U.S. Department of Health and Human Services. (2001). *Youth violence: A report of the surgeon general.* Washington, D.C: Author.

U.S. Department of Justice. (1998). *National crime victimization survey. Criminal victimization 1997: Changes 1996–97 with trends.* 1993–97. Washingtons, D.C: Bureau of Justice Statistics.

Volokh, A. & Snell, L. (1998). *School violence prevention: Strategies to keep schools safe.* Reason Public Policy Institute Policy Study NO. 234. Retrieved January 4, 2004 from: http://www.rppi.org/ps234.html.

Vossekuil, B. Reddy, M., Fein, R., Borum, R., & Modzeleski, W. (2000). U.S.S.S. safe school initiative: An interim report on the prevention of targeted violence in schools. Washington D.C.: U.S. Secret Service, National Threat Assessment Center.

Chapter 2

Conceptualizing Violence

Herbert H. Krauss

The Ubiquity of Violence

Violence has always been with us. Before humans learned to objectify their experiences, concretize them symbolically, and transmit them in ideograph, they had mastered the ability to prey on one another. Human remains in Atapuerca, Spain provide evidence of European cannibalism 800,000 years ago. By the middle Paleolithic period (150,000 to 40,000 B.C.E.) there are indicators that human-induced trauma in humans had mounted significantly (Walker, 2001). After reviewing the bio-archeological evidence, Walker (2001, p. 573) concluded "No form of [human] social organization, mode of production, or environmental setting appears to have remained free of interpersonal violence for long." The most influential of human moral narratives, the Old and the New Testaments, the Koran, and the Bhagavad Gita, are replete with descriptions of human violence, some of which are held forth as exemplary exercises of power employed for the good.

Modern times have not seen humans put violence aside. Not counting incidents of intentional starvation, of violence against ethnic or political subpopulations, or of purposely lethal "re-education" programs carried out as instruments of public policy, from 1945 until 1997 when Summerfield (1997) tallied them, there were more than 160 wars and armed conflicts. And the twenty-first century has certainly gotten off to a bloody good start.

In American society, violence is pandemic. Focusing upon violence perpetrated by and against the young, the National Incidence Study of

11

the National Center of Child Abuse (1996) found 23.1 per 1,000 children, 18 years old or younger were maltreated. Of these, 3.2 per 1,000 suffered sexual abuse. The National Committee for the Prevention of Child Abuse Survey of 1997 reported that 15 of 1,000 children are victims of child abuse. Clearly, the rates at which children have direct experience with violence are enormous. In some US neighborhoods over one-third of pre-teens and teens have been directly victimized by community violence (Margolin & Gordis, 2000). In their review of the literature Margolin and Gordis (2000) came across one investigation, based on parental reports, that estimated that in the US inner city neighborhood surveyed, 84 percent of first and second graders witnessed community violence (e.g., shootings, stabbings, gang chases, drug use, etc.) and 21 percent were directly victimized. The comparative statistics for fifth and sixth graders were 90 and 35 percent, respectively. When the children themselves were asked, the fifth and sixth graders indicated 97 percent had seen community violence and 59 percent had been victims of it.

Our schools are havens compared to the neighborhoods in which they are embedded; only 10 percent of reported incidents of non-fatal violence against those 12 or older occurred in school buildings or on school property (Mattaini et al., 1996). Yet they too can be quite violent. In a survey of 12 schools in an economically depressed area of Chicago, Kellam (1990) concluded that the incidence of moderate to severe aggression in first grade varied from under 10 percent to more than 30 percent. Within-school variation was even higher, no doubt due largely to pupil "tracking," with some classes reporting an incidence of violence under 10 percent and others over 65.

In addition to experiencing violence, either as victim or observer, our society embeds its children in a matrix of imaginary aggression. Video games and movies aside, children can get a full dose of violence just by watching television. The American Psychological Association (1993) estimated that US children between the ages of two and eleven watch approximately 28 hours of television per week and teenagers around 23 hours (children of lower socio-economic classes watch more). During primetime about five to six violent acts per hour are depicted. On Saturdays, with its heavy loading of cartoons, the number rises to between 20 and 25.

In spite of the society's enthrallment with imaginary, albeit increasingly graphic and realistic, representations of violent behavior, few wish to live in a culture in which the threat of violent harm is imminent and real or for their loved ones to live in one. To reduce the likelihood that we or those to whom we are close become its victims, effective action to reduce violence is needed. This requires a way to understand violence.

It is imperative that we understand our circumstances, our condition, by adopting, discovering, or creating conceptualizations that enable us to attend to, form, and organize the streams of impressions we receive into structures of meaning. The root reason we need, seek, and produce such structures is that our ability to abstract information accurately from our environment and act on that information increases our odds of survival. And we have survived. But it is also obvious that sometimes, perhaps as unintended consequences or perhaps as necessary sub-routines in a process and strategy so central to survival, meaning-making takes on a life of its own. Because of this, because human beings are not born with a store of infallible information sufficient for their survival, and because all of the data that we process is colored by and weighted with our hopes, fears, desires, and aims as individuals and as members of collectives, taking the appropriate lesson from what we perceive and finding the proper conceptualization to further our interests is far from easy as the history and current state of epistemology attests. This task is made more daunting if the data set to be appreciated is large and complex, and, more challenging still, if a methodology adequate to assessing the correspondence between what is conceived or formulated as present and what indeed is present is itself a work in progress.

This is indeed the case with violence. Violence is defined variously, perceived multifariously, and studied in diverse ways. The perspective from which this essay views violence and attempts to visualize its meaning is that provided by the work of Kenneth Burke (e.g. 1966, 1969a, 1969b). Burke's conviction is that drama and its production and performance affords an apt analogy for comprehending why people act as they do. For this reason he termed his paradigm dramatistic. Before discussing dramatistics, however, violence and the most current construction of its meaning on the "world stage" will be considered.

THE WORLD HEALTH ORGANIZATION'S VIEW OF VIOLENCE

The Forty-Ninth World Health Assembly adopted Resolution WHA 49.25 in 1996. That resolution expressed "great concern" over a "dramatic worldwide increase in the incidence of international injuries affecting people of all ages and both sexes, but especially women and children...," and declared violence a "leading worldwide public health problem" (cited in Krug, Dahlberg, Mercy, Zwi, & Lozano, 2002, p. xx). It urged member states to assess the incidence and nature of violence within their borders and to send this information to the World Health Organization (WHO) along with a report of the initiatives undertaken to deal with violence and its sequellae. WHO also requested that its Director General take steps to "(1) describe violence's typology and assess its causes and consequences, (2) evaluate the efficacy of programs designed to prevent violence and ameliorate its effects, (3) promote national and transnational efforts to reduce violence and its deleterious influence on human well being, and (4) send to the Executive Board a plan for developing a science-based public health approach to violence prevention" (cited in Krug et al., 2002, p. xx).

The World Report on Violence and Health (Krug et al., 2002) was intended to be an important, albeit partial, response to the charge of Resolution WHA 49.25. Directed to researchers and practitioners, it defined *violence* as

> The intentional use of physical force or power, threatened or actual, against oneself, another person, or against a group or community, that either results in or has a high likelihood of resulting in injury, death, psychological harm, maldevelopment or deprivation. (WHO Global Consultation on Violence and Health, 1996)

WHO's definition of *violence* is purposely broad, denoting not only the intentional use of physical force which harm, but also the malintentioned use of the influence inherent in unequal social and institutional power relationships (e.g., parent and child) which harm, and the malintentioned failure to present harm. Thus, falling within WHO's definition of violence are intentioned physically violent acts and "neglect and all types of physical, sexual and psychological abuse, as well as suicide and other self-abusive acts" (Krug et al., 2002, p. 5).

WHO's definition of violence is also quite complex in that it includes a notion of *intent* and because it applies that notion unevenly. Willed action is an essential component of every act of violence; however, the act is deemed violent by WHO even if its perpetrator did not intend the harm that ensued. The intentional use of physical force, for example, is deemed a violent act if it either results in harm or is likely to do so even if its initiator failed to appreciate accurately its full potential for ill.

Undoubtedly, WHO's primary aim in requiring an assessment of the initial impetus for an individual's act (was the act intentionally undertaken or was it the result of happenstance) was to make possible a differentiation between a violent act and a "true" accident. (Bear in mind WHO reserves to itself the ability to substitute its view of an action for an agent's report as to why it was undertaken, for example, when WHO believes culpable negligence is behind the act. Culpable negligence defines an act as violent if the act produces harm). In introducing *intention* in its definition of violence, however, WHO also implicitly promulgates a volitional model of human action. Such a model depicts individuals as purposeful. Nonetheless, in separating one's intent in undertaking an action from one's view (or his or her society's view, for that matter) of its likely outcome in its definition, WHO appropriated to itself the right to say what is and is not violence. WHO's aim in this was to substitute an universal *"enlightened public health paradigm"* (emphasis is mine) for that used by the individual or the individual's indigenous culture to understand and deal with violence. Cultures clearly differ among themselves in their conceptualizations of violence (e.g., Naroll, 1983; Rohner, 1975; Barton, 1969) and what a given society holds as normal at one time might be considered violence at another (e.g., Harris, 2001; Miller, 1993).

Striking one's pupils to enhance their performance, to cite one instance, is considered violence by WHO whether or not the teachers of a given society at a given time might judge doing so to be culturally sanctioned acts of discipline.

In three significant respects WHO's approach to violence is superior to others. One advantage is that it allows the work of compiling potentially consistent statistics on violence (e.g., prevalence, incidence, cost) both across societies and within a particular society to begin. It permits, within the limits of the reliability and validity of those estimates, the reasoned analyses of violence and the patterns of its occurrence, analyses which might lead to a deeper understanding of etiology, and inform primary, secondary and tertiary prevention efforts. A second advantage is that WHO's involvement makes violence an issue of international concern whose amelioration requires an international initiative led by an international organization, WHO, with the moral force and institutional resources necessary to orchestrate and direct the public health efforts needed to, if not eliminate violence, reduce its likelihood and its deleterious effects. The third advantage is that it potentially extends to large populations of individuals whose statuses typically make them more vulnerable to harm (the elderly, women and children, and the marginalized, for instance) various moral and institutional protections from violence for which they would otherwise not be eligible.

Acknowledging its assets, however, in no way minimizes its defects, real and potential. These include:

1. The lack of a compelling reason to believe that a public health model is appropriate for understanding and treating violence. Clearly public health professionals, as trained currently, have much to contribute to the secondary and the tertiary prevention of collective violence, their role in its "primary" prevention is far from clear.

2. In reserving to itself the right to substitute its universally applicable and "enlightened" definition of *violence* for that of the indigenous society, WHO is embarking upon an agenda and a course of action designed to change established social values as well as reduce violent acts. Putting aside the striking hypocrisy in insisting on respect for diversity and the tolerance

of cultural and religious differences while at the same time working to ensure cross-societal value homogeneity, even well-intentioned as efforts at value "reform" often produce unintended consequences which prove counterproductive. Just as there are untoward consequences for "defining deviancy down" (Moynihan, 1993), there may also be for defining *normality* down.

3. WHO's determination to classify as violent behaviors not viewed as such in a given society will also undoubtedly make reliably operationalizing WHO's conceptual definition of violence more challenging. Compounding the difficulties is WHO's inclusion of intent in its definition. If, for example, what is perceived as an accident in one society is considered the unintended consequence of mental illness in another, and culpable negligence in yet a third, how should the act be categorized?

4. The aggregation of instances of behavior judged violent by one society with those classed otherwise by another society may produce additional problems. The acts considered violent might have radically different etiologies than those phenotypically similar, but designated as normal. For example, alcohol abuse may contribute significantly to the probability of child battering in societies which construe hitting a child as markedly deviant and violent and not at all in societies in which it is deemed normal and proper to discipline children by striking them when they fail to show proper respect for elders. Aggregating into one class – *child beating* – instances from both societies would probably obscure variables associated with each of the two types of "violence" against children and, thereby, make primary prevention more difficult.

In spite of its problems, however, any fair summary assessment of its program to define, understand, and reduce violence would, after a careful weighing of its likely benefits and liabilities, conclude that on balance WHO has indeed provided a useful and valuable rubric for grappling with violence.

Demographics of Violence

WHO estimated that in 2000, 1.6 million people worldwide died from self-inflicted, interpersonal, or collective violence (violence committed to advance a particular social or political agenda). This yielded an overall age-adjusted incidence rate of 28.8 per 100,000 (Krug et al., 2002). Of these total deaths, 31.3 percent (8.8 per 100,000) were attributed to homicide, 49.1 percent to suicide (14.5 per 100,000) and 18.6 percent (5.2 per 100,000) to war.

Once created, databases such as the one from which the above statistics were drawn proliferate, because they suggest and make possible answers to such questions as the following:

Q. Are violence related deaths more common in low to middle-income countries than high-income countries?

A. They are by a ratio of more than two to one (32.1 deaths per 100,000 for the former and 14.4 deaths per 100,000 for the latter).

Q. Is murder related to gender?

A. It is. The age-standardized rate of males dying of homicide is 13.6 per 100,000. For women it is 4.0 per 100,000.

Q. Do homicide rates vary jointly as a function of age and gender?

A. They do. The rate at which men die of homicide rises precipitously within the age category of 15 to 29 (from 2.1 per 100,000 to 19.4 per 100,000) and then gradually diminishes (for males 60 and above it is 13.0 per 100,000). The rate at which females are murdered at each defined age division hovers at about 4.4 per 100,000 except for ages 5 to 14 where it is 2.0 per 100,000.

Q. Are there cross-national differences in the rates with which youths are murdered?

A. Indeed there are. In WHO's sample, rates of youth homicide were highest in Latin America (e.g., Columbia, 84.4 per 100,000; El Salvador, 50.2 per 100,000), the Caribbean (e.g., Puerto Rico, 41.9 per 100,000) and some south-eastern European countries (e.g., Albania, 28.2 per 100,000) and lowest in Western Europe (e.g., France, 0.6 per 100,000; Germany 0.8 per 100,000; United Kingdom, 0.9 per 100,000) and far Eastern Asia (e.g., Japan, 0.4 per 100,000). The U.S.'s youth homicide rate is 11.0 per 100,000. Almost all other countries with rates above 10.0 per 100,000 are "developing" or in the midst of a rapid social or economic change.

Researchers have consistently found homicide rates to be linked with such characteristics as nationality, ethnicity, religion, gender, age, social status, socio-economic condition, family of origin and their combinations. The relationships found between these variables and homicide are far from exceptional. Somewhat different but stable associations between this set of social identifiers and the incidence of many other behavioral sequences which WHO defines as self-directed or interpersonal violence – suicide, rape, child abuse or neglect, wife beating, and so on – have also been established. These results demand adequate explanations. To date, of those advanced none has won general acceptance.

Even less is known about collective violence. This is in spite of its early appearance in human history and the consistently mounting death toll attributable to it since then. The first documented instance of collective violence was uncovered at a Mesolithic site in Bavaria where approximately 7800 years ago 38 humans, mostly women and children, had been bludgeoned to death (Walker, 2001). The 25 largest incidents of collective violence in the twentieth century took, directly and indirectly, approximately 191 million lives (Rummel, 1994). In fact, fewer empirical predictors (e.g., a gross mal-distribution of economic resources, rapid demographic change, Krug et al., 2002) of collective violence have been identified for collective than interpersonal violence.

That no acceptable comprehensive theory of violence has emerged ought not be taken to mean that progress in understanding behavior that is violent has not been made. Solid information has been developed about the precursors and predictors of violent acts at each "level" of human organization from the biological to the trans-societal. What is missing is a frame of reference for fashioning a working and unified model of violence, one that would suggest how the materials already at hand might best be utilized and where any necessary additional constituents might be found or obtained. Optimists believe that such a perspective will be found or devised; pessimists believe that no theory encompassing violence can be constructed that will not collapse of its own weight and that success in understanding violent behaviors will come from concentrating investigative efforts on particular projects far less grandiose, on frontal lobe functioning in murderers (Raine, 1993), for example. Of course, there is no reason to presuppose that both the search for a grand theory and focal research cannot be pursued profitably at the same time. Nor is there reason to believe that the progress made utilizing these rather distinct approaches to violence will not prove to be mutually beneficial.

VIOLENCE AND BIOLOGY

Initial assays of a phenomenon focus upon its most salient characteristics as they are viewed by those intent on describing them. These perceptions are only, in part, a function of the phenomenon, itself. They are also influenced by the investigative techniques available and the meaning that the phenomenon holds for its investigators after being filtered through their cognitive biases and pre-existing commitments. Violence is no exception. The earliest scientific attempts to render it intelligible emphasized its biological etiology. There were obvious reasons for this. One, already alluded to, was its historical and, indeed, contemporary ubiquity. Violence appeared to be a "natural" part of life. A second followed from the observation that aggressive behavior was more common in some people than others, and in some animals, more than others. The discovery that aggressiveness could be "bred into" or out of animals (dogs, for example) was well known. The leap from "breeding produces aggressive dogs" to "breeding produces aggressive humans" was not large, especially since aristocratic societies organized on the basis of inheritance took for granted that blood mattered. Third, intensely experienced emotions such as rage were believed more "basic" than those less moving. Once induced, rage invariably overmastered calm repose and logic and reason as well. Fourth, there was Darwin who provided intellectual and scientific support to that whole train of thought.

William James (cited in Geen, 1998, p. 317) declared, "Our ancestors have bred pugnacity into our bones and marrow and thousands of years of peace won't breed it out of us." Lombroso affirmed that he could detect a constellation of physical features in violent criminals, sloping foreheads, long arms, full lips, and twisted noses. These he construed as atavisms to humans of the more primitive past (Niehoff, 1999). For Francis Galton, the mental and moral characteristics of violent criminals were controlled by hereditary just as were height and eye color (Niehoff, 1999). After examining thirty women who killed their own children, Spurzheim concluded that their brain centers for "philoprogentitive-ness" (love of children) were underdeveloped (Niehoff, 1999). Freud's position on aggression changed in the course of his years. As he saw more of war and man's capacity for violence and his physical vitality waned, he moved from a frustration-leads-to-aggression position to one in which a death instinct was central. At root, he argued, we kill each other to avoid turning our destructive wishes and impulses against ourselves (Geen, 1998). Writing in a vein that Freud would have found congenial, Lorenz (1966) held that aggressive behavior was triggered by specific environmental stimuli. Once released, aggression-specific energy builds up anew until it is discharged once more.

Current research leaves little doubt that certain patterns in which violent, aggressive behavior is expressed have as determining factors the organism's biological heritage or condition. In other researches, biology plays an indirect yet important role, and in yet others a trivial or walk-on part at best. It is also clear that in all instances, even those in which its contribution dominates that of all others, the part played by biology in violence is much more complex than imagined previously.

Evidence that violence can have non-trivial biological underpinnings is derived from many sources. One is violence's demographics. Violent crime across time and culture is male by a ratio greater than four to one (Barash, 2002), for example. Aggression, especially among polygamous mammals, humans among them, is disproportionately male. Among polygamous mammals, males are characteristically larger and more assertive than females, males have higher mortality rates, and enter senescence earlier than females; typically, females reach sexual maturity before males. "When those characteristics appear in other species, biologists readily interpret them as indicating male competition for access to females" (Barash, 2002, p. 8) and, consequently, for genetic survival. Therefore, so the argument goes, male aggression is likely genetically based. Further support for the conviction that the potential for violence is rooted in genetics is adduced from investigations which indicate that individual differences in traits such as aggressiveness and assertiveness, altruism, empathy, and nurturance have high heritability (Geen, e.g. 1998).

The rapidly accumulating animal and human research which through ablation, stimulation, and imaging has identified some of the brain structures and paths involved in some acts of aggression also underscores the important role the brain plays in violent behavior. Besides the brain's Papez circuit (angulas gyrus and hippocampus, anterior thalamus, mammillary body), the hypothalamus and amygdala have also been implicated. Current thinking holds two paths are involved in processing stimuli associated with threat and, thence, some forms of violent action. One loops through the frontal cortex and the other goes more directly from the sensory thalamus to the amygdala. The first adds perceptual and experiential details to information processed in the latter (Niehoff, 1999).

As knowledge about the biological correlates of aggressive behavior has accumulated and research focused upon those relationships has become more finely tuned, a more nuanced consideration of the contribution biology makes to violence has emerged. We know now that aggression in infrahumans is more complicated than originally thought. For example, the aggressive responses of animals differ as a function of the type of threat posed (e.g., a threat to their young vs. status threats vs. external pain, etc., Archer & Gartner, 1984). It has become clear as well that a complex configuration of emotions and behaviors well beyond those directly associated with aggression can be elicited when an animal is threatened *in vivo*. As Silverberg and Gray (1992, p. 31–32) found in their studies of dominance maintenance in primates:

> Clearly dominance structures can no longer be structured as mere summaries of dyadic assault records.... Affiliative acts (including peace-making) seem important in structuring primate groups. However, the level of affiliative behavior does not seem to be inversely correlated with the level of agonistic behavior, perhaps because some affiliative behavior is rewarding in ways other than the service of conflict resolution. On the other hand, violence can have 'pro-social' (group structure preserving) consequences, but always with some cost to losers.

Furthermore, a demonstration that biological processes are closely tied to the proximal expression of violent behavior does not mean that environmental factors are not casually involved. As Denno (1990, p. 4) concluded in his report on the Biosocial Project, an investigation in which over 1,000 individuals deemed at risk for violence were studied from birth to adulthood,

> Crime and violence appear to stem from such a tight weave of both biological and environmental influences on behavior that the dominance of any single discipline in explaining violence cannot be justified. For example, results in this book show that what might appear to be a strictly biological trait, such as hyperactivity or severe learning difficulty may be the product of exclusively environmental origins, e.g. lead poisoning.

The evolving consensus even among those who heavily weigh the contribution biological factors make to aggressive behavior is that "biological variables are best understood as moderator variables in human aggression. Each of the biological factors discussed here – evolutionary history, genetic inheritance, and level of hormone activity – contribute to the base level of aggressiveness of the individual and thereby helps to determine the type and magnitude of responses to situational provocations" (Geen, 1998, p. 321).

Bear in mind that even this rather modest conclusion about the part played by biology in human violence requires qualification, for it is a summary judgment of the results obtained by ethologists, neuroscientists, and behaviorally oriented psychologists using investigative paradigms that focused upon the nature and elicitation of *angry aggression*, outwardly directed actions evoked by the presence of the threat of predation, physical discomfort or other aversive conditions in an animal biologically predisposed to react strongly to them. While *angry aggression* may have instrumental qualities, for example, terminating or eliminating threat, studies of *angry aggression*, may contribute little insight about aggression driven by instrumental motives, aggression which may or may not be attended by negative emotions and which has aims more complex than, say, immediate defense against predation– making the world safe for democracy, or eliminating oppression, or asserting inalienable rights, or just maintaining the normal way of doing things, for example. Understanding instrumental violence surely requires more details about the environment, more knowledge of motivation, and more information about how information is processed and represented than simplistic research paradigms can yield in themselves.

In spite of the accumulating evidence that higher order social variables significantly influence the expression of violent behaviors, there are some who remained convinced that the application of a basically reductionistic methodology that emphasizes the role played by biological processes offers the best prospects for understanding violence. Wilson is one.

In *Consilliance: The Unity of Knowledge* (1998) Wilson, socio-biology's most important polemicist, argues:

> The full understanding of utility [decision making or choice] will come from biology and psychology by reduction to the elements of human behavior followed by bottom up synthesis, not from the social sciences by top-down inference and guess work on intuitive knowledge. It is in biology and psychology that economists and other social scientists will find the premises needed to fashion more predictive models, just as it was in physics and chemistry that researchers found premises that upgraded biology (p. 206)

An example of his approach is his explanation of the violence between the Tutsi and Hutu peoples which boiled over once more in Rwanda in 1994 when units of Rwanda's army comprised mostly of Hutus murdered more than half a million Tutsis and moderate Hutus. In the wake of an avenging army of Tutsis, two million Hutu refugees fled Rwanda, thousands of whom subsequently fell to starvation and disease. Acknowledging that "On the surface it would seem, and so was reported by the media, that the Rwandan catastrophe was ethnic rivalry rum amok," Wilson (1998, p. 288) argued, "This is true only in part. There was a deeper cause, rooted in environment and demography." What happened, according to Wilson, was that Rwanda had exceeded its carrying capacity. Food production was

> overbalanced by population growth. The average farm size dwindled, as plots were divided from one generation to the next. Per capita grain production fell by half from 1960 to the early 1990s. Water was so overdrawn that the hydrologists declared Rwanda one of the world's twenty-seven water-scarce countries. The teenage soldiers of the Hutu and the Tutsi then set out to solve the population problem in the most direct possible way. (Wilson, 1998, p. 288)

Wilson's diagnosis is mistaken and ought to be rejected, not because to hypothesize that the scarcity of resources contributes to the likelihood of violence is unreasonable; all too often it does. Nor should it be scrapped because the "scientific" methodology which has proved so productive for the physical and the biological sciences cannot be applied with profit in the social sciences and the humanities; it obviously can. It should be discarded because one cannot build a plausible explanation of human action given the potentially non-singular set of possible cognitively and historically contrived life worlds actualizeable at any given time, if one restricts oneself to information solely about the physical or chemical biological components or sub-routines that must, of necessity, underlie any of the set of possible life worlds that might be realized. The necessary failure of such simplistic reductionistic formulations becomes even more transparent when one considers that operating chacteristics of the instantiated life world exert significant downward influence upon the simpler, lower level constituents of that larger higher system. Any changes in function thus induced are, in turn, fed back to alter the operating characteristics of the higher, as the following example illustrates:

> TAM, Sudan, January 22 – Hope is gaining ground on the front lines of Africa's most expansive – and exhaustive battlefield, where Sudanese have killed and maimed other Sudanese in an area the size of Europe for 20 long years.
>
> •   •   •
>
> At their commander's order, about 100 of the youngest fighters dropped their rifles... stripped off their camouflages uniforms and ran around in the hot sun like children. Actually they were children, the youngest no more than 10.
>
> •   •   •
>
> Southerners have long resisted attempts by the government to impose Shariah, the Islamic legal code, on them. Oil has exacerbated the north-south conflict as the government has piped the south's rich underground deposits to the north without sharing the wealth.
>
> •   •   •
>
> The negotiators have agreed to let southerners decide... whether they want to separate altogether... They have also decided to divide the nation's oil wealth evenly.
>
> •   •   •
>
> Pushing hard from the sidelines has been the Bush administration, which has made resolving Sudan's war a top priority.
>
> •   •   •
>
> Sudan and particularly the south... has suffered immensely from the long war. Public buildings are in ruins. Paved roads are nonexistent, isolating the south from the region.... Only a quarter of the south's children are enrolled in schools.... Experts estimate that as many as two million land mines remain hidden. Just as dangerous, AIDS... is expected to skyrocket when soldiers and refugees flock back home.
>
> •   •   •
>
> It is optimism that gives strength to the young men hacking through the bush outside Yarol... Using a narrow dirt path as their guide, the villagers have cleared miles... from Yarol to a place called Ramciel.... Southerners envision it... their future capital.
>
> Today it is nothing more than a collection of shrubs and trees around a lowering rock... But southerners have high hopes. They see fountains atop the dry earth, broad boulevards and maybe even skyscrapers.
>
> •   •   •
>
> Pipe dreams, probably. But international donors preparing to flood southern Sudan with assistance should peace eventually break out are not thrilled with building a new capital while people are suffering so... (Lacy, 2004, p. A10).

VIOLENCE AND SOCIAL PSYCHOLOGY

Those enamored by primarily biological, reductionistic accounts of violence might profit from reading one of the foundational texts of modern sociology—Durkheim's (1951) *Suicide: A Study in Sociology*. Written in 1897, Durkheim chose suicide to demonstrate that an explanation of self-destructive behavior based upon societal forces was possible and that the science of sociology could better account for suicide than any other competing explanations.

> But it seems hardly possible to us that there will not emerge... from every page of this book... the impression that the individual is dominated by a moral reality greater number, than himself: namely, collective reality. When each people is seen to have its own suicide-rate, more constant than that of general mortality, that its growth is in accordance with a coefficient of acceleration characteristic of each society; when it appears that the variations through which it passes at different times of the day, month, year, merely reflect the rhythm of social life; and that marriage, divorce, the family, religious society, the army, etc. affect it in accordance with definite laws, some of which may even be numerically expressed – these states and institutions will no longer be regarded simply as characterless, ineffective ideological arrangements. Rather they will be felt to be real living, active forces which, because of the way they determine the individual, prove their independence of him; which if the individual enters as an element in the combination whence these forces ensue, at least control him once they are formed. Thus it would appear more clearly why sociology can and must be objective, since it deals with realities as definite and substantial as those of the psychologist or the biologist (Durkheim, 1951, pp. 38–39).

While their have been challenges to the validity of some of its details, no one has invalidated the thrust of his argument. Using a primitive and intuitive form of factor analysis, Durkheim showed that rates of suicide within and across societies varied reliably as a function of certain demographic social markers – marital status, religious participation, and gender, for instance. From their patterns of co-occurrence, Durkheim derived a remarkable typology of suicide – fatalistic, altruistic, anomic, and egotistic – reflective, he believed, of the influence of the extent to which certain characteristics of modernity affected a given social group or society.

Contemporary social psychology can be viewed as two distinct fields: one more akin to psychology and concerned with the behavioral, affective processes of individuals, or, at most, the workings of small groups; the other more closely related to sociology and focused upon the interaction between the individual or groups of individuals and the larger units of society in which they are embedded and with which they interact (Heimer & Matsueda, 1997). On the whole, the former field has limited its interest in violence to angry aggression and has constructed two representations of it. The first posits that noxious circumstances can precipitate aggressive behavior. They do so by eliciting the emotional states which automatically trigger aggressive behavior. This position, exemplified by Berkowitz (e.g., 1963), is known as *neo-associationalism*: "neo-associationalism theory considers emotion, cognition, and behavior to be parallel processes that stem from negative affect; each process may influence the other" (Heimer & Matsueda, 1997, p. 226). The second accentuates the contributions of higher order cognitive processing to the expression of angry aggression. Once one is required to take, for example, cognitive appreciations of threat into models of violence, models necessarily become complicated. Questions about how the "threatfulness" of circumstances is learned, and, once learned, how such appreciations become linked to actions arise. So do puzzles about how one's attributions and actions influence others and the extent to which one's anticipation of that influence is recursive.

Contemporary sociological theorizing about aggression falls into three not entirely mutually exclusive major categories (Heimer & Matsueda, 1997): (1) Control and disorganizational theories which, following Durkheim's (1951) lead, see violence as one "natural" or prescribed result of certain social configurations. (2) Learning and subcultural theories which hone in upon how within a culture individuals or subgroups come to acquire behavioral repertories linked to violence. (3) Labeling theories which de-emphasize the significance of initial conditions and stress that being identified as belonging to a certain social category and being treated, thereafter, as if that attribution is warranted produces or maintains violent behavior.

Representative of the first category of research, Naroll (e.g., 1983) demonstrated that as "moral nets," attachments to formative reference groups reflecting a culture's central values, weakened a society's rate of crime, homicide, and suicide increased. Yoblonsky's (1962) depiction of socialization into gang life exemplifies the second, and Schur's (1971) presentation of the consequences of being viewed as dangerous, is illustrative of the third.

Beyond the sociological level of analysis remain yet others. One such is Levy's (1996) demonstration that to understand war, one must not only take into account the structure of a country's political system, its policy making process, and its public opinion but also the nature of the international system in which it is embedded with its particular distribution of military, political, and economic power, its pattern of military alliances, how smoothly and predictably the international system operates, and so on. "Wars occur," Levy (1996, p. 6) concludes, "not only because some states prefer war to peace; they also occur because of the unintended consequences by those states that prefer peace to war, and that are more interested in minimizing their losses than maximizing their gains, but are willing to take considerable risks to avoid losses."

WHO's Ecological Model of Violence

WHO's own model for understanding violence, though fundamentally empirical, is far less reductionistic than Wilson's. Labeled *ecological*, WHO sees

Violence is the result of the complex interplay of individual, relationship, social, cultural and environmental factors.

•   •   •

The first level of etiological model seeks to identify the biological and personal history factors that an individual brings to his or her behavior.... The second level ... how proximal social relationships – for example, relations with peers, intimate partners and family members – increase the risk for violent victimization and perpetration of violence.... The third level ... community contexts in which social relationships are embedded – such as schools, workplaces and neighborhoods – and seeks to identify the characteristics of three settings that are associated with being victims of perpetrators ... The fourth and final level ... examines the larger societal factors that influence rates of violence....

•   •   •

Larger societal factors include:

- cultural norms that support violence as an acceptable way to resolve conflicts; ...
- norms that entrench male dominance over woman and children; ..
- norms that support political conflict.

Larger societal factors also include the health, educational, economic, and social policies that maintain high levels of economic or social inequality between groups in society (Krug et al, 2002, pp. 12–13).

The advantage of WHO's ecological model over Wilson's approach is patent: It mines the rich vein of genetic, biological, and neuro-psychological research relevant to violence without overemphasizing, by fiat, its importance. It encourages the demonstration that variables, not usefully reduceable to their physical or biological parameters, ideas for instance, can influence the expression of violence. In doing so, it has the correlated potential for facilitating our comprehension of the multiple paths through which biology influences violent behavior as well as directing investigators to explore the significance of social structures in the production of violence, delineate their components, and detail their operations—a set of tasks prerequisite to success in understanding etiology of violence, lowering its incidence, and reducing its harm.

BURKE'S DRAMATISTIC MODEL OF VIOLENCE

No one raised in the ethos of the modern physical and natural sciences and aware of their signal accomplishments takes as a goal adding unnecessarily to the number and the complexity of the explanatory devices required to measure, map, and delineate a phenomenon, let alone relishes introducing murky constructs of debatable reliability and questionable validity into the explanatory schema designed to account for it. The only rational argument one can convincingly offer for doing so is that it is necessary, and, if one does not, no veridical view of the phenomenon is possible. This is clearly the case with violence. If violence is to be understood and prevented, the interaction of variables as diverse in structure and action as the gene and conceptual nervous system, as the individual and the culture in which he or she is embedded, will have to be considered.

Even when it is admitted that "social" variables must be considered if violence is to be explained, a basic problem yet remains. It is, to paraphrase Simpson (1951, p. 26), to form meaningful, convincing, useful, and truthful narratives of the life histories of those who commit violent acts and those who are victimized by them out of a sophisticated, nuanced understanding of the biological, psychological, and social processes which can and do induce, perpetrate, or aggravate the potential for or expression of violence. This is a difficult undertaking at best as are all exercises that are fundamentally studies of the individual.

It is simplified considerably, however, because, at any given historical moment, the range of basic, distinct cultural forms actualized is quite constrained, even when one takes into account that those absorbed in that instant and those not might disagree about what is an important difference (e.g., are both Protestants and Catholics Christians?). Of course, much more is known about the *whys* and *wherefores* that restrict variability in the physical world (e.g., why Planck's constant is constant) or in the biological world (e.g., how the human genotype limits the human form) than in the social world. And, certainly, different mechanisms ensure that physical, biological, and social systems emerge and develop as they do. What is clear, however, is that whether one considers kinship structures, methods of government, modes of inheritance, division of labor, or other like patterns of cultural expression, only a small number of those that can be imagined are ever actualized, and of those that are actualized, significantly fewer yet are found with any cross-cultural frequency. Within a society, strong forces, both institutional (e.g., laws) and those less formal (e.g., imitation), operate to restrain behavioral and cognitive diversity. The pressures to conformity that they exert reduce to a few the statuses that are actually available, the number of roles that can be realistically enacted and the variety of styles with which they can be convincingly played, and the ends that can be desired. At any given time, consequently, potent dynamisms act to provide a limited number of shared, similar, or mutually comprehensible leit motifs and ensure that substantial communalities in thought, affect, and action exist among groupings and clusters of individuals from the same society and from different societies.

The ability to compare and contrast the influence identifiable cultural forms and contexts exert on behavior within and between societies also provides insight into the circumstances that make certain behavioral configurations more likely. An analysis of cross-cultural data drawn from a survey of 90 preliterate societies, for example, permitted Ross (1993, p. 2) to infer

> In societies where early socialization is harsh and physically punishing, when it has little affection or warmth, and where male gender-identity conflict is high, both internal and external conflict and violence are higher. Individuals who have experienced early lack of affection and harsh treatment have much more trouble establishing warm cooperative bonds with others as adults and are more prone to view behavior of others as hostile and threatening. Projecting threat and aggression onto others – both inside and outside one's society—provides an easy justification for one's own violent actions. Finally, although those three dimensions of socialization are conceptually related, according to the results, each makes a statistically independent contribution toward explaining conflict. (pp. 102–103)

In contradistinction

> The low conflict society is not one without disputes and differences, but more often one where differences that arise are managed in such a way that extreme rancor, polarization, and outright violence are avoided... Low-conflict societies are not simply those with less wealth and hence fewer resources for people to fight over... Nor are low-conflict societies more likely to be centralized, powerful states that limit internal fighting... Low conflict societies have a psychocultural environment that is affectionate, warm, and low in overt aggression, and relatively untroubled by male gender identify conflicts. These patterns, established in early relationships are likely to produce dispositions facilitating the peaceful resolution of disputes. (pp. 187–188)

Hence, given information about how a well-defined normative sample of individuals behaves in certain circumstances, it is often possible to accurately predict how others with similar characteristics will behave in similar circumstances. Depending on the question, "Who is most likely to beat his wife?," for example, and sufficient information about the variables associated with wife-beating, one might be able to provide a valid answer without necessarily knowing all that transpired in the life of each particular husband and wife combination.

To aver this is not meant to imply that an individual's every action, every thought, or every choice is potentially knowable or foreseeable. For as Bahktin (Morson, 1991, p. 206) concluded, because, "The great-isms assume that everything," to use Bahktin's pejorative term,

> is subject to 'transcription'... They consequently overlook that in human life what is often most important, what usually contains the soul of activity and the meaning of events.... Real life, true historically, and genuine individuality are to be found in what is left over – in the 'surplus'—after all rules are applied and all generalizations have been exhausted. In that surplus we find the singular world in which we create, become aware, in which we live and in which we die.

Or, as he sometimes put the point, theoretism necessarily loses the event-ness of events.

Burke (e.g., 1966, 1969a, 1969b) provides the most appropriate frame for a "grand theory" of violent behavior on the horizon. Burke's frame makes it possible to view harmful acts as their perpetrators and victims see them and to recognize and allow for the "eventness" of events. Unlike biosociological theorists whose "scientism" has dominated social science for some time, Burke does not aim to explain all of human behavior in terms of causal, reductionistic, materialistic, or genetic constructs, true for all times and in all places. He does not describe human activity as if it were elicited from a robot predetermined in word and act by scientific laws (a paraphrase of Bahktin found in Morson, 1991, p. 208). But, neither does he deny that, at root, we are animals and as such we are biological creatures subject to the relevant laws discovered by the natural and the physical sciences. Burke (1966, p. 16) begins his system-building by asserting, "Man is the symbol-using (symbols-making, symbol-misusing) animal inventor of the negative (or moralized by the negative) separated from his natural condition by instruments of his own making goaded by the spirit of the hierarchy (or moved by the sense of order) and rotten with perfection."

To aver that humans are symbol-using animals in the age of "cognitive science" is a commonplace. So, too, is the reminder that we remain animals. However, the two statements taken together are provocative, and in juxtaposing them, Burke challenges us to consider which of our motives derive from our animality, which from our symbolicity (his word), and which are compounds of the two. The phrase "inventor of the negative" underscores the importance to us of the notion of the negative. Negatives do not exist in nature:

> The quickest way to demonstrate the sheer symbolicity of the negative is to look at any object, say, a table, and to remind yourself that, though it is exactly what it is, you would go on for the rest of your life saying all the things that it is not, 'it is not a book, it is not a house . . .'. (Burke, 1966, p. 9)

The negative's importance lies in that it stands at the heart of the injunction "Thou shall not." For Burke, "The negative begins not as a resource of definition or information, but as a command, as 'Don't'" (Burke, 1966, p. 10). As such it makes choice, character, and morality possible.

> *Action* involves *character*, which involves *choice* – and the form of choice attains its perfection in the distinction between Yes and No (shall and shall-not, will and will-not). Though the concept of sheer *motion* is non-ethical, *action* implies the ethical, the human personality. Hence the obvious close connection between the ethical and the negativity as indicated in the Decalogue. (Burke, 1966, p. 11)

Burke's clause, "separated from his natural condition by instruments of his own making," underscores the centrality of culture in forming and creating human existence:

> [E]ven the most primitive of tribes are led by inventions to depart somewhat from the needs of food, shelter, and sex as defined by the survival standards of sheer animality. The implements of husbandry, with corresponding implements of war, make for a set of habits that become a kind of "second nature," as a special set of expectations, shaped by custom, comes to seem "natural." (Burke, 1966 p. 13)

His "goaded by the spirit of hierarchy," implies that cultures are invariably marked by orderings and differentiations, and his last, "rotten with perfection," depicts humans as driven to actualize their beliefs and symbols and the implications thereof in the external world.

There are five key elements in Burke's (1969a) system: *act, scene, agent, agency,* and *purpose.* He believes knowledge of (1) What was done? (*act*), (2) Where or when was it done? (*scene*), (3) Who did it? (*agent*), (4) How did he or she do it? (*agency*), and (5) Why? (*purpose*) is requisite to any full reconstruction of an individual's motive and behavior. Although it seems quite simple, Burke's scheme has intricacy, even if one puts aside its dynamic possibilities: for example, the agent's acts may change the scene, and perhaps, the agent.

> Our term, "agent," for instance, is a general heading that might, in a given case, require further subdivision as an agent might have his act modified (hence partly motivated) by friends (co-agents) or enemies (counter-agents). Again, under "agent" one could place any personal properties that are assigned a motivational value, such as "ideas," "the will," "the fear," "malice," "intuition," "the creative imagination." A portrait painter may treat the body as a property of the agent (an expression of personality), whereas materialistic medicine would treat it as 'scenic,' a purely "objective material," and from another point of view it could be classed as an agency, a mean by which one gets reports of the world at large. Machines are obviously instruments (that is, agencies); yet in their vast accumulation they constitute the industrial scene with its own set of motivational properties." (Burke, 1969a, pp. xix–xx)

Further compass is added to his system when it is recognized that it is possible to inquire about and gain insight into the higher levels of organization that shape the operation of dramatistic's five key elements, for instance, the nature of the play that is being produced. Is it Theater of the Absurd, a Morality Play, Classical Greek Tragedy or Comedy, a Comedy of Manners, or Slapstick? One might also ask: is the drama is scripted tightly for its genre? Is it well directed? By whom? Might another present it differently? Is it good theater? For whom is it written—Pacino, Schwarzenegger, Chaplin? Who is the intended audience? Has it stood the test of time? And on and on and on.

While no one is likely compiling "A Compendium of Plays of Violence, Volume I," the presence of such a volume would, without doubt, add to the understanding of violent acts and aid in devising the strategies necessary to reduce both them and their noxious consequences.

THE ST. BARTHOLOMEW'S DAY MASSACRE OF 1572

One way to illustrate the dramatistic approach is by example. This might be done with a play—an epic of social realism—about a child's preparation (á la *Karate Kid*) for the struggle for survival in an "economically disadvantaged" neighborhood, physically isolated and morally alienated from the "larger society."

> [F]undamental values concerning the expression of anger not only were part of the child-rearing values of their mothers but were also part of the life experience . . . assertiveness and self defense were necessary aspects of their survival and self-esteem in this environment as as their daughters' . . . these mothers actively sought to "toughen" their young children by modeling aggressive behavior (often in the context of evocative verbal accounts to others in their children's presence), selective reinforcement of justified aggressive outbursts by their offspring, teasing their daughters to provide mock "practice" aggressive episodes, using social referencing processes to heighten the children's anger when self-defense seemed warranted, rewarding self-control when aggression was unjustified or inappropriate, and using discourse to interpret, comment, threaten, challenge, warn, or pacify their children. All these practices reflect exogenous models of emotional regulation. . . . (Miller & Sperry, 1987, in Thompson 1990, p. 2)

The example chosen, however, is the Saint Bartholomew's Day Massacre of 1572. (The account provided relies heavily on Lincoln,1989, and Manetsch, 2001.) If objectivity is the aim, it is often better to view from a distance.

The massacre is set in France in the period Protestants consider The Reformation. Throughout Europe, a revolutionary struggle is being played out. On its face, the struggle is for the souls of men. In that sense, what follows may be thought of as a morality play, and, for most Catholics, it ends, as it ought, with the triumph of Christ over Satan. Most Protestants view the final act differently. Some accept God's verdict and convert to Catholicism. For the greater number, alternative interpretations arise. Some flee, metaphorically so to speak, from Egypt. Others go underground to continue their struggle against the idolatry of the Church. Yet others retreat to Protestant strongholds for the security they offer or to continue the Holy War.

Behind the sectarian clash of arms and fueling it is a conflict for political and economic hegemony. The death of King Henri II in 1559 brought on a crisis of governance. Of the sons that succeeded him, Frances II (1559–60) died young, and Charles IX (1560–74) and Henri III (1571–89) were too easily influenced by powerful noblemen and their mother, Catherine De Medici. Concurrently, there was an explosive growth of Protestantism in France. By 1562, Protestants numbered 2 million. Not only were they growing more numerous, they were more prosperous, more urban, and more likely to be found in the higher strata of the professions and crafts. They affected a distinctive, austere lifestyle. They did not fast on Fridays or during Lent. Their dress was severe; they did not play cards, throw dice, or dance. Further, most viewed Catholics as idol worshipers who were estranged from Christ, and they did not keep that opinion hidden.

Between 1562 and 1572 in France, three religious wars between the two communities of faith had already been fought to a stalemate. Besides these wars, there had been hundreds of sectarian riots. Violent suppression was the order of the day, instigated and furthered by sermon and example. After the last of that bloody decade's religious wars (1568–70) an attempt was made to achieve peace through the marriage of the foremost Protestant Huguenot Prince, Henri of Navarre, and Margaret of Valois, the sister of King Charles IX.

The *dramatis personae* include, beside King Charles IX, his wife, Catherine De Medici, Prince Henri of Navarre, the groom, and Margaret of Valois, the bride, the following: Bishop Simon Vigor who violently opposed the marriage; Henri, duke of Guise who led the militant Catholic League; Pope Gregory XIII; admiral Coligny and Henri of Conde, Protestant leaders who wished legal recognition and freedom of worship for Protestants; groups of Protestant nobles; Catholic nobles; various Catholic mobs; sundry Protestants and altruistic individuals who succored some of the massacre's victims.

On 18 August 1572, Henri of Navarre married Marguerite de Valois. It was surely not what Marguerite de Valois wished, for she refused to answer "oui" during the ceremony at Paris' Notre Dame Cathedral and to consumate the marriage the King was compelled to force her to move her head in assent. Bishop Vigor is reported to have preached, "God will not endure this detestable union" (Menetsch, 2001, p. 10).

While considerable efforts were undertaken by the King to normalize the wedding, he was not able to do so. The duc de Anjou, the Chief Catholic Marshall, caused a play to be produced as part of the festivity in which Protestants try to enter Heaven and are cast into Hell. On the following night another theatrical was produced in which the King and his brothers, dressed as Amazons, war with Navarre and other leading Protestants, attired as Turks, and defeat them.

On 22 August, after a visit to the King, an attempt was made on Coligny's life. He was wounded, rushed to safety, and surrounded by Protestant leaders. When the King and his council visited him, they found him distrustful of their intentions and threatened vengeance against his attackers if they were not soon brought to justice. On the 23rd, the royal council met and with the King's concurrence decided to preemptively eliminate the Huguenot leadership in Paris. A list of those to be purged was drawn up. "Now is the hour," the duc de Guise proclaimed, "in which, by the grace of the King, we must avenge ourselves on the race of the enemies of God" (Lincoln, 1989). On Sunday, 24 August, as the Feast of Saint Bartholomew's was ushered in by church bells, the massacre began. By dawn, the 200 listed were murdered and Navarre and Conde were under house arrest. In Paris, three days of riot, murder, and pillage followed, in spite of the King's call for order. More than 2,000 were killed. During the next three months, the carnage spread across France as if it were ripples on water, leaving another 10,000 dead.

On receiving reports of the massacre, Pope Gregory XIII ordered a Jubilee held in Rome on 11 September 1572 and every year thereafter. To further commemorate the event, he had medallions struck. On one side was his image and on the other was an image of the Exterminating Angel of God with the inscription "Slaughter of the Huguenot Vermin."

Even from the sketchiness of detail available in the narrative, one can grasp how dreadful and absorbing the times must have been. What is clear is that in addition to the significant influences their biological constitutions, temperaments, aptitudes, and childhood experiences exerted in preparing them to assume their roles, the *dramatis personae* of the Massacre were tightly scripted into intricate and deadly interaction, held in place by powerful social forces and ideas. To believers, and to some degree all believed, at contest was their immortal souls. To preserve for all eternity their place and that of their loved ones in the presence of God, many, Catholic and Protestant alike, were prepared to kill and be killed. Intrinsically intertwined with the sectarian struggle was a competition between Catholic and Protestant for social, economic, and political hegemony. Beneath that lay the traditional clash of noble with King, and below that the primeval war of order against anarchy. These were revolutionary times in which no one could rest secure.

To today's audience, it is obvious that opportunities to avoid the Massacre were present. Then, so bound were the actors to the plot and to each others' performances that they did not choose to or feel able to break the storyline. The bride cannot bring herself to assent to a marriage of state, neither can the Duke de Guise and key elements of the Catholic aristocracy of his faction. For his part, Admiral Coligny and the Protestant nobility cannot allow the assassination attempt against him to go unanswered or trust the King to ensure justice be done. The King is unable to overcome his weakness of character, and, faced with Coligny's lack of support, he cannot withstand the power of the Catholic nobility. He must realign with them and order preemptive action or risk the loss of his throne and another stalemated civil war. For the King's men, to refuse the order to liquidate the 200 is unthinkable or deadly. Of course, transcending the play, however unlikely, is always possible. Some lesser players, in the course of things, do; some Catholics with great personal danger do rescue Protestants at risk.

From the information presented, we cannot know the exact compound of motives that propels each actor. We can assume for some, religious fervor is primary; for others, revenge; for others, secular riches and power; for others, personal security; and for others, pure political calculation; but for most it is the result of a shifting dynamic of each of these desires.

How does the play end? For most Catholics, well. For most Protestants, poorly. The King has succeeded at least temporarily in solidifying the throne. For Navarre, who survives the Massacre, the end remains to be rewritten. Eventually, he succeeds in revising it.

REFERENCES

American Psychological Association. (1993). *Violence and youth: Psychological response.* Washington, D.C.: Author.
Archer, D. & Gartner, R. (1984). *Violence and crime in cross-national perspective.* New Haven: Yale University Press.
Barash, D.P. (2002). Evolution, males, and violence. *The Chronicle of Higher Education, XLVIII,* 37, B7–B9.
Barton, R.F., (1969). *Ifugao law.* Berkeley, CA: University of California
Berkowitz, L. (1963). *Aggression: Its causes and consequences.* Philadelphia: Temple University Press
Burke, K. (1969a). *A grammar of motives.* Berkeley: University of California Press.
Burke, K. (1969b). *A rhetoric of motives.* Berkeley: University of California Press.
Burke, K. (1966). *Language as symbolic action.* Berkeley: University of California Press.
Denno, D.W. (1990). *Biology and violence.* New York: Cambridge.
Durkheim, E. (1951). *Suicide: A study in sociology.* Spaulding, J.A. & Simpson, G. (trans.). New York: Free Press.
Geen, R.G. (1998). Aggression and antisocial behavior. In D.T. Gilbert, S.T. Fiske, & G. Lindzey (Eds.). *The handbook of social psychology, Vol. 2* (4th Ed.) (pp. 317–356). New York: McGraw Hill.
Harris, W.V. (2001). *Restraining rage.* Cambridge: Harvard University Press.
Heimer, K. & Matsueda, R.L. (1997). A symbolic interactionist theory of motivation and deviance: Interpreting psychological research. In D.W. Osgood (Ed.). *Motivation and delinquency* (pp. 221–276). Lincoln, Nebraska: University of Nebraska Press.
Kellam, S.G. (1990). Developmental epidemiological framework for family research on depression and aggression. In G.R. Patterson (Ed.). *Depression and aggression in daily interaction* (pp. 11–48). Hillsdale, NJ: Erlbaum.
Krug, E.G., Dahlberg, L.L., Mercy, J.A., Zwi, A.B. & Lozano, R. (2002). *World report on violence and health.* Geneva: World Health Organization.
Lacy, M. (2004). Rebels, many teens, disarm in Sudan's south. *New York Times, 153,* 52, 741, p. A10.

Levy, J.S. (1996). Contending theories of international conflict: A levels of analysis approach. In C.A. Crocker & F.O. Hampson, F. (Eds.). *Managing global chaos*. Washington, D.C.: US Institute of Peace.

Lincoln, B. (1989). *Discourse and the construction of society*. New York: Oxford.

Lorenz, K. (1966). *On Aggression*. New York: Harcourt, Brace and World.

Manetsch, S.M. (2001). The Saint Bartholomew's Day Massacre. *Christian History, 20, 3, 8–15*.

Margolin, G. & Gordis, E. B. (2000). The effects of family and community violence on children. *Annual Review of Psychology, 51*, 445–479

Mattaini, M.A. & Twyman, J.S., Chin, W. & Lee, K.N. (1996). Youth violence. In M.A. Mattaini & B.A. Thyer (Eds.). *Finding solutions to social problems* (pp. 75–111). Washington, D.C.: American Psychological Association Press.

Miller, P.J. & Sperry, L. L. (1987). The socialization of anger and aggression. *Merrill-Palmer Quarterly, 33*, 1–31.

Miller, W.I. (1993). *Humiliation*. Ithaca: Cornell University.

Morson, G.S. (1991). Bahktin and the present moment. *American scholar, 60*, 201–222.

Moynihan, D.P. (1993). Defining deviancy down. *American Scholar, 62*, 17–30.

Naroll, R. (1983). *The moral order: An introduction to the human situation*. Beverly Hills, Ca. Sage.

Niehoff, D. (1999). *The biology of violence*. New York: The Free Press.

Raine, A. (1993). *The psychopathology of crime*. New York: Academic Press.

Rohner, R. (1975). *They love me, they love me not*. New Haven: HRAF Press.

Ross, M.H. (1993). *The culture of conflict*. New Haven: Yale University Press.

Rummel, R.J. (1994). *Death by government: genocide and mass murder since 1900*. New Brunswick, NJ: Transaction Publications.

Schur, E.M. (1971). *Labeling deviant behavior*. New York: Harper & Row.

Silverberg, J. & Gray, J.P. (1992). Violence and peacefulness as behavioral potentialities of primates. In J. Silverberg & J.P. Gray (Eds.). *Aggression and peacefulness in humans and other primates* (pp. 1–36). New York: Oxford University Press.

Simpson, G. (1951). Editor's introduction. In E. Durkheim (1951). *Suicide: A study in sociology*. New York: Free Press.

Summerfield, D. (1997). The social, cultural and political dimensions of contemporary war. *Medical Conflict Survivors, 13*, 3–25.

Thompson, R.A. (1990). Emotion and self-regulation. In Thompson, R.A. (Ed.). *Socio-emotional development* (pp. 367–467). Lincoln, Nebraska: University of Nebraska Press.

Walker, P.L. (2001). A bio-archaeological perspective on the history of violence. *Annual Review of Anthropology, 30*, 573–599.

WHO Global Consultation on Violence and Health (1996). *Violence: a public health priority*. Geneva: World Health Organization (document WHO/EHA/SPL.POA. 2).

Wilson, E. (1998). *Consilience*. New York: Knopf.

Yoblonsky, L. (1962). *The violent gang*. New York: Irvington Publishers.

Chapter 3

A History of Violence in the Schools

Elizabeth Midlarsky and Helen Marie Klain

Violence in the Schools: Historical Perspectives

American children spend approximately 35 hours per week in school (Volokh & Snell, 1998). In recent decades, schools have been portrayed as unsafe, a theme reinforced in movies such as *Blackboard Jungle* and *Lean on Me*, and in the news media. Indeed, on a daily basis, we are confronted with stories in the news about children and adolescents who are victims of aggression or crime in school, or who are victimizers. School shootings have been reported in Pearl, Mississippi; West Paducah, Kentucky; Jonesboro, Arkansas; Jefferson County, Colorado, and many other places. To cite some specific examples:

- In February 1996, in Moses Lake, Washington, a junior high school honor student shot and killed his math teacher and two students with a high-powered rifle (Staff, 1996).
- In 1996 in Lynville, Tennessee, a teenager fired a rifle into a school hallway, killing a teacher and a student (Staff, 1996).
- In May 1998, in Springfield, Oregon, a student was expelled after bringing a .32 caliber handgun to school. On the following day, he killed his parents at home, and then fired at fellow students and staff, in the school cafeteria (National School Safety Center, 1999).

In addition to the violent deaths are the non-fatal but serious ways in which both students and teachers are victimized. Crimes at school include rape, sexual assault, robbery, and aggravated assault (Resnick et al., 1997).

The response to what has appeared to be an increase in the prevalence, and certainly the dangerousness, of school violence has been to characterize it as a major public health problem (National Institutes of Health, 1994). Polls of the American public have indicated that violence in the schools is among the greatest concerns in the nation (Rose & Gallup, 2000). Ridding schools of violence and drugs became an important goal during the 1990s, as reflected in the government statement: "By the year 2000, every school in America will be free of drugs and violence and the unauthorized presence of firearms and alcohol, and offer a disciplined environment conducive to learning" (U.S. Department of Education, 1993). Nevertheless, even in this new millenium, violence in the schools has continued to provoke attention and concern (Reddy et al., 2001).

It seems right to assume that school violence in particular—and youth violence in general—are areas of great concern, in need of concerted prevention and intervention efforts. But is it also right to assume that "[h]istorically, our schools have been relatively safe havens from violence. . . . [whereas] more recently there has been an epidemic of youth crime (Elliot, Hamburg, & Williams, 1998)"?

The use of the term "epidemic" may be appropriate, as it is used differently here than when referring to physical health. Practitioners in the field of public health ordinarily use "epidemic" to refer to a contagious mechanism that spreads a disease from person to person. When people in the public health field refer to an epidemic of school violence, what they mean is that school violence is evoking more trauma in society than it has in the past (Moore & Tonry, 1998). The use of the term "history," though, is vague and could be misleading in this context.

While the existing data on school violence indicate that it did increase through much of the decade of the 1990s, virtually none of the recent work addresses the earlier history of this phenomenon. Additionally, even though nominally rigorous research methods have been used, methodological flaws abound in the way that the longitudinal data on school violence were collected (cf. Cornell & Loper, 1998; Kingery, Coggeshall, & Alford, 1998). Information about violence in the schools before the middle of the twentieth century is even less frequently based on systematic research efforts. The early history of school violence is known largely through archival records and anecdotes, gathered through means that rarely resemble modern research. Nevertheless, it can be useful to turn to archives and historical accounts in order to determine whether school violence is actually a new and unique phenomenon, either in prevalence or in dangerousness. If not unique, it may, instead, be yet another sociobehavioral phenomenon that has waxed and waned in response to varying social conditions. These conditions may then be amenable to understanding and ultimately to some degree of control.

At this juncture, then, schools are often portrayed as more vulnerable and dangerous than ever before in our history. The killings reported during the past decade have been perceived as unprecedented. Yet, in actuality, schools may not be any more violent than they were in the past, and they may really be less violent than in other historical periods (De Mause, 1974; Prothrow-Stith & Quaday, 1996). Without disputing that school violence is a serious problem, this chapter aims to dispel the myth that it is an apocalyptic phenomenon unique to our time and place in history. The introduction of a historical perspective will, it is hoped, permit us to approach this very real problem more evenly. This chapter is therefore designed to present a review of the historical evidence of violence both by students and by teachers. We then consider factors that may be contributing to the problem, and discuss implications for future work.

HISTORICAL EVIDENCE OF STUDENT VIOLENCE

"Have you had a rebellion lately, eh, eh?"—George III (1760–1820) to Eton school boys (Volokh & Snell, 1998, p. 1)

Student initiated school violence can be categorized into four types that have been evident throughout history. First is the act of rebellion. Rebellious episodes are often characterized by an impromptu clash during which malicious intent is absent. The second consists of action out of anger. These cases have a focused agenda and goal. Third, students behave violently out of protest. Violent protests are based on a belief or cause for which the protagonists demonstrate, object symbolically, or engage in physical violence. The fourth and the most unnerving type of school violence is the random act of violence. Here the choice of victims is not associated with the motive, and the acts are very difficult to predict.

Early Evidence of Student Violence

Student misbehavior and violence of all four types have occurred in the schools throughout recorded history (Aries, 1962). Clay tablets dating back to 2000 BC have been found with descriptions of student misbehavior and disruption in Sumer, an ancient civilization in Mesopotamia (Volokh & Snell, 1998).

In medieval schools, teaching focused mainly on religion and the re-cruitment of future ecclesiastics. Youths were also commonly taught trades through apprenticeships that usually lasted seven years (Crews & Counts, 1997). Even with an extensive curriculum of religion and skill-building, students were reported to be turbulent, rebellious, and violent (Beker & Rubel, 1980).

Contrary to the notion that students began bringing weapons to school only in very recent years, European students commonly carried weapons to school during the seventeenth century. Preteens swore, had sex, smoked, and even dueled with pistols. In France, for example, school children were usually armed. They fought with one another and beat their teachers. Re-volts and riots were common in the schools; passersby tried to avoid walk-ing past the schools out of fear of being attacked by students. In 1646, armed school boys staged an attack at the Jesuit College of La Flèche to free a fellow student who was being held for punishment. During a struggle between the school headmaster, the school servants, and the students, a musket went off shooting a student in the abdomen. In the same year, two pupils were killed on separate occasions during battles between the Humanities class and the Philosophy class at Aix College. In 1649, students barricaded themselves in Die College. They fired pistols, tore up school books, threw benches out of the windows and attacked passersby with swords. At Beaune in 1661, an Oratorian father was assaulted by his pupils at school, an attack that resulted in serious injuries. At times, teachers had no choice but to call in military forces to restore order (Aries, 1962). It is noteworthy that the mid-17th century was a time of upheaval throughout Europe, not the least of which were the Thirty Years' War and the English Civil War. Weapons and models of destructiveness were therefore prevalent.

School violence appeared to be particularly widespread during pe-riods wherein education became compulsory for previously unschooled students. Neither the students nor their teachers had any positive attach-ment to one another nor to the schools. Disciplinary problems were ram-pant and were addressed through corporal punishment. In contrast to the opinion that leniency leads to chaos, the harsh discipline applied in ear-lier times led, quite literally, to bloodshed. One example is found in the "ragged schools" in England where, in response to the adult violence,

> [t]he floors were sprinkled with blood, benches broken down, lesson boards torn asunder, the scholars tumbling over each other in wild confusion, the mas-ter with his clothes torn, teachers obliged to escape for their lives out of the windows, and over the roofs of houses. (Ashley-Cooper, 1847, p. 129)

These cases are evidence that school violence is not a recent phe-nomenon. Based on the documentation, these accounts of school violence may be classified as acts of youthful rebellion. These episodes of violence appear to lack malicious intent; they likely arise from the unruly chaos and mischief of adolescent behavior.

Student Violence in Colonial America: 1647–1779

Religion had a dominant presence in the goals of education in the 17th and 18th centuries. However, colonists made school a setting for more than ecclesiastical recruitment. Teachers were also expected to instill values and morals in children. Pamphlets encouraging the education of children were distributed with the following goals:

> (1) never permit children to be alone, since they are not fit to govern themselves; (2) discipline, do not pamper children; (3) teach modesty; (4) train children to work; teach them diligence in some lawful trade; (5) above all teach respect for and obedience to authority. Disobedience leads inevitably to dishonor, disease, and death. (Empey, 1979, pp. 12–13)

Even with the focus on discipline and values, school violence was present in the colonies. This violence may have been provoked, at least in part, by the environment in the larger community—which was chaotic and volatile. Whatever the source of the violence, though, violence was rampant in the schools and tended to be motivated by rebellion, protest, and anger. Schoolmasters (i.e., teachers) were often chosen because they were big enough and tough enough to handle the older teenage boys. These older boys often took pleasure in beating their masters or kicking them out of town. In 1669, a Massachusetts student threw his schoolmaster down twice, attacked him with a chair and threatened to break his neck. The schoolmaster brought the attack to the attention of the colonial tribunal to ensure public punishment of the student (Bybee, 1982). The colonies were also the setting of over 300 student mutinies each year. These mutinies consisted of students chasing the teachers out of school houses and locking them out (Volokh & Snell, 1998). Not surprisingly, it was often difficult to find teachers to staff the schools.

Student Violence in the Emerging Nation: 1780–1860

The purpose and fundamental goals of the education system changed with the birth of the new nation. After the Revolutionary War, the newly won sense of freedom permeated the schools. Schools were quickly becoming agents of "republicanism." The formal goals of education during this period included promoting virtues such as discipline, sacrifice, simplicity, and intelligence, as well as incorporating the concepts of liberty and government (Kaestle, 1983). One observer noted that "There is as little disposition on the part of American children to obey the uncontrovertible will of their masters as on the part of their fathers to submit to the mandates of kings" (Mann, 1934, p. 288).

During this early post-revolutionary period, American schools remained chaotic and disorderly. Horace Mann (1934) reported in 1843 that during the early nineteenth century, over 400 Massachusetts school houses were "broken up" as a result of disciplinary problems. Even American universities were the settings of acts of student violence. Princeton University experienced many violent episodes. In 1802, students set fire to their library and completely destroyed it. In 1823, riots and explosions were seen on campus. The chaos did not end until one half of the graduating class had been expelled. In total, Princeton saw six campus rebellions between 1800 and 1830 (Baker & Rubel, 1980). The University of Virginia was also the setting for a violent campus riot in the early nineteenth century. That riot ended only after a professor had been killed and armed police seized the campus (Rosenthal, 1971).

Thus, in the late eighteenth and early nineteenth centuries, the emerging American nation sought to define its role and identity within the global community. This endeavor may have been expressed in the acts of rebellion and protest evident in both in the society at large and, in microcosm, within the American schools.

Student Violence during the Industrial Revolution: 1860–1920

After the Civil War, schooling was finally accepted as an important element of daily life for children. Thirty-one states had made education compulsory by 1900. The educational system was designed to disseminate "Americanism". Children participated in school governments, sang patriotic songs and recited the Pledge of Allegiance in the schools of the late 1800s (Crews & Counts, 1997). Dewey (1897) stated that the fundamental function of education should be to socialize the child to function productively in the changing society.

Although the educational system during this period aimed to create productive members of society, school violence remained a threat. The lack of discipline, poor teaching methods and disruptive and violent student behavior caused many in the late 1800s to describe American schools as "wild and unruly" (Crews & Counts, 1997). In 1870, a Massachusetts school teacher, Etta Barstow, was stoned by four of her students. The stoning took place in retaliation for the teacher's earlier act of locking the students out of the schoolhouse when they refused to return upon being called in from the lunch break. As such, it was a case of violence motivated by anger. The brutal stoning weakened Etta Barstow's health and contributed to her untimely death (Carr, 1870).

In the 20th century violence continued, with the form changing along with the changing times. During this period Princeton University was once again the setting of a violent student protest. In 1914, students set fire to campus buildings in protest against the university's system of teaching (Baker & Rubel, 1980).

In 1917, the "Gary, Indiana platoon system" was introduced in New York City schools to deal with increases in both the number and nature of student enrollment (e.g., unprecedented increases in East European immigrants). This plan, known as the "Gary Plan," attempted to better utilize the New York City school buildings to accommodate the changing student population. It entailed a reorganization of the classroom structure and layout by combining certain classes into one classroom (Crews & Counts, 1997). This idea was too radical and inconvenient for some students, many of whom were immigrants who were struggling to perform well in school. They believed that the Gary Plan would make learning even more difficult for them and would decrease the quality of education in the schools. In the politically charged atmosphere than existed in 1917, school children protested in the name of their political cause. Between 1,000 and 3,000 angry students staged a strike, picketing and throwing stones at the windows of Manhattan's P. S. 171 on Madison Avenue, in response to the Gary Plan. The students who did not participate in the picketing were beaten, and their schoolbooks were burned. Eventually, the rioting spread to public schools in Brooklyn and the Bronx with more than 10,000 students joining in the protests. The strikes did not stop until police guards arrested fourteen of the student leaders (Baker & Rubel, 1980; Crews & Counts, 1997).

These documented cases of student violence help us understand that during the Industrial Revolution, American schools were in an uneasy state. Students began to take an active role in shaping the methods and the quality of their education. They acted in protest against actions that they believed were not conducive to learning. The students felt that education was important, and they voiced their concerns. Student riots and picket lines of this era are examples of violent protests against perceived injustice.

Student Violence in the Early Twentieth Century: 1920–1950

The values of the American public changed dramatically during the early 1920s. The "Roaring Twenties" was a decade of prosperity and pleasure. Fearing mischief that could be engaged in by affluent, idle youth, the goals of education during the twenties were described as the provision of "moral education, character education, education for citizenship and for the wise use of leisure time" (Palmquist, 1929, p. 11).

Directly following this prosperous era were the stock market crash and the Great Depression. When student delinquency occurred during this era, the main forms that it took were truancy and excessive lying (Crews & Counts, 1997). Interestingly, there was a paucity of school violence and of other serious school disturbances during the Depression years. However, the lack of school violence is likely due to the fact that many children had to leave school and work (Baker & Rubel, 1980). It is also suggested that with the onset of World War II school children were more obedient because they understood the danger that their nation was in and felt a civic responsibility to respect authority (Shepherd & Ragan, 1992).

Student Violence in the Modern Era: 1950–2004

After World War II, the nation developed goals for education that included the promotion of equal opportunity between the races and the sexes, and meeting the scientific and technological needs of the Cold War (Shepherd & Ragan, 1992). Additionally, Crow and Crow (1950) listed four new objectives of the education system as: (1) self-realization, (2) human relationships, (3) economic efficiency and (4) civic responsibility. Even with these new idealized objectives, school violence has crept back into the schools.

The immediate post-World War II era was politically sedate. However, this relative quietude did not yield student compliance. The overall national climate encompassed urban strife and the anomie of suburban life. The developing unrest fueled student protests, rebelliousness, and crime in and outside of the schools. In the 1950s, students became very active in social movements including movements concerned with school segregation and racial equality. In some cases, these social movements led to violent protests, which involved outbreaks in the schools. The most notable instance of this period occurred in Little Rock, Arkansas in 1957 when nine black students attempted to enter their new schools that had previously been attended only by white students. An angry mob of students and parents protested the racial integration outside of the school. The 1950s also witnessed an increase in school assaults and vandalism (Crews & Counts, 1997).

During the 1960s, the term "school violence" was coined as a result of the growing problem of violence in the schools. Between the years 1964 and 1968, assaults on teachers increased from 253 to 1,801. During the same time period, weapons offenses in schools increased from 396 to 1,508 (Beavan, 1967). A Congressional hearing on school violence reported that among 757 major school districts there were approximately 200 student deaths classified as school-related in a single year. The increase in violence during this period may be attributed to the increase in the number of students enrolled in school as the "Baby Boom Generation" were entering high school during this decade (Crews & Counts, 1997).

Racism and civil rights clashes were evident in schools throughout the 1960s. Black students felt that schools did not honor black cultural and political heroes in history classes and that schools did not adequately deal with issues concerning black culture. The students voiced their concerns to school administrators and to the public, but their complaints were rarely heard. Their frustration in the education system often reached a climax in public demonstrations and riots (Baker & Rubel, 1980). Also in the late 1960s, students protested political events such as the Vietnam War. Radical political student groups emerged in the late 1960s which often demonstrated on school grounds, commonly resulting in violent clashes (Crews & Counts, 1997).

In the summer of 1966, one of the first reported acts of random school violence occurred. Charles Whitman, a student from the University of Texas, took aim at students and faculty from the twenty-eighth floor of the university library tower. During a 96 minute shooting rampage, Whitman fatally shot thirteen people and wounded thirty-one (Altman & Ziporyn, 1967).

It was in the 1970s that violence in the schools was first included among the top ten concerns in the annual Gallup poll of public attitudes toward schools (Gallup, 1978). This growing concern was fueled by documented increases in violence in the schools. Between 1970 and 1973, there was a 19.5% increase in homicides on school grounds, an 85.3% increase in student to student assaults, a 77.4% increase in student to teacher assaults, a 54.4% increase in weapons confiscated on school grounds, and a 40.1% increase in rapes and attempted rapes (Goldstein, Apter & Harootunian, 1984). In 1978, teenagers were at a greater risk of being victims of violence at school than anywhere else (Crews & Counts, 1997). The school violence of this decade could be described as acts of rebellion and anger. Violent gangs present in the schools during this period were responsible for a majority of the crimes and deviant behavior occurring in the classroom (Baker & Rubel, 1980).

The increase in juvenile criminality during the 1980s is often attributed to the advent of crack cocaine (Simonsen, 1991). In addition, substantial federal funding cutbacks in the 1980s resulted in a greatly reduced quality of education in the public schools (Spring, 1990). Students in public schools adopted a "get tough" philosophy and their behavior mirrored their philosophy. A survey of students between the ages 12–19 conducted in 1989 found that 9% reported being the victim of crime in or around their school and 2% experienced one or more violent crimes (Crews & Counts, 1997). It should therefore come as no surprise that school violence in the 1980s was viewed as a major social problem.

In the 1990s educational goals still focused on socializing students to become productive members of society. In 1996, Elam, Rose and Gallup stated:

> One of the principal goals of education is to produce individuals capable of clear moral judgment and self-control. However, this goal will be difficult for the school to achieve due to the ever-present occurrences of school violence. (p. 43)

For example, during the 1990s nearly 20% of students reported carrying a weapon to school, and an estimated 270,000 guns were brought to the schools on a daily basis (Crews & Counts, 1997). Between July 1, 1997 and June 30, 1998 alone, 60 violent deaths in the United States were school related. Of these 60 violent deaths, 48 were homicides, and 12 were suicides. During the same period, the 253,000 reports of nonfatal student to student violence included rape, assault, and robbery. Between 1994 and 1998, teachers were the victims of 668,000 violent crimes at school, a number which translates to 83 crimes per every 1,000 teachers each year (Kaufman et al., 2000).

At Thomas Jefferson High School in Brooklyn, New York, in 1992, a 15 year old student got into an argument with two of his fellow classmates. Later in the week, he came to school with a gun and fatally shot them (Volokh & Snell, 1998). Over fifty Thomas Jefferson students were killed during the early 1990s, with many of the deaths taking place on school grounds. Many of the deaths were related to drugs and gangs (Volokh & Snell, 1998). The most shocking and infamous case of school violence to date is the Littleton, Colorado massacre of 1999 in which two students planted bombs in their school before fatally shooting 12 students and one teacher, injuring twenty more and then eventually killing themselves (Best, 2002).

HISTORICAL EVIDENCE OF TEACHER VIOLENCE

"A boy has a back; when you hit it he understands"—A pedagogical maxim of the 1800s (Baker & Rubel, 1980, p. 10)

"All cruelty springs from weakness."—Seneca 4BC–65AD

While the spotlight is typically on wild and unruly behavior by students, it is important to note that teachers also have long exhibited violent behavior. Indeed, the earliest recorded incidents of school violence consist of teacher violence—in the form of behavior referred to as "corporal punishment." Corporal punishment has been an accepted practice, and has often been mandated by school authorities. It is generally defined as the intentional inflicting of pain as the penalty for an offense (Hyman & Perone, 1998).

One way to understand corporal punishment, an extreme form of discipline, is that it has been used to assert the power and authority of school teachers and officials. As caregivers of school children, specifically given the charge to educate them, this authority has been viewed as a necessity. In the face of serious student misbehavior, especially violence, power assertion has been the rule. Even if only one student-offender is punished, then this punishment is expected to "send a message" to all students and to the community that the authority vested in the school is still secure (Foucault, 1979). Particularly unfortunate is the fact that throughout much of the history of American schools, many teachers have been so poorly paid that they took teaching jobs by default (in other words, it was the only job that they could get). As few teaching resources and little training in pedagogy were available, rote memorization was the primary means of instruction. Corporal punishment was therefore used not only to punish, but as a way to force bored students to engage in rote learning of required materials (Hyman & Wise, 1979). It is also unfortunate that only 27 states prohibit the use of corporal punishment today.

Early Evidence of Teacher Violence

In the ancient world, children were expected to be attentive and hard-working at all times when in school. Thus, it wasn't unusual for teachers to whip children for laziness or for daydreaming. In Ancient Egypt, teachers were given complete control over their charges. Students who were sleepy, slow, or talkative were beaten with a rod. In Pre-Columbian America, the Incas beat students who disobeyed—even though only sons of rulers and noblemen attended school. However punishment could only be administered once a day, and the maximum consisted of ten strokes to the soles of the feet (Bauer, 2002).

The Use of Corporal Punishment in Colonial America: 1647–1779

In the early colonial period, teachers spent more time trying to maintain order than imparting knowledge. Religion and obedience were emphasized in early American schools, often to the exclusion of academic subjects. Puritan beliefs set a standard for morals and character. These beliefs were ingrained in the community through the social agent of the schoolhouse. Teachers were hired for their flawless characters, rather than for their level of education or interest in teaching. The primary duty of teachers in colonial America was to maintain good order in the classroom. Indeed, they often spent more time maintaining order in the classroom than teaching. Teachers were given absolute authority in the schoolhouses and they demanded obedience. Corporal punishment was commonly used to control the students. The students were ordered to learn from repetitive drilling, and those who were unable to learn were punished (Baker & Rubel, 1980). Any punishment that the students had to endure was considered justified by the Puritan community. Indeed, The Puritan settlers took the responsibility to educate their children very seriously. Education in reading the Lord's gospel, as well as the rules of the community would, they believed, be the means for rescuing children from evil and insuring their eternal salvation. These convictions echoed Proverbs, XIII, 24,

> He that spareth the rod hateth his son
> But he that loveth him chastiseth him betimes.

In colonial America, reports of corporal punishment in the schools were common and seen as a way to create a better youth. The dominant belief that human nature is intrinsically evil justified the use of power assertion to subdue the young. Punishments during this time included being hit on the knuckles with a ruler for talking in class, to being pulled from the seat by the ear for falling asleep, being forced to clean the blackboard or schoolyard trash for tardiness, or being threatened with eternal damnation! For very serious misbehavior, the pillory or whipping post were used, or even the branding iron. A child who stole might be branded "T" for thief, and a "B" might be used to punish blasphemy (Crews & Counts, 1997). Teachers were often chosen for their toughness, as the biggest teenage boys enjoyed beating and kicking the teacher out of town. Even when teachers were averse to harsh discipline, they felt that they had no choice. Some teachers underwent considerable suffering under these conditions (Baker & Rubel, 1980).

College students, who tended to be older teenagers, were not exempt from corporal punishment. In 1645, two Harvard College students were badly beaten by the schoolmaster for burglary. In 1672, another Harvard College student was publicly whipped, suspended, and forced to eat his meals alone and naked. His crime was blasphemy. At the end of the 17th century, students of Harvard College were given routine corporal punishments for crimes such as "lack of piety, sexual indiscretion and having long hair" (Baker & Rubel, 1980).

Corporal Punishment in the Emerging Nation: 1780–1860

After the Revolutionary War, American citizens were given individual liberty. However, there was a fear that too much liberty would lead to anarchy and chaos (Crews & Counts, 1997). Education was seen as a way to bridge the gap between personal and national freedom and maintaining the social order. Teachers often had to control bored, mischievous and unmotivated pupils on a daily basis. Teachers often chose to maintain order in the classroom through threats, intimidation, humiliation and physical abuse (Baker & Rubel, 1980).

In 1793, a schoolhouse was built in Sunderland, Massachusetts. This schoolhouse is noteworthy because it was the first schoolhouse with a whipping post built into the floor of the building (Hyman & Wise, 1979). During the same period, paddling devices and whips were prominently displayed in the classroom as a reminder that punishment would follow disobedience. Often, when students were off-task, the schoolmaster would simply point to the devices and order in the classroom would be restored (Hyman & Wise, 1979). Hauberle was an American school headmaster for more than 50 years. He took pride in the number of beatings and physical punishments that he administered. He published a list of the finest accomplishments of his career and cited that he administered 911,527 blows with a cane, 124,010 blows with a rod, 20989 blows with a ruler, 136,715 blows with his hand, 1,111,800 raps on the head and ordered 613 kneelings on a triangular piece of wood. Teachers of this era also used confinement to punish unruly pupils. It was common to send a student into a windowless closet, known as a "dungeon," for an extended period of time (Baker & Rubel, 1980). Burton (1833) described his experiences in the classroom and the harsh punishments the students endured:

> She kept order; for her punishments were horrible, especially to us little ones. She dungeoned us in that windowless closet just for a whisper. She tied us to her chair-post for an hour. A twist of the ear, or a snap on the head from her thimbled finger reminded us that sitting still was the most important virtue of a little boy in school. Some students were ferruled on the hand, some were whipped with a rod on the back, some were compelled to hold out, at arms length, the largest book which could be found till muscle and nerve, bone and marrow were tortured with the continued exertion. (p. 25)

In 1837, Horace Mann was elected to be the first Secretary of the Massachusetts Board of Education (Crews & Counts, 1997). He reportedly visited a small school of 250 students for a five day period. During this short period of time, he witnessed 328 floggings (Mann, 1934). The first state court case to address the authority given to teachers and their means of disciplining students was *State v. Pendergrass* in 1837. In this case, a six year old girl was beaten with a switch until she had red marks on her body. It was ruled that the teacher had not exceeded the limits of authority because the child suffered no permanent injury (Bybee, 1982).

The Use of Corporal Punishment in the Industrial Revolution: 1860–1920

During the Industrial Revolution, children were beginning to be treated differently than adults. Child labor laws were enacted to protect children from harsh working environments and long hours (Crews & Counts, 1997). In 1899, Illinois opened a court created specifically to deal with juvenile cases. This court was established as a result of the public's recognition that children were indeed different from adults and should be held to different standards (Simonsen, 1991).

States began to make education mandatory for children out of the growing need for an advanced and intelligent society (Baker & Rubel, 1980). To deal with the increase in student enrollment and curriculum standards, teachers and school administrators were trained in education and classroom management. Corporal punishment was still accepted as an appropriate form of punishment, if it was used as a last resort. It could be administered for acts of violence or inappropriate behavior, but not for poor academic performance. With the growing comprehension of children's needs and educational practices, some educators started to view corporal punishment as cruel and unusual punishment regardless of the offense (Baker & Rubel, 1980). In 1867, New Jersey became the first state to ban the use of corporal punishment in the classroom. It is interesting to note that before the ban was fully implemented, there were 9,408 documented whippings in the Newark, New Jersey school system of 10,000 students (Hyman & Wise, 1979).

Corporal Punishment during the Early Twentieth Century: 1920–1950

After World War I, teaching emerged as a career for which higher education was required (Crews & Counts, 1997). It was no longer seen as a temporary position for untrained workers. The Great Depression forced many children to leave school to help support their families (Baker & Rubel, 1980). Thus, while juvenile delinquency, such as theft and vandalism, increased outside of the school, violence decreased within schools (Crews & Counts, 1997). As student misbehavior in the schools decreased, therefore, the need for corporal punishment by teachers decreased as well (Baker & Rubel, 1980). While lawmakers were starting to recognize that corporal punishment was harsh, cruel and unnecessary in the schools, paddling remained a common occurrence, at least in certain states (Simonsen, 1991).

Corporal Punishment in the Modern Era: 1950–2004

In a 1969 poll conducted by the National Education Association, 65% of elementary school teachers and 55% of secondary school teachers favored the "judicious use" of corporal punishment in the schools. During 1973 and 1974, there were approximately 40,000 cases of corporal punishment documented in the school records of California alone (Hyman & Wise, 1979).

In 1976, three Missouri students were caught with cigarettes on school grounds. As punishment, there were given the choice of either eating the remaining 18 cigarettes or undergoing a paddling. The boys chose to eat the cigarettes to avoid the pain of the beating. All three of them ended up in the hospital for three days with kidney infections and ulcers from eating the cigarettes (Hyman & Wise, 1979).

In 1977, a 14 year old Florida student was beaten by school administrators for leaving the school auditorium too slowly. He was beaten about the neck, head, arm, leg and back with a belt and paddle, resulting in cuts that required sutures, as well as bruises and scars. His father took the school to court, claiming that the beating violated his son's Eighth Amendment right against cruel and unusual punishment, and his Fourteenth Amendment right of due process. The U. S. Supreme Court found that corporal punishment did not violate the Eighth Amendment because it had been used in education for centuries. The Court also ruled that the punishment did not violate the right to due process because prior notice would hinder the schools' ability to administer the punishment (*Ingraham v. Wright, 97, S. Ct. 1977*; in Hyman & Rathbone, 1993). In light of this ruling it may not be surprising that corporal punishment still occurs in schools today.

In 1987, a second grade student was tied by her waist and legs to a chair for almost two days in school to keep her from misbehaving. She was not allowed to eat, drink, or use the bathroom during her punishment. The teacher claimed that she was using an "instructional technique" rather than corporal punishment (*Jefferson v. Ysletta Independent School District, 5th Circuit, 1987*; in Hyman & Rathbone, 1993). In 1989, an eight year old boy was paddled by his teacher. During the paddling his arm broke. His teacher claimed it broke when the boy squirmed to avoid the blows. His parents believe that it was broken when the child was yanked up from the floor by his arm (*Crews v. McQueen, Ga. Ct Apps. 1989*; Hyman & Rathbone, 1993).

Today, 23 states still deem corporal punishment in the school to be an acceptable means of punishment for disobedience and offensive acts in the classroom (Arcus, 2002). The issue of corporal punishment remains controversial today. According to its supporters, corporal punishment is seen as a way to teach students morals and proper behavior, as well as communicating societal norms and expectations (Hyman & Rathbone, 1993). Its detractors claim that corporal punishment constitutes unnecessary and even gratuitous violence in the schools (Crews & Counts, 1997).

FACTORS CONTRIBUTING TO SCHOOL VIOLENCE

The thesis of this chapter is that historically, the American school as a safe haven has been a goal rather than a reality. American schools, like schools in virtually all places and historical eras, have rarely been peaceful. The amount of violence has ebbed and flowed but never disappeared. The nature of the violence and its causes have probably been as diverse as the surrounding cultures and the social forces in operation within them.

While it is evident that school violence has been present in schools since students first came into being, it is unclear what factors create such an unruly and violent environment. Certainly, there are factors that have remained present throughout history which may contribute to the amount of violence in schools. Possible predictors of school violence include, to begin with, one of the means that has been used historically to combat student misbehavior—corporal punishment. Other factors include bullying, intrapersonal factors (such as emotional disturbance, exposure to violence in the home, and substance abuse), media exposure, and the availability of weapons.

It is believed by some researchers that the socialization of children by violent means such as corporal punishment creates an environment in which violence is accepted as a norm (Arcus, 2002; Straus, 1994). Children raised in this environment are more apt to learn that the powerful control the weak through authoritarian means, including violence. They are less likely to be empathic, and to care for others, than are those socialized through gentler means (Midlarsky, Supraner, & Krauss, submitted).

Children raised in an environment in which power assertion is the primary means of disciplining are likely to be aggressive and violent; it may be no coincidence that the states reporting the highest rates of school paddling also report having the greatest number of juveniles awaiting capital punishment in the state judicial system (Arcus, 2002). It has also been reported that states with the highest rates of homicide committed by children tend to have the highest rates of corporal punishment (Straus, 1989; see Figure 2). Arcus (2002) also found that children are more likely to die in school shootings in the states that permit the use of corporal punishment than states that prohibit corporal punishment. It was also found that the more physically punitive the methods of discipline of that state were, the more likely that a student would die in a school shooting (Arcus, 2002). However, the direction of causation is not clearly established. It is possible that states with more punitive practices are reacting to exogenous societal conditions which increase the prevalence of violence in their schools.

Another important predictor of school violence is victimization by school bullies. Being the target of bullies is a predictor of bullying others, suicidal thoughts, and suicide. Bullying behaviors include taunting, destruction of personal property, and physical aggression by a powerful individual or a group. Bullying has occurred in schools from the beginning of formal schooling and has been reported in countries ranging from Kenya, to Norway and Japan. The one factor that is present in all cases of school shootings is that the shooters had all been bullied (Batsche & Knoff, 1994; Olweus, 1993).

Certain intrapersonal factors have been shown to predict violent school behavior in students. Harper and Ibrahim (2000) found that violent youth behavior is correlated, among other things, with poor social skills and with substance abuse. Goldstein and Huff (1993) found that intergenerational antisocial behavior was also related to youth violence and aggression. It has also been found that anger, depression, and deficits in coping skills are related to acts of violence by students (Flannery & Singer, 1999). Capozzoli and McVey (2000) add that Conduct Disorder, parental abuse, and stress are related to violent behavior in youths.

The media and entertainment industries may also contribute to school violence today (Felson, 1996; Flannery & Singer, 1999; Reiss & Roth, 1993). A study conducted by Lichter, Lichter and Amundson (1999) at the Center for Media and Public Affairs examined the frequency of violent images in popular entertainment. They found that when movies, television programs, and music videos are all taken into account, violent images were shown an average of 14 times per hour on average. It is very difficult to establish causal effects between viewing violent images and engaging in violent behavior. However, evidence suggests that violence in popular entertainment may well promote violent youth behavior (Felson, 1996; Flannery & Singer, 1999; Reiss & Roth, 1993). Capozzoli and McVey (2000) theorize that violence in the media desensitizes the youths to the horrors of murder, by "normalizing" it. The media have also been blamed for copycat crimes in the schools (Cohen, 1999; Kostinsky, Bixler & Kettl, 2001; Maeroff, 2000). One week after the massacre in Littleton, Colorado, at least one copycat threat was reported in each of 49 states. In Pennsylvania alone, more than 60 threats of violence against schools or students were reported. Four weeks after the massacre, over 350 students were arrested nationwide on charges related to threats of school violence, a dramatic increase from the weeks before the Colorado incident at Columbine (Kostinsky, et al., 2001).

Another factor that may be related to school violence is the availability of guns and other weapons. Researchers have found that juveniles have easy access to guns, and that an expressed fascination with weapons is related to school violence, particularly among males (Flannery & Singer, 1999). In 1997, the results of a survey indicated that approximately one third of all households in the United States have guns, and two thirds of gun owners have more than one gun (Cook & Ludwig, 1997). Furthermore, twenty percent of gun owners in a recent survey reported that they keep a loaded gun in their homes at all times, and the gun is frequently not secured. However, accessibility to guns owned by adults and kept in the home is not the only problem. While the federal law restricts the sales of guns to minors by licensed gun dealers, some states allow children as young as 12 years old to legally possess semi-automatic weapons as well as other firearms (Ward, 1999). It is sometimes argued that without such easy access to firearms, many acts of school violence in recent years would not have taken place (Flannery & Singer, 1999).

IMPLICATIONS AND CONCLUSIONS

This historical survey reminds us of the dangers of oversimplification as we consider the etiology of school violence. Factors associated with violence in the schools have varied widely across eras and places. Thus, while population density, diversity, and poverty are associated with violence in some places and times, in others they are not. In the late nineteenth century, New York had a large and extremely poor and heterogeneous population of immigrants, many of whom were clustered in the Lower East Side. Yet, the amount of violence was very low, both in the streets and in the schools. The "mean streets" of New York are safer than York was in the thirteenth century. The Greek mountains were far more violent than the streets of London. During the Thirty Years' War, there was a great increase in school violence, and during World War II, there was a decrease. These and many other historical facts tend to indicate that questions about violence in the schools have no easy, "one size fits all" answers.

What is abundantly clear is that school violence cannot be explained by any single cause. Like most complex social phenomena, it is multiply determined (Gilligan, 2001). School violence has existed through all of the eras in which there has been formal schooling. Whether the students have been children of noblemen and rulers or children of families in poverty, taught by untrained or trained teachers, violence has occurred. There has never been a period in which parents could send their children to school, confidently (and correctly) assuming that they would be safe from violence both by their peers and by their teachers.

In societal contexts that apparently have never been completely free of conflict and violence, perhaps it is to be expected that violence would permeate the schools. Today, public officials reassure us both that school violence is on the decline and that our schools are quite safe, relative to the surrounding communities. And perhaps our schools, while not truly serving as safe havens, have more protections against violence than most other settings within our turbulent world. Our job, however, is to foster the development of schools that can create the moral leaders of a peaceful society, rather than serve as reflections of the troubles that currently exist.

REFERENCES

Altman, J. & Ziporyn, M. (1967). *Born to raise hell*. New York: Grove Press.
Arcus, D. (2002). School shooting fatalities and school corporal punishment: A look at the states. *Aggressive Behavior, 28*, 173–183.
Aries, P. (1962). *Centuries of childhood*. New York: Alfred A. Knopf, Inc.
Ashley-Cooper, A., Seventh Earl of Shaftesbury. (1847). The ragged schools. *Quarterly Review, 79*, 127–141.

Baker, K. and Rubel, R.J. (1980). *Violence and crime in the schools*. Lexington, MA: Lexington Books.

Batsche, G. & Knoff, H. (1994). Bullies and their victims. *Psychological Review, 23*, 165–174.

Bauer, S. (2002). *Ancient times*. New York: W. W. Norton.

Beavan, K. (1970, February 13). School violence on the increase. *New York Times Educational Supplement, 2856*, 16.

Best, J. (2002). Monster hype. *Education Next, 2(2)* 50–55.

Bielick, S. Chandler, K., & Broughman, S.P. (2001). *Homeschooling in the United States: 1999*. U.S. Department of Education. Washington D.C.: National Center for Education Statistics.

Burton, W. (1833). *The district school as it was*. Norwood, MA: Norwood.

Bybee, R.W. (1982). *Violence, values, and justice in the schools*. Boston: Allyn & Bacon.

Capozzoli, T.K. & McVey, R.S. (1999). *Kids killing kids: Managing violence and gangs in schools*. Boca Raton, FL: St. Lucie Press.

Carr, V. (1870). The stoning of Etta Barstow. *The Canton Town Report*. Retrieved January 28, 2004 from http://www.canton.org/history/barstow1.htm.

Cohen, A. (1999). Criminals as copycats. *Time, 153(21)* 38–39.

Cook, P.J. & Ludwig, J. (1997). Guns in America: National survey on private ownership and use of firearms. *Research Brief*. Washington D.C.: U.S. Department of Justice.

Cornell, D.G. & Loper, A.B. (1998). Assessment of violence and other high-risk behaviors with a school survey. *School Psychology Review, 27*, 317–330.

Crews, G.A. & Counts, M.R. (1997). *The evolution of school violence in America*. Westport, CT: Praeger.

De Mause, L. (1974). The evolution of childhood. *Journal of Psychohistory, 1*, 403–575.

Dewey, J. (1897). My pedagogic creed. *The School Journal, LIV*, 77–80.

Elam, S., Rose, L. & Gallup, A. (1996). The 28th annual Phi Delta Kappa/Gallup poll of the public's attitude toward public schools. *Phi Delta Kappan, 78*, 1, 41–59.

Elliot, D.S., Hamburg, B.A., & Williams, K.R. (1998). Violence in American schools: An overview. In D. S. Elliot, B. A. Hamburg, & K. R. Williams (Eds.), *Violence in American schools* (pp. 3–28). New York: Cambridge.

Empey, L.T. (1979). *The future of childhood and juvenile justice*. Charlottesville, VA: Virginia University Press.

Falk, H.A. (1941). *Corporal punishment: A social interpretation of its theory and practice in the schools of the United States*. New York: Columbia University.

Felson, R.B. (1996). Mass media effects on violent behavior. *Annual Review of Sociology, 22*, 103–128.

Flannery, D.J. & Singer, M.I. (1999). Exposure to violence and victimization at school. *Choice Briefs, 4*, 1–11.

Foucault, M. (1979). *Discipline and punish*. New York: Vintage Books.

Furlong, M., Morrison, G.M., Chung, A., Bates, M., & Morrison, R.I. (1997). *School violence: Children's needs*. Bethesda, MD: National Association of School Psychologists.

Gallup, G.H. (1978). The 10th annual Gallup poll of the public's attitude toward public schools. *Phi Delta Kappan, 60*, 1, 33–45.

Gilligan, J. (2001). *Preventing violence*. London: Thames & Hudson.

Goldstein, A., Apter, B., & Harootunian, B. (1984). *School violence*. Englewood Cliffs, NJ: Prentice Hall.

Goldstein, A. & Huff, C.R. (1993). *The gang intervention handbook*. Champaign, IL: Research Press.

Harper, F. & Ibrahim, F.A. (2000). Violence and schools in the USA: Implications for counseling. *International Journal for the Advancement of Counseling, 21*, 349–366.

Hyman, I.A. (1990). *Reading, writing and the hickory stick: The appalling story of physical and psychological abuse in American schools*. Washington, DC: Lexington Books.

Hyman, I.A. & Perone, D.C. (1998). The other side of school violence: Educator policies and practices that may contribute to student misbehavior. *Journal of School Psychology, 36(1)* 7–27.

Hyman, I.A. & Snook, P.A. (1999). *Dangerous schools: What we can do about the physical and emotional abuse of our children.* San Francisco: Jossey-Bass Inc.

Hyman, I.A. & Wise, J. (1979). *Corporal punishment in American education.* Philadelphia:Temple University Press.

Hyman, R.T. & Rathbone, C.H. (1993). *Corporal punishment in schools: Reading the law.* Topeka, Kansas: National Organization on Legal Problems of Education.

Kaestle, C.F. (1983). *Pillars of the republic: Common schools and America society: 1780–1860.* New York: Hill & Wang.

Kaufman, P., Chen, X., Choy, S.P., Ruddy, S.A., Miller, A.K., Fleury, J.K., Chandler, K.A., Rand, M.R., Klaus, P., & Planty, M.G. (2000). *Indicators of school crime and safety, 2000.* Washington, DC: U.S. Departments of Education and Justice.

Kingery, P.M., Coggeshall, M.B., & Alford, A.A. (1998). Violence at school: Recent evidence from four national surveys. *Psychology in the Schools, 35,* 247–258.

Kostinsky, S., Bixler, E., & Kettl, P. (2001). Threats of school violence in Pennsylvania after media coverage of the Columbine High School massacre. *Archives of Pediatrics and Adolescent Medicine, 155 (9)* 994–1001.

Lichter, S.R., Lichter, L.S., & Amundson, D. (1999). *Merchandizing mayhem: Violence in popular culture.* Washington, D.C.: Center for Media and Public Affairs.

Maeroff, G.I. (2000). *A symbiosis of sorts: School violence and the media.* Choice Briefs, 7, 1–9.

Mann, H. (1934). Seventh annual report to the Massachusetts State Board of Education, 1843. In Ellwood Cubberly, Ed. Readings in public education in the United States: A collection of sources and readings to illustrated the history of educational practice and progress in the United States (pp. 287–288). Boston: Houghton Mifflin.

National Institutes of Health. (1994). *Report of the panel on NIH research on antisocial, aggressive, and violence-related behaviors and their consequences.* Bethesda, MD: author.

National School Safety Center. (1999). *School associated violent deaths. In-house report.* Westlake, CA: NSSC.

Palmquist, T.R. (1929). The school's responsibility in the problem of crime. *The Kansas Teacher, 30(1)* 7–16.

Parker-Jenkins, M. (1999). *Sparing the rod: Schools, discipline and children's rights.* London: Trentham Books Limited.

Prothrow-Stith, D. & Quaday, S. (1996). Communities, schools, and violence. In A. M. Hoffman (Ed.), *Schools, violence, and society* (pp. 153–161). Westport, CT: Praeger.

Reddy, M., Borum, R., Berglund, J., Vossekiul, B., Fein, R. & Modzeleski, W. (2001). Evaluating risk for targeted violence in schools. *Psychology in the Schools, 38,* 157–172.

Regoli, R.M. & Hewitt, J.D. (1994). *Delinquency in society: A child-centered approach.* New York: McGraw-Hill.

Reiss, A.J. & Roth, J.A. (1993). *Understanding and preventing violence.* Washington, D.C.: National Academy Press.

Resnick, M.A., Bearman, P., Blum, R., Bauman, K., Harris, K., Jones, J., Tabar, J., Beuhring, T., Sieving, R., Shew, M., Ireland, M., Bearinger, L., & Udry, J. (1997). Protecting adolescents from harm: Findings from the national longitudinal study of adolescent health. *Journal of the American Medical Association, 278,* 823–832.

Rose, L. & Gallup, A. (2000). The 32nd annual Phi Delta Kappa/Gallup Poll of the public's attitudes toward the public schools. *Phi Delta Kappan, 82,* 41–66.

Rosenthal, C.F. (1971). *Social conflict and collective violence in American institutions of higher learning.* Washington D.C.: U.S. Department of Commerce.

Rothman, E.P. (1977). *Troubled teachers.* New York: David McKay Company, Inc.

Shepherd, G.D. & Ragan, W.B. (1992). *Modern Elementary Curriculum*, 7th ed. Harcourt, Brace, & Jovanovich.

Simonsen, F.E. (1991). *Juvenile justice in America* (3rd edition). New York: Macmillan.

Spring, J. (1990). *The American school: 1642–1990* (2nd edition). New York: Longman.

Staff. (1996, March 3). Shooting at school prompts new concerns about violence. *The New York Times*, p. 8.

Straus, M. (1989). *Corporal punishment and crime: A theoretical model and some empirical data.* Indianapolis, IN: Indiana University.

Straus, M.A. & Donnelly, D.A. (1994). *Beating the devil out of them.* New York: Lexington Books.

Supraner, I. Midlarsky, E., & Krauss, H. (2005). Family backgrounds of Holocaust via reserves (submitted).

Tonry, M. & Moore, M.H. (1998). Youth violence in America. In M. Tonry & M.H. Moore (Eds.), *Youth violence* (pp. 1–26). Chicago: University of Chicago Press.

U.S. Department of Education. (1993). *Reaching the goals. Goal six. Safe, disciplikned, and drug-free schools.* Washington, DC: U.S. Department of Education, Office of Educational Research and Improvement.

Volokh, A. & Snell, L. (1998). *School violence prevention: Strategies to keep schools safe.* Reason Public Policy Institute policy study No. 234. Retrieved January 4, 2004 from: http://www.rppi.org/ps234.html.

Ward, J.M. (1999). *Children and guns.* Washington, D.C.: Children's Defense Fund.

Chapter 4

Warning Signs
School Violence Prevention

June F. Chisholm and Alfred W. Ward

In the days and weeks following the Columbine shootings, I walked around school seeing things in a totally different light. I didn't just stroll down the halls with my usually oblivious "I-didn't-get-enough-sleep" attitude. I really looked at the people walking next to me, in front of me, and in back of me. All I kept thinking was, "Any one of these people could shoot me at any second." I knew it was highly unlikely but after watching CNN's coverage of Columbine for hours, I came to the realization that as ridiculous as it may seem, it could happen at my school. It could happen at any school.

Melanie Ratchford (2000)

Since violence was declared a public health issue in 1985 by then Surgeon General of the U.S., C. Everett Koop, the incidence of violence has continued to mount, and in most recent years it has become a significant problem within the school system (Kingery, Coggeshall, & Alford, 1998). Research on the impact of violence in the schools has confirmed that this form of violence has created an enormous threat to the emotional, physical, and spiritual well being of children who are not only victims of violence but are perpetrators as well (Batsche & Knoff, 1994; Chisholm & Ward, 2004; Chisholm, 1995; Dwyer et al., 1998). Metal detectors, security guards, and, most recently in New York City, the police are commonplace in those schools where the outbreak of violence occurs daily. This paper reviews the violence and violence prevention research designed to identify proximal (individual/behavioral) and distal (societal/environmental) warning signs of violence. Also discussed is the collaborative violence prevention initiative launched by the American Psychological Association and Music Television (MTV) to inform the public about warning signs of potential violent acts so that schools remain safe, secure environments for learning, free from violence.

PERSPECTIVES ON VIOLENCE

A review of the literature indicates no single cause for violence. Indeed, violent behavior is best understood as the result of a multitude of interconnected events and circumstances (Gottfredson, 1997; Sheras, Cornell, & Bostain, 1996). Theories and research on violence have explored and attempted to understand this phenomenon from different perspectives, ranging from the micro level (e.g., the psychology of the offender) to the macro level (e.g., a focus on society itself by examining sociopolitical, economic, and cultural factors). Figure 1 presents an etiological model of violent behavior (modified from Gottfredson, 1997), identifying proximal and distal type predictors of problem behaviors as well as factors (protective and risk) that potentially mediate or moderate (Frazier, Tix, & Barron, 2004) predictor/outcome relationships. This model conceptualizes the etiology of violence as a complex nexus of circumstances that demand a commensurate approach to strategies of prevention. We will now review various components of the model presented in Figure 1. Many of the variables categorized in this model will be discussed more fully in later sections.

Representative problem behaviors towards which prevention programs are typically targeted include criminal and delinquent acts such as theft, illegal acts of aggression, sale of drugs and alcohol, as well as poor school performance, high-risk sexual activity, alcohol and drug use, dropout, and truancy. The model recognizes the overriding importance of the economic context (local labor markets) in which schools exist. Economic context variables constitute an array of distal predictors such as income level and employment rate, which relate in complex ways with the incidence of criminal behavior. Community, school, and family variables constitute a set of distal environmental predictors. In particular, school-based factors may include availability of drugs and alcohol, availability of weapons, a focus on academics, strength of leadership, clarity about behavioral norms, consistency of rule enforcement, and climate of emotional support (i.e., teacher/student relationships) (Gottfredson, 1996; Martinez & Richters, 1993).

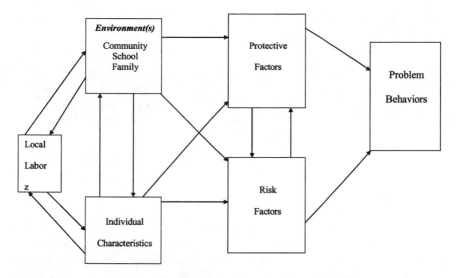

Figure 1. An Etiological Model of Violent Behavior. (*Source*: Modified from Gottfredson [1997]. School-Based Crime Prevention. In L.W. Sherman, D. Gottfredson, D. MacKenzie, J. Eck, P. Reuter, and S. Bushway *Preventing Crime: What Works, What Doesn't, What's Promising*, [Chap. 5]. Retrieved from http://www.ncjrs.org/works/chapter5.htm.)

Individual characteristics represent a proximal set of predictors pertinent to an evaluation of prevention. Useful individual proximal predictor variables include attachment to school, commitment to education, school performance, peer relationships, impulsiveness, and social competency skills. One goal of empirical research is to identify those variables that can be categorized as resiliency factors. A general model of resiliency, as well as examples (Coles, 1995), will be discussed later.

Models of resiliency are closely related to protective and risk factors that mediate or moderate the relationship between predictor (whether distal or proximal) and problem behavior outcomes. Protective factors, when present, weaken the relationship between predictor and negative outcome. Such factors might be distal, such as the presence of after-school programs, or proximal, such as strong social competency skills. Risk factors, when present, strengthen the predictor/negative outcome relationship. Again, such factors may be distal, such as an unstable family structure, or proximal, such as high impulsivity levels. Resiliency research typically attempts to isolate those proximal individual characteristics that buffer the deleterious effects of certain predictors (as, for example, exposure to community violence) on subsequent problem behavior.

Violent youth have been studied extensively in psychology, and many of the theories and clinical insights formulated years ago are still relevant today (Bushman & Baumeister, 1998). According to May (1972) violence is a uniting of the self in action. He writes,

> It is an organizing of one's powers to prove one's power, to establish the worth of the self. It is risking all, a committing all, an asserting all. But it unites the different elements in the self, *omitting* rationality. This is why I have said above that the uniting of the self is done on a level that bypasses reason. Whatever its motive or its consequences may be within the violent person, its result is generally destructive to the others in the situation. (p. 188)

Lefer (1984) discusses why some individuals can restrain themselves from inflicting injury while others cannot. Depending on the strength of repression, suppression, inhibition, reaction formation, rationalization, and conscience, a violence-prone individual (VPI) may be categorized as 1) one who uses violence as a means to an end without a need for justification; 2) one who uses violence as a means to an end but must justify it to his/her conscience; 3) one who is violent only in a dissociated or drugged state; or 4) one who becomes symbiotic with another violence-prone individual (VPI) and aids the other in committing violence. There were significant differences among the types of violence-prone individual (VPI) in their dreams. Their dreams often reenacted the violence inflicted upon them and their intimates in childhood and youth.

The motives that may generate aggression and violence result from the objective nature of events as well as the way these events are construed. The meaning given to these events is based on past experience, world views, personality, and views handed down by society via parental socialization and family experience (Frick & Christian, 1999; Dwyer et al., 1998; Shields et al., 1994; Staub, 1989). Sheldon and Eleanor Glueck's (1950) seminal longitudinal research in delinquency found that the quality of the home environment distinguished between delinquent and non-delinquent boys. Much research on family violence has determined a link between severity of childhood abuse and later victimization of others (Pynoos & Nader, 1988; Lewis, Lovely, Yeager, & Della Femina, 1989).

Research in the 1990s examined the relationship between exposure to chronic community violence and various stress reactions (e.g., post traumatic stress symptoms, dissociation, and antisocial behavior (including violent acts) among inner-city adolescents (Bell & Jenkins, 1993; Richters & Martinez, 1993; Coles, 1995; Hoch-Espada, 1997). It is hypothesized that the impact of exposure to chronic violence traumatizes the child or adolescent. This individual who, without treatment, may become desensitized to acts of violence, develops a habitual pattern of coping with chronic, albeit unpredictable, violence which perpetuates the violent climate by which he/she was once threatened. Hoch-Espada (1997) found a relationship between exposure to violence, stress, and antisocial behavior. She speculates that youth who engage in aggressive behavior may be attempting to master their own feelings of helplessness they experienced while being traumatized. She writes, "In behavioral reenactments of the trauma, these youth play the vacillating roles of both victim and victimizer" (p. 128). This idea, the compulsion to repeat, is a psychodynamic concept discussed years ago in the writings of Freud. These studies raise questions about the trends toward more punitive measures for dealing with violent youth. "The truant, the juvenile delinquent, and/or the disobedient adolescent son may require therapeutic intervention before and/or in place of punitive consequences. Unless violent and criminal behavior is treated differently, with attention to the underlying PTSD (Post Traumatic Stress Disorder) component, a perpetuation of violence will continue to occur" (Hoch-Espada, 1997, p. 131).

Juvenile delinquents are not the sole perpetrators of violence within our schools and neighborhoods. Unfortunately, an increasing number of children lack the guidance of a mature, nurturing parent in the home or an empathic teacher in the school; they are left to fend for themselves in regards to how to think about their experiences and how to deal with powerful emotions. Today many young people resort to acts of violence as a means of dealing with high levels of stress, anxiety, fear, frustration, and anger (Dwyer et al., 1998; Walker, Colvin, & Ramsey, 1995). Gorkin (1997) describes the "four angry I's": 1.) Injustice (a person views him or herself as being a victim of unfairness), 2). injury (a person has a sense of feeling disrespected and insulted), 3). invasion (one's personal space is perceived to be violated and/or one's psychological integrity is being threatened) and 4. intention (one is determined to do something about the above either reflexively or purposefully). Many children, despite reporting having witnessed or otherwise having been exposed to violence, do not develop the stress reactions mentioned above. Identifying the factors which buffer and protect these children from developing stress reactions is the thrust of the literature on resilience (Coles, 1995; Howard, 1996; Hoch-Espada, 1997; Dwyer et al., 1998).

The perennial problem for teachers, especially those in public schools, is how to achieve the goal of bringing a large number of children who vary in terms of academic achievement, behavior, motivation, interests, ethnic/cultural backgrounds, likeability, maturity, and intelligence to criterion levels of academic competencies within a specified time frame (e.g., the academic year). Sarason (1982) writes, "I have never met a teacher who was not aware of and disturbed by the fact that he or she had not the time to give to some children in the class the kind of help they needed—and the need for help, it should be emphasized, is frequently not due to any basic intellectual defect" (p. 187). The teacher, therefore, feels constrained by the pressure to follow a schedule (e.g., lesson plans and the overall curriculum) regardless of whether or not the class is with her (Hyman & Perone, 1998; Sarason, 1982). There are many factors associated with the potential for violence in the schools, including a high level of teacher dissatisfaction; a low level of parent involvement and proactive problem-solving; an adversarial relationships between school personnel and the parents of problem children; an atmosphere in which bullying and teasing behavior is tolerated; high suspension rates and disciplinary referrals; a high number of dropouts in nearby middle and high schools; gang activity; drug and alcohol use; and low overall academic achievement (Twemlow, 2000; Twemlow & Sacco, 1999; Twemlow, Sacco, & Williams, 1996; Hazler, Hoover, & Oliver, 1991).

PRODROMAL SIGNS OF VIOLENT BEHAVIOR IN THE CLINICAL LITERATURE

The clinical literature discusses the difficulties mental health providers face in their efforts to assess the potential for violence towards self or others (Monahan, 1984; Schneidman, 1985; Chiles & Strosahl, 1995; Volavka, 1995). Indeed, studies have found that clinicians' judgments and laypersons' judgments of potential future violence are based on the same information, and, although accuracy of prediction can be problematic (Ennis & Litwack, 1976; Rice & Harris, 1995), several factors have been associated with violent behavior, including 1) past criminal and violent behavior, gender, age, childhood history variables and diagnostic variables (Rice & Harris, 1992); 2) use of drugs, temper outbursts, frequent arguments, physical fights, becoming easily annoyed or irritated, threatening to harm self or others, access to weapons (Gardner, Lidz, Mulvey, & Shaw, 1996).

PREVENTION STRATEGIES

Theoretical perspectives on prevention have conceptualized the causes of violence and the best ways to combat it within frameworks which once again range in scope from micro-level to macro-level contexts (e.g., intrapersonal, interpersonal, group, behavior setting, organization/institution, community, society). Psychologists adhering to one or more of these perspectives have sought competency-based training programs, social advocacy, and grass roots community development as viable solutions to this social problem (Gottfredson, 1997; Sheras et al., 1996).

For example, Cole's (1995) view of children at risk for antisocial and/or violent behavior reiterates other findings from research, focusing on the intrapersonal/interpersonal contexts, which include low tolerance for frustration, impulsivity, anger, attention deficit problems, academic frustration, poor problem solving strategies, and low expectations for non-aggressive means to resolve problems. Their families display poor parental management and dysfunctional communications, unclear family boundaries, inconsistent roles and rules of discipline, and contradictory behavioral standards (Frick & Christian, 1999). Lefer (1984) suggests that preventive strategies should address the needs of the younger population in terms of their feelings of alienation, of lack of impact and invisibility when not committing acts of violence, and their feelings of helplessness and depression.

Major complementary goals of prevention program development are to reduce risk factors for violent behavior and increase protective factors (Sherman, 1997). Such goals are central to programs categorized as primary prevention (Reiss & Roth, 1993). As stated earlier, risk and protective factors can be either distal or proximal and can alter the predictor/outcome relationship through either mediation or moderation. The methodological literature points to substantive differences between mediating and moderating effects (Frazier et al., 2004). A mediator is defined as a variable that explains the relation between a predictor and an outcome (Baron & Kenny, 1986). Using the language of path analysis, a variable mediates when the direct path between predictor and outcome is small relative to the indirect path between those two variables via the mediator. Moderators, on the other hand, alter the strength and direction of the relationship between the predictor and the outcome (Baron & Kenny, 1986). Evaluating moderator-predictor interaction effects addresses the degree of relationship alteration. For example, let's assume that the predictor is a school-based intervention program with two levels, intervention and control, and the outcome is well-being. In a first case, researchers wish to examine the mediating effects of the distal variable, family cohesion. If the path between intervention and well-being is low relative to the indirect path through family cohesion, mediation is exhibited. One interpretation of such a finding might be that intervention relative to control led to increased family cohesion, which resulted in higher well-being. Now let's examine the proximal variable, gender, as a moderator. A typical question asked in this case is whether the intervention program was differentially effective by gender. Evaluating a gender by intervention interaction effect addresses this question. One interpretation of such a significant interaction effect could be that the increases in well-being between intervention and control were higher for females than males.

As stated in an earlier section, resiliency research typically attempts to isolate those proximal individual characteristics that buffer the deleterious effects of certain predictors on subsequent problem behavior, in other words, identifying proximal protective factors. Resiliency models often ask a question typical of moderation: What individual difference variables attenuate the predictor/negative outcome relationship? Figure 2 presents a general strategy for addressing resiliency, using as examples exposure

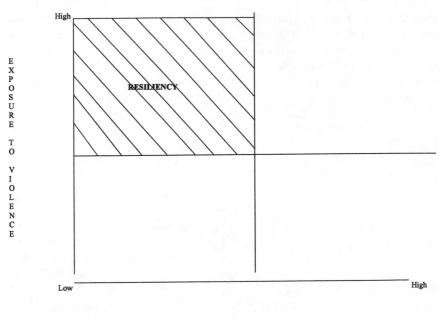

Figure 2. General Strategy for Addressing Resiliency.

to violence as the predictor and symptoms associated with Post-Traumatic Stress Disorder (PTSD) as outcomes. Examining the characteristics of those individuals falling into the upper left quadrant of the figure (high exposure, low PTSD) relative to the other quadrants constitutes a major goal of resiliency research. For example, Coles (1995) examined the moderating effect of the perceived hopelessness of an urban adolescent sample on the relationship between exposure to community violence and PTSD symptoms. Overall, he found statistically significant and strong (moderate effect size) relationships between predictor and outcome. He created a "resilient group" by isolating participants into the high exposure/low PTSD quadrants. He found that the "resilient" group had significantly lower hopelessness scores than the "non-resilient" group (the other 3 quadrants). Neither Figure 2 nor this example advocates creating groups from interval-level data, a practice of artificial dichotomization discouraged by methodologists (Frazier et al., 2004; Baron & Kenny, 1986). If the moderator under investigation is continuous, it is better to examine the predictor-moderator interaction within a multiple regression model (see Frazier et al., 2004, for more detail on how this is accomplished).

Examples of secondary and tertiary prevention strategies for violence conceptualized within these contexts have included approaches that identify youth at risk for violence, develop conflict resolution/ management strategies in the school, monitor educational progress/ personal development, improve cognitive and affective skills of high risk children and remediate aggressive behavior in children with a history of aggression (Grossman et al., 1997; Prothrow-Stith, 1987).

Research on effective school-based preventive interventions include 1) cognitive-behavioral interventions in which programs focus on interpersonal cognitive problem-solving (e.g., interpreting social cues, formulating alternative solutions to social situations) and 2) behavioral social skills training programs that teach specific behaviors related to resisting peer pressure, accepting criticism, etc. (Hyman & Perone, 1998).

In studying environmental sources within the schools associated with violence, researchers have found that the size of the school and the ratio of the number of people who seek to participate, relative to the capacity of the setting to accommodate people, and the minimum number of persons required for the setting to be maintained are significant determinants of student participation, level of satisfaction with their personal competencies, and, conversely, students' sense of alienation/isolation and rejection (Gottfredson, 1997; Sheras et al., 1996).

School-based preventive interventions that address the complex relationship between school processes and school climate with academic achievement and rates of delinquent behavior have found favorable results. Social process interventions which focus on changing the social environment in the school have been successful with respect to increasing student participation and academic performance (e.g., modifying teacher behavior in the classroom to facilitate bonding with low achievers) (Dwyer et al., 1998).

PRIMARY PREVENTION INITIATIVES

Prothrow-Stith (1991) writes: "The destructive lessons parents teach when they are physically and psychologically abusive to their children and when they allow their children to be physically and psychologically abusive to others, in conjunction with our society's glorification of violence, the ready availability of guns, and the drug culture are an explosive combination that set our children up to be the perpetrators and the victims of violence" (p. 145).

As with other public health concerns like tuberculosis, smoking cigarettes, and AIDS, reducing and hopefully eliminating the impact of school violence requires comprehensive, multifaceted strategies all of which recognize the pervasiveness of the problem. Prothrow-Stith (1991) recommends intervention strategies at the primary, secondary, and tertiary levels of prevention. A primary preventative initiative, for instance, might focus on the industries which, operating according to the profit motive, are making money by producing and marketing products that contribute to our violence ridden society. That is to say, that one needs to examine those industries that are directly or indirectly connected to the proliferation of violence. For example, the manufacture, marketing, and distribution of guns are lucrative. Unfortunately, the number of children who died between 1983 and 1993 because of gunfire nearly doubled and gun crime among juveniles has risen steeply (The State of America's Children Yearbook, 1997).

As a society, we need to reconsider why the production and sale of guns to the general public (especially handguns and assault weapons) that have the sole purpose of causing injury or death is sanctioned. For those who argue that it is a constitutional right to bear arms, perhaps legislation and sanctions could be imposed on the industry to make "smart guns." As James Wilson suggests, the technology exists whereby guns can be equipped with devices which render them inoperable when fired by someone other than the licensed owner.

Another industry under scrutiny and seemingly on the defensive about its role in promoting a climate of violence in American society is the media and entertainment industry (Palermo, 1995). Aggression and violence in America have become idealized, as evidenced in television programs, films, video, and other media. The mass media and entertainment industries are being called to task for their "glorification of violence" and gratuitous inclusion of violence on television and in movies. After several decades of research involving more than 1,000 studies on the relationship between media violence and aggression, six professional societies–the American Psychological Association, the American Academy of Pediatrics, the American Academy of Child and Adolescent Psychiatry, the American Medical Association, the American Academy of Family Physicians and the American Psychiatric Association–signed a joint statement about the dangers of exposing children to media violence (Bushman & Anderson, 2001). Another primary prevention approach to curtail school violence would be to have professionals involved in raising public awareness through rigorous advocacy campaigns about the importance of maintaining and improving the education and services provided for youth and their families. Several projects were launched in the 1990s to help achieve that goal, including an initiative of the American Psychological Association in conjunction with MTV. The American Psychological Association is a scientific and professional organization representing psychology in the United States with 159,000 members including educators, clinicians, consultants, researchers, and students. MTV is part of MTV Networks, a unit of Viacom, Inc., which operates cable television programming services.

In 1999, they collaborated on a special broadcast of *Warning Signs* a program which delves into the thoughts, fears, and attitudes adolescents and young adults have about violence. This 30 minute broadcast aired several times during the month of April, 1999, and subsequently became a video which, along with written material (e.g., guide, brochure, sample material for presentations, media alerts, and materials for conducting other local activities), has been made into an outreach kit. The kit is used by psychologists participating in the APA's national public education campaign network to help them conduct community outreach events, particularly *Warning Signs* forums for youth and other interested parties in local communities throughout the United States.

The guide in the kit entitled, "Warning Signs: fight for your rights: take a stand against violence" presents scientific and clinical information on violence and violence prevention in an easily readable format for the general population (e.g., guidance counselors, school principals, parents, students, teachers, community leaders, public officials, etc.). The content areas covered are organized around the following headings–Reasons for violence; Recognizing violence warning signs in others; What you can do if someone you know shows violence warning signs; Dealing with anger; Are you at risk for violent behavior?; Controlling your own risk for violent behavior; and Violence against self.

The information in the section on recognizing violence warning signs in others is shown in Table 1

One of the authors (Chisholm) has been involved in several of these forums in which the video is shown and followed by discussion. One forum I facilitated, which was open to the public, was cosponsored by a university in New York City and the APA. In attendance was a cross section of individuals (e.g., high school principals, assistant principals, guidance counselors, parents, teachers, high school students, college students, university faculty, and community activists) interested in decreasing violent incidents in the schools. Another forum I was invited to facilitate was conducted as part of a day long staff development training at a local high school where there had been concern about violence in the school (which already had installed metal detectors and bag searches by security).

Several common themes emerged from these two forums, including 1.) the need for a community-wide effort to create safe school environments; 2.) the need for personnel who are responsive to all children, and who actively support positive relationships between school staff and students, school staff and parents; 3.) recognizing early warning signs (e.g., bullying, teasing), imminent warning signs (e.g., detailed threat, self-injurious behaviors); and 4.) developing a prevention and response plan.

While the forums generated few solutions, the discussions were animated, expectations were raised, and participants pledged to network with

Table 1. Recognizing Violence Warning Signs in Others

Often people who act violently have trouble controlling their feelings. They may have been hurt by others. Some think that making people fear them through violence or threats of violence will solve their problems or earn them respect. This isn't true. People who behave violently lose respect. They find themselves isolated or disliked, and they still feel angry and frustrated.

If you see these immediate warning signs, violence is a serious possibility

    Loss of temper on a daily basis
    Frequent physical fighting
    Significant vandalism or property damage
    Increase in use of drugs or alcohol
    Increase in risk-taking behavior
    Detailed plans to commit acts of violence
    Announcing threats or plans for hurting others
    Enjoying hurting animals
    Carrying a weapon

If you notice the following signs over a period of time, the potential for violence exists:

    history of violent or aggressive behavior
    Serious drug or alcohol use
    Gang membership or strong desire to be in a gang
    Access to or fascination with weapons, especially guns
    Threatening others regularly
    Trouble controlling feelings like anger
    Withdrawal from friends and usual activities
    Feeling rejected or alone
    Having been a victim of bullying
    Poor school performance
    History of discipline problems or frequent run-ins with authority
    Feeling constantly disrespected
    Failing to acknowledge the feelings or rights of others

Source: American Psychological Association (2002).

others and work collaboratively to maintain safe schools. At the conclusion of these presentations, I summarized their concerns and suggested the following key ideas for them to keep in mind:

1. Accept your responsibility for being an advocate for the total well being of the children in your school–maximize not only learning of the 3 R's, but also their emotional, cognitive, social, and spiritual functioning.
2. Convey an awareness and attitude that children are coming to learn at school which is *your place* of work and *your home away from home—NOT THEIRS!*
   - Provide orientation about rules for getting along (good citizenship, information about procedures, expectations, etc).

3. It is your responsibility to *know* your kids, whom you have "invited" into your home away from home, AND to *know* your staff.
4. Network with key personnel, include parents, and other volunteers for the Herculean task of adequate, appropriate supervision throughout the day.
5. Work at primary, secondary, tertiary models of prevention.

At the conclusion of these forums I told the story about an equal opportunity (author unknown):

> This is a story about four people: Everybody, Somebody, Anybody and Nobody. There was an important job to be done and Everybody was asked to do it. Everybody was sure Somebody would do it. Anybody could have done it, but Nobody did it. Somebody got angry about that because it was Everybody's job. Everybody thought Anybody could do it, but Nobody realized that Everybody wouldn't do it. It ended up that Everybody blamed Somebody when actually Nobody asked Anybody.

In conclusion, the moral imperative is clear. Recognizing school violence as a phenomenon existing within the *culture* of our schools, which mirror some disturbing trends in contemporary American culture, is essential. Sarason's (1982) observations about the "problem of change" within the school system is apropos to our understanding about the "problem of violence" in schools: "Far from being peculiar to schools, the problem of [violence] is the problem of every major institution in our society, and that fact alone suggests that our conceptions [about how to reduce violence] have deep roots in the nature of our society" (p. 44). As the story about Everybody, Somebody, Anybody, and Nobody suggests, all of us have a stake in eliminating violence in our schools; the success of our efforts depends on each and every single one of us.

References

American Psychological Association (2002). *Warning Signs*. Retrieved January 21, 2004, from http://helping.apa.org/warningsigns/

Baron, R.M. and Kenny, D.A. (1986). The moderator-mediator variable distinction in social psychological research: Conceptual, strategic, and statistical considerations. *Journal of Personality and Social Psychology, 51,* 1173–1182.

Batsche, G.M. & Knoff, H.M. (1994). Bullies and their victims: Understanding a pervasive problem in the schools. *School Psychology Review, 23,* 165–174.

Bell, C. and Jenkins, E. (1993). Community violence and children on Chicago's southside. *Psychiatry, 56,* 46–54.

Bushman, B. & Anderson, C. (2001). Media violence and the American public: scientific facts versus media misinformation. *American Psychologist., 56,* 6/7, 477–489.

Bushman, B.J. & Baumeister, R.F. (1998). Threatened egotism, narcissism, self-esteem and direct and displaced aggression: does self-love or self-hate lead to violence? *Journal of Personality and Social Psychology, 71(1),* 219–229.

Cangtor, R. Kivel, P. & Creighton, A. (1997). *Days of respect. Organizing a school wide violence prevention program.* Alameda, CA: Hunter House.

Children's Defense Fund (1997). *The state of America's children, yearbook 1997.* Washington, D.C.

Chiles, J. & Strosahl, K. (1995). *The suicide patient.* Washington, DC: American Psychiatric Press.

Chisholm, J.F. (1995). Violent Youth: reflections on contemporary child rearing practices in America as an antecedent cause. In L. Adler & F. Denmark (eds), *Violence and the prevention of violence.* New York: Praeger Press, pp. 47–59.

Chisholm, J.F. & Ward, A.W. (2004). Violence in the USA. In L. Adler (ed), *Violence Around the World: International Perspective,* New York: Praeger Press, in press.

Coles, H. (1995). *Effects of chronic violence on inner city junior high school aged children.* Unpublished doctoral dissertation, Pace University.

Cornell, D.G. & Loper, A.B. (1998). Assessment of violence and other high-risk behaviors with a school survey. *School Psychology Review, 27,* 1–14.

Dwyer, K., Osher, D., Warger, C., Bear, G., Haynes, Nl, Knoff, H., Kingery, P., Sheras, P., Skiba, R., Skinner, L. & Stockton, B. (1998). *Early warning, timely response: a guide to safe schools: the referenced edition.* Washington, DC: American Institutes for Research.

Ennis, B.J. & Litwack, T.P. (1976). Psychiatry and the presumption of expertise: flipping coins in the courtroom. *California Law Review, 62,* 693–752.

Forehand, A., Biggar, H. & Kotchick, B.A. (1998). Cumulative Risk across family stressors: short and long term effects for adolescents. *Journal of Abnormal Child Psychology, 26,* 119–128.

Frazier, P.A., Tix, A.W. & Barron, K.E. (2004). Testing moderator and mediator effects in counseling psychology research. *Journal of Counseling Psychology, 51(1),* 115–134.

Frick, P.J. & Christian, R.E. (1999). Age trends in association between parenting practices and conduct problems. *Behavior Modification. 23(1),* 106–128.

Garbarino, J. (1995). *Raising children in a socially toxic environment.* San Francisco: Jossey-Bass.

Gardner, W., Lidz, C.W., Mulvey, E.P. & Shaw, E.C. (1996). Clinical versus actuarial predictions of violence in patients with mental illnesses. *Journal of Consulting and Clinical Psychology, 64, 3,* 602–609

Glueck, S. & Glueck, E. (1950). *Unraveling Juvenile Delinquency,* Cambridge, Mass: Harvard University Press.

Goldstein, A. & Conoley, J.C. (1997). *School violence intervention: a practical handbook.* New York, NY: The Guilford Press.

Gorkin, M. (1997). The four faces of anger. *Treatment Today.* vol 9, no 3, p. 57–58.

Gottfredson, D. (1996). An empirical test of school-based environmental and individual interventions to reduce the risk of delinquent behavior. *Criminology 24,* 705–731.

Gottfredson, D. (1997). School-based crime prevention. In L.W. Sherman, D. Gottfredson, D. MacKenzie, J. Eck, P. Reuter, & S. Bushway (eds). *Preventing Crime: What Works, What Doesn't, What's Promising.* Retrieved January 21, 2004, from http://www.ncjrs.org/works/chapter5.htm

Grossman, D.C., Neckerman, H.J., Koepsell, T.D., Liu, P., Asher, K.N., Beland, Kl, Frey, K. & Riaria, F.P. (1997). Effectiveness of a violence prevention curriculum among children in elementary school: a randomized controlled trial. *Journal of the American Medical Association, 277,* 1605–1612.

Hazler, R.J., Hoover, J. & Oliver, R. (1991). Student perspectives of victimization by bullies in school. *Journal of Humanistic Education and Development, 29,* 143–150.

Hoch-Espada, A. (1997). *Post-traumatic stress, dissociation, and antisocial behavior in inner-city adolescents.* Unpublished doctoral dissertation, Pace University.

Howard, D. (1996). Searching for Resilience among African-American youth exposed to community violence: theoretical issues. *Journal of Adolescent Health, 18,* p. 254–262.

Hunter, L. & Elias, M., (1998). School violence: prevalence, policies, and prevention. In A.R. Roberts (ed.). *Juvenile justice: policies, programs and services.* Chicago: Nelson-Hall, 71–92.

Hyman, I.A. & Perone, D.C. (1998). The other side of school violence: educator policies and practices that may contribute to student misbehavior. *Journal of School Psychology, 30,* 7–27.

Kingery, P.M. Coggeshall, M.B. & Alford, A.A. (1998). Violence at school: recent evidence from four national surveys. *Psychology in the Schools, 35,* 247–258.

Larson, J. (1994). Violence prevention in the schools: a review of selected programs and procedures. *School Psychology Review, 23,* 151–164.

Lefer, L. (1984). The Fine Edge of Violence, *Journal of the American Academy of Psychoanalysis, Vol 12(2),* 253–268.

Lewis, D.O. Lovely, R., Yeager, C. & Della Femena, D. (1989). Toward a theory of the genesis of violence: a follow-up study of delinquents. *Journal of the American Academy of Child and Adolescent Psychiatry, 28,* 431–436.

Martinez, P. & Richters, J. (1993). The NIMH community violence project II: Children's distress symptoms associated with violence exposure. *Psychiatry, 56,* 22–35.

May, R. (1972). *Power and Innocence: A Search for the Sources of Violence.* New York: W.W. Norton.

Monahan, J. (1984). *Predicting Violent Behavior.* Beverly Hills, CA: Sage.

Noguera, P.A. (1995). Preventing and producing violence: a critical analysis of responses to school violence. *Harvard Educational Review, 65,* 189–212.

Palermo, G.B. (1995). Adolescent criminal behavior: is TV violence one of the culprits: *International Journal of Offender Therapy and Comparative Criminology. 38,* 11–22.

Poland, S. (1994). The role of school crisis intervention teams to prevent & reduce school violence & trauma. *School Psychology Review, 23,* 175–169.

Prothrow-Stith, D. (1987). *Violence prevention curriculum for adolescents.* Newton, MA: Education Development Center.

Prothrow-Stith, D. (1991). *Deadly Consequences.* New York: Harper Perennial.

Pynoos, R.S. & Nader, K. (1988). Children that witness the sexual assaults of their mothers. *Journal of American Academy of Child and Adolescent Psychiatry. 27(5),* p. 567–572.

Ratchford, M. (2000). Lessons learned from Columbine. *Newsday,* April 19th, Wednesday, A37, A39.

Reiss, A.J. & Roth, J.A (eds) 1993 *Understanding and Preventing Violence.* Washington, DC: National Academy of Sciences.

Rice, M.E. & Harris, G.T. (1992). A comparison of criminal recidivism among schizophrenic and nonschizophrenic offenders. *International Journal of Law and Psychiatry, 15,* 397–408.

Rice, M.E. & Harris, G.T. (1995). Methodological development: violent recidivism: assessing predictive validity. *Journal of Consulting and Clinical Psychology, (63) 5,* 737–748.

Richters, J. & Martinez, P. (1993). The NIMH Community Violence Project: I. Children as victims of and witnesses to violence. *Psychiatry, (56) 7.*

Sarason, S. (1982). *The culture of the school and the problem of change.* Boston: Allyn & Bacon.

Schneidman, E. (1985). *Definition of suicide.* New York: Wiley.

Sheras, P.L. Cornell, D.G. & Bostain, D.S. (1996). The Virginia youth violence project: transmitting psychological knowledge on youth violence to schools and communities. *Professional Psychology: Research and Practice, 27,* 401–406.

Sherman, L.W. (1997). Thinking about crime prevention. In L.W. Sherman, D. Gottfredson, D. MacKenzie, J. Eck, P. Reuter & S. Bushway (eds). *Preventing Crime: What Works, What Doesn't, What's Promising.* Retrieved January 21, 2004, from http://www.ncjrs.org/works/chapter2.htm

Shields, A.M. Cicchetti, D. & Ryan, R.M. (1994). The development of emotional and behavioral self-regulation and social competence among maltreated school-age children. *Developmental and Psychopathology, 6,* 57–75.

Staub, E. (1989). *The Roots of Evil: The Origins of Genocide and Other Group Violence.* Cambridge: University press.

Twemlow, S. (2000). The roots of violence: converging psychoanalytic explanatory models for power struggles and violence in schools. *Psychoanalytic Quarterly, (69)4*, 741–785.

Twemlow, S.W., Sacco, F.C. & Williams, P. (1996, Summer). A clinical and interactionist perspective on the bully-victim-bystander relationship. *Bulletin of the Menninger Clinic, 60(3)*, 296–313.

Twemlow, S.W., Sacco, F.C., (1999). A multi-level conceptual framework for understanding the violent community. In: *Collective Violence: Effective Strategies for Assessing and Intervening in Fatal Group and Institutional Aggression*, ed. H.V. Hall & L.C. Whitaker. New York: CRC Press, 566–599.

Volavka, J. (1995). *Neurobiology of violence.* Washington, DC: American Psychiatric Press.

Walker, H.M., Colvin, Gl & Ramsey, E. (1995). *Antisocial behavior in school: strategies and best practices.* Pacific Grove, CA: Brooks/Cole.

Chapter 5

Developmental Aspects of School Violence
A Contextualist Approach

ROSEANNE L. FLORES

INTRODUCTION

Over the last decade we as a society have witnessed an increasing number of violent acts committed against and by children. In the home, in their communities, or in society at large, children are exposed on a daily basis to increasing levels of violence. Within the home environment, many children are either witnesses to the abuse of a parent or are the recipients of abuse themselves. Within their communities they are often exposed to violence in their neighborhoods and in their schools. And at the larger societal level they are exposed to violence through the media, television, the movies, and music, to name but a few sources. The exposure to violence through these diverse mediums has affected youth from infancy through adolescence. The consequences of this onslaught of ongoing violence had been a dramatic influence on both children's cognitive and social emotional functioning. Children exposed to violence have experienced severe changes in their behavior, such as sleep disturbances, irritability, withdrawal, inability to focus and pay attention, as well as academic failure. It has been argued that depending on the development of the child, exposure to violence will produce different outcomes.

Previous research has demonstrated that the development of violence in children is dependent on the interaction among a myriad of factors, such as biological propensities, ineffectual parenting strategies, poverty, cognitive functioning, social emotional functioning, the cultural milieu, and the intrusive presence of the media. To date there has been no one universal theory that can account for the interaction between these various factors; however, Bronfenbrener's ecological systems approach (1998; 2000) poses a possible model for attempting to explain how the various levels within the child and across environments can interact often leading to violent behavior. The purpose of this chapter is to examine how the interaction between multiple environmental contexts impact children's development of violent behavior, with a specific focus on school violence.

Monica is a three year old girl who has just been dropped off at a daycare center. Her mother gives her a kiss goodbye and leaves her with the childcare provider. The door closes and the car drives away. Monica goes to place her coat in her cubby. She walks over to Cathy who is playing with a doll, one of Monica's favorite toys. Monica pushes Cathy on the floor and takes the doll. Cathy bursts into tears.

Jeffery is an eight year old African American boy. He has just moved into his new neighborhood. His parents moved here because they wanted a safer environment and good schools for their children. It is Jeffrey's first day at the new elementary school. As he walks through the hallway he hears some boys screaming at him, "We don't want no black kids around because our parents told us they decrease our property values!" Jeffrey is afraid and quickly goes to his locker; there he finds that his locker has been defaced and scrawled across the front are curses and derogatory slurs. Jeffrey returns home to his family at the end of the day only to say that he does not wish to return to school.

Martha is a 14 year old girl. She has just found out that Carla is dating her boyfriend. Martha is enraged. At lunchtime she follows Carla into the bathroom and begins screaming and cursing at her. Carla tries to leave the scene, but before she can Martha pulls out a knife and stabs her. Martha runs from the bathroom. Carla is dead.

These scenes and others like them have become everyday occurrences in our nation. More than at any other time in the history of America, we have become concerned with expression of violence in our communities, and more specifically, in our schools. From the point of view of the public, schools should be safe places where children can learn, grow, and aspire to do great things. The occurrence of violence in schools cannot be tolerated because by its very existence it will destroy the fabric of learning, and the growth and development of our children. But what exactly do we mean by school violence? This is a very difficult question to answer, because the definition of school violence has changed over the course of time. Moreover, researchers, educators, politicians, and the general public have varying views. Historically, school violence meant youth who committed crime (Furlon & Morrison, 2000). More recently, school violence has been redefined to incorporate aspects of victimization, aggression, antisocial behavior, perpetration of violence, and criminal activity among other aspects of behavior (APA, 1993; Flannery, 1997). Although this new definition appears to view school violence as being multifaceted, understanding that violent behavior is comprised of many dimensions is not enough because violent behavior happens along a continuum (Flannery, 1997) as can be seen from the scenarios narrated at the beginning of this chapter. Very young children tend to exhibit aggressive behaviors, such as biting, hitting, and kicking, as in the case of Monica. Children in elementary and middle school have a tendency to engage in bullying or physical fighting, as in the case of Jeffery. And finally, pre-adolescents and adolescents tend to engage in physical and sexual assault such as date rape, gang activity, and assault with a deadly weapon, as in the case of Martha and Carla. Understanding the developmental aspects of violent behavior can allow us to explore how exposure to violent behavior in the community, school, home, and larger society affects children throughout their development. Understanding these issues is critical if we are to provide an adequate school-based prevention and intervention program.

Over the last decade we have witnessed an increasing number of violent acts committed against children and by children. Whether in the home, in their communities, or in society at large, children are being exposed on a daily basis to increasing levels of violence. In the home, they may be exposed to domestic violence (Appel & Holden, 1998). In their communities they may be exposed to violence in their neighborhoods and in their schools (Jordan, 2002). And at the larger societal level they are often exposed to violence through the media, i.e., through television, movies, newspapers, magazines, books and music. The exposure to violence through these sources has affected youth from infancy through adolescence. The consequences of this onslaught of ongoing violence have had a dramatic influence on both cognitive and social emotional functioning. Children exposed to violence have experienced severe changes in their behaviors, such as sleep disturbances, irritability, withdrawal, inability to focus and pay attention, as well as academic failure (APA, 1993). As might be expected depending on the context and the child's age, exposure to violence will have different outcomes.

According to the previous research the type and variety of violence has increased. For example, Carter, Weithorn, & Behrman (1999) have reported that child abuse occurs in 30–60% of family violence cases where children are involved. Moreover, every year 3–10 million children witness some act of domestic violence (Carter et al., 1999). In addition, the National Center for Children Exposed to Violence (2003) reported that there has been a 41% increase in the number of cases of abuse and neglect toward children. With respect to community violence, the United States has the highest rate of childhood homicide, suicide, and firearm related deaths among all industrialized nations (National Center for Children Exposed to Violence, 2003). In schools, acts of violence have also increased. The United States Department of Education (2002) has reported that 57% of high school students have been expelled from school due to carrying firearms; 33% of middle school students and 10% of elementary school children have also been involved in expulsions due to carrying firearms. In addition, children also continue to be exposed to high levels of violence in the images they are exposed to through the media. As can be seen from the above mentioned statistics, children are not only the victims of violence; they have also become the perpetrators of violence. Thus it appears that the victim becomes the victimizer.

DEVELOPMENTAL PRECURSORS TO VIOLENT BEHAVIOR

So how does violent behavior develop? There is no easy answer to this question because there appears to be a myriad of factors that can attribute to the development of violent behavior, such as biological propensities, ineffectual parenting strategies, poverty, cognitive and social emotional functioning, cultural milieu, and the intrusive presence of the media to name a few. To date there has been no one universal theory that can account for the interaction between these various factors; however, Bronfenbrener's ecological systems approach (1998; 2000) poses a possible model for attempting to explain how the various levels within the child and across the environment can interact and lead to violent behavior.

In his ecological model, Bronfenbrenner views children as developing within a complex system of relationships which are affected at multiple levels by the surrounding environment. He views biology as interacting with the environment and has more recently referred to his model as a bioecological approach. According to this approach the environment is viewed as a series of nested structures that includes home, school, and neighborhood settings in which children spend their everyday lives. Each layer is viewed as having a critical impact on the child's development. According to this theory there are five subdivisions that can influence child development. They are the microsystem, the mesosystem, the exosystem, the macrosystem, and the chronosystem.

The *microsystem* is the innermost layer of the system which refers to the activities and the interaction patterns within the child's immediate environment. According to this model in order to understand child development we must understand that the interactions in the child's environment are bi-directional, that is, adults influence the child's behavior, but the child also influences the adults' behavior. As the parent-child interaction becomes more stable over time, it will have a lasting impact on the child's development. Parent-child relationships can also be affected by third parities. Thus interactions between mother and father will influence the child. For example, if the father treats the mother in an abusive manner in front of the child, the parent interaction will influence the development of the child. Moreover, as the abuse continues to unfold, the child and mother may begin to engage in abusive interactions with the father, (Appel & Holden, 1998). If left unchecked, these learned interactions will be passed on from one generation to the next.

The next subsystem is the *mesosystem*. This subsystem is comprised of at least two microsystems, such as the home and school. Within this system what happens in one microsystem influences another microsystem. For example, how a child learns to read in the classroom is also influenced by how what goes on in the home. If a behavior occurs in more than one setting it becomes a consistent part of the child's repertoire. Understanding this subsystem can play a major role in understanding the development of violent behavior.

The next subsystem is the *exosystem*. The exosystem involves the social settings that do not actually contain children, but nevertheless affect their experiences in their immediate setting. For example, although the formal settings in which parents work do not have a direct influence on their children's lives, they do indirectly affect the quality of the child's life. For example, if parents do not have alternative care for their children when they become sick, they may have to take off from work. Depending on the type of employment the parents may have, this could cost them time as well as money. The lack of money could lead to bills not being paid and additional stress, which in turn could affect the child. Similarly, if the parents cannot pay for after school care, this may increase their stress, which could also indirectly influence the child's development. The exosystem could also be as informal as the parents' social network. Previous research has demonstrated that families who have fewer support systems show higher levels of child abuse and increased levels of violence (National Research Council, 1993).

The fourth subsystem is the *macrosytem*. The macrosystem is not a specific context. Instead it consists of values and laws, customs, and resources within a particular culture. For example, if quality education, i.e., safe spaces that provide a true education, is a priority for a nation then that will benefit the child's environment, at the physical as well as the social level. Children will be in safe and engaging environments and parental stress will decrease because they will not have to worry about where their children are and if they will succeed.

Finally, the fifth and last subsystem is the *chronosystem*. The chronosystem involves changes in the environment due to a temporal dimension. These changes can happen within the child. For example, as children get older they shift from being dependent individuals to independent thinkers who are capable of modifying and creating their own experiences and settings. How this happens is dependent on the biological, intellectual, physical and social capital that children have available to them. In this part of the model children are the producers and products of their own environments. However, if what has been developed previously is based on a negative foundation, this will negatively influence children's ability to achieve.

DEVELOPMENTAL PRECURSORS WITHIN CONTEXTS OF VIOLENT BEHAVIOR

According to previous research, one of the strongest predictors of whether a child will engage in violent behavior is a previous history of violence. This violence is generally situated in the home and influences behavior within other social settings, such as the school. If one uses Bronfenbrenner's model as a mechanism for understanding the development of this behavior then one could argue that what is occurring is that the initial violent act begins within the microsystem, either within the parent-child bond or within the parent-parent bond, which in turn influences the behavior of the child. Because violent behavior is usually persistent, the aggressive behavior has time to develop and become enduring. Depending on the biological factors that both the parent and child possess, the above interactions could become extremely volatile. For example, a child who has a high activity level and is impulsive may react very differently in a violent situation than would a child who has a moderate activity level (APA 1993). In addition to the developmental history of violence, other developmental factors that can have a direct influence on the child's behavior are the child rearing practices engaged in within the family as well as additional family factors. For example, previous research has demonstrated that children who are the target of harsh, physical, inconsistent punishment tend to develop consistent patterns of aggressive and violent behavior (APA, 1993). There is a tendency for them to use the same aggressive behavior patterns with their peers in other contexts. Therefore what is learned at home will influence what the child would do in other contexts, i.e., school. Using Bronfenbrenner's ecological model, one possible way to explain aggressive activity in school would be to talk about the interaction between two microsystems (home and school) within the mesosystem in which children exposed to violence in the home could be said to have a tendency to reproduce the behavior in school. However, it should be noted that not all violent home environments lead to violent outcomes. For example, it has been found that in spite of the dangerous and violent environments in which families often live, some parents have been able to shield their children from violence. These families have served as critical support systems for their children, providing them with warm, nurturing, and stable home environments, thus giving them the necessary means to cope with the violence in their homes and community (Randolph, Koblinksky, & Roberts, 1996).

Another set of factors that influences development and is the focus of the present paper is the interaction between school environments and aggressive behavior that begins in early childhood. Previous research has demonstrated that poor early socialization and aggressive behavior, which is often learned at home, can lead to poor academic performance and the development of inappropriate peer relationships within the school environment. Again using Bronfenbrenner's theory as a framework, what children are exposed to early on in the home, in this case violent behavior, will eventually become internalized and if sustained will be generalized to other contexts. Thus, as the previous examples have shown, in order to fully understand a child's development of aggressive and violent acts, it is necessary to view them as they unfold across multiple contexts.

Another crucial factor that is sometimes overlooked is the influence of culture on environmental contexts. As our nation continues to become more diverse there will undoubtedly be families whose home culture conflicts with the culture of the community. For children this conflict will play itself out in school. When this happens there will often be a mismatch between what is expected at home and what might be expected in school, i.e., a mismatch between microsystems. If the conflict is not adequately resolved it can lead to frustration on the part of the child and influence academic performance as well as social emotional functioning. If the parents are unable to interact with the school, if, for example, they do not speak English, or if they are not accustomed to the ways of American school culture, their children may fall through the cracks. Children who find themselves in this position may look to their peers, who might also have succumbed to school failure, for advice and comfort. Feeling isolated from mainstream society these children may begin to engage in antisocial behaviors. Thus it is crucial that if we want to create an effective school violence prevention and intervention model, culture must be taken into account (Jordan, 2002).

INTERACTION BETWEEN COMMUNITY AND SCHOOL VIOLENCE

Until recently the vast majority of research has examined school violence as if it were separate and apart from community violence. In 2002, the National Institute of Child Health and Development cosponsored a workshop with various agencies within the National Institute of Health as well as outside agencies in order to examine the current status and gaps within research, practice and policy with respect to children exposed to violence. One of the areas under discussion was the relationship between community and school violence. The participants agreed that reducing the discussion of school violence by focusing mainly on violence that occurs in schools would be a great mistake (Workshop on School Children Exposed to Violence, 2002). Children's behaviors are the product of multiple interactions that take place in multiple settings. If we only focus on what occurs in the schools we run the risk of not addressing all of the possible causes of school violence and therefore limit the possibilities for eradicating violence in schools.

Another area which is related to school violence and which has been not been addressed in the research is what happens after school. According to the 1999 National Report Series, what is important is not the violence that occurs during the day, because for the most part schools are safe, but rather what happens after school. For many children, there are no adults waiting for them when they return home from school. Many children supervise themselves and often their younger siblings as well. While not all children engage in delinquent behavior after school, children who have few resources and are prone to negative behaviors run the risk of getting into serious trouble. These children may become either the victims of crime or the perpetrators of crime. According to this report more, violent crimes are committed after school hours on school days and non-school days than during the evening hours. In addition, young people are more at risk of being the victim of a violent crime at the end of a school day than at any other time. Thus because there is a greater potential for children to either become victims of crime or perpetrators of crime at the end of the school day, there is a need for establishing interventions that not only focus on violence in the schools but also violence that occurs after school.

SUMMARY AND CONCLUSIONS

The focus of this chapter has been on understanding the developmental precursors of school violence within multiple contexts. Using Brofenbrenner's approach, it has been argued, that development occurs in multiple contexts and that these contexts are interactive. It has also been argued that in order to understand the phenomenon that we have termed "school violence," we need to understand how violence within homes (i.e., parental and caretaker interactions) and within the community (i.e. neighborhoods) coincide with and influence what goes on in the schools. It has been emphasized that it would be erroneous to view schools as separate entities that exist apart from their communities. Schools often represent the political, cultural, ethnic, and economic fabric of the community and what goes on inside the doors of each building is often indirectly, if not directly, tied to the larger community. In addition, it was also emphasized that there is a need to pay attention to what goes on after school. Many children become victims of violence not during the school day, but after they leave school. With so few children returning home to adult supervision, there are more opportunities for children to be involved in activities that can lead to violent acts, such as aggravated assaults, sexual assaults, or bullying. Therefore, I believe that any program that is designed to address school violence should also take into account after school violence.

As has been mentioned throughout the chapter, it is my belief that in order to understand the developmental aspects of school violence, we must look beyond their manifestation in the classroom, using a more contextual and interactive perspective. This perspective will allow us to design more integrative interventions that will target not only school environments but home and community environments as well. For example, if we can figure out how to reduce home and community violence by helping to eliminate some of the stressors in those environments that can lead to violence, then perhaps we can help prevent those acts of violence in schools that are related to those contexts. In line with the aforementioned recommendation, one stressor that working parents often face is what to do with their children between the hours of three and six in the evening. Because we know that a vast majority of violence takes place not in the schools themselves, but rather after school, one of the targets of intervention should be providing youth with supervised after school activities that would allow them to channel their energy into appropriate activities. This would reduce the stress and hopelessness that many parents experience, and it would also contribute to a safer environment for the children as well as the community at large. Understanding human development is a complex process that requires understanding human behavior at multiple levels. Previous research in the area of school violence has attempted to understand this phenomenon by talking about warning signs that occur at various stages of development. While I think it is important to recognize that children exhibit different behaviors at various stages across the life cycle, I believe it is also important to recognize that those developmental signs occur as a result of interactions across multiple environmental contexts. Future work in this area should look to identifying and measuring developmental aspects of violence within and across different cultural, ethnic, class, community, and family settings.

REFERENCES

American Psychological Association. (1993). *Summary report of the American Psychological Association Commission on Violence and Youth* (Vol. 1). Washington, DC: Author. (ED 379 056).

Appel, A.E. & Holden, G.W. (1998). The co-occurrence of spouse and physical child abuse: A review and appraisal. *Journal of Family Psychology*, 12(4), 578–599.

Bronfenbrenner, U. (2000). Ecological theory. In Kazden (Ed.), *Encyclopedia of psychology*. Washington DC & New York: American Psychological Association and Oxford University Press.

Bronfenbrenner, U. & Morris, P.A. (1998). The ecology of developmental processes. In W. Damon (Series Ed.) & R.M. Lerner (Vol. Ed.), *Handbook of Child Psychology: Vol. 1. Theory* (5th ed.). New York: Wiley.

Carter, L.S., Weithorn, L.A, & Behrman, R.E. (1999). *Future of children. Special Issues: Domestic Violence and Children*, 9(3), 4–22.

Flannery, D.J. (1997). School violence: Risk, preventive intervention and policy. Urban Diversity Series. No. 109. New York: Teachers College. ERIC Clearinghouse on Urban Education. (ED 416272).

Furlong, M. & Morrison, G. (2000). The school in school violence: Definitions and facts. *Journal of Emotional Disorders*, 1-18. Retrieved February 23, 2004. http://www.findarticles.com/cf_0/m0FCB/2_8/62804295/print.jhtml.

Jordan, K. (2002). School violence among culturally diverse populations. In L.A. Rapp-Paglicci, Roberts, A.R. & Wodarski, J.S. (Eds.), *Handbook of Violence*. New York: John Wiley & Sons. Inc.

National Center for Children Exposed to Violence. (2003). http://www.neceu.org/violence/statistics/statistics-abuse.html.

National Research Council (1993). *Understanding child abuse and neglect*. Commission on Behavioral and Social Sciences and Education, Panel on Research on Child Abuse and Neglect: Washington, DC: National Academy Press.

Randolph, S.M., Koblinsky, S.A., & Roberts, D.D. (1996). Studying the role of family and school in the development of African American preschooler in violent neighborhoods. *Journal of Negro Education*, 65(3), 282–294.

Workshop on Children Exposed to Violence: Current status, gaps, and research priorities (2002, July). National Institute of Health.

U.S. Department of Education, (October, 2002). *Gun-Free Schools Act Reports: School Year 1998–1999*. Retrieved February 20, 2004, from National Children Exposed to Violence database.

U.S. Department of Justice: Office of Juvenile Justice and Delinquency Prevention. (1999, November). *Violence After School*. Washington, DC: Author.

Chapter 6

Gender and Ethnicity Issues in School Violence

Darlene C. DeFour

As I write this chapter the Mayor of New York City, Michael Bloomberg, has announced the twelve most violent schools in New York City. He said that these schools would be provided with additional security officers. He also announced a "no violence tolerance" policy. Any act of violence would result in the immediate dismissal of the student. The majority of these schools are in Black and Latino communities. Male students perpetrate a majority of the types of violence that result in the school being placed on this list. However, the incidents that have placed school violence in the headlines across the country were acts committed almost entirely by white males (e.g., Columbine).

By the year 2050 over half the population of the United States will be comprised of people of color. The population of the state of California is already over 50% people of color. Other states that are nearing this percentage are Arizona, New Mexico, Texas, and New York (White, 2003). As a result of this shift in demographics, we will not be able to ignore issues of ethnic and cultural diversity in schools, and we must also take a look at how these demographics impact violence in schools.

These changes in the demographics of the country make it imperative that we understand issues of diversity. Hall (1997) indicated that psychology would become obsolete if the field did not respond to the changes in the demographics of the country. She pointed out that it is essential that there be wide scale changes in research, training, teaching, and practice. If this did not happen then the field would not be able to provide appropriate services to the majority of the population and would become useless. Similarly, psychological theories and research must be broadened to reflect the diversity of the population. The same is true for how we view problems in the schools, including school violence. Exposure to school violence is not the same for all groups. Some research suggests that black and minority youth, compared to white youth, are more likely to be victims of violence in elementary and junior high school settings (Hill, 1998, as cited in Stevenson, Herrero-Taylor, Cameron, & Davis, 2002). Therefore, it behooves us to examine how gender and ethnicity relate to school violence.

In this chapter we will first look at definitions of school violence and how taking gender and ethnicity into account would impact these definitions. We then look in more detail at gender and violence. Particular attention will be paid to how school violence manifests itself with girls. Next, we look at ethnicity and school violence. Finally, we will briefly consider two interventions designed to decrease school violence that take gender and ethnicity into account.

DEFINING SCHOOL VIOLENCE

How Should Violence be Conceptualized and Defined?

The wave of mass shootings that have been in the news headlines has made school violence resurface as a major public health concern, in spite of the fact that the amount of school violence appears to have decreased nationally (Astor, Pitner, Benenishty, & Meyer, 2002). The newspaper descriptions of this violence suggests to the general public what types of acts are considered violent. How the violence is described in these accounts would lead a person to believe that the violence occurred because of some personal defect in the perpetrator or because of neglectful parents (e.g., Today Show interview, May 19, 2004). The focus of these stories is on physical violence. However, by concentrating on physical violence the deleterious effects of nonphysical aggression (e.g., spreading rumors to harm others) are not taken into account. It has been hypothesized that this form of aggression occurs more frequently in girls, and although not flashy (it isn't reported in a news headlines), it can also be damaging (Crick et al., 2001). Although it is comedy, the recently released movie *Mean Girls* may make the general public more aware of this form of aggression.

How school violence is defined is important. Its definition will impact the scope of what is studied. What behaviors should we be concerned about? How should we intervene to prevent it? Should it be conceptualized as "school violence" or "violence in schools" (Furlong & Morrison, 2000)?

Furlong and Morrison define school violence as "looking at schools as a physical location for violence that originates in the community" while violence in the schools is defined as viewing the schools as a system that produces or intensifies problems of the people within it. In my view, it is not useful to conceptualize violence as one or the other. We should use both lenses to view school violence.

Some researchers have called for taking an ecological systems view to looking at school violence (e.g., Holtappels & Meier, 2000; Jordon, 2002). An ecological view is a theoretical perspective that maintains that human behavior is best understood in terms of the interaction between a person and his or her environment (e.g., Bronfrenbrenner, 1979; Rappaport, 1977). It also conceptualizes institutions as systems that are embedded within larger systems. As a result of this, what happens in an institution will impact as well as be impacted by the larger system within which it is nested. In addition, arrangements within the particular institution will influence the behavior of its inhabitants. In thinking about schools, this means that some of the violence that takes place inside of them will start with the environmental conditions of the community of which they are a part. An example of this form of school violence may be when an ex-boyfriend of a female student (who does not attend her school) goes to her school and fatally shoots her because she broke up with him. Or, larger societal factors can enter the school context. For example, after 9/11 Muslim students in many communities feared for their safety inside as well as outside of school. Of greatest risk were female students who were easily identifiable because of their form of dress. In some cases, the violence results from the school location itself. Spencer et al.'s (2003) work tells us that we cannot draw an imaginary dividing line between school and non-school locations. What happens to children outside of school in terms of exposure to violence may produce fear that results in violent behavior in the school (e.g., bringing a knife to school). Students may be indirect victims of violence. They may be aware of someone in their neighborhood who was victimized. They may live in communities where violence is commonplace. Thus being located in a community where there are high rates of violence will clearly impact violence in the school. As Anderson et al. (2001) point out, more than fifty percent of all school-associated violent death's occurred during transition times during the school day—either at the beginning of the day or at the end of the day or during lunch-time.

In the school shootings that have been recounted in the national news, some of the roots of those incidents may have come from relationships that occurred in the context of the school. In addition, there are specific aspects of schools that can promote or diminish violence. There are situations where people within the school system may be able to identify and intervene to stop violent incidents before they occur. Therefore, we should view schools as a context in which outside forces affect levels of violence.

Underwood, Galen, and Paquette (2001) point out that aggression is hard to define because it takes place within a social context. The context within which it occurs will strongly influence how particular acts are defined. They also suggest that we examine how social context is defined. Underwood et al. maintain that defining and understanding aggression are complicated by the fact that what is meant by social context is varied. Social context has been used to refer to "the culture, in which the kids are developing, the physical settings in which children interact, to the grade or ages or particular identities of other people present to the activities that that they are engaged in to the proximal events leading up to the aggressive act."

In addition to social contextual processes that impact definitions of violence, social judgments influence perceptions of violence and aggression. Ethnic and racial stereotypes influence how the actions of group members are interpreted. Stereotypes of groups can determine whether a particular act is labeled "violent" based on who performs it. Research suggests that people of color are perceived as more violent and aggressive than whites (Allport & Postman, 1947; Duncan, 1976). We should consider how this might effect judgments in school settings. Are minor infractions perceived differently based on the ethnicity of the actors?

GENDER AND SCHOOL VIOLENCE

Girls and Violence

> Sheila goes to her locker and finds a note. The note says, "Sheila is a bitch." Every student in the hallway has the same note.

> Mary feels terrible. All of the girls who were her friends last week and have been for the last year are no longer talking to her. They don't want her to sit with them at lunch.

General Information

As is the case outside of school settings, there appear to be gender differences in the types of violence/aggression experienced, the frequency of violence exposure, and the types of violent acts carried out. In addition, there are gender differences in the locations in schools where violence is experienced (Astor & Meyer, 1999). Results of research (Weiler, 1999) suggest:

- Girls experience physical and verbal sexual harassment more often than boys
- Girls participate in social aggression

- Girls are less likely to be in gangs than boys
- Girls are more likely to use knives than guns

Moskowitz et al. (2002) observed gender differences in the types of violence-related injuries received as well as where the injuries were experienced for adolescent girls and boys. Girls were two times more likely than boys to be stabbed than shot. In addition, girls were more likely than boys to experience these injuries at home or in school rather than in a public place. This indicates that the school is a place where girls are directly affected by violence.

Researchers have also noted that within schools there may be particular areas that girls fear for their safety (Astor & Meyer, 1999). While both boys and girls identified hallways as places of concern, girls reported more instances of violent events. Girls also characterized more areas of the school as unsafe than did boys. Girls also reported more of the violent events. The research pointed to "undefined public spaces" as being perceived by girls as particularly dangerous. Undefined public spaces are places that are in the open (or communal) but don't appear to be the responsibility of any individual or group. In non-school settings this includes building lobbies, stairwells, hallways, and elevators. In the Astor and Myers (1999) study, unsafe public spaces identified by students included hallways, gyms, locker rooms, playgrounds, auditoriums, and cafeterias during lunch periods. They also identified as violent locations areas around the school just before classes or right after school ended.

The girls in the study reported that they had personal knowledge of acts of violence in places that they indicated were violent areas in the school. "The majority of the girls reported being aware of, witness to, or victims of sexual harassment and rape in many of those undefined areas before, during, and after school hours. Most of these reported instances were related to dating situations between boys and girls" (Astor & Meyers, 1999, p. 208).

Unlike previous research, Astor and Meyers (1999) found a significant amount of violence occurred between girls. However, as in previous research, the students and teachers perceived that the characteristics of violence among girls were different from other types of school violence. This was largely because the aggression often came out of conflicts that were deep-rooted and multifaceted.

RELATIONAL AGGRESSION

As indicated above the differences in school violence of girls and boys go beyond the quantity of violent acts that are performed. There have been some suggestions that the types of violence in the schools as is manifested among girls is distinct from other forms of school violence. School violence is not always physical. Defining violence as mere physical acts would leave out forms of violence that may occur more frequently to girls. In addition to physical acts, nonphysical forms of violence and aggression can have deleterious effects on both the victim as well on the social climate of the school. Researchers have noted that these forms of aggression may be more difficult to detect and thus come under less scrutiny by teachers and school administrators (Crick et al., 2001). Astor et al. (1997) noted that even when physical aggression takes place among girls, it is deemed to be different from other forms of school violence because of the milieu in which it develops. It evolves in a context much like that of nonphysical aggression. A variety of terms and definitions have been used to characterize aggression that is not physical:

1. *Indirect aggression:* a noxious behavior in which the target person is attacked not physically or directly through verbal intimidation but in a circuitous way, through alienation (Lagerspetz, Bjorkqvist, & Peltonen, 1988)
2. *Social aggression:* manipulation of group acceptance through alienation, ostracism or character defamation (Cairns, Cairns, Neckerman, Ferguson, & Gariepy, 1989)
3. *Relational aggression:* "harming others through purposeful manipulation and damage to their peer relationships" (Crick & Grotpeter, 1995).

In social aggression the goal is to destroy the person's self worth or social standing in the group. Galen and Underwood (1997) indicate that this comes in a variety of forms. The victimizer can use indirect forms including negative facial expressions or body language. Another indirect form would be in cases where the victim is excluded from a social circle or rumors are spread about him or her.

The research results are mixed as to whether there are gender differences in terms of who are more frequently the victims of this behavior. Some studies find girls are more frequently victims of this form of aggression, while others find no difference, and a few studies find boys showing more relational aggression. Research results suggest that there may be developmental differences that would account for whether boys or girls exhibit more relational aggression (Crick et al., 2001).

Underwood (2003) maintains that the existence of gender differences in this form of behavior is probably not the important question. It is more important to understand how this aggression functions. This is the case when considering relational violence in the school context. It is critical to consider gender differences when thinking about school violence. There is some suggestion that being victimized by this type of violence versus being violent in this way is more closely linked than physical aggression is with physical victimization (Crick et al., 2001). Crick et al. (2001) also suggest that the methodology used may influence study results. Studies using peer and teacher reports more frequently yield mixed results, while observational studies show girls as being more frequently victimized.

Effects of Relational Violence

More research is now focusing on the victims of relational aggression (Crick et al., 2001). The goal of much of this research is to assess how being a victim of relational aggression affects a person's adjustment. Research results show that relational victimization does affect well-being and social adjustment. Investigators conducted studies to see if relational victimization added unique information about adjustment beyond that provided by physical victimization. Study findings indicate that it does in fact provide additional information. In a review of studies that considered the impact of relational victimization Crick et al. assessed its contribution in three different relationship contexts (peer, friendship, and romantic relationships) at three developmental periods (preschool/early childhood, middle childhood and adolescence). For preschool children, results of research suggest a relationship between peer relational victimization and poor peer relationships and rejection by peers, internalizing problems, and a lack of prosocial skills. Middle childhood relational victimization is related to poorer psychological adjustment (Crick & Grotepeter, 1996). It is also related to social adjustment problems (being rejected by peers, being submissive, and being lonely). It may also be predictive of later relationships with peers. In adolescence, relational victimization is also associated with poorer mental health (e.g., depression). According to some research, victims of relational aggression have also talked about committing suicide and not wanting to attend school (Owens, Slee, & Shute, 2000).

As Crick et al. (2001) point out:

> In sum, regarding relational victimization within the peer context is beginning to yield important findings, demonstrating that this form of victimization is positively associated with a myriad of negative social/psychological adjustment outcomes from early childhood to adolescence. In general it appears that relational victimizations with the peer group is most to be associated with poor peer relationships (e.g., peer rejection) internalizing problems (e.g., depression), and externalizing problems (e.g., lack of self-restraint, antisocial personality features). (p. 206)

Relational aggression was also found within friendships. Thus although friendships are frequently viewed as sources of support, they can also be the site of aggression. In fact, this is one reason why this form of aggression can be very painful for the victim. Relational aggression also appears to provide additional information when trying to predict externalizing problems in girls (Crick et al., 2001). It is also a predictor of clinical symptomology (depressed affect and borderline features) in romantic relationships.

Research findings also suggest that there may be gender differences in the impact of indirect/relational aggression. Girls appear to be more effected by this behavior than are boys (Crick et al., 2001). Finally, there is some evidence that some children who are victims are also children who engage in relational aggression.

Relational aggression is particularly important in the school context. Children spend the majority of their time in this setting. Relational aggression can poison the social climate of the school. Having high rates of relational aggression can make the environment of the school tense. There are reports of students not wanting to come to school because of it. Since it often happens in student networks it is difficult for school officials to intervene. Relational aggression in schools is not uncommon. Many schoolchildren children experience it to some degree. Being a frequent victim appears to be what is important (Crick et al., 2001). How do teachers and counselors know when to start intervention? How might this relate to problems with physical violence in schools?

Physical Aggression and Violence

Girls are less likely to be physically aggressive, but some girls do engage in fights (Weiler, 1999). There is a paucity of literature that looks at how and why girls fight. Physically aggressive behaviors that take place in schools usually involve fighting, bullying, and carrying weapons (Weiler, 1999). However, the majority of these aggressive behaviors are both performed by males and are directed at males. As Weiler (1999) points out, the percentage of girls committing violent acts in school is not trivial. For example, in schools characterized by large numbers of boys carrying weapons, there is a correspondingly high rate of girls who also carry weapons.

Smith and Thomas (2000) conducted a study in which they compared violent and nonviolent girls. Data was collected from a national survey in which they were trying to outline the characteristics of violent versus nonviolent youth. Violent girls were those who "had been suspended from school for fighting or bringing a weapon to school, or charged with a violent offense from the juvenile justice system." All other girls in the sample were considered "nonviolent." The results of their research indicate that the girls who were classified as violent were more likely to dislike school and view school discipline as unfair. Almost thirty-two percent of the violent girls indicated that school "feels like jail." The violent and the nonviolent girls also differed in terms of what made them angry. The violent girls' anger was not focused on anything specific, while nonviolent girls' anger was focused on some specific act of injustice. Ninety-one percent of violent girls as opposed to 50% of the nonviolent girls said yes when asked, "Have you ever felt angry enough to hit or hurt someone?" This feeling was associated with loneliness, unfair treatment by adults, not being liked by classmates, number of hours watching television and somatic anger symptoms.

When girls fight physically it is frequently viewed as different from boys' aggression. The rate of increase in antisocial behavior by girls exceeds that for boys (Weiler, 1999). Girls' engagment in violent crime may be more strongly associated with depression. There are different developmental paths that lead to violence for women and men and there is a great need for longitudinal investigations of physical aggression in girls as well as boys (Underwood, Galen, & Paquette, 2001).

School Violence as It Effects Other Female Members of School Settings

Usually when gender issues and school violence are discussed the focus is on how boys and girls are impacted in different or similar ways. Frequently ignored in these discussions is how gender affects the experiences of violence for others who are part of the school setting. Women comprise the majority of the teachers, the school social workers, and the school psychologists. Limited research attention has been paid to their experiences. Almost all of the programs that have been developed to ameliorate school violence have focused on the experiences of students.

Astor, Behre, Wallace, and Fravil (1998) have pointed out the limitations of such an approach. Teachers, social workers, and school psychologists have different perceptions of the problems than students. However, their work conditions are effected by school violence. In many cases it has been serious enough for some school social workers to consider leaving their jobs (Astor et al., 1997).

Violence and Boys

Two 12 year-old boys (Joe and Jack) are walking down the hallway during the change of classes. One "accidentally" bumps into the other. The boys then push and shove each other. Voices are raised. "What did you do that for?" "What is wrong with you?" "I will show you." A fistfight starts. The Dean of Students comes to break it up. Both boys are taken to the Dean's office.

On the way home from school Joe's friends call him a "punk" for letting Jack get away with hitting him. The day after this incident Joe brings a gun to school and looks for Jack.

Most of the research that has been conducted on school violence has been on male students. Some of what we know about male students and violence indicates:

- Boys are much more likely than girls to be physically aggressive at school
- Boys are more often both the victims and perpetrators of school violence
- Boys fight more than girls
- Boys are more likely to be in gangs
- Boys are more likely to use guns (Weiler, 1999)

Researchers have attempted to provide theoretical explanations for these behaviors. Some investigators believe that males perform violent acts as a way of expressing their masculinity (Kenway & Fitzclarence, 1997). They view this as particularly true for men who have limited power and control in the larger society. Kenway and Fitzclarence believe that schools and other societal institutions have supported this form of expressing masculinity. Others have called this ideology "hypermasculinity" (Mosher & Sirkin, 1984). According to Mosher and Sirkin hypermasculinity has three elements: a) endorsing callous attitudes toward women, b) viewing violence as manly, and c) viewing danger as exciting. Hypermasculinity has been associated with aggression in a variety of social domains, such as dating and school (e.g., Truman, Tokar, & Fischer, 1996).

Stevenson (2002) maintains that masculinity may manifest itself in young black men in the form of anger or in the form of being cool and detached. They recognize how they are perceived by the larger society. They are viewed by some as dangerous people who do not contribute to society. They are either overly observed in public settings (followed in stores when they are there to purchase something, stopped and searched by the police) or ignored. What forms might this intense scrutiny and these non-verbal messages about worthiness take in school settings? Franklin's work suggests that feelings of invisibility by black males can have numerous implications for behavior. "Invisibility is an inner struggle with feeling that one's talents, abilities, personality, and worth are not valued or recognized because of prejudice and racism. Conversely, we feel visible when our true talents, abilities, personality, and worth are respected" (Franklin, 2004, p. 4). Reactions to feeling invisible include internalized rage, frustration, loss of hope and anger. Violence can result from pent up anger.

ETHNICITY AND SCHOOL VIOLENCE

Exposure to school violence is not the same for all groups. Current research suggests that black and other minority youth when compared to white youth are more likely to be victims of violence in elementary and junior high school settings (Hill, 1998 as cited in Stevenson et al., 2002). As is generally the case, males of color are more exposed to nonsexual aggression than are girls (Anderson et al./ 2001). In addition, exposure to societal ills such as community violence, poverty, racism and sexism will also impact reactions to violence. Soriano and Soriano (1994) point out that a significant amount of school violence is the result of cultural ignorance and insensitivity. Changes in societal demographics can result in students needing to interact with others from different cultures. Cultural misunderstandings can take place due to unawareness of the social rules of the other's culture. If students feel disrespected, violence might erupt. In addition, teachers and administrators may work with students who come from backgrounds with which they may not be familiar. Even students and faculty from the same ethnic background may not understand one another due to class and generational differences. Theoretical approaches to understanding school violence must take into account the significance that culture and ethnicity may play in school settings. Stevenson (2002) maintains that few researchers consider culture as an important issue to examine in aggression intervention research.

Spencer and her colleagues (Spencer, 1999; Spencer, Dupree, Cunningham, Harpalani, & Munoz-Miller, 2003) have built on the work of Bronfrenbrenner (1979) and developed an identity-focused cultural ecological (ICE) model called the Phenomenological Variant of Ecological Systems Theory (PVEST) that has been used as a conceptual framework to examine human developmental processes. They have applied this framework while conducting research across a variety of domains including school adjustment for African American youth and vulnerability to violence. Unlike other approaches, this perspective takes into account culture, context, and normative developmental processes at the same time.

PVEST contains five components: (1) risk and protective factors, (2) net stress engagement, (3) reactive coping strategies, (4) emergent identities: stable coping response, and (5) coping outcomes. Risk and protective factors are those aspects of a person's life that may make him or her vulnerable to negative outcomes as well as those which might shield the person from negative outcomes. Examples of risk factors are living in poverty, race and gender discrimination, and exposure to racial and gender stereotypes. Exposure to these risk factors can be buffered by the individual's perception of himself or herself. "Age and stage-dependent self- and other-appraisal processes are involved (i.e., what one thinks or assumes others think about him or her) and are dependent on social-cognitive processes" (Spencer, 1999, p. 45) While risk and protective factors largely deal with a person's perceptions, net stress refers to real or actual experience of situations that may test a person's psychosocial identity and well-being. For example, experiences with discrimination, neighborhood violence, and negative feedback from teachers are significant stressors for minority youth. Net stress is alleviated by the social supports the person has available to help handle these challenges. This could include social support from adults that may serve to buffer the stressors that youth of color are exposed to. Once the stress is experienced the person then responds and attempts to cope with it by using reactive coping methods. The methods that youth may use to cope can be adaptive or maladaptive. Some examples of maladaptive coping responses include exaggerated gender role displays (e.g., hypermasculinity or "male bravado") and social withdrawal. Adaptive strategies include as asking for help, social engagement, and self-acceptance. As these methods of coping continue to be used over time they become "stable coping responses" or "emergent identities."

> Emergent identities define how individuals view themselves within and between their various contextual experiences. The combination of cultural/ethnic identity gender role understanding, and self and peer appraisals contribute to and define one's identity. Identity lays the foundation for future perception and behavior, yielding adverse or productive life-stage, specific coping outcomes. Productive outcomes include good health, positive relationships, and high self-esteem, while adverse outcomes include poor health, incarceration and self-destructive behavior. (Spencer et al., 2003, p. 36)

Stevenson et al.'s (2002) work based on this model shows how maladaptive coping for young African American males may manifest itself: "cultural and ecological demands on the gender identity of development of black youth often judge concern or fear for one's safety as 'sweet,' 'soft,' and weak" (p. 474). In order to counteract the appearance of weakness an African American boy will use a personae where he presents himself as "hard" and displays a heighten form of particular interpretation of masculinity: "I am cool;" "Nothing bothers me;" "I am not afraid of anything." Young men who cope in this way frequently will not tell adults when they are in danger. They also may cope with their suppressed fear by carrying a weapon. They may fight, as in the hypothetical situation above, to prove that they are men.

Caldwell, Kohn-Wood, Schmeelk-Cone, Chavous, and Zimmerman (2004) looked at the relationship between racial discrimination and identity and violent behavior in African American youth. The results of their research suggest that coming into contact with discrimination predicted violent behavior in both male and female young adults.

GENDER AND ETHNICITY IMPLICATION FOR SCHOOL VIOLENCE INTERVENTIONS

Interventions to prevent school violence should incorporate issues that are relevant to both gender and ethnicity. Stevenson (2002) talks about the importance of developing and utilizing long-term culturally relevant interventions. There are some promising programs that allow for this. For example, Astor, Benbenishty, and Meyer (2004) state that the development of school violence programs should be based on data and tailored to fit a specific school. In addition, students and teachers should be involved. The method they developed allows schools to assess whether specific forms of school violence are occurring. It also allows schools to see who the victims and the victimizers are. Are girls or boys the victims of particular types of violence? Programs can then be developed to match the school's need. The school can then select the forms of violence that are relevant.

Stevenson (2002) has developed a program that is culturally specific. It is designed to help African American youth manage anger during athletics. The program Preventing Long-term Anger and Aggression in Youth, is an intervention research program designed for African American youth who have had difficulties with aggressive behavior in the past. The program uses Spencer's (1999) identity-cultural ecological model as a conceptual framework. The program attempts to incorporate features that are part of the cultural realities of the youth.

What would Mayor Bloomberg think of these programs? The goal of Mayor Bloomberg's decision to place more security guards in schools that were considered dangerous was to reduce the amount of violent crime. A recent article in the New York Times (Gootman, 3-24-2004) notes that the amount of crime in the targeted schools has dropped by 9%. According to this article the number of serious assaults, weapons possessions, and other serious criminal incidents in schools since the implementation has dropped from 3.3 per day to 3.02 since this plan was implemented. The 9% decrease in crime in those schools is probably a result of the increase in citing non-criminal incidents. In addition, there is no mention if the percentage decrease was the same for all of the targeted schools. Has the social climate changed in those schools? Has there been a decrease in the number of students who fear coming to school? If so, is it the same for male and female students? What about other forms of violence? Were they reduced as well? What is the social climate like in those schools? These are questions that need to be addressed.

References

Allport, G.W. & Postman, L.J. (1947). *The psychology of rumor.* New York: Holt.

Anderson M, Kaufman J., Simon T.R., Barrios L, Paulozzi, L., Ryan G, Hammond R, Modzeleski W, Feucht T, Potter L, and School-Associated Violent Deaths Study Group. (2001) School-Associated violent deaths in the United States, 1994–1999. *JAMA; 286:* 2695–2702.

Astor, R.A., Behre, W.J., Wallace, J.M., & Fravil, K.A. (1998). School social Workers and school violence: Personal safety, training, and violence Program. *Social Work, 43(3),* 223–233.

Astor, R.A., Benbenishty, R. & Meyer, H.A. (2004). Monitoring and mapping student victimization in schools. *Theory into Practice, 43,* 39–49.

Astor, R.A. & Meyer, H.A. (1999). Where the girls and women won't go: Female students', teachers', and social workers' views of school safety. Social Work in Education, 21, 201–219.

Astor, R.A., Pitner, R.O., Benbenishty, R., & Meyer, H.A (2002). Public concern and Focus on school violence. In L. A. Rapp-Paglicci, A.R. Roberts and J.S. Wodarski (Eds.), *Handbook of violence* (pp. 362–302). New York, NY: John Wiley & Sons.

Bronfrenbrenner, U. (1979). *The ecology of human development.* Cambridge, MA: Harvard University Press.

Cairns, R.B., Cairns, B.D. Neckerman, H.J. Ferguson, L.L. & Gariepy. J. (1989). Growth and aggression: 1. Childhood to early adolescence. *Developmental Psychology, 25(2),* 320–330.

Caldwell, C.H., Kohn-Wood, L.P., Schmeelk-Cone, K.H., Chavous, T.M. & Zimmerman, M.A. (2004). Racial discrimination and racial identity as risk or protective factors for violent behaviors in African American young adults. *American Journal of Community Psychology, 33,* (1/2), 91–105.

Crick, N.R. & Grotpeter J.K. (1996). Children's treatment by peers. Victims of relational aggression and overt aggression. *Developmental and Psychopathology, 8,* 367–380.

Crick, N.R., Nelson, D.A., Morales. Cullerton-Sen, C. Casas, J.F., Hickman, S.E., (2001). Relational victimization in childhood and adolescence—I hurt you through the grapevine. In J. Juvonen and S. Graham (Eds.), *Peer harassment in school: The plight of the vulnerable and the victimized* (pp. 196–214). New York, NY: Guilford Press.

Duncan (1976). Differential social perception and attribution of intergroup violence: Testing the lower limits of stereotyping of blacks. *Journal of Personality and Social Psychology, 34,* 590–598.

Franklin, A.J. (2004). From brotherhood to manhood: How Black men rescue their relationships and dreams from the invisibility syndrome. John Wiley & Sons, Inc.: Hoboken, NJ

Furlong, M., and Morrison, G. (2000). The school in school violence: Definitions and facts. *Journal of Emotional & Behavioral Disorders, 8(2),* 5–16.

Gootman, E. (2004, March 25). Crime falls as citations surge in schools with extra officers. *New York Times.* Retrieved March 26, 2004, from http://www.nytimes.com

Hall, C.C.I. (1997). Cultural malpractice: The growing obsolescence of psychology with the changing US population. *American Psychologist, 52,* 642–651.

Holtappels, H.G. & Meier, U. (2000). Violence in schools. *European Education. 32,* 66–80.

Jordon, K. (2002). School violence among culturally diverse populations. In L. A. Rapp-Paglicci, A.R. Roberts and J.S. Wodarski (Eds.), *Handbook of violence* (pp. 326–346). New York, NY: John Wiley & Sons.

Kenway, J, & Fitzclarence, L. (1997). Masculinity, violence and schooling: Challenging 'Poisonous Pedagogies'. *Gender & Education, 9(1),* 117–134.

Lagerspetz, K., M. J., Björkqvist, K., & Peltonen, T. (1988). Is indirect aggression typical of females? *Aggressive Behavior, 14(6),* 403–414.

Molidor, C. & Tolman, R.M. (1998). Gender and contextual factors in adolescent dating violence. *Violence Against Women, 4(2),* 180–194.

Mosher, D. L. & Sirkin, M. (1984). Measuring a macho personality constellation. *Journal of Research in Personality, 18,* 150–163.

Moskowitz, H., Griffith, J.L., DiScala, C. & Sege, R. D. (2002) Serious injuries and deaths of adolescent girls resulting from interpersonal violence: Characteristics and trends from the United States. Journal of the American Academy of Child & Adolescent Psychiatry, 41(2), 181. Abstract retrieved November 5, 2003, from PsycINFO database.

Owens, L., Slee, P., Shute, R. (2000). 'It hurts a hell of a lot. . .' The effects of indirect aggression on teenage girls. *School Psychology International 21*, 359–376.

Rappaport, J. (1977). Community psychology: Values, research and action. New York: Holt, Rinehart & Winston.

Smith, H., & Thomas, S. P. (2000). Violent and nonviolent girls: Contrasting perceptions of anger experiences, school, and relationships. *Issues in Mental Health Nursing, 21 (5)*, 547–575.

Spencer, M.B. (1999). Social and cultural influence in school adjustment: The application of an identity-focused cultural ecological perspective. *Educational Psychologist, 34*, 43–57.

Spencer, M.B., Dupree, D., Cunningham, M., Harpalani, V., Munoz-Miller, M. (2003). Vulnerability to violence: A contextually-sensitive developmental perspective on African American adolescents. *Journal of Social Issues, 59*, 33–49.

Stevenson, H. C. (2002). Wrestling with destiny: the socialization of anger and healing in African American males. *Journal of Psychology and Christianity. 21*, 357–364.

Stevenson, H.C., Herrero-Taylor, T. Cameron, R., Davis, G.Y. (2002). "Mitigating Instigation: "Cultural phenomenological influence of anger and fighting among "Big-Boned" and "Big-Faced" African American youth. *Journal of Youth and Adolescence, 31(5)*, 473–485.

Soriano, M. and Soriano, F. I. (1994). School violence among culturally diverse populations: Sociocultural and institutional considerations. *School Psychology Review, 23(2)*, 216–235.

Truman, D.M., Tokar, D.M., and Fischer, A.R. (1996). Dimensions of masculinity: Relations to date rape supportive attitudes and sexual aggression in dating situations. *Journal of Counseling & Development, 74*, 555–562.

Underwood, M. (2003). *Social aggression among girls*. Guilford Press: New York.

Underwood, M., Galen, B. R., Paquette (2001) Top ten challenges for understanding gender and aggression in children: Why can't we just get along? *Social Development, 10*, 248–266.

Weiler, J. (1999). An overview of research on girls and violence. Retrieved May 29 2002 from Columbia University, Institute for Urban and Minority Education Website: http://iume.tc.columbia.edu/choice/briefs/choices01.html

Wekerle, C. and Wolfe, D. A. (1999). Dating violence in mid-adolescence: Theory significance, and emerging prevention initiatives. *Clinical Psychology Review, 19(4)* 435–456.

White, J. (2003) Paper presented at the 3rd annual conference sponsored by the Institute for the Study of Race and Culture. 30 Years of Racial Identity Theory. What Do We Know and How Does it Help? Boston University, Boston, MA.

Chapter 7

Sexual Violence in the Schools

Beatrice J. Krauss, Herbert H. Krauss,
Joanne O'Day, and Kevin Rente

It is clear that in school and on the way to school youth routinely encounter teasing, disrespectful remarks, or unwanted/uninvited touching that is sexual in nature (American Association of University Women Educational Foundation, 1993, 2001; Stein, 1999). Often, the perpetrators are their classmates, other students, and less frequently school staff—instructional staff, janitors, bus drivers and other adults associated with school (American Association of University Women Educational Foundation, 2001; Stein, 1999). Surprisingly often, the events occur within as well as across gender, but most often include a male perpetrator and a female victim (Fineran, 2002; Rickert, Vaughan, & Wiemann, 2002). In multiple surveys, youth assert that much of this behavior occurs publicly and evokes little reaction from either other students or school staff (American Association of University Women Educational Foundation, 1993, 2001; Fineran & Bennett, 1998).

For the youthful victims, there is often confusion and embarrassment, a change in their relationship to school and the academic goals of school, as is true for their reactions to more general and milder forms of teasing, bullying and disrespect (American Association of University Women Educational Foundation, 2001). Absenteeism, poorer grades, depression, and anxiety often ensue; suicidality and other mental health problems (Ackard & Neumark-Sztainer, 2002) as well as a propensity for later re-victimization have been documented (Coker et al., 2000; Humphrey & White, 2000; Smith, White, & Holland, 2003). For vaginal/penile assault, unplanned pregnancy is a concern. The current concentration of

HIV (Centers for Disease Control and Preventions, 1999a; Krauss et al., 2001; Rosenberg & Biggar, 1998) and other sexually transmitted infections among adolescents and youth (Martin, Clark, Lynch, Kupper, & Cilenti, 1999; Rickert et al., 2002; Steele, 2000) make potential health sequelae of sexual assault quite serious.

The struggle of youth to understand what has happened to them and go on is mirrored in the adult world as the adults responsible for their guidance and safety begin to sort out their own terminology regarding source, severity, intent of physical or emotional harm, location, and even the sexual content of events (Fineran, 2002). On the basis of their definitions, adults also formulate policy and response.

The adult language about sexually charged and harmful acts is evolving. It includes terms such as rape, attempted rape, sexual assault, sexual harassment, domestic violence, date rape, dating violence, acquaintance rape, hate crimes and violence against sexual minorities, intimate partner violence, child abuse, peer abuse, peer violence, sexual violence in schools, sexual exploitation, and sexual violence (Ackard & Neumark-Sztainer, 2002; Fineran & Bennett, 1998; Stein, 1999). Some of these terms have legal connotations, e.g., sexual violence, sexual harassment, while others have developed from social science research in which either the type of sexual violence, its predictors or its after-effects seem to vary by relationship of victim to perpetrator, characteristics of the victim, by duration or by setting, e.g., late vs. early childhood abuse (e.g., Maker, Kemmelmeier, & Peterson, 2001).

Some evolving terms, e.g., peer sexual violence, rely on a growing understanding of the social world of the young. Unlike sexual violence among adults where much violence occurs within intimate or formalized relationships, youth sexual violence may occur in relationships that are transitory; the "dating" of "dating violence" may refer to social forms that are passé to older students or irrelevant to younger students (Krauss et al., 2001); or students may be harmed by classmates who are relative strangers rather than intimates. Peer sexual violence may occur during childhood, but is distinct from child sexual abuse. Child sexual abuse statutes are quite detailed, but often imply "contact or interaction between a child and an adult when the child is being used for the sexual stimulation of that adult or another person" (National Center on Child Abuse and Neglect, 1981). Childhood sexual abuse may be committed by another minor when that person is either significantly older than the victim (often defined as more than five years) or when the abuser is in a position of power or control over the child (Ackard & Neumark-Sztainer, 2002; National Center on Child Abuse and Neglect, 1981).

Since in the majority of cases at school, the perpetrator of sexual violence is likely to be another student, one whose own experience or witness of harm may lie behind his or her hurtful and sexually-charged act (Clarke, Stein, Sobota, Marisi, & Hanna, 1999), adults struggle to achieve a balance between the "soft" responses—teaching, counseling, conflict-resolution—that would heal both victim and perpetrator, and the "hard" responses—discipline, zero-tolerance policies (pre-existing and mandatory prescribed punishments)—that would deter such events from occurring within the school environment (National Education Association, 2004). "Hard" and "soft" responses are also involved in preventing the perpetuation of "hostile environments" where pervasive and persistent sexual harassment and sexual violence are likely to occur. Hard responses include sign-ins, weapons searches, metal detectors, hall patrols, police presence and other security techniques (National Education Association, 2004), while soft responses include training of all school staff and students to recognize and manage interactions that may be harmful, e.g., to understand "flirting vs. hurting," in the language of one training program (Stein & Sjostrom, 1996). And training programs must take account of what is required of youthful victims in school disciplinary, civil or criminal proceedings.

The specific acts that define *sexual violence*—sexual assault, attempted rape or rape—originate in definitions handed down from criminal law. Their determination depends upon overt signs of intent, force, injury, or, in the case of rape, penetration and lack of consent. Consent is particularly complex, with standards varying by state and jurisdiction. Consent is dependent on mental states (e.g., someone who is drunk cannot consent), the age of the victim (e.g., in some jurisdictions someone 16 or under cannot consent), and age difference between victim and perpetrator (e.g., in some jurisdictions a youth five years or more younger than the perpetrator cannot consent). Many school-age youth within a state or jurisdiction are wholly ignorant of these definitions and standards (Yee, O'Day, O'Sullivan, & Krauss, 2000).

Other terms (e.g., the "unwelcome, uninvited, and unwanted") that define acts of *sexual harassment* generally, depend on an understanding of youth's internal intentions and reactions. In law, proof of that intent may require that students come forward, document and complain about their treatment or document and complain about the failure of school authorities to address and rectify the incidents that are happening to them. To date, the Supreme Court has heard three cases regarding sexual harassment or violence where the plaintiffs intended to place responsibility on schools and collect damages for harassment or violence that occurred within schools. The Court decided for the plaintiff in two (*Franklin v. Gwinnett County Public Schools*, 1992; *Davis v. Monroe County Board of Education*, 1999) and cited the victim's lack of complaint to school authorities in the third case (*Gebser v. Lago Vista Independent School District*, 1998).

The current chapter will focus on sexual violence in the schools, which is understudied and is a difficult area to study. Sexual harassment in the schools has been comprehensively reviewed by Stein (1999). Stein considers all forms of harassment and hate crime directed toward sexual minorities as sexual violence, but concludes that current understanding labels sexual harassment as the general term, with sexual violence—assault, attempted rape or rape—representing more severe forms of harassment. Sexual violence, according to that understanding, is distinguished by the availability of criminal action remedies in which individuals, the perpetrators, are held liable. These criminal proceedings are available in addition to actions taken by the school, the Office of Civil Rights of the U.S. Department of Education, civil proceedings that apply to all sexual harassment, and other criminal proceedings that apply to child abuse.

The chapter will begin with a definition of sexual harassment and violence, indicate the prevalence of school violence and the difficulties in determining its prevalence, summarize recent research on effects of sexual violence in adolescence, briefly outline the landmark Supreme Court decisions that have changed the school liability and school response landscape, present a sampling of school policy and remedy responses, and end with a unique perspective on school violence from the viewpoint of school nurses and students who have participated in an in-depth study of adolescent sexual behavior and the social settings in which it occurs.

DEFINITIONS

Sexual Harassment

Sexual harassment is a form of sex discrimination that violates Title VII of the Civil Rights Act of 1964. It has been extended by judicial precedent, under Title IX, to students in federally funded educational institutions or institutions where students receive federal financial aid (U.S. Department of Education Office of Civil Rights, 1999). The Office of Civil Rights of the US Department of Education (1997, available also at http://www.ed.gov/about/offices/list/ocr/docs/ocrshpam.html, accessed 2004) notes,

> sexual harassment is illegal–Title IX of the Education Amendments of 1972 (Title IX) prohibits ... sexual harassment .... Title IX protects students from unlawful sexual harassment in all of a school's programs or activities, whether they take place in the facilities of the school, on a school bus, at a class or training program sponsored by the school at another location, or elsewhere. Title IX protects both male and female students from sexual harassment, regardless of who the harasser is.
>
> Sexual harassment can take two forms: *quid pro quo* and *hostile environment*. *Quid pro quo harassment* occurs when a school employee causes a student to

believe that he or she must submit to unwelcome sexual conduct in order to participate in a school program or activity. It can also occur when an employee causes a student to believe that the employee will make an educational decision based on whether or not the student submits to unwelcome sexual conduct. For example, when a teacher threatens to fail a student unless the student agrees to date the teacher, it is quid pro quo harassment. . . . It does not matter whether the student refuses to submit to the teacher's demands and suffers the threatened harm, or does what the teacher wants and thus avoids the harm. In both cases, the harassment by the school employee is unlawful . . . .

Hostile environment harassment occurs when unwelcome sexually harassing conduct is so severe, persistent, or pervasive that it affects a student's ability to participate in or benefit from an education program or activity, or creates an intimidating, threatening or abusive educational environment. A hostile environment can be created by a school employee, another student, or even someone visiting the school, such as a student or employee from another school (U.S. Department of Education, Office of Civil Rights, 1997).

Harassment can be visual (e.g., leering, gestures), verbal (e.g., derogatory comments, propositions) or physical (unwanted touching, physical assault). The victim does not have to be the person harassed but could be anyone affected by the offensive conduct. Further, the harasser's conduct must be unwelcome.

Sexual Violence

In most surveys administered to youth or school staff about sexual violence, the terms attempted or completed rape, as well as sexual assault or battery are used to reflect familiar terminology. Sexual violence, however, in most states now, is defined by the gender-neutral term "sexual assault." Sexual assault is the use of force, threat or coercion, physical or psychological, to make a person engage in sexual activity without that person's consent (American Medical Association, 1995). The legal department of the Planned Parenthood Federation of America (1998, accessed 2004) explains sexual assault to teens in this way:

[T]he following acts are considered crimes in most states when they are committed with physical force or with a threat to hurt the victim or another person. These acts are also crimes if the victim is physically helpless and can't give consent. For example, when the victim is drunk or asleep and unable to refuse sex.

- Penetration of a victim's anus or vagina. The penetration may be by a body part, such as finger or penis, or by an object.
- Penetration of the victim's mouth by a man's penis.
- Intentionally touching a victim's intimate parts, such as buttocks, inner thigh, breasts, genital area. (or the clothing covering those body parts)
- Forcing a victim to touch someone else's intimate parts.
- Cunnilingus: contact between the mouth of one person and the vulva of another.

Under older laws a crime was not committed unless the attacker used violent force that overcame the victim's "resistance." In most states this is no longer the case. A crime has been committed when the victim is touched or penetrated without her (or his) consent (http://www.teenwire.com/index.asp? taStrona=http://www.teenwire.com/warehous/articles/wh_19981201p060 .asp, accessed 2004).

Prevalence of Sexual Violence in U.S. Schools

The ideal survey to determine the prevalence of sexual violence in schools would query youth directly about experiences of perpetration or victimization under conditions that preserve anonymity and foster accuracy in reporting. The ideal survey would have concrete and easily understood descriptors of sexually violent acts, and would gather enough particulars about incidents, including their locale (i.e., school or neighborhood), to inform prevention efforts. Sampling techniques would allow generalization.

Unfortunately, such data are limited. One early and one recent study carried out by Harris Associates meets most of these criteria (American Association of University Women Educational Foundation, 1993, 2001). However, even their recent survey of 2,064 public school students falters by use of unique terminology for forms of sexual harassment and failure to clearly define and incorporate sexual assault. Sexual assault is approached through questions such as the following: "forced you to do something sexual other than kissing," (reported as often or occasional by 3% of 8th through 11th grade girls and 5% of boys in those grades in 2001), "touched, grabbed or pinched you in a sexual way" (reported by 29% of girls and 20% of boys), "pulled off or down your clothing" (reported by 4% of girls and 6% of boys), and "intentionally brushed up against you in a sexual way" (reported by 28% of girls and 20% of boys). This report notes an increase in sexual harassment of boys since 1993, a decline in reports of teacher or staff harassment, and, although now most students know about sexual harassment policy at their school (about 70% of students), estimates of sexual harassment and sexual violence have not abated nor have youth estimates of the negative impact of harassment on their daily school life. Yet, only 11% of those who experienced harassment said they told a teacher and 9% another school employee (American Association of University Women Educational Foundation, 2001).

Other prevalence estimates for sexual violence in schools are derived from triangulating among several data sources, each of which are problematic, because of reporting biases, focus on only one form of sexual violence, placing several forms of violence together into one category or failing to note where the violence occurred.

Some data sources are open to underreporting biases, because they are based on use of criminal justice statistics and only capture cases that have come to the attention of the justice system (e.g., Devoe et al., 2003). These sources, also, may fail to discriminate sexual violence from other forms of serious violence (e.g., Devoe et al., 2003, include rape and sexual assault in a serious violent victimization category that includes robbery and aggravated assault; no table in their report separates rape and sexual assault from other forms of serious violence). Some surveys ask youth directly about incidents of victimization, thus avoiding potential underreporting, but, to date, fail to ask for the locale of those incidents (e.g., Youth Risk Behavior Surveys, Grunbaum et al., 2003). Equally open to underreporting is a survey conducted in 1996–97 among principals of a representative sample of U.S. elementary, middle and secondary schools (National Center for Education Statistics, 1998). This study, however, is clear about sexual violence, its incidence during one year (rather than prevalence among the student population over their lifetime), and where it occurred.

In the summer of 1997, 1,234 principals in the 50 states and the District of Columbia were asked to report on the incidence of crime and violence in their school in the previous academic year. They were asked specifically about the number of incidents that involved contact with law enforcement, that involved students as victims or perpetrators, and that occurred during school hours or at school sponsored events or activities. "Rape or sexual battery" was among these incidents, categorized among suicide, physical attacks or fights with weapons, or robbery as serious or violent crimes. Sexual battery was defined as "an incident that includes rape, fondling, indecent liberties, child molestation, or sodomy. These incidents should take into consideration the age and developmentally appropriate behavior of the offenders and are severe enough to warrant calling the police or other law enforcement representative" (National Center for Education Statistics, 1998).

Results were weighted to represent all U.S. public schools. Approximately 4,170 instances of rape or sexual battery, or about 10 instances per 100,000 students, were estimated from reports. Incidents were estimated to have occurred at about 3 percent of schools. Slightly less than half occurred at the high school level, 34 percent at the middle school level and 17 percent in elementary schools. Moderate-sized (300–999 students, 48% of incidents) to large (over 1,000 students, 44% of incidents); urban or urban fringe (73% of incidents); and Southeast, Central or Western schools (88% combined) were most likely to have reported incidents.

A South Carolina study of the prevalence of severe dating violence, based on student report, indicates that sexual violence may be more common than principal report suggests, but fails to denote the location of that violence (Coker et al., 2000). Using 5,414 responses of 9th to 12th graders from the South Carolina Youth Risk Behavior Survey, the authors estimate that 12.1% of youth report they were victims or perpetrators of severe dating violence, 7.6% as victim and 7.7% as perpetrator. More girls than boys were involved in severe dating violence, 14.4% v. 9.1%.

A Minnesota study of 81,247 students in grades 9 to 12 notes that approximately 9% of girls and 6% of boys report that they had experienced date violence or rape (Ackard & Neumark-Sztainer, 2002). Again, where the violence occurred was not reported.

Results of these two studies are consistent with a review of research from the early to mid-90's (Fineran & Bennett, 1998). The studies reviewed "all had questions regarding the physical forms of sexual harassment, which include sexual assault. All three studies documented that 10 percent to 20 percent of the students experienced these behaviors and that girls experienced these behaviors more than boys" (Fineran & Bennett, 1998). University of North Carolina women offered data retrospectively about their high school years in the context of another study on dating violence. Their recollections indicate about 7% experienced attempted rape and 13% forcible rape during adolescence (Smith et al., 2003). Again, the locale for incidents is not mentioned.

Some resolution of these disparate figures may be possible by looking at victimization at school and away from school. A recent report (Devoe et al., 2003) combines Bureau of Justice Statistics and National Center for Education Statistics to estimate the serious violent crime in 2001 among youth by the location of its occurrence. Approximately, 64% of the approximately 451,000 incidents of serious violence that affected youth ages 12–18 (rape, sexual assault, robbery and aggravated assault) were reported as happening away from school, while 36% happened at school. Younger children, 12–14, were more likely to be victimized at school, while older children, 15–18, were more likely to be victimized away from school. The combining of other forms of violence into one category makes these figures difficult to interpret with regard to sexual violence alone, and only partially resolves the discrepancy between criminal justice statistics, school report statistics and prevalence estimates derived from self-report.

Other data, gathered outside K-12 schools and colleges, also suggests sexual violence is more prevalent than criminal justice statistics indicate. Sexual violence may occur later, or in different venues, or data to date on violence in schools may represent substantial underreporting or unwillingness to bring serious incidents to the attention of school authorities. In a survey of over 1,000 recent army enlistees, mean age 26, where explicit queries defining terms were made (Martin, Rosen, Durand, Knudson, & Stretch, 2000), 29.9% of women reported they had experienced attempted rape during their lifetime, 22.6% experienced completed rape and 29.2% other unwanted sexual contact. The figures for men were 1.8%, 1.1%, and 5.8%, respectively. There was no information about the locale or the age at which incidents occurred. These figures are consistent, however, with the increasing and cumulative lifetime reports of women in the University of North Carolina study whose reports on incidents during adolescence and prior to college were retrospective, but whose reports on continuing victimization were longitudinal (Smith et al., 2003).

Whether in or out of school, youth are the most likely victims of sexual assault in the U.S. Estimates suggest 3.5 per every 1,000 youth age 12 to 15 experience sexual assault; 5.0 per 1,000 for youth 16 to 19; 4.6 per 1,000 for youth 20–24; and 1.7 per 1,000 for those 25 to 29. Adolescent female victims are estimated to outnumber males 13.5:1 (American Academy of Pediatric Committee on Adolescence, 2001).

THE EFFECTS OF SEXUAL VIOLENCE

Multiple physical and mental health effects of sexual violence have been documented. There is little, if any, data on effects particular to incidents that have taken place at school, although studies of school-based sexual harassment indicate avoidance of school and fear of being harmed at school are common (American Association of University Women, 1993, 2001; Stein, 1999).

Physical effects are anticipated depending on the nature of the assault. Physicians treating adolescent victims of sexual assault recommend screening or prophylaxis for common sexually transmitted infections, possible pregnancy prophylaxis, substance use and mental health screening along with treatment of injuries and collection of forensic data (American Academy of Pediatrics Committee on Adolescent Care, 2001; Steele, 2000).

Multiple mental health effects—a greater likelihood of suicidal thoughts and attempts, eating disorders, lowered self-esteem and general well-being—have been documented among a sample of students exposed to peer sexual violence (dating violence and rape) even after other abuse by adults was controlled for (Ackard & Neumark-Sztainer, 2002). Additional studies suggest sexual violence is associated with increased substance use (Coker et al., 2000; Martin et al., 1999), lower quality of life (Coker et al., 2000), vulnerability to post-traumatic stress disorder and more frequent somatic complaints (Martin et al., 2000).

The research on vulnerability to re-victimization is complex. The target adult condition—sexual victimization, other physical victimization or both—varies from study to study as does the type of victimization entered as a predictor (childhood sexual abuse, adolescent sexual abuse, child abuse in adolescence, dating violence, rape). Peer sexual victimization appears to be a predictor of adult physical or sexual assault victimization (Ackard & Neumark-Sztainer, 2002), peer violence victimization appears to be a predictor of later or co-occurring sexual violence victimization (Smith et al., 2003), while childhood sexual abuse or early adolescent sexual victimization appear to be predictors of adult sexual re-victimization (Humphrey & White, 2000; Maker et al., 2001).

A growing literature indicates that sexual and physical violence co-occur, both for victims (Martin et al., 1999; Smith et al., 2003) and perpetrators (Clarke et al., 1999; Ozer, Tschann, Pasch, & Flores, 2004) co-temporaneously or in a victim/victimizer cycle. Victims tend to experience both physical and sexual assault, while, especially among boys, perpetrators tend to carry out both sexual and other forms of assault. There is some indication that girls as victims and boys as perpetrators both experience negative mental health effects of sexual violence (Coker et al., 2000).

SUPREME COURT DECISIONS

In 1992, the U.S. Supreme Court held that, in the case of a high school student who had been subjected to "continual sexual harassment and abuse by a teacher" (*Franklin v. Gwinnett Public Schools*, 1992), a "damages remedy is available for an action brought to enforce Title IX." In short, school districts could be sued for teacher-student sexual harassment that prevented a student from full participation in educational programs or activities in schools receiving federal funds.

In 1998, the Court heard the case of a high school student who had a sexual relationship with a teacher. The school district had no harassment policy in place as required by federal guidelines, nor had the student complained to the teacher's superiors. The plaintiff sought to recover damages under Title IX. The Court held for the school district (*Gebser v. Lago Vista Independent School District*, 1998).

Within six years of the Franklin decision, the Court extended its understanding from teacher-student harassment to student-student sexual harassment (*Davis v. Monroe County Board of Education*, 1999). In so doing, it clarified both student and school district responsibilities. In the brief for the plaintiff, a fifth grader in Hubbard elementary school, her counsel wrote:

> [O]n behalf of her minor daughter, LaShonda D., Mrs. Davis alleges that LaShonda was sexually harassed in school by another student and that the Board knowingly tolerated, condoned, and was deliberately indifferent to the misconduct, in violation of Title IX of the Education Amendments of 1972....
> In the first of several instances, starting in December of 1992, a classmate identified as 'G.F.' repeatedly attempted to touch LaShonda's breasts and vaginal area and told her in vulgar terms that he 'want[ed] to feel her boobs' and 'want[ed] to get in bed' with her. Both LaShonda and her mother reported these incidents to [a] classroom teacher....

The harassment persisted. Incidents during ensuing months were witnessed or reported to other teachers, a coach, and the principal. The brief continues:

> With no response forthcoming from the school, in May 1993, G.F. was charged with and pled guilty to sexual battery. Throughout this five-month pattern of sexual harassment, neither the teachers nor the Board ever disciplined G.F. In addition, the Board had no policy prohibiting the sexual harassment of students in its schools at this time; nor did it have any plan of action or guidance to assist employees in handling, or students in reporting, such misconduct. Additionally, the Board did not provide any training to its employees instructing them on how to respond to incidents of sexual harassment of students. The sexual harassment LaShonda endured, and the refusal of the school to take steps to end it, interfered with her ability to benefit from the education the Board provided at Hubbard. LaShonda's ability to concentrate diminished, causing her grades, previously all A's and B's, to suffer. In addition, the harassment affected her mental and emotional well-being, as evidenced by a suicide note she wrote, which her father found in April 1993.

Writing for the majority, Justice Sandra Day O'Connor, held:

> A private Title IX damages action may lie against a school board in cases of student-on-student harassment, but only where the funding recipient is deliberately indifferent to sexual harassment, of which the recipient has actual knowledge, and that harassment is so severe, pervasive, and objectively offensive that it can be said to deprive the victims of access to the educational opportunities or benefits provided by the school.

Schools receiving federal funds or whose students receive federal funds were on notice to develop policy and practice to manage sexual harassment and sexual violence.

SCHOOL POLICY

Guidelines for preventing and reacting appropriately to school-based violence or adolescent sexual violence have been authored by the American Academy of Pediatrics (2001), the American Civil Liberties Union (2001), the American College of Obstetrics and Gynecology (2000), Human Rights Watch (2001), the National Association for Secondary School Principals (2000), the National Education Association (2004), the U.S. Department of Education Office of Civil Rights (1997, 1999) and others. An issue briefing on school violence is posted as well for the National Association of School Nurses (2000).

These guides, and their many spin-off publications, are aimed variously at parents or students, teachers and other school personnel, school administrators, school boards, state and federal legislators, health and mental health professionals, and local, city, state and federal departments of education. Most guides approach sexual violence under a general framework of school safety—sexual violence and sexual harassment are among many behaviors that threaten students' feelings of safety (e.g., National Association of School Nurses, 2000; National Association of Secondary School Principals, 2000; National Education Association, 2004). A few approach sexual violence from the perspective of sexual diversity and sexual minority rights (American Civil Liberties Union, 2001; Human Rights Watch, 2001), especially informative, since, to date, Title IX does not provide protections for sex discrimination except as it leads to sexual harassment.

The Department of Education's Office of Civil Rights (1999) provides an 18-point checklist for a comprehensive approach to sexual harassment that incorporates hate crime:

- Board members, district administrators, and the superintendent recognize the urgency of the problem of unlawful harassment and hate crime, identify people and agencies that can help them develop effective prevention and response strategies, and compile a library of useful materials
- School officials select personnel to work on creating an effective anti-harassment program in consultation with parents, students, and community groups
- Compliance coordinators are appointed and trained
- School personnel assess the school climate to determine the prevalence and types of harassment that may exist and the potential for hate-motivated violence
- School district adopts a written anti-harassment policy or reviews and revises existing policies for accuracy, clarity and legal compliance; the policy is clearly communicated to all members of the school community; and school personnel and students are held accountable for their actions
- School district develops a formal grievance procedure and takes steps to make sure it is working properly
- Instructional personnel use or supplement the district's curriculum and pedagogical strategies to foster respect and appreciation for diversity
- School sites institute, improve, or expand age appropriate student activities to prevent or reduce prejudice and conflict
- School district and individual school sites institute specific measures to respond immediately and effectively when harassment occurs to stop the harassment and prevent recurrence
- School officials flexibly apply response mechanisms to both the victim and the perpetrator, taking into account the parties' ages and the context of the behavior

- School personnel continually monitor the school climate and promptly address problems that could lead to harassment or violence or that indicate that harassment could be occurring
- Appropriate school officials become familiar with pertinent civil and criminal laws at the state, local, and federal levels, so that they are able to recognize possible civil rights violations, hate crimes and other criminal acts
- Schools develop guidelines and procedures for collaboration with law enforcement officials, make appropriate referrals to outside agencies, and designate liaison personnel
- Crisis intervention plans are in place to minimize the possibility of violence or disruption of the educational process
- District-level personnel and individual school sites form continuing partnerships with parents and the community to prevent hate crimes and harassing behaviors
- Staff training and professional development programs support the district's anti-harassment efforts
- All harassment incidents are carefully documented and incidents are reported to outside authorities as required
- District regularly assesses the effectiveness of its anti-harassment efforts (U.S. Department of Education Office of Civil Rights, 1999)

These recommendations are supplemented by guidance based on the Family Educational Rights and Privacy Act about when a victim or perpetrator's privacy rights might be offset by due process concerns.

Examination of other guidelines reveals additional recommendations. Human Rights Watch (2001) calls for new legislation to incorporate sex discrimination into sexual harassment protections; asks for procedures that require a response from school personnel even when a student does not file a complaint; wishes all school staff (cafeteria workers, bus drivers, etc.) trained in sensitivity to sexual harassment and sexual minority issues; wants staff to be trained on how to intervene in observed incidents of hate crime or harassment; requests affected students to be consulted about school responses to incidents (e.g., a decision to move a student to another class); suggests confidentiality procedures be strengthened (e.g., "outing" without permission); encourages greater access for students and staff to information about sexual minorities; and recommends respect for diversity be taught in the earliest grades.

In its preamble to a model anti-harassment policy, the American Civil Liberties Union (2001) positions sexual harassment and sex discrimination within other forms of discrimination—on the basis of race, disability, religion, marital status, etc. It also calls for strengthened reporting systems and well-publicized protections for those who file a grievance. Like the National Education Association (2004), the American Civil Liberties Union (2001) suggests the ultimate remedy for school-based sexual harassment and violence is at hand:

> To prevent harassment in the first instance, staff members should teach—teach why harassment is wrong and teach that tolerance and respect are essential to a free society. In response to an act of harassment, staff members should intervene immediately to stop the harassment and, if appropriate, should punish the harassment promptly, consistently, and proportionately to the seriousness of the act. But the response should not end there; rather, staff members should deter future harassment with continuing lessons of tolerance and respect.

Other guides suggest that prevention efforts involve "zero tolerance" in key areas—weapons and drugs, for example (National Association of Secondary School Principals, 2000) and address some of the underlying reasons for sexual violence through curricular, school climate, mental health, and advocacy efforts (National Association of School Nurses, 2000; National Association of Secondary School Principals, 2000; National Education Association, 2004). Some of the recommendations from these education professionals are for smaller schools and smaller classes; alternative classes; codes of conduct; programs for peer mediation, anger management and conflict resolution; and more mental health services. Advocacy issues include gun control (National Education Association, 2004) and reduction of media violence (National Association for Secondary School Principals).

It is the medical professionals, however, who explicitly underline the sociocultural context of sexual violence (American Academy of Pediatrics Committee on Adolescence, 2001). The medical provider should be prepared that for the victim of sexual assault, "[e]xploration of gender roles and relationship parameters (e.g., exploitative, nonconsensual vs. healthy) are critical."

THE IDEAL VERSUS THE REAL

For the last three years, several of the authors have been conducting in-depth interviews with 12–24 year old youth in a high HIV prevalence (10%) neighborhood in New York City. We have been asking youth about the social settings where they meet and have romantic or sexual relationships. From interviews with youth, we have inferred a sea-change in heterosexual relationships, at least among a substantial minority of young people. The change is marked by casual attitudes toward sexual experimentation by both boys and girls, status games about number and type of partners, pervasive public disrespect across gender, and seeming normalization of these behaviors and attitudes (Krauss, O'Day, Godfrey, & Rente, 2003). Much of what we have heard could be called sexual violence.

What we have observed is not limited to one locale, but has been reported in many states, in urban and rural locations, in social science or public health research (Freudenberg et al., 1999), in journalistic reports (Franks, 2000; Jarell, 2000; Sales, 1997), and in anthropological observations (Dash, 1996; Dietrich, 1998). The behaviors have been associated with clusters of sexually transmitted infections or HIV (Centers for Disease Control, 1999b, 2000; Rothenberg et al., 1998; Welych et al., 1998). A few examples will illustrate. The youth quoted below are generally talking about gathering in groups at unsupervised apartments or houses for hours or for day-long events where sex with one or more partners evolves from alcohol and substance use and just being together, or about sexual events that are planned; others know the sex is happening:

> "Some of the time we plan what will happen and sometimes it just happens. We're drinking and smoking blunts and weed. We get all woozy. We're dancing and we start touching. We see what other people are doing. Things just happen."

> "I came to the party prepared to wear her down, to beg her for hours if I had to." "I knew if I made her feel bad at first, called her names, I'd have a better chance later."

> "I could say afterward I had sex with one of the most popular guys."

> "If I had sex with several guys and had a baby, no one would know whose it was; it would be mine."

> "There were ten guys there; I didn't think I could leave."

> "She was a 'walkable.' That means she was good-looking and you wouldn't mind being seen with her, walking her to the subway, after you had sex with her."

Unknowingly, schools have been in collusion.

> "It is easy to hold [these kind of] hooky parties because our school only takes attendance in first period and most of our parents are in the WEP program so no one is home."

Schools were used as points of meeting and organizing for these gatherings; sometimes flyers advertising parties were handed out at school; sometimes sexual relationships continued in unsupervised areas of schools, such as furnace rooms or stairwells.

We asked five school-based health providers who had rotated between schools and averaged seven years of practice with youth if any youth had reported such activities to them. These individuals made it clear that young people were unlikely to report such gatherings to them because of well-known, stringent requirements for notification of other school personnel and parents.

One of our respondents was "kicked out of school" after making unwanted sexual advances and inappropriately touching a girl's breast and vagina at school. After he requested oral sex, the girl complained to school personnel. Our respondent went through the disciplinary proceedings, was assigned to an alternative school, and still believes administrators plotted to get him kicked out of school, jealous of his popularity and good grades.

Our "real life" examples indicate how important it is to begin sexual violence prevention with tolerance and respect—across gender, across age, across other categories of diversity, and within one's self. Such education needs to start early. School and community response, as Human Rights Watch (2001) suggests, must take account of the social realities facing potential victims or victimizers and work especially hard to make the mechanisms that would support reporting—"a telling environment" as the National Education Association (2004) puts it—protected.

ACKNOWLEDGMENTS: Beatrice Krauss, Joanne O'Day and Kevin Rente are at the Hunter College Center for AIDS, Drugs and Community Health. Herbert Krauss is at Pace University. Beatrice Krauss is a professor of Urban Public Health at Hunter College Center for Community and Urban Health as well as executive director of the Center. We would like to gratefully acknowledge the continuing contributions of the youth of New York City's Lower East Side. Research was supported by the National Institute of Mental Health (R01 MH62975). Correspondence concerning this chapter should be sent to Beatrice Krauss, Hunter College, 425 E. 25th Street, New York, New York 10010. E-mail: bkrauss@hunter.cuny.edu.

REFERENCES

Ackard, D.M. & Neumark-Sztainer, D. (2002). Date violence and date rape among adolescents: associations with disordered eating behaviors and psychological health. *Child Abuse and Neglect*, 26(5), 455–73.

American Academy of Pediatrics Committee on Adolescence. (2001). Care of the adolescent sexual assault victim. *Pediatrics*, 107, 1476–1479.

American Association of University Women Educational Foundation. (1993). *Hostile hallways: The AAUW survey on sexual harassment in America's schools*. Washington, DC: Harris/Scholastic Research [Research Report 923012].

American Association of University Women Educational Foundation (2001). *Hostile hallways: Bullying, teasing and sexual harassment in school*. Washington, DC: Harris Interactive [ERIC Document Reproduction Service No. ED 454 132].

American Civil Liberties Union (2001). Model anti-harassment and discrimination policies for schools [Online]. Available: http://www.aclu.org/LesbianGayRights/Lesbian GayRights.cfm?ID=9214&c=106.

American College of Obstetrics and Gynecology. (2000). *Drawing the line: A guide to developing effective sexual assault prevention programs for middle school students*. Washington, DC: Author.

American Medical Association. (1995). *Strategies for the treatment and prevention of sexual assault.* Chicago: Author.

Clarke, J., Stein, M.D., Sobota, M., Marisi, M. & Hanna, L. (1999). Victims as victimizers: physical aggression by persons with a history of childhood abuse. *Archives of Internal Medicine, 159,* 1920–1924.

Centers for Disease Control and Prevention. (1999a). HIV/AIDS surveillance supplemental report. *5*(3), 1–12.

Centers for Disease Control and Prevention. (1999b). Cluster of HIV-positive young women – New York, 1997–1998. *Morbidity and Mortality Weekly Report, 48,* 413–416.

Centers for Disease Control and Prevention. (2000). Cluster of HIV-infected adolescents and young adults – Mississippi, 1999. *Morbidity and Mortality Weekly Report, 29,* 861–864.

Coker, A.L., McKeown, R.E., Sanderson, M., Davis, K.E., Valois, R.F. & Huebner, E.S. (2000). Severe dating violence and quality of life among South Carolina high school students. *American Journal of Preventive Medicine, 19,* 220–227.

Dash, L. (1996). *When children want children: The urban crisis of teenage childbearing.* New York: William Morrow and Company.

Davis v. Monroe County Board of Education, 527 US 629 (1999).

DeVoe, J.F., Peter, K., Kaufman, P., Ruddy, S.A., Miller, A.K., Planty, M., Snyder, T.D. & Rand, M.R. (2003). *Indicators of school crime and safety: 2003.* Washington, DC: U.S. Departments of Education and Justice [NCES 2004–004/NCJ 201257].

Dietrich, L.C. (1998). *Chicana adolescents: Bitches, 'ho's, and schoolgirls.* Westport, CT: Praeger.

Fineran, S. (2002). Sexual harassment between same-sex peers: Intersection of mental health, homophobia and sexual violence in schools. *Social Work, 47,* 65–74.

Fineran, S. & Bennett, L. (1998). Teenage peer sexual harassment: Implications for social work. *Social Work, 43,* 55–64.

Franklin v. Gwinnett County Public Schools, 503 U.S. 60 (1992).

Franks, L. (2000, February). The sex lives of your children. *Talk Magazine,* 102–107, 157.

Freudenberg, N., Roberts, L., Richie, B.E., Taylor, R.T., McGillicuddy, K., Greene, M.B. (1999) Coming up in the Boogie Down: Lives of adolescents in the South Bronx. *Health Education and Behavior, 26*(6), 788–805.

Gebser v. Lago Vista Independent School District, 524 US 274 (1998).

Human Rights Watch. (2001). *Hatred in the hallways: Violence and discrimination against Lesbian, gay, bisexual, and transgendered students in U.S. schools.* New York: Author.

Humphrey, J.A. & White, J.W. (2000). Women's vulnerability to sexual assault from adolescence to young adulthood. *Journal of Adolescent Health, 27,* 419–424.

Jarrell, A. (2000, April 2). The face of teenage sex grows younger. *New York Times,* Section 9, pp. 1, 8.

Krauss, B.J., Friedman, S.R., O'Day, J., Yee, D.S., Mateu-Gelabert, P., Flom, P.L., Sandoval, M. & Bula, E. (2001, July). *Social contexts of adolescent sexual behavior: Risk in high HIV seroprevalence neighborhoods.* Paper presented at the AIDS Impact Conference, Brighton, England.

Krauss, B.J., O'Day, J., Godfrey, C. & Rente, K. (2003, July). *Peer pressure is like the weather: People talk about peer pressure but rarely do they operationalize it.* Presented in Poster Session at the NIMH Conference on Role of Families in Preventing and Adapting to HIV/AIDS, Washington, DC.

Maker, A.H., Kemmelmeier, M. & Peterson, C. (2001). Child sexual abuse, peer sexual abuse, and sexual assault in adulthood: A multi-risk model of revictimization. *Journal of Traumatic Stress, 14,* No. 2, 351–368.

Martin, L., Rosen, L.N., Durand, D.B., Knudson, K.H. & Stretch, R.H. (2000). Psychological and physical health effects of sexual assaults and nonsexual traumas among male and female United States Army soldiers. *Behavioral Medicine, 26,* 23–33.

Martin, S.L., Clark, K.A., Lynch, S.R., Kupper, L.L. & Cilenti, D. (1999). Violence in the lives of pregnant teenage women: Associations with multiple substance use. *American Journal of Drug and Alcohol Abuse, 25*, 425–440.

National Association of School Nurses. (2000). *School violence: Issue briefing* [Online]. Available: http://www.nasn.org/briefs/violence.htm

National Association of Secondary School Principals. (2000). *Position paper—safe schools* [Online}. Available: http://www.principals.org/advocacy/ps_safe_sch.cfm.

National Center on Child Abuse and Neglect. (1981). Child sexual abuse: incest, assault and sexual exploitation. Washington, DC: U.S. Government Printing Office.

National Education Association. (2004). *School safety* [Online]. Available: http://www.nea.org/schoolsafety.

Ozer, E.J., Tschann, J.M., Pasch, L.A. & Flores, E. (2004). Violence perpetration across peer and partner relationships: co-occurrence and longitudinal patterns among adolescents. *Journal of Adolescent Health, 34*,64–71.

Planned Parenthood Federation of America (2004). *What is rape? Some legal definitions* [Online]. Available: http://www.teenwire.com/index.asp?taStrona=http://www.teenwire.com/warehous/articles/wh_19981201p060.asp.

Rickert, V.I., Vaughan, R.D. & Wiemann, C.M. (2002). Adolescent dating violence and date rape. *Current Opinion in Obstetrics and Gynecology, 14*, 495–500.

Rosenberg, P.S. & Biggar, R.J. (1998). Trends in HIV incidence among young adults in the United States. *Journal of the American Medical Association, 279*, 1894–1899.

Rothenberg, R.B., Sterk, C., Toomey, K.E., Potterat, J.J., Johnson, D., Schrader, M. & Hatch, S. (1998). Using social network and ethnographic tools to evaluate syphilis transmission. *Sexually Transmitted Diseases, 25*(4), 154–160.

Sales, N.J. (1997, September 29). The sex trap. *New York Magazine,* 27–33.

Smith, P.H., White, J.W. & Holland, L.J. (2003). A longitudinal perspective on dating violence among adolescent and college-age women. *American Journal of Public Health, 93*, 1104–1109.

Steele, R.W. (2000). Prevention and management of sexually transmitted diseases in adolescents. *Adolescent Medicine, 11*, 315–26.

Stein, N. (1999). *Incidence and implications of sexual harassment and sexual violence in K–12 schools.* Wellesley, MA: Wellesley College Center for Research on Women. (Adapted by permission from Stein, N. (1999). *Classrooms and courtrooms: Facing sexual harassment in K–12 schools.* New York: Columbia Teacher's College Press.

Stein, N. & Sjostrom, L. (1996). *Flirting or hurting? A teacher's guide on student-to-student sexual harassment in schools* (grades 6–12). Wellsley, MA: Wellsley College Center for Research on Women.

U.S. Department of Education, National Center for Education Statistics. (1998). *Violence and discipline problems in U.S. Public Schools: 1996–97.* Washington, DC: Author [NCES 98–030].

U.S. Department of Education, Office of Civil Rights (1997). *Sexual harassment: It's not academic.* Washington, DC: Author [ERIC Document Reproduction Service No. ED 423609].

U.S. Department of Education, Office of Civil Rights. (1999). *Protecting students from harassment and hate crime: A guide for schools* [Revised.] Washington, DC: Author [ERIC Document Reproduction Service No. ED 431246].

Welych, L.R., Laws, B., Fiorito, A.F., Durham, T.H., Cibula, D.A. & Lane, S.D. (1998). Formative research for interventions among adolescents at high risk for gonorrhea and other STDs. *Journal of Public Health Management and Practice, 4*(6), 54–61.

Yee, D.S., O'Day, J., O'Sullivan, L. & Krauss, B.J. (2000, November). *Sex in group settings among adolescents in a high HIV seroprevalence neighborhood: Moving from anecdote to understanding.* Presented at the American Public Health Association Annual Meeting, Boston, MA.

Chapter 8

A Transgenerational Perspective on Peace and on Violence Prevention

The Role of Older Persons and Grandparents in the Culture and Development of Peace and Non-Violence

ASTRID STUCKELBERGER

THE BACKSTAGE OF VIOLENCE: SOCIO-DEMOGRAPHIC DYNAMICS

Violence in youth and violence in schools has mostly been approached and studied from an individual or societal perspective. In this context, the family is considered merely as the nexus of development and interaction of two generations (parent-children).

The fact that today's population architecture has dramatically changed over the past century in terms of socio-demographic composition demands that we look at the social coherence of this new situation. By demonstrating this fundamental transformation by facts and figures, this article will break myths about the new architecture of society and the mutation of the extended family system and then synthesize and discuss different findings addressing inter-generational and transgenerational aspects of violence.

In order to understand the profound mutation our society is living through and the consequences of this new architecture of society for the

119

younger generations, a general overview of three major areas of this change will be described: 1) the structural changes of the population, 2) a more specific view on the ageing of the population, and 3) the transformation of the family and of genealogical relations.

This article will address violence in schools from a new and innovative perspective, by taking a macro-view on the issue of violence and peace as well as a micro-view on the individual role and responsibility the older generation has in building a non-violent society. The argument has two objectives:

1. The first objective is to underline the importance of understanding the world in which the younger generations live and grow today by describing key elements of the new architecture of our society, but also to demonstrate the dynamics of today's family which consists of four to five generations and its consequences on intergenerational relations. The role of grandparenthood and of older persons is too often not considered or underestimated when addressing the younger generations' problems or when building a sustainable family and social policy.
2. The second objective is to see what role and interventions the elderly can play at the individual and collective level in their commitment to participate in individual, local and global peace and non-violence processes. This aspect has not yet been considered, and this article wishes to bring light to the specific interaction between ageing generations and non-violence/peace with a discussion based on existing facts and a scientific perspective on psycho-social and behavioral dimensions of the population and the individual ageing process.

This innovative approach wishes to contribute to a set of efficient and sustainable solutions that could eradicate violence for future generations.

THE NEW ARCHITECTURE OF OUR WORLD

In 1999, the United Nations Population Fund launched their yearly report, "State of the World Population," on the theme, "Six Billion: A Time for Choices" announcing that an estimate of six billion people are alive in the world and highlighting the critical decisions facing the international community as we enter the twenty-first century: "This slow demographic change calls for policy choices." This report underlines key figures, which should stand as the background evidence when considering any societal or policy issues (table 1).

Table 1. Architecture of the World Population: A Brief Fact Sheet

In general

- Number of inhabitants: in 1960s = 3 billion; in 2000 = 6.1 billion; in 2050 = 9.3 billion
- Annual Rate Growth: 1.3 % per year or 77 million people/year. Six developing countries account for half of this annual growth: India (21%), China (12%), Pakistan (5%), Nigeria (4%), Bangladesh (4%), and Indonesia (3%)
- Youth (15-24): the biggest-ever generation of young people with a number of 1.05 billion young people
- Elderly (60+) : the biggest-ever generation of older persons with an estimated number of 420 million at midyear 2000, 795,000 added each month during the year.

Growing number of generations

- The population of the elderly will triple from 606 million to 2 billion by the year 2050, the number of nonagenarians and centenarians is increasing worldwide, older generations are proportionally increasing. Those age groups are proportionally the fastest growing segments of the population
- 4 to 5 generations live together, out of which 2 to 3 can be considered in the older generation or at retirement age
  Each generation is living with certain cohort and historical specificities from which emerges new situations such as:
  - "digital homeless generations" – i.e., older generations that will never be technologically connected,
  - "generations of war" - i.e., youth generations having only lived a life of war, or
  - "generation wipe out" – i.e., one to two generations having in majority died due to wars or epidemics such as HIV/AIDS
- Continuing urbanization and international migration creates policy challenges: half of all people live in cities, compared to a third in 1960. Worldwide, cities are growing by 60 million persons per year. Today, there are 17 mega cities – with 10 million people or more. The distribution by generations is unbalanced between urban and rural areas, as younger generations tend to migrate to cities for seeking better job opportunities.

✓ Today, the number of children under the age of 15 is less than the number of elderly.
✓ By 2050, the number of younger will be the half of the number of elderly people.
✓ This millennium will host four to five generations living together, each with their cultural history and pace of development.

Some key elements for generations living in either region:

More developed regions (population: 1.2 billion)

- Little change over the next 50 years
- Low fertility levels
- population decline: by mid-century, it is projected that 39 countries will have a smaller sized population than today: Japan and Germany (each 14% smaller), Italy and Hungary (each 25% smaller) and the Russian Federation, Georgia and Ukraine (each between 28% and 40% smaller)
- Living arrangements: tendency to one-generation household or living alone.

Less-developed regions

- Population: rise from 4.9 billion in 2000 to 8.2 billion in 2050
- Declines in fertility: in the absence of such declines, the population of less-developed regions would reach 11.9 billion; fertility is projected to decline markedly in the future.

(Continued)

Table 1. (*continued*)

- Rapid growth of population is still expected among 48 countries classified as least developed: population expected to nearly triple from 2000 to 2050: passing from 658 million to 1.8 billion
- Rapid urbanization: by 2015, projections state there will be 26 megacities – 10 million and more – 22 of them in less-developed regions, 18 in Asia alone
- Living arrangements: tendency of the older generation to live with adult children.

Sources: UNFPA (1999). UN Population Division (2000); Kinsella and Velkoff, US Census Bureau (2001).

Structural Changes of the World Population

The world no longer looks the same way as it did to our ancestors: not only are our statistics more and more accurate in viewing a "State of the World," but we can today easily grasp a global picture of the world population and its key trends. Today's youth lived in a different world, a global world, and this reality can be the cause or the consequence of some of the behaviors we observe; furthermore, when one reflects on the genealogy of youth and their complex family history, many have relations with different parts of the world; for example, one generation might be living in United States, the other one in Europe, while the older generation lives and remains in its homeland in South America, Africa or Asia. Many have in their ancestors and family history – whether they are aware of it or not – some tales of wars and violence. Thus it is important to seize the "picture" of the major changes at hand in the world at the moment: more people are living on the same territory, with fewer children, migrating to cities or different countries, and living longer. When looking closer at the data provided by reliable international sources (UNFPA, 1999; UN Population Division, 2000; US Census Bureau, 2001) and captured in the short fact sheet (table 1), the following facts can be underlined:

- The world's population has quadrupled in the last 100 years and has doubled in 40 years from 3 billion in 1960 to 6 billion in 1999; a billion was added in only the 12 last years.
- *The worldwide tendency is towards fewer children per couple, but more generations*: women have fewer children than ever before as access to family planning provides women with more choices, improving and allowing more control over the number and the spacing of childbirths. Although the population is still increasing by about 78 million people per year, the actual rate of growth has slowed down from 2.4 to 1.3 per cent in 30 years. The generally sustained decrease in total fertility rates in industrialized nations since at least 1900 has

resulted in current levels below the population replacement rate of 2.1 live births per woman in most such nations. Looking at the youth/old generation ratio, there are more young people and older people alive than ever before: Even with the existing large numbers of young people, the elderly population aged 60+ has already exceeded in numbers the population of the younger generation (below age 15) and by 2050, for every child there will be two elderly persons.

- Population growth has slowed down, stopped, or decreased in Europe, North America and Japan. Today, the population growth of those countries only increases as the result of the immigration of the work force and the naturalization of migrant families. *International migration and continual urbanization* creates policy challenges. Half of the world's population today lives in cities, compared to a third in 1960. Worldwide, cities are growing by 60 million people each year and by 2030, it is predicted that over 60% of people, i.e., 5 billion, will live in urban areas or megacities. Thus, in all regions, international migration is moving close to the top of policy agendas, as the numbers of migrants increase: between 1965 and 1990, migration expanded form 75 million to 120 million. Migrant workers send more than US $70 billion home each year in remittances. More and more migrants are women. The consequences of population mobility on the development of younger generations, on the links between generations and the family architecture have been underestimated: they modify the transmission of culture and knowledge, transfer of financial assets and the systemic patterns and roles of each member of the family, as will be demonstrate further in this article.

Why would it be relevant to demonstrate world facts and figures when addressing local or national issues? The point is that with migration, mixed marriages, and intercultural lineages, local issues are affected directly or indirectly by today's global issues, and if solutions do not consider the global picture, local solutions might only have a short-term effect. Violence and peace are issues that concern all sectors of societies; addressing only one sector while ignoring other core elements would be like pouring water in a bucket full of holes.

In this context the theory defended in this article is that older generations have a crucial role for youth development–a transgenerational effect. Such effects are apparent, for example, in the perpetuation of memories and the many forms of violence or non-violence throughout its descendants, or through its active or preventive role as grandparent or great-grandparent.

A closer look at who are the older persons today is necessary to avoid ageist attitudes too often carried out in our society and to break the myths about the negative images of ageing with scientific findings.

The Ageing Phenomenon and Its Consequences for Youth

One of the most important challenges the world faces in the 21st century is responding to the economic, financial and social implications of the changing demographics in our ageing societies.

Denver Summit of the 8 (G8) in 1997

Population Ageing and Its consequences

Global population ageing is emerging as a phenomenon never yet witnessed in the history of humanity. The spectacular increase in human life expectancy associated with lowered fertility and improved health is generating growing numbers and higher proportions of an older population and extending the duration of life to exceptional ages. This mutation has been referred to as the "Silent Revolution" or the "Age Quake," reflecting the lack of attention of the media and society has paid to it. The effect of technology on globalization has introduced the idea of a society centred more on the values of what is "new," "young," and "fast," while the far-reaching effects of the "silent revolution" are not uttered but are already felt by every individual, family, neighborhood and nation throughout the world.

To further draw the new architecture of the world, what portrait of the Ageing World can one make today?

The most recent data from the Population Division, Department of Economic and Social Affairs of the United Nations (2000) and to the US Census Bureau (Kinsella & Velkoff, November 2001), reveals the following:

• *Dramatic increases in longevity,* which caused global life expectancy to climb 20 years since 1950, to 66 years in 1999. Life expectancy at birth exceeds 78 years in 28 countries. The population of the United States will age rapidly when the baby boomers (people born between 1946 and 1964) begin to reach age 65 after the year 2010; by the year 2050 the population 65 and over is projected to be slightly above 20 percent (compared with about 13 percent today). In contrast, some African countries (e.g., Malawi, Swaziland, Zambia, and Zimbabwe) where the HIV/AIDS epidemic is particularly devastating, the average life expectancy at birth may be 25 years lower than it otherwise would have been in the absence of HIV/AIDS; however, the proportion of older persons is still growing as the survivors still have a relatively high life expectancy of 65 in those regions. Thus, low life expectancy at birth does not mean that the possibility of living to higher ages has eroded.

• *The numbers and proportions of older persons, potential (great-) grandparents, have increased.* Since 1950, the proportion of the world's population over 60 has changed from one in thirteen to one in ten. By the year 2050, one in five will be 60 years or older. Europe remains the oldest regions in the world, followed closely by North America. Country wise, Italy has the highest proportion of elderly people with 18.1% 65 or over. By 2020, the Japanese population will be the oldest in the world, with 31% over 60 years of age, followed by Italy, Greece and Switzerland. The global population 65 and over was estimated to be 420 million people as of midyear 2000, an increase of 9.5 million since midyear 1999. The net balance of the world's elderly population grew by more than 795,000 people each month during a year. Projections for the year 2010 suggest that the net monthly gain will be in the order of 847,000 people. China has the largest elderly population, numbering nearly 88 million in 2000 (Kinsella & Velkoff, 2001).

• *Some developing countries are ageing at a faster pace than developed countries (figure 1).* By 2020, five of the ten countries with the largest populations of older persons will be in the developing world: China, India, Indonesia, Brazil and Pakistan. Although industrialized nations have higher percentages of elderly people than do most developing countries, 59% of the world's elderly now live in developing countries in Africa, Asia,

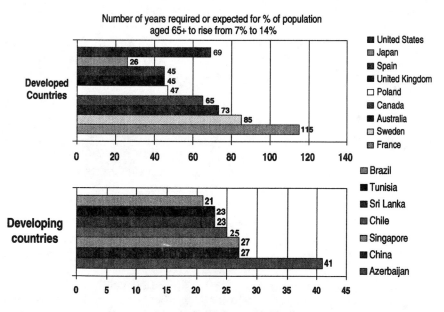

Figure 1. Speed of population ageing (*in years*).

Latin America, the Caribbean, and Oceania. By 2020 also, the population of older persons from developing countries will rise by nearly 240% from the 1980 level. For example, it took only 23 years for countries such as Chile or Sri Lanka to raise its population of 65+ year-olds from 7% to 14% while it took 116 years (5 times more years) for the same growth. *Striking differences exist between regions*: for example, 1 in 5 Europeans being 60 years or older, as compared to 1 in 20 Africans. The older population is still predominant in rural areas, but it is increasingly more urban. This point is important, as it will affect the structure of migrant family ascendants.

• *The older population itself is ageing*. The "oldest old" the fastest-growing component of many national populations. The world's growth rate for the 80+ population from 1999 to 2000 was 3.5 percent, while that of the world's elderly (65+) population as a whole was 2.3 percent, and the growth rate was 1.3 percent for the total population. Currently, persons 80 years and older constitute 11% of the population 60 and above. In contrast, by 2050, 27% of the older population will be over 80 years old. Past population projections often have underestimated the improvement in mortality rates among the oldest segment and actual numbers of tomorrow's oldest segment could be much higher than presently anticipated.

• *The majority of older persons are women (55%)*; among those who are 80 years or older, 65% are women. They make up the majority of the oldest segment and the elderly widowed, and are most frequently the care-givers of the older persons in all parts of the world. Although there are more elderly women than elderly men in the vast majority of countries, there are exceptions, such as India, Iran, and Bangladesh. Today's generation of older women is less likely to be literate, but younger generations of women are increasing their level of education. In China in 1990, for example, only 11% of women 60 and over can read and write, compared with half of men 60 and over.

Improvement of the Individual Process of Ageing and Its Consequences for Youth

The longer life phenomenon presents major improvements in the ageing process of the individual. People all around the world are getting older, are in better health and remain active longer, thus play a longer lasting role in the family and can contribute longer to the social system.

Scientific findings of this last decade have revolutionized the negative model of the belief in an irreversible decline that comes with age. Although stereotypes and stigmatisation of age remains, many of the prejudices and remaining myths and fictions on ageing are being challenged today by new studies. Table 2 reports concisely scientific facts countering some of the classical myths and fictions carried out in society.

Table 2. Fiction and Facts about Ageing

Fiction: The stereotype *The typical "ageist attitude"*	Facts *based on scientific evidence*
"To be old is to be sick, dependent and senile"	The majority of older persons are in good mental and physical health. Statistics show that the majority of retirees, even at 80 years old, are independent and live at home. In the developed world, as the younger generations of retirees have benefited from the improvement of public health and social security measures, they age with better health, higher education, a sound economic situation, and pursuing social activities and contacts.
"In old age, it is too late to do anything"	The newest findings show that good health can be maintained and that the process of physical and mental decline can be reversed through active measures. Interventions at higher ages can improve physical and mental health (i.e., several studies on persons 75 years old and older showed that physical activity strengthens the muscles and increase the bone mass and that mental activity prevents mental degenerative diseases).
"The secret of ageing well is in the genes"	Our ageing process can be modulated at each stage of our lives. Twin studies with adopted and non adopted subjects have shown that the influence of genes diminishes with age and other factors such as life experience and culture have a stronger effect.
"The elderly can't learn anything"	At all ages, one can learn, develop and expand knowledge and skills. Concepts such as continuous education or Life Long Learning (LLL) are now well established; for example, Universities of 3rd Age and Seniorweb networks have flourished around the world.
"Older persons can't direct their lives, are not productive and are a burden to society"	Today the generations of retirees are healthy, active and creative; most of them can and want to participate in society, they have a role and responsibility in the way they use their full citizenship, as well as in the way they transfer their assets and memories. For example, the American Association of Retired People (AARP) counts today more than 30 millions members and stands as one of the strongest political lobbies in the United States.
There is "No cash return" when investing in the elderly*	Older persons do contribute to the economy of the nation and the family through informal work and volunteering, through financial transfers to younger generations, and also as consumers. They diminish the costs of conflict and violence in younger generations by being models in maintaining cohesion in the family, such as prioritising human values, restoring healing memories and history, and transmitting a sense of security in life.

*New stereotype from author.
Source: Adapted from Rowe and Kahn (1998).

Adjusting our images of ageing with the newest reality brought by scientific evidence can only contribute to the image we have of our own ageing, but it can also help us comprehend the untapped potential of an active ageing population to participate to societal issues. Breaking ageist attitudes removes barriers between generations and gives a better understanding of the possible and necessary interactions with youth. Living longer has allowed more members of the family to be alive at the same time – we are now witnessing a multigenerational society which brings very new dynamics for the younger generations to interact with generations older than ever before in history.

A MULTI-GENERATION SOCIETY: FAMILY SYSTEM IN MUTATION

Portrait of a Four to Five Generation Society

Considering the state of the world and the spectacular increase in longevity, the new architecture of society must be outlined with two key components:

1. the extension of inter-generational lineage and living descendants
2. the restriction of intra-generational links as there are fewer siblings and children with fertility decline

In other words, the structure, the backbone, of our society has expanded from 2 or 3 generations existing concurrently during the last century, to 4 to 5 generations at the present, while the number of children and potential brothers/sisters has decreased, which is affecting family dynamics and all dimensions of life.

The existence of up to 5 generations living at the same time is today a possible reality. At the population level, evidence shows that four-generation families are becoming increasingly common (e.g., Lehr, 1998; Soldo, 1996) and the ageing of the baby-boomers may produce a great-grandparent boom in many countries. This is not only the case in the developed world: population statistics show that the average growth rates of higher age groups are increasing in all regions of the world (figure 2). The developing world is potentially more inclined to find a 4 or 5 generation structure, as the average age of the mother at the birth of a first child is lower. This fact has implications when dealing with the youth of migrant families: the architecture of their families can include living grandparents and great grandparents with a given role. Figure 2 clearly shows that, even in the least developed regions, the most striking growth rate is among the ages of 80+ and 60–79: the parents, grandparents and

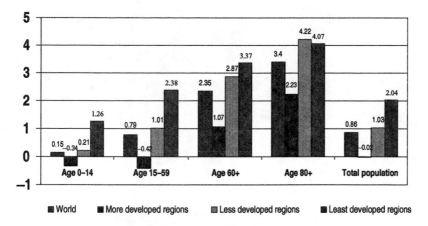

Figure 2. Population average annual growth rates by age group and by region. (*Source*: UN Population Division, *World Population Prospects: The 2000 revision*.)

great-grandparents of today. No longer can an increasing population of older persons be narrowly defined as a single group. The age of grandparents can now ranges from 35 to 123 years old, and their grandchildren from newborns to retirees. Consequently, new legislation will be needed to address and solve conflicts between generations, and intergenerational legal issues will be increasingly important.

The number of centenarians is increasing worldwide. In 1999, 145,000 centenarians were estimated to be alive, and 2.2 million are estimated in 2050, a 15-fold increase. According to researchers in Europe, the number of centenarians has doubled each decade since 1950 in industrialized countries, and (when data is available) developing countries seem to follow the same trend. Using reliable statistics from ten Western European countries and Japan, Vaupel and Jeune (1995) estimated that some 8,800 centenarians lived in these countries as of 1990, and that the number of centenarians grew at an average annual rate of approximately 7 percent between the early 1950s and the late 1980s.They also estimate that, over the course of human history, the odds of living from birth to age 100 may have risen from 1 in 20 million to 1 in 50 for females in low-mortality nations such as Japan and Sweden.

Thus one finds more and more frequently two generations at retirement age and the duration of a life as a retiree is increasing in all regions of the world (table 3). As an illustration, the official world record of longevity held by a French woman, Mrs. Jeanne Calment, who lived up to age 123 in relatively good health. This might even make us suspect the future potential of 6 living generations with 3 generations at retirement age

Table 3. Effective Retirement Age and Duration of Retirement 1950–1990

Region	Effective retirement age		Expected duration of retirement	
	1950	1990	1950	1990
Japan	66.2	65.5	12.0	17.8
North America	65.9	62.6	13.1	18.1
Oceania	65.3	60.0	13.2	20.5
Nothern Europe	67.2	61.9	12.2	18.7
Southern Europe	69.0	60.1	10.5	19.9
Western Europe	65.7	59.3	12.8	20.7
Central/Eastern Europe	65.0	59.2	12.8	18.6
Average W/o Central and Eastern Europe	66.5	61.8	12.4	19.0
All countries	66.0	61.0	12.5	18.9

Source: Gillion, Turner, Bailey and Latulippe (2000). *Social Security Pensions, Development and Reform.* International Labour Office, Geneva.

(Allard et al., 1994); the latest 1999 census in Vietnam counted nearly 4,000 centenarians which highlights the tendency of considering them to be a 'visible' group even in developing countries (Central Census Steering Committee, 1999).

The changes described in the structure of the world population, in the ageing of the population, and the emergence of a society consisting of four to five generations can only convince us of the emergence of a new architecture of the world with important implications for the social and family system. Beside facts about the structure, some important mutations can also be observed in the dynamics of this multi-generational society: living longer also brings a higher risk of experiencing changes or cyclic events during a life course that can potentially affect child development: multiple employment or careers, multiple marriages, or divorce.

Complexity of Family Patterns

It is only through understanding how generations interact and evolve together that one can grasp the elements necessary for any sustainable policy or action in society. The difficulty is to move from a static picture, the photographic cliché of society - as presented in the first part (statistics, census, etc.), to a more lively view, a motion picture showing us the unfolding of society (cohort and longitudinal studies, qualitative approach). The picture enriched by a motion picture gives us a more accurate understanding of society and its dynamic; with this logic in mind, evidence-based policy would by definition acknowledge the need for dynamic policies.

Table 4. Mutation of the Genealogy and Family Pattern:
from Old to New Genealogies

Traditional architecture	Current architectural tendency
Strong mortality at all ages	Increase of life expectancy and decrease of fertility
2 to 3 generations	4 to 5 generations
0 to 1 generation at retirement age	2 to 3 generations retirement age
Predominance of	
Intra-generational links	Inter-generational lineage increases
Many siblings	Few brothers/sisters
Numerous descent	Weak descent at each generation
Traditional family	Nuclear family or single parent
Generations living together or near	Generations living apart or abroad
Homogeneous family	Heterogeneous family –"Recomposition" of the family
One life cycle with unique events	Repetition of life cycles (divorce/mariage, jobs, etc.)
Transmission of values	
Traditional education and socialization	Peers + new informal education (ICT*, mass media)
Shared economic management	Independent economy between generations
Genealogy-dependent survival	State-dependant survival
Women at home - Man-centered career	Men and women work outside the home
Hierarchy of age - the Elder	Multiple hierarchy (economic, technological, etc.)
Unidirectional life course	Complexities of life course pattern
Unidirectional genealogies	Multiplication of genealogies
Metamorphosis of solidarity —multiple generation society	

An important component of this new architecture, shown in Table 4, is the transition of the traditional family structure towards heterogeneous forms of genealogies and generation arrangements, but also the shift from a homogeneous structure of generations within society to an increasing heterogeneity of generations.

Many factors influence this transition and illustrate the many possible extended family systems a child might be living in today:

• *Older persons are more likely to be married or re-married than in the past and have children at late ages.* Not only do individuals live longer, but they have more freedom than ever to be parents at any age for men and at higher ages for women (the record age of giving birth for women is of 67 years in Italy and becoming a father has reached record ages of as high as 104 years in Iran). Over the last two or three decades, the marital status of the elderly has changed: with an increased proportion of married older men and women, and a decreased proportion of widowers. Some of the change is attributable to improved survival of both husbands and wives (Myers, 1992) but also to different marital experiences of birth cohorts such as those resulting from war. In most countries few elderly are not married.

• *Increase in divorce and remarriage rates at all ages:* although currently rates of divorced elderly people tend to be low, the future cohorts of the elderly will have higher proportions of divorced/separated people. With the increase in divorce and marriages worldwide, it becomes increasingly common to find parents who during their life course become grandparents and then parents again, breaking with the stereotype of the traditional "one marriage for life" pattern. Due to extended longevity, there is a stronger potential to repeat the family cycle of "marriage-childbirth-divorce," the timing being limitless for men; this mix of timing challenges the classic genealogies. A child nowadays can experience very complex situations: the child might have many half brothers and sisters ranging from his age to the age of one of his parents; have multiple grandparents and great-grandparents (including the grandparents-in-law); or have a parent of the age of his school friends grand sister or grandparents, etc...

• *Importance of grandparents:* the importance of grandparents is not trivial and is gaining importance. In some countries women and men provided care for their grandchildren - from babysitting to being a custodial parent. Survey data for the United States from the mid 1990s indicate that 9% of all Americans with grandchildren under age 5 were providing extensive care giving (minimum 30 hours/week or 90 nights/year) (Fuller-Thomson & Minkler, 2001). In 1995 in the United States, 29% of preschool children whose parent(s) work or were in school were cared for by a grandparent (typically the grandmother) (Smith, 2000). Many grandparents find themselves becoming the sole providers of care for their grandchildren. One reason for this is the migration of the middle generation to urban areas to find work. These "skip-generation" families are found in all regions of the world and may be quite prevalent. Another reason for the increase in the number of children living in households headed only by grandparents can be attributed to several current trends (e.g., divorce, HIV/AIDS, drug abuse and child abuse). In 1997 in the United States, 3.9 million children, 5.5% of all children under age 18, lived in a household maintained by their grandparents (Casper and Bryson, 1998).

• *Effect of epidemics on generations:* today in some regions, *an entire generation might be wiped out* by crises such as epidemics or wars. For example, children orphaned by HIV/AIDS is a matter of great concern: not only do the children depend on older relatives for their care, but when separated and not returned to their elders or relatives, they could also be at risk of becoming street children or entering the social assistance system and head towards lifelong extreme poverty. Other striking figures are those of the suicide rates in older age groups, which are higher than in any younger age group (WHO, 1999). This in itself could be considered a mental health epidemic that might affect future generations by becoming a model with the risk of euthanasia being legalized.

• *Urbanization and migration as a generation splitting factor.* The tendency toward urbanization is increasing worldwide as mentioned above and leads to the separation of young people from their grandparents, who previously played a role in their traditional education and socialization. It also causes new financial flows between developed and developing countries if retirement is lived in a different country, or if working migrants return to their home country after retirement.

Finally, it appears clearly today *that traditional extended families are gradually disappearing*. Recent data confirm this tendency worldwide. For example, in the Middle East, as is the case in Egypt, 85% of all households are now nuclear families (UNFPA, 2001).

The most striking mutation one can observe is that *the complexity of family ties and lineages is dramatically spreading* in all corners of the world, not only because of the steady decline of fertility, but also due to the changing patterns of women's lives. Society allows more choices and more mobility, but also witnesses a higher rate of divorce at all ages. New situations arise: for example, most of today's retirees did not get to know their grandparents, and they have many more brothers and sisters than the following generations; in contrast, most children of today get to know their four grandparents and even their great-grandparents, and they have fewer siblings of the same father than any generation which ever lived. Many families today include half-brothers and half-sisters who live in different places, which further complicates the picture (i.e., in France - Toulemon, 2001).

The mutation of traditional family patterns and the links between generations is clearly provoking a reform of the classical genealogy (Table 4) but also of the way society and policy will have to deal with it without taking the place of the family. It is no longer possible to build a genealogical tree without being confronted by complex situations and the social or legal framework for solving those situations is often not yet in place. For example, recently the Geneva State Court of Justice in Switzerland has reported an alarming tendency of divorced parents who are giving their resignation as legal parents and they are requesting that the custody of their children be withdrawn from them. The motive is that their children have become uncontrollable and are no longer obeying the family or social rules; they address the court by affirming that the state, "has to take care of our children, we no longer know what to do with them" (Tribune de Genève, March 2002). New programs to empower parents to apply their rights as parents will be put in place. These are just emerging symptoms of a new society where the state will have to look very carefully into preserving the responsibility of its citizens toward their ascendants and descendants.

As one acknowledges the growing "complexities of the traditional genealogies," the challenge ahead lies more in the regulation and adjustment of the dynamics between generations than in solving the challenges of old age alone. The socio-economic interdependency of generations in building a sustainable society calls for a systematic approach with more generation-integrated or generation-adjustment components. The non-adjustment of generations bears a definite risk: the future conflict and clash between generations.

CONFLICT AND VIOLENCE BETWEEN OR THROUGHOUT GENERATIONS: FROM THE STRUCTURAL TO THE DEVELOPMENTAL PERSPECTIVE

Data about conflict or peaceful interaction between generations are rare and results are contradictory. The new architecture of the family genealogies, as described above, has given rise to debates on the potential conflicts and opportunities between generations (table 5). In this context, a fundamental issue when discussing the process of conflict and violence or peace is to first clarify the concept of generation and its definitions and then to highlight research areas where psycho-social research and theories contribute to our subject, either on the inter-generational aspect or the individual development aspect. The following section will provide reflections on findings supporting a potential for structural violence between generations as well as the transpersonal and transgenerational dimension in transmitting violent or peaceful behaviors and values from generation to generation. Conflict and violence are closely linked. From a psycho-social perspective, internal or external conflict is the source of self-development of violence, but also acting out of self-injury. Therefore the term conflict will be used here in order to include a broader approach to violence. For the same reason, peace - as a concept encompassing a broader concept then non-violence or conflict resolution - will be used to express the psycho-social dimension bestowing a state of balance for the individual and society.

Table 5. Potential Conflicts and New Opportunities between Generations:
Some Examples

Conflicts	Opportunities
Technological clash: information vs. experience	*Sustainability*: transmission of living skills
ICT*: mutual ghetto of generations	*Younger generations as teachers of ICT*
Historical culture: local vs. global (or mixed)	*Ageing as reference models of life/death*
Socio-demographic: complexity of family ties	*Retiree's role and responsibility for future generations*
Burning issues:	• as promoters of peace and violence prevention
• Unequal distribution of social welfare and goods	• protectors of the environment
• Absence of Inter-generational rights	• defenders of universal values
• Development concept to become generation-specific	• spiritual guides and leaders
• Retirement age as a ghetto economy	• models of wisdom
• Employment vs. free voluntary work of the retirees	*Older generations as contributors to youth's future*
• Health care rationing (i.e., age discrimination in access to high-tech care, transplants, etc.)	• volunteering - time and experience
• Juventocracy or Gerontocracy: Younger or Older generations as leaders	• sharing their life expertise - strategic and conflict management competencies
• Conflict of values? Economy vs. Humanity	• adding life networks and experience
	• transmitting values to the children of tomorrow – way to live and to die
	• enhancing global solidarity - new concept of service

*ICT: term to describe the new Information and communication technology.

STRUCTURAL PERSPECTIVE: LINK AND TRANSMISSION FROM GENERATION TO GENERATION

The concept of generation is similar to the methodological concept of cohort: in essence, humans born and raised at different times have experienced different life events, which can have long-term consequences for them (figure 4). For example, major worldwide events occurring at a specific point and place in history have had profound impacts on particular segments of a population or a specific generation; for example, when large numbers of males are killed at relatively young ages by wars or conflicts, the survivors become a discrete group. The same must be kept in mind when considering the evolution and ageing process of a given population affected by disasters and conflicts and touching generations at different stages of their development (i.e., consequences of the war in Iraq). For example, some generations of youth have only known war (e.g., the youth of

Afghanistan has experienced 23 years of war), or some generations have lived through a sudden trauma that mark their life development (e.g., the Holocaust or the Rwanda genocide). This aspect is fundamental when considering sustainable social and policy development of a population.

The definition of generations usually takes into account two main levels of definition:

1. *Micro level*: generation within the family context (time framework: genetic identity)
2. *Macro level*: generation within the larger context of society (time framework: socio-political identity)

The MicroLevel

Based on genetic identity the generation is defined by sequences of organisms deriving from a common ancestor, and each sequence creates a generation. This is the classical concept underlying the construction of the genealogical tree.

Potential conflicts arising in the context of lineage can take many forms depending on which and how many generations are involved: interpersonal, economic conflicts, family issues such as grandparent custody in the case of divorce, and transgenerational violence.

The MacroLevel

A generation is defined herewith in the social and cultural context as living in a common period of time in the history of humankind. In other words, a generation is defined by its socio-cultural mark – this definition can be considered as belonging to a *cultural-anthropological approach*. Each generation composes a succession of different individuals in society bound to specific social, cultural, economic or political common experiences (methodologically, this division of time is similar to a cohort or a period). The time frame of such a generation depends on the impact of those events or experiences (i.e., the Hippie generation).

Conflict and peace arise at both levels: within the family context at the micro-level, conflicts can continue from one generation to another, but they can also arise at the macro-level, where an entire segment of the population is affected by war or conflicts, thus perpetuating a different collective behavior which affects the following generation.

Reviews of the concepts of conflict or the peace process at the micro-level or macro-level inevitably overlap. War, genocide, and natural disaster affect not only a generation at the macro-level but at the micro-level as well. On the other hand, some micro-level conflicts might not seem to affect the macro-level directly, although it is important to keep in mind that micro-level conflicts might affect the long-term lineage of future generations within the family.

When considering time dynamics, the importance of lineage in generations must be emphasized: mechanisms of transmission exist within society which may account for variation within the larger society (Back, 1995). This transmission is not so much linked to genetic factors but to psycho-social factors influencing over time the life course of the individual and the group. Studies on generations have proved that transmission of values occur within a family (i.e., Bengston et al., 1985); furthermore, from the psycho-analytical point of view, the transmission of psychological distresses and unsolved conflicts are perpetuated from one generation to another (Kaës et al., 1993). Thus, one can postulate that peace and conflict does transmit from generation to generation - at the conscious and subconscious level - and that the role of elders is key to perpetuating a memory of peace versus war, conflict versus reconciliation, hatred versus forgiveness, etc.

Theories on transmission of models of behavior and values between generations have not yet been given much attention. Some researchers and anthropologists have studied this link in very different contexts. Put side-by-side in a synthetic analysis, those findings provide serious elements to say that the older generation has an impact on the younger generation. The idea of this chapter is precisely to bring some basic reflections from scientific findings and psychosocial theories on how generations at the micro- and macro-level live and interact with each other in a peaceful or conflicted way and how this affects younger and future generations.

In 1971, in her famous book *A Study of the Generations Gap* (1970, 1971), Margaret Mead describes the evolution of links between generations in a tri-dimensional perspective of the past, present and future models of interaction between children, parents and grandparents. Her approach provides an interesting framework for understanding the possible development of conflict or peace between generations:

- *The Post-figurative Model* (traditional context): this is the traditional model where children are educated by their parents and are in contact with their grandparents both of whom are role models of different stages of life. This model predominates in cultures with little mobility and a strong sense of timeless continuity and identity. Authority stems from the tradition of the past and the ancestors.
- *The Co-figurative Model* (war, migration context): this model emerges with a disruptive event – war, revolution, migration, new

technologies – where children live a completely different experience from that of their parents, grandparents and other older members of their community. In this context, the younger generations can no longer learn from their grandparents from whom they are often separated, and they must create new closer models. In this model, children don't live with or see their grandparents and great-grandparents regularly, and their parents maintain a dominant role. Parents look for models among their peers, while their children look for new existing models of grandparents in their surroundings.

• *The Prefigurative Model* (today's generation gap and high-tech context): younger generations are taking on new authority in the unfolding of their future and parents often learn from their children. Grandparents no longer play the role of transmitters of traditions; there are no or few possible links and communication between generations as parents belong to a past world and children to a radically new world that is unknown to their elders. The new generation is finding its own modeling through the mass media and modern technology. Margaret Mead emphasizes, "We know that we are facing a youth that will never experience what we have experienced and that we will never experience what they have experienced." Grandparents and even parents do not play an important role in transmitting knowledge as the speed of change and the advancement of technology do not allow sufficient time to incorporate and learn the new in order to be able to face the modified conditions of the environment. In this situation, a generation gap is clearly at hand. The "technology versus tradition" clash of generations is a risk.

Gerard Mendel studied the relations between adolescents with older generations in a psycho-analytical approach. This author links the crisis between generations to an Oedipal-type of crisis against the father figure due to the dominance of technology. The refusal of the inheritance and of the father figure creates a divide more than a conflict between generations and empowers youth as a political force in society (Mendel, 1963). Recently, Mendel has stressed the crisis of authority in society, especially of sacred authority. This author stresses in particular that the father figures can no longer help solve the archaic anxieties brought by society and globalization (Mendel, 2002). In a society that encourages individualism, the problem is how to keep cohesion in society while giving a sense of social responsibility to people. He suggests new ways to palliate the negative effects of modernization and the advancement of technology in society by humanizing and completing the psycho-familial pattern as well as by developing a new psycho-familial personality, not so much based on kinship as on social bounds, taking in charge of one's own life according to one's own values.

The socio-psychoanalytical view of Gérard Mendel, as well as the anthropological view of Margaret Mead, brings a very interesting perspective to the development of generations, which is in line with the mutation from the traditional family structure to the new architecture of the family, and, consequently, of generations. It seems quite evident that the individual can no longer be separated from the generation and from the global context in which we are living. Nowadays, Margaret Mead's post-, co- and prefigurative models of generations gives us a tool to re-think how to improve the world of future generations. For example, it would be worth studying if violence and the lack of identity of youth are linked to their loss of identity in society and in particular with the older generations. In other words the loss of one's place in the genealogy could weaken the stability or the existence of a reference system. Violent behaviors could well express the search for a role and reference in the family and in society. Some burning issues stemming out of the rapid pace of modernization of our societies have already provoked in many ways the questioning of a common reference system between generations, which if not solved could degenerate and become matters of serious concern.

Conflicts and Opportunities between Generations

As just described, the dynamics between generations and the mutation of the family affects the way members in society live and the way they develop a culture of conflict: either towards potential violence or towards conflict management and peaceful resolution. We propose to take two examples of the most striking societal changes and their consequences, which are mentioned by several authors as sources of potential intergenerational conflicts: 1. economy-based conflicts and 2. technology-based conflicts.

Economy-Based Conflicts between Generations

According to former Minister of Health of Germany and Professor of Gerontology Ursula Lehr, conflicts between generations will not so much be generated by demographic change but by economic constraints (1998). Today we can witness contrasting systems of economic solidarity throughout the world: the increasing multi-generational social structure requires important adjustments of the social and economic system to ensure the equal distribution of social welfare between generations. For example, the lower the age at which retirement pension benefits can be received, the longer society needs to ensure financing the retirement duration (table 3). In the case of scarce retirement benefits or no pension system, the retiree will have to find other financial resources in order to live and survive (through his/her descendants, work or other means). As the duration of the phase of retirement is increasing worldwide, the social welfare system has started to question and pressure the population to increase the age of retirement or reduce the pension benefits.

In countries with strong social welfare systems, governments are slowly replacing the traditional family-based inter-generational economic system with a tendency towards a more individual-based financing. In this relatively new approach, the welfare state is increasingly taking a key role in the management of the micro-family economy (i.e., social security, health and disability insurance, homelessness, unemployment, divorce regulation, etc.). Consequently, new forms of collective solidarity are developing (ensured by the state), and other forms of family solidarity are vanishing, as they are not encouraged to keep it. Ties between generations no longer depend on an obligatory economic interdependence and younger generations do not feel the urge of reciprocity as strongly as former generations. While inheritance is still the main form of legalized economic transfer today we increasingly see legal conflicts between more than two generations, underlining the lack of legal framework for a multi-generational legislation.

The form of economic exchange is also modified: as life expectancy has been rising, inheritance is an event that occurs later in life for family members. In developed countries, especially where social security guarantees a minimal wage to retirees, mutual exchange can take the form of kin-free and more social or global solidarity. According to research conducted in Germany on transfers among living kin (Kohli, 1998), inheritance happens at a time of life when the recipient is no longer in real need of it (i.e., to establish a household or start a family). Kohli also stresses that money transfers are part of an ongoing process of family relationships with its different dimensions of solidarity, but also with all its complications and conflicts. Nevertheless, economic transfers (inheritances) are partly done before death. Kohli describes the family as a component of the "new welfare mix" assuming, in the best cases, an important and complementary role the state cannot play on its own. Finally, transfers remain predominantly in the family and flow from the older to the younger members of the family, which is also the case in lower income families. What is given is directly proportional to what retirees receive in pensions. Poverty reduction programs would benefit greatly from taking into account this dynamic dimension between generations by supporting the long term flow and preservation of financial assets and transfers among members of a family.

On the other hand, increased life expectancy in the context of an intergenerational perspective requires that we view development not just form the angle of old people, but also from that of an extended youth period

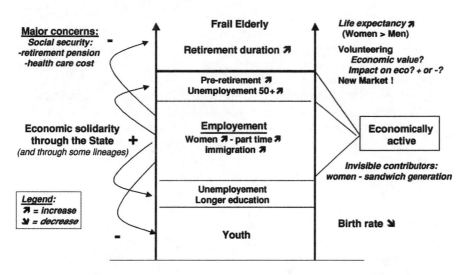

Figure 3. Economic inter-dependency in a 4 to 5 generations society.

(longer period of education, marriage and family at higher ages) which is also costly to society – and from that of a reduced period of professional work – with pre-retirement schemes (Figure 3).

Today, new symptoms of generational mis- or maladjustments are emerging and they are publicly expressed with dissatisfaction and mis-understanding. For example, a frequent debate taking place in developed countries is that the old person constitutes a "pension burden" – this argument stems from the materialistic perspective and is not rationally justified as elders are not responsible for the declining birth rates of the new generations (and consequently the declining working force contributing to pension systems). In addition, they have put in 40 to 45 years of work while contributing to their retirement wages, had fewer choices, and a briefer education than today's active population. Another recent criticism addresses the accountability of the older generation towards the younger generation, for example reproaching elders who leave debts and problems for the younger generations they did not want or are not responsible for. The question of accountability could well be one of the future motives for conflict and a divide between generations, especially in situations of war and the degradation of the environment. The state of the world the younger generations is receiving might well become a justified reproach that the older generation should anticipate. Thus, in its hands, it is important that future calculations of economists consider the time dynamics of an individual life course, as well as the cohort, generations, and period effects on social and human development.

ICT Development-Based Conflicts

Conflicts can also emerge from the *rapid pace of technological changes and modernization* of our Society. The new (M)ICT society (Media Information and Communication Technology) is about to create a new generation of "homo technicus." A German study emphasized that both the young and the old felt that they were not understood by the other party (Lehr, 1998). Those findings confirm the existence of the model that Margaret Mead described as the pre-figurative model. It announces a possible cultural and technological clash between generations if care is not given to the development of socio-cultural cohesion in society while developing the economy of a country (table 3, figures 4 and 5). New discussions about the right to development will need to address the issue of including and addressing all ages and generations. The speed of development of each generation is different and would require different policies of development or generation-adapted policies. Some thinkers have predicted that the future wars will be between the "fast" and the "slow," between the "ICT-rich" and "ICT-poor" (ICT = information and communication technology). This remark is particularly relevant when taking the ageing population into consideration, as the decline in the speed performance during the ageing process is in complete contradiction with the required speed of development that is impinging on us. The same can be said about life experiences: what the elders of today have lived and experienced is very different from that of the younger generation: let us not forget that the older generation has lived through remarkable changes with the invention of the television, radio, airplanes, phones, electronics, computers, and the internet while the younger

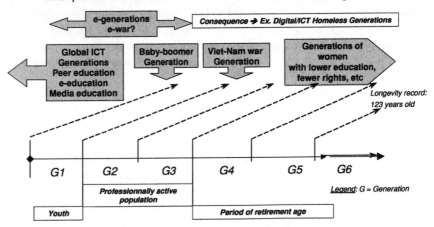

Figure 4. Dynamics of generations divide: The time link.

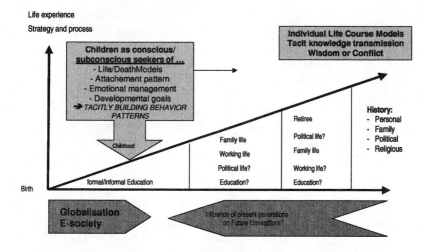

Figure 5. The treasure of Time ... of life transmitting memories and values.

generation has lived with modern technology since birth. Socialization has also changed; for the older generation the mapping of the world was local-national, and traveling beyond the village or the country was exceptional. Today the mixing of cultures and the open window of the media/internet on the world is giving children a more global view and the awareness of living in a global village with a common future. Even in the arts, children films are viewed internationally, from Pokémon to Harry Potter and others, children today have access to the same information, which was not the case of the elderly when they were children (figure 4). The children of today are living with a global and universal feeling of one planet. Because of the mass media they see what is happening on the other side of the planet, and, almost instantly, they are aware of their neighbor, whether he/she is next door or at the far end of China, Australia, Patagonia or Iceland. From this perspective, one can wonder about how generations can communicate and what it is they can share together. One should also question the value system generations have in common, what is changing and what is continuous in time, what has to be sustained or even what should not be developed in future generations.

What every individual indisputably has in common is the life process itself, which ageing is a part of, and through life experiences each person will age and form his/her own life events and history, his/her own strategies of conflict resolution, his/her own sense of coherence his/her in life. These personal treasures gathered throughout time are transformed into memories and values with peaceful effects on the future generations, or with hatred perpetuated throughout their lives and those of future generations (figure 5). Thus the personal dimension of the individual can have a tremendous effect on his/her descendants. Research has not yet measured the effect of the transmission of memories or the wishes of the elderly before death, the "philosophical testimony," on to the following generations. The powerful impact of the will and wish for hatred or peace of a dying elderly person on his/her descendants – at the conscious and subconscious level – can certainly have an impact on the behavior of the descendants, especially in cultures with strong traditions of respect toward their elders. Psycho-analytical theories have well demonstrated the strong impact of non-resolved family conflicts on the ill or in abnormal behaviors of children and adults. Sucide and active euthanasia reflects such issues.

Despite findings on the conflicts between generations, some researchers have found different results and insist on good relations between generations today (e.g., Attias-Donfut et al., 2002; Roux et al., 1996). These contradictory results might confirm the theory of the cultural lag, formulated by Ogburn in 1922, who stressed that good social integration and good contacts between the generations result from structural conditions in society that have existed earlier. The negative effects of the processes of industrialization and urbanization do not have immediate effects, but instead are felt after a couple of generations.

Finally, conflicts between generations can take place at different levels of society (economic, social or cultural) and take many forms (intra-individual, in the family, within society, or at the national and international level). What is important is to recognise that each generation is interdependent and that they must work together in order to improve the state of the world. It is in the hands of the elders and the younger generations to understand and grasp the opportunities to create a common vision and agenda for the future. If the older or the younger generation would take on the agenda of society on their own, without considering the inter-dependency of all other generations, the risk of a generation conflict will increase. No generation could dispute that it is in our interest to build a viable and sustainable future for the world, thus anticipating conflicts and their resolutions and bringing or ensuring peace between generations is a prerequisite for any sound policy or plan of action.

NEED FOR A TRANSGENERATIONAL THEORY ON CONFLICT AND VIOLENCE

Developmental Psychology Perspective: Life Course Patterns of Violence

Understanding the development of the individual within his/her life course cannot be separated from the concept of generation and cohort. The methodological trap is that research and science provide us with a unidirectional and static view of either a picture at one point in time of individuals or populations (statistics through for example census, transversal studies), or a more dynamic picture with many photographs at different points in time - those snapshots representing the evolution of the same group of individuals (i.e., longitudinal studies) or with the same selection criteria (i.e., cohort studies). The difficulty lies within grasping the unfolding motion picture of the many axes (the population studied, the sub-groups within a population, each age group, the broader image of generations all moving in time from childhood to old age and the evolution of the techno-political context), especially in a time of rapid changes and mutation.

Understanding human life in a holistic view requires that developmental psychology includes a "life course dimension" when addressing children or adolescent issues. Furthermore, a systemic approach also requires that "linked lives" are taken into consideration, the lives of persons linked to those children and adolescents. This chapter focusses on the role of older persons and grandparents in transmitting patterns of conflict and violence or peace to younger generations and a life span development approach explains some deeply engrained behaviors and patterns and legitimates the inclusion of older persons in a plan of action for violence prevention.

In general, developmental psychology deals with the individual throughout his/her life, and studies the description, explanation and modification of the ontogenesis of inter-individual age-related changes of mind and behavior, from conception to death; it aims at identifying the range of conditions of individual plasticity or modifiability of development (Baltes & Smith, 1995). Numerous specialties have emerged that concentrate on either age-graded periods (infancy, childhood, adolescence, adulthood, old age, centenarians) or on domains of functioning and processes (physical growth, cognitive development, memory development, personality development, social development, spiritual development, etc.). Interestingly enough, some authors have questioned the goal of development and what really develops throughout a life course (Miller, 1993). Many theories have surfaced, all giving a different perspective of the course of development. Theories range from giving focus to social behaviors and personality (Freud, Jung, Erikson, as well as social learning theory, ethology) to thinking and cognitive structures (Piaget, Baltes as well as information processing theories, problem-solving, conflict-resolution), to perception (Gibson) or culturally constructed systems of knowledge (Vygotsky-contextualism).

In the area of ageing, developmental psychology is relatively new and gerontologists have further questioned what is the most important goal of ageing. While some authors came up with the concept of "successful ageing" which combines three elements: survival (longevity), health (absence of disability) and life satisfaction (happiness) (Palmore, 1979). Recently more attention has been given to the subjective appraisal of life linked to psychological mechanisms and processes such as coping, resilience, beliefs or wisdom. Discussions have also taken place in order to include the process of dying well or addressing the quality of the end of life as a developmental task (e.g., Lawton, 2001).

Findings have shown very positive aspects of ageing beyond expected ages: individuals feel they are "survivors" and thus a certain elite of society which empowers them with a sense of exception with privilege with a renewed sense of physical and psychological well-being (Perls, 1995). One could actually reverse the "life time system" to a "death time system" and argue that the perception of the proximity of death is proportional to one's urge to be at peace with oneself and the world. Although the topic of the psychology of inner peace is not yet recognized, linking it to the ageing process is crucial.

This contribution does not claim to make a review of developmental psychology and ageing, but to highlight certain areas of research in human development. It give some insights into new ways in which psychology could further advance scientific investigation and progress in terms of more precise constructs concerning the development of peaceful versus distressful states of being. Two approaches will be discussed:

1. The stress-coping model, in particular the psycho-dynamic theory associated to inner distress leading either to aggressive behavior or to conflict resolution problem-solving strategies
2. The concept of wisdom as it refers traditionally to old age and associated with the attainment of higher skills of problem-solving and peaceful being.

Insight 1: Stress and Coping: From Inner Distress to Social Expression

Peace and conflict can be considered as a result of intra- and interpersonal forms of stress and coping. Stress can arise either from the social context or by internal unresolved conflicts. An individual with unresolved inner conflicts and who is not at peace with himself, or cannot cope with life, is more inclined to develop aggressive behavior (towards himself or others) or mental health disorders which will affect the family and society at large.

Although the terms "stress" and "coping" refer to different notions, they are related in the sense that coping is a positive response to stress. Coping refers to those things people do or avoid doing to prevent themselves from being harmed by stressful experiences which includes taking direct action to resolve problems as well as thoughts or actions intended to control the impact, either in the way the problem is perceived or in the emotional response to the stressor (Pearlin et al., 1990). Failure to cope with a situation can on the other hand generate not only inner conflicts, but externally expressed aggressive behaviors. Thus, considering the inner dimension of internal conflict or peace, stress and coping theories can grandly contribute to the understanding of the process at hand and give clues for the prevention, intervention and reconstruction of individual development.

As Leonard Pearlin (1993) himself acknowledges: "Stress researchers experience some confusion and despair about the concept of stress and its study, however it is acknowledged that it is not the core meaning of the concept that is confusing, for there is general agreement that stress refers to 'a response of the organism to a noxious or threatening condition,' the doubt and disagreement arise with regard to where and how to identify this response." Another difficulty is the fact that different people experiencing similar life conditions are not necessarily affected in the same manner, which has led to a focus on the concept of coping. Pearlin notes that stress results also from the individual's "reading" of the environment in situations related to fear of crime, fear of strangers, or simply fear of being lost in an unfamiliar section of town. As stress studies move outside the laboratory, these sorts of questions will become more readily apparent to researchers confronted with real world settings and will hopefully help to tackle today's new situations.

The conceptual basis of stress has been used in three different ways in the process of stress: (a) the difficulties that people face, (b) the psychological distress that results from those difficulties and (c) the mediating relationship between these two (Lazarus & Folkman, 1984). The stress – generated by stressors – refers to problems, hardships and other circumstances that have the potential to adversely affect people's well-being and inner peace. For example, an area that has received attention are the "extreme stressors" such as variety of form of victimization, involving the violation of social norms and moral standards. Interpersonal physical and psychological violence involves several sources of stress such as the experience of a violent situation, but it is also involved in the aftermath of a violent trauma and sets a number of secondary stressors in motion such as the post-traumatic stress syndrome (Pynoos, Sorenson & Steinberg, 1993). Another area of study has considered the individual and collective stress resulting from diverse holocausts and genocides (Eitinger & Major, 1993). Some gerontologists have developed new concepts such as the one of "aintegration" on the basis of post-traumatic experiences of Holocaust survivors and expanded it to a personality concept (Lomranz, 2001). The concept of "aintegration" calls for acceptance of inconsistencies, ambiguity and paradox, openness to contradictions, while maintaining mental health, development and creativity. All these require a paradigmatic change of thinking (e.g., from solving all conflicts to living peacefully with conflicts, expansion of openness, decline in manipulation, coercion, etc.). Lomranz emphasizes that elders who represent post-modern society and cultures have been robbed of their role as "transmitters of culture," which is partly a result of the absence of life-sustaining values in late adulthood. They, nonetheless, transmit what they are used to being: either liberal or conservative, promoters of peace or promoters of cruel power and wars. Many of these adult developmental processes become major in the wake of traumatic experiences such as wars, collective trauma or fear and their consequences.

In general, research on stress and ageing investigates how adults successfully negotiate – via effective coping strategies, defense mechanisms, problem-solving, optimism – life challenges, events and crises, and life/health threats that accompany growing old. Although there is no doubt that later life is a period at higher risk of being affected by losses in health, reduction of the social network, and participation in major roles, those changes appear to have less impact on the elderly than on younger persons (Kasl, 1992). Very little is known about what is stressful to the elderly and their adaptive strategies facing conflict situations. Very little is known also about the impact an older person experience has on future generations, such as in the case of suicide or active euthanasia. Drawn from an in vivo ethological observation in Kenya, sudden and unexpected death of the older generation affects the younger generation's stability: the experiment done in a natural park in Kenya showed the "uncontrollable and hysterical" behavior of young elephants after killing the old elephants for reasons of restricted territory; this lead the natural park to adopt a policy of killing the whole lineage of elephants rather than just one generation of elephants.

Some elements of response stem from the psychodynamic theory of stress researchers such as Diehl, Coyle and Labouvie-Vief (1996) have advanced in their work on coping in the elderly; in some recent studies they contrasted coping and defense strategies across age and gender groups. The findings show that older adults use a combination of coping and defense strategies, indicating greater impulse control and the tendency to positively appraise conflict situations. Adolescents and younger adults use more outwardly aggressive and psychologically undifferentiated strategies, indicating lower levels of impulse control and self-awareness. Women use more internalizing defenses than men, suggesting that men and women face different developmental tasks in the process to maturity in adulthood and thus to coping strategies. Those findings also underline the differences between men and women in conflict resolution situations, knowing that their subjectivity and coping mechanisms throughout their life courses differ

(Stuckelberger, 1997, 1998; Stuckelberger & Höpflinger, 1996). Women do not react in the same way when facing a health threat as demonstrated in studies on subjective health. Women tend to adopt an active coping strategy and base their action on the belief they can be active agents of change while men tend to adopt a passive and escapist strategy based on the belief that things will resolve on their own with time; women carry out a type of self-intervention and use multiple coping strategies, in contrast to men, who do not operate in the same way or rely less on self-intervention (Stuckelberger, 2000).

Other elements of response to the link between stress, violence and peace can be found in *Society as a Stressor*: classical studies viewed society and culture as a reservoir of personal stress and maladjustment. Anthropologists, in particular, have been very sensitive to discrepancies between the real and the ideal, the differences between the principles and beliefs to which a society claims adherence and those that are reflected in the actions of members of society. To the extent that individuals internalize both the idealized values and the discrepant norms regulating actions, they would presumably be hosts to inner conflict detrimental to their well-being (Pearlin, 1993). Nevertheless, societies are both sources of stress and sources of patterns by which people avoid stress or recover from stress. The evolution of communication reveals similar trends: the media and entertainment is today considered as a source of stress and of violence promotion to the point that the World mental health association has created a working group in Finland "Media for mental health" (http://www.wfmh.org/wmhday/wmhd2002/sec1fvt_media .htm); Canada has put in place the Media Awareness Network (http:// www.media-awareness.ca/english/index.cfm). Also, six prominent US medical groups (American Academy of Pediatrics, American Academy of Child & Adolescent Psychiatry, American Psychological Association, American Medical Association, American Academy of Family Physicians and the American Psychiatric Association) warn of the developmental impact of entertainment violence on children (US Congressional Public Health Summit, 2000):

- Children will increasingly exhibit anti-social and aggressive behavior.
- Children may become less sensitive to violence and those who suffer from violence.
- Children may view the world as violent and mean, becoming more fearful of being a victim.
- Children will desire to see more violence in entertainment and real life.
- Children will view violence as an acceptable way to settle conflicts.

Margaret Mead's pre-figurative models correspond well to thinking of media and entertainment as a source of education for the younger generations. Unfortunately, there is still little research on the stress-creating violence from media and entertainment.

Finally, an element of explanation can be found in the models of today: Considering the range of generations existing at the same time, the older generation is the least violent. Available evidence consistently indicates that older persons have the lowest rates of criminal acts and is arrests for all types of crimes. It is important to note that the most crimes for which older persons are arrested are for minor offences (Cutler, 1995). This provides a good basis for involving the elderly in creating models of society or peace initiatives. It is also important to note that at a macro-level, the paradoxical observation about some world or national leaders well beyond retirement age: while some of the political or religious leaders are models of peaceful leaders for future generations, others display models of leadership prone to violence. UN Secretary-General Kofi Annan recently reminded the Israeli and Palestinian leaders, both over 70 years old, that they have a special and urgent responsibility to chart a path back to negotiations leading to a peaceful settlement of the conflict, without which there will be no security for either people. "They have a responsibility to lead," he said. "History will judge them harshly, and their people will not absolve them, if they fail to do so" (UN Press Release, 6 March 2002). This statement stresses the older generation's responsibility for the younger and future generations.

The stress-coping theory analysis states that stress does not always have detrimental or maladaptive effects. More theoretical analysis and empirical research is needed in order to know under what conditions stress has favorable versus unfavorable effects on the quality of decision-making and long term behavior. In other words, when is stress transformable into peace or positive societal transformation? And when does it mutate into aggressiveness and violence? And what are the ingredients to build the best response and outcome?

Insight 2: Wisdom: Seeking the Common Good and Common Interest

Wisdom has been considered one of the highest forms of knowledge and personal functioning throughout the history of mankind. It has a very strong interpersonal and social aspect with regard to both its application and the consensual recognition of its existence. Wisdom is an antonym of war and violence and a synonym of peace and serenity. Research and theory on the sources and conditions associated with the development of wisdom across the life span is one of the least developed fields of investigation. Wisdom has been identified through its assessment as 1) a personality characteristic (e.g., Erikson), 2) a post-formal thinking process (i.e., Piaget), or 3) an individual's problem-solving performance with regard to difficult problems involving the interpretation, conduct, and management of life (e.g., Baltes, Smith & Staudinger, 1992). Erikson, in his epigenetic theory of personality development, identified the achievement of integrity and wisdom as the last and highest form of personality functioning (Baltes and Staudinger, 1993, Sternberg, 1990, Erikson, 1959: Erikson, Erikson & Kivnick, 1986; Jung, 1971). Achieving this last stage requires, on the one hand, successful mastery of the previous life tasks and, on the other hand, accelerative and supportive conditions associated with the social environment: it requires the full expression of mature identity, including the transcendence of personal interests, mastering one's own finitude, and attention to collective and universal issues. A few studies have appeared and reported that older age groups are characterized by higher levels of integrity than young and middle-aged subjects (e.g., Whitbourne et al., 1992). Baltes and Staudinger (1993), two of the pioneers in research on wisdom have developed a model outlining a set of factors and processes that need to cooperate for wisdom to develop: the cognitive and emotional-motivational processes as well as certain experimental factors associated with the interpretation, conduct, and management of life. An exceptional coalition of several sources and experimental combinations of circumstances are required for wisdom to be generated. The study of wisdom is bound to be complex as it involves the need to understand the richness of a person's inner life and processes such as knowledge and procedural knowledge about life, value relativism, awareness and management of uncertainty, eclectic frame of reference and meta-coping skills.

Balance Theory of Wisdom

Although most developmental approaches to wisdom are ontogenetic, other views have taken, for example, a philogenetic or evolutionary approach, arguing that constructs such as wisdom must have been selected over time, at least in a cultural sense (Csikszentmihalyi & Rathunde, 1990). A further view of wisdom worth mentioning - as it refers to the direct and practical aspects of peace or violence – is the *balance theory of wisdom* (for a review, see Sternberg, 1998; Sternberg & Lubart, 2001) which hold the core notion of "tacit knowledge" as action-oriented knowledge acquired without direct help form others, that allows individuals to achieve goals they personally value (Sternberg, 1999). The interesting parameter used in tacit knowledge is a form of "knowing how" rather than of "knowing that" (Ryle, 1949). To help someone develop tacit knowledge, one must provide mediated learning experiences, rather than academic abilities and direct instruction or information as to what to do and when (Sternberg, 1999). From a developmental standpoint, this view suggests that *wisdom is not taught so much as indirectly acquired*. While practical intelligence deliberately seeks outcomes that are good for oneself regardless of the interests of others, wisdom seeks good ends for oneself, and also good outcomes for others. With wisdom, one seeks a common good, realizing that this common good may be better for some than for others. As Sternberg and Lubart (2001) mention "an evil genius may be academically intelligent, he may be practically intelligent, he cannot be wise." Problems requiring wisdom always involve at least some elements of intrapersonal, interpersonal and extra-personal interests. In this view, wisdom is defined as the application of tacit knowledge toward the achievement of a common good through a balance among (a) intrapersonal, (b) interpersonal, and (c) extra-personal interests in order to achieve a balance for adaptation to existing environments, the shaping of existing environments and the selection of new environments. The ideal problems for measuring wisdom, in the light of balance theory, are complex conflict-resolution problems involving multiple competing interests and no clear resolution of how these interests can be reconciled.

Gerotranscendance

Along with the concept of wisdom, a new interesting theory of "Gerotranscendance" was developed by Lars Thornstam (1989, 1992). His theory suggests that human ageing encompasses a general potential towards gerotranscendance which is a shift in meta-perspective, from a materialistic and rational vision to a more universal and transcendental one, normally followed by an increase in life satisfaction. He cites Harald Ofstad (1972), a Norwegian philosopher, who views our society as looking down upon and holding in contempt those who are unproductive, ineffective, and dependent, such as old people in society. However, the values of Western society also derive from the old Hebrew tradition where old age and wisdom are held in high esteem, thus contradictory to the decreasing value given to the elderly today. As a result, the general population holds a value-dependent tendency to adopt a wretched perspective about elderly people, which is also found within gerontology.

Another area of research in this field concerns religious and spiritual behaviors. Research on the spiritual dimension of the human being such as beliefs, faith, religious practice or rituals and spiritual motivation are providing more and more evidence of their impact on successful coping in ageing and in death management (for a review see Pargament, 1997). This area can also further contribute to the reflection on peace and violence; it will not be tackled here as it involves a more complex situation that calls for the simultaneous analysis of the political implication of religion on human behavior, of collective and individual belief systems.

Carrying the Bones of the Ancestors

Where is the common man today who offers protection to his family, people, and nation through promoting peace? Where is the common man who is committed and hardworking – who although he may be unemployed continues to work for the everyday essentials of living and for training the children, youth and young adults. Confusion has now set in among the common man. With today's cross-cultural, high technology, choice-filled and multi-society mode of attaining more than just enough to get along in life, the common man's image has been weakened, This has often pressured him to become corrupt, i.e., and make excuses to the point of becoming an artifact or a relic in his own world.

Indigenous Leader's Statement, given at the Peace Summit of Religious and Spiritual Leaders, United Nations, August 2000.

It is difficult to measure the increase/decrease in the wisdom of the peoples of the world. However, the level of conflict and wars has certainly escalated in the world. Sternberg and Lubart (2001) do press psychologists to take the measurement of wisdom and the formulation of theories and theory-based measures of wisdom much more seriously. The work at hand is often dwarfed by work on intelligence. The authors' state: "Perhaps we even need to think about how we, as psychologists, might create experiences that would guide people to develop wisdom, much as we have been concerned in some quarters about developing intelligence. Perhaps if schools put into wisdom development even a small fraction of the effort they put into the development of an often inert knowledge base, some of the conflicts that have arisen so quickly would also quickly disappear."

For a New Approach: Transgenerational Developmental Psychology

Today's adult developmental theory is still focussed on a static view of age-ing and ignores the generation effects. Major adult developmental theories either idealize the ageing process or emphasize the pathological aspect of ageing, minimizing their psycho-social role in the lineage. Modern culture has often robbed the elderly of their role and responsibility – a very famous writer of Africa once said, "If an elder African dies, it is a whole Library that is burning" (Hampatê Ba). In the same way, aboriginal culture has many indigenous people wove a special respect to the elders and to the dead ancestors, which provides the backbone of the value system guiding all decisions. Indigenous populations used to say, "All decisions are to be made for the seven generations to come."

Researches have shown that the behavior of parents affects the behavior of their children even far beyond the time of education, for example: smoking, alcoholism, suicide, sexual abuse, transgenerational violence, all have long-lasting affects and are reproduced from generation to generation. Many research areas have emphasized the importance of transmission between generations, some of the main areas linked to peace and conflict transmission are:

Social Learning Theories

Social learning theories are certainly the version of learning theory that and are the most relevant in intergenerational psychology most clearly influences current developmental thinking and research. Watson and Skinner, key figures of behaviorism and social learning theories in psychology, had visions of a better society and humanity. If changing the environment can change behavior, there are exciting possibilities for human society. According to learning theory, personality – or the self – is a repertoire of behavior created by an organized set of contingencies. Skinner, wrote: "The behavior a young person acquires in the bosom of his family composes oneself; the behavior he acquires in other surroundings, say, the armed services composes another. The two selves may exist in the same skin without conflict until the contingencies conflict – as they may, for example, if his friends from the services visit him in his home." Several theories of personality are classified as social learning theories. Bandura (1977) disagrees with Skinner as he sees the child as an active, thinking being who contributes in many ways to his/her own development. The child is an originating agent, free to choose the models he/she will attend to and hence will have some say about what he/she will learn from elders. In Bandura's cognitive social learning theory observational learning requires the observer to actively attend to, encode, and retain the behaviors displayed by social models. Children are active information processors, who organize experience by making mental notes about their strengths and weaknesses and about the likely consequences of their behavior. For example, new findings are proving that not only do children follow implicitly throughout their lives the pathological behavior of their parents, but if parents make a positive change in their behavior, the children will also change their behavior. A study on the cessation of smoking has proved that the cessation of smoking of the parents was significantly linked to the children's pattern of taking up or quitting smoking (Farkas et al., 1999). Thus, not only do negative patterns have an impact, but positive behavior also does, which gives ground to postulate that positive models of change of older generations do influence the behavior of younger generations, which enhances the responsibility of the older generation in many ways.

Emotional Transmission—Patterns of Attachment and Dependency over Generations

Bowlby, the pioneer of attachment psychology, believes that attachment theory is not only a theory of child development, but it is a lifelong phenomenon (e.g., Bowlby, 1988). Some research shows that present thoughts about the past are assumed to influence the quality of adults' relationships of attachment with their children. There is evidence for the intergenerational transfer of individual differences in patterns of attachment in different continents (see Sperling & Berman, 1994 for an overview; Parkes, Stevenson-Hinde & Morris, 1991; Van Ijzendoorn, 1995). These studies conclude that there is substantial intergenerational transmission of individual differences in an attachment pattern. In about 75% of families, the classification of the parents' mental representation of how they themselves were attached to their parents is in agreement with measures of the attachment relations they currently have with their infants. In about 25% of the families, parents classified as secure in their mental representations of the past were nevertheless diagnosed as having an insecure relationship with their infant, and vice versa. Although one can still question what is the cause and what is the effect, one can talk about intergenerational concordance or congruence instead of intergenerational transmission of the quality of attachment relations (Demetriou, Doise & van Lieshout, 1999).

Transgenerational model of violence of adult and elder abuse suggests that violent behavior – as perpetrator or victim - learned within the family is transmitted from one generation to the next. According to this view, abusers grow up in violent families only to reenact the parent-child cycle of violence once the dependency roles shift from child to parent (Wilber & McNeilly, 2001). Transgenerational violence is based on findings that perpetrators of domestic violence are more likely to have grown up in violent homes where they witnessed spousal abuse and/or were victims of child abuse themselves. In the same way, battered women, as well as their abusers, are more likely to batter their children. According to Quinn and Tomita (1997), the rate of transmission of abusive violence from one generation to the next is estimated to be about 30% compared to a 3% rate of abusive violence in the general population. The same pattern applies for alcoholism, suicide and other behavioral disorders leading to self-violence or outwardly-directed violence. Another form of violence derived from domestic violence recently starting to raise interest is "financial elder abuse" especially in the case of patients suffering from cognitive impairment or under mental health treatment.

Generativity Theory: The Motivational Factor of Social Transmission

In the psychosocial theory of development over the life course, Erikson (1963, 1982) described a series of eight stages of crisis in personality growth, of which generativity versus stagnation was the seventh. Generativity represents the component of the individual's personality that develops to incorporate concern beyond the self to the needs, interests, and well-being of future generations. The unfavorable resolution represented by "stagnation" involves a selfish interest in oneself to the exclusion of others who may follow. The psychosocial crisis stages Erikson defines are set in terms of pairs of polar opposites, such as generativity vs. stagnation or the most favorable vs. the least favorable resolution of the crisis. The ability to achieve a favorable resolution of a stage depends in part on the combination of biological, psychological and social forces that operate at a given time.

Creative endeavors in which the individual leaves something behind for the benefit of future generations also is seen a form of generativity. Not only in terms of commitment to parenting and providing for one's own children, but in a larger sense generativity may be expressed as the involvement in helping future generations, for instance, through a career dedicated to teaching, to improving the environment, the political climate or social welfare and to achieve a peaceful society.

The concept of generativity has not been subjected to empirical testing. A series of longitudinal studies, however, tried to measure this dimension. The findings of these investigations support the hypothesis that generativity is positively associated with well-being and adaptation in a larger sense and that favorable development in the area of family life is associated with success at work for men (i.e., Vaillant, 1977; Vaillant & Milofsky, 1989). Furthermore, the development of a sense of generativity may be strongly related to other changes in personality and the self, such as a greater sense of self-assurance, and the ability to cope in a flexible way with life stresses. Constructs, such as role involvement and satisfaction, personality, identity and coping, lead themselves more readily to empirical investigation than the more generic and perhaps elusive notion of generativity. The concept remains a useful one for heuristic purposes and a stimulus for further inquiry regarding the notion of change and continuity throughout the life course (Whitbourne et al., 1992).

The above section brings evidence to confirm that maintaining peace and non-violence include in youth must as much the relations between generations as the sound development of the individual throughout his/her life course.

On the other hand, putting the findings together one can conclude that through its behavior, through its pattern of attachment, and by its problem-solving attitude, each generation has an implicit and explicit impact on future generations. As violent patterns of behavior perpetuate in generations to follow, peaceful patterns of behaviors will also perpetuate in generations to follow. Therefore, the decisive influence of one generation upon another in matters of inner/outer peace and conflict calls for the older generation to assume moral responsibility with regard to the younger generations. This is valid as much in the post-, co-, as in the pre-figurative model. Older persons do have a duty and responsibility towards younger generations: they set a reference, a model or anti-model of coping with life and facing death of violence, of peace. We are all getting older, day by day; it is our destiny to develop and gain life skills up to the and of life. "Elder" in the sense of a wise and naturally authoritative figure within the family and society should be the ideal we all strive for. Elders are essential to the cohesion of society. Not only are elders transmitters of tacit knowledge, of life experiences, of history, of life crisis management, they are also the roots of our society. Thus, in order to find our true common values for peace and justice, it is of paramount importance to restore the role of the elder in society and build a cohesive common vision for the future.

CONCLUSION

Today the increase in violence in schools and in youth in general concerns the whole of society. Violence in youth is but an expression of a dysfunctional society, a symptom of an unbalance that older generations have a duty to analyze. In this context, while professionally active generations are important actors, the two to three generations of retired people do play an important role as agents improving society as was demonstrated in this chapter.

Older people are key to violence prevention and to the promotion of a culture of peace: first, by the legacy they leave to future generations collectively, but also personally with their implicit or explicit "moral testimony;" second, by the simple fact that, throughout their lives, they participated in and witnessed history at a personal level as well as at the levels of the family and society. In living the history of their own nation, the older generations have experienced the profound impact of oar, violence and war on society and on their families. Canadian General Romeo Dallaire, who witnessed the genocide in Rwanda and lived himself with posttraumatic syndrome for years, delivers speeches today that call for a non-violent society where older generations have a duty to stop war and violence (see quotation below). He reckons that the massacre of more that one million Tutsi by the Hutu people over the course of three months was the consequence of the development of hate transmitted from generation to generation, starting form the time when the Belgium occupier gave more privileges to the Tutsi people (ref. Film, The Just Man, 2002). Restoring and healing collective memories and social justice is thus of paramount importance for the future of our world. The way in which the collective memory of war, violence, and the peace process is transmitted to the following generations is a powerful and indisputable factor of social transformation:

1. Either by encouraging a spirit of forgiveness and of reconciliation within society (political), within the family (socio-genealogical) and within the self (psychological)
2. Or on the contrary, by increasing the hatred fear and the will of revenge of one generation on to another one, through daily attitudes, behaviors and words – e.g., through informal education of war, but also through the behavior patterns of violence and insecurity as the norm

Generations of Peace—Importance of the Elders of Today

"We cannot continue to believe that war is the ultimate dimension of discipline and of destruction of the world ... the elders of the world cannot accept that the youth of the world is being sacrificed and trained to self destruction, be abused in war, being instruments of war, soldiers, that they are targets of a new era of conflict. The elders can coalesce and bring to an end the intolerable use and abuse of younger generations. Elders can build the power, the lobby, to bring it all to an end. Elders today have to keep up with our youth, to be credible to our youth."

> Lieutenant General Romeo Dallaire, former commander of the United Nations Observer Mission in Uganda and Rwanda during the Genocide Speech given at the World Congress on Gerontology in Vancouver (July, 2001)

The beliefs – including the false beliefs – conveyed from one generation to another can without any doubt become a source of individual or collective violence or a warranty of peace in the nation and in the world. One way to overcome discord, hatred and violence is through the commitment of ageing individuals to become conscientious role models and to represent key values of forgiveness, reconciliation and peace. The elders have the choice to conscientiously address their responsibility towards youth: (1) to leave the fruits of their work and achievement behind them: a world of peace or destruction for the next generations, (2) to leave an image of the way to live and die that will influence their peers and descendants positively, (3) to transmit through their attitudes and behaviors a mental imprint of living in peace with the self, the family and the nations.

In this context a transgenerational approach to violence in schools would bring a new light and new solutions to restore the identity of youth in society today. Throughout the world, some schools have allowed people from the older generations to give courses, but they have not yet included them as agents of conflict management or violence prevention. Older generations could also at the personal level achieve a better understanding and communication with disruptive behavior and violence in children where parents' or peers' direct interactions fail. In order to begin a process of including the transgenerational perspective, a first draft of an *Intergenerational Plan of Action for Conflict and Violence Prevention in Schools* is proposed in which the older generations have a role to play. This plan is applicable in schools and takes into account the inner dimensions of peace and security as well as the outer dimension and expression of non-violence and peace, two aspects that alone can guarantee a long-term sustainable strategy. The mutual benefit of the inter-generational component will not only benefit youth, but also the elderly by restoring their role and making it possible for them to serve society.

The Second United Nations World Assembly on Ageing, which took place in Madrid in April 2002, offered an opportunity to address the issue of the Ageing Population and World Peace with a proposed plan of action at the macro-level to involve the elders in all efforts to (a) prevent conflict and violence, (b) promote peace at the inner and outer level, and (c) empower future generations for peace and teach them the skills to maintain a state of peace (Stuckelberger, 2002). Here the proposed plan aims at applying peace strategies at the micro-level with a specificity to school settings. Those ideas and reflections wish to be captured by those who most need it, nurtured by professionals and further refined and developed by youth, as the youth of today holds the seeds of wisdom for tomorrow's world.

Quotations to Insert in the Pages and Texts

"We will disarm the world only if we proceed to inner disarmament"
ANONYMOUS
"There is no way to peace, peace is the way"
MAHATMA GANDHI
"Be the peace you want to see"
ANONYMOUS

First Draft Proposal for a Plan of Action

Intergenerational Plan of Action
for Conflict and Violence Prevention in Schools

1. Label schools or sections of schools "Healthy" or "Peace Promoting Schools."
2. Bring the older generations of retirees into schools and empower them in their role and responsibility as contributors of non-violent and peaceful behaviors in life. For example, they can share how to use conflict resolution skills by telling true stories to learn from and concrete situations in the family and society.
3. Bring into schools older persons from different cultures and religions who have witnessed the horrors of violence and war (i.e., General Dallaire, former UN corps in Rwanda) and have them discuss real cases.
4. Create Circles or Platforms of understanding and reconciliation between older and younger generations.
5. Build within the school curriculum a new education line with a range of possible courses with specific aims:
   - in order to "demystify violence:" teach the logic of conflict and escalation of violence through examples or by no. 2, 3 and 4. A psychologist could join in giving more theoretical and scientific approaches to complement.
   - *in order to cope with situations when facing violence*: offer courses on human psychology, emphasizing the commonalities and differences in communication skills and conflict management at all ages but also in different settings and cultures.
   - *in order to secure the mind and build tolerance with oneself and others*: teach courses that address the human being and humanity, courses on what is life (the life course and the ageing process), on cultural differences and belief systems in the world, on societal changes. Inter-religious platforms could join in this group and teach objectively the different religious cultures
   - *in order to heal and give tools to self-healing of potential violence and aggression*: list and analyze the fears of the students; teach self-help and calming techniques of the mind; sport activities could also include more self-defense courses and martial arts to canalise better violent energies.
   - *In order to raise awareness on the violent effect of certain media and entertainment* create a media awareness network and a participative course where students could carry out auto-analysis of their own pattern of media and ICT responsiveness. Include reality-check excercises.
6. Find an innovative system of identifying potential victims and portrayers of aggression to prevent or intervene in time – i.e., creation of a Council

of the Elders or Council of the Wise in the school to which children can securely report their fears, anxieties and worries at the personal, family and friends level. Find a way to informally or formally nominate god-mothers and godfathers for children with no inter-generational identity reference.

7. Have socially lawyers and attorneys work for conciliation within the family when establishing the will and "philosophical testimony" of older generations in order to prevent perpetuating conflicts/violence – develop case models.

8. Give awards promoting peaceful and non-violence behaviors with ancestors' figures and models such as a "Ghandi Award" for youth think also of "Peace Aut" "Music for Peace" Award.

9. Create a Mass Media Award of Violence Prevention in Schools, which would help develop the concept of "healthy media" with a hit parade of the best/worst for violence prevention/promotion. Older generations could witness the formidable changes from their own childhood.

10. Make psychology a part of the school curriculum, especially courses which are potentially instruments for behavioral change for all generations.

A Plan of Action for Non-Violence and Peace: A Collective Vision, a Common Agenda

The idea of this conclusion is to raise a new action-oriented policy for a Peace agenda that fits in the priority issues of the global society we live in. In order to guarantee peace, issues will have to be addressed in such a way as to avoid disruption or conflicts between generations, and in order to guarantee long term peace, a common vision for all generations will have to be addressed.

Priorities Linked to World Peace: Building a Common Agenda and Plan of Action

The importance of the dynamics between generations is key component in sustaining social and human development. Thus the role of older generations within the global agenda has to be addressed at many levels.

- *Health*: Equality between generations in access to and distribution of medical, social and economic resources.
- *Poverty alleviation* programs during the entire life span, but also the setting up of long term and sustainable anti-poverty programs linking many generations.
- *The HIV/AIDS epidemic* is a good example for proving the need for building inter-generational dimensions in development,

anti-poverty programs and policy-making. The AIDS epidemic at the end of 2000, showed alarming numbers (figure 8), the global estimates are of 36.1 million people with HIV/AIDS (UNAIDS, 2001). This epidemic is not only wiping out one or two entire generations, but it has created a whole generation of children without parents but with grand-parents: today, 13.2 million children 14 and younger have been orphaned by AIDS in all parts of the world (figure 9).

Elements of a Plan of Action for Peace Including Older Generations

1. **Empowering the elders in their role and responsibility as contributors of peace:** Bring the elders of today and all of us tomorrow to play a key role in building and promoting a culture of peace within the family and the 'global village' they live in. From their own internal/external peace-making process - through memories and actions, through reporting the 'history' linked to war/peace - the elders set models of how to engage or not in the peace process: either through building reconciliation or through perpetuating conflicts. The responsibility of elders in leaving behind a legacy of peace or war can empower their children, grand-children and society as a whole. Thus, subtle and powerful models of behavior (life and death) influence future generations - an area that has very rarely been addressed or investigated. Given the worldwide increase in longevity, policy on ageing should enable the elderly to bring their human expertise in improving the state of the world not only for tomorrow but also for the generations to come.

2. **Create a platform involving older and younger generations,** in order to build a coalition for promoting Peace and acting subsequently towards peace at different levels:
   - *at the individual level:* setting educative programs including new aspects such as wisdom (see Sternberg above), inner peace, conflict resolution within, peaceful behavior.
   - *at the family level:* intra and inter-generational peace, by building cohesive family planning with more than 2 generations, respecting the gender balance.
   - *at the societal level:* organizing groups for Peace, but also getting groups of elders involved in politics for a Peaceful world and setting up parliamentarian groups of Youth and Elders – Create a Circle of Wise Elders at the local, national and why not at the UN? Involve elder religious and spiritual leaders or retired political leaders in addressing the issue and participating in the Peace Plan agenda.

- *at the political level*: (i) identify all elders ruling the world and call them to be peace promoters; (ii) bring up the issue of peace process negotiation on a long term basis; (iii) construct of instruments to prevent conflicts, preserve and build a peaceful society, such as mapping peace projects (Stuckelberger, 2004).

3. **At the level of the mass media:** create awards for the best article that enhances inter-generational cohesion and peace initiatives by the elderly. Urge the media, through scientific arguments, to take responsibility for the psychological damage created by the negative and sometimes terrifying images and news 'freely' launched with no ethical guidelines as to their impact on younger and older generations.

4. **Educate** our communities about the urgent need to provide tools and instruments to enhance understanding of worldviews and wisdom as an education complementary to intellectual knowledge. Educating children and all generations to care for the common good of the planet such as peaceful resolution of conflicts at all levels or the protection of the natural environment and all forms of life, which is a component of peace.

5. **Set up an organization of Young-Old Volunteers for Peace** which could provide interventions in different situations: preventing war, during war or post-war reconstruction.

6. **Women as active agents of peace, and especially older women** considering the high proportion of women in older ages, they should be involved in civil societies initiatives of peace as well as the planning of peace missions from the outset. Peacekeeping personnel should be trained in their responsibilities towards women and children. The prejudice and discriminating image of older women will have to be dispelled as they are the main portrayers of care in younger generations and in the very old generation.

7. **Integrate elders into UN peace operations** could include
   - a plan for incorporating the issues of the elderly into all aspects of its work from presention to peacemaking and peace building
   - more retirees and women retirees, appointed as special representatives

8. **Psychology as an instrument for international intervention:** psychologists should bring the very needed perspective of human development psychology perspective to all UN priorities. More particularly, psychologists and policy psychologists will be asked to work more and more on issues related to psychological reconstruction of men, women, children and the elderly who have suffered major traumas collectively (wars, bombing, terrorist attacks, etc.) or individually (violence, rape, abuse, etc.). The new situation

psychologists face today is fear, insecurity and collective trauma, such as children who have only lived war situations.

9. **Psychology of Peace** and inter-generational psychology are two areas that strongly need more research, theoretical and practical models. Psychologists can be involved at different levels: in the prevention of conflicts and wars, in the many forms of interventions during conflict and post-conflict situations, as well as in the individual peace-restoring and peace-building psychology. Psychology could greatly contribute in furthering reflection form its own theoretical or heuristic models.

10. **Responsible Living:** Ageing is inseparable from the notion of social participation and the responsibility of the elders towards the generations to come. The cultural and spiritual heritage that the older generations leave behind them is in a way the state of the world they have collectively co-created. The younger generations are living by the life example and through being educated in a spirit and a culture of war or of peace.

References

Allard M., Lèbre V. et Robine J.M. (1994). *Les 120 ans de Jeanne Calment, doyenne de l'humanité*. Paris: Le Cherche Midi Ed.

Attias-Donfut C., Lapierre N. et Segalen M. (2002). *Le nouvel esprit de famille*. Editions Odile Paris: Jacob.

Back, K. (1995). Generations. In G.L. Maddox (Ed.), *The Encyclopedia of Ageing* (2nd edition) (pp. 395–396). New York: Springer.

Baltes P. and Smith J. (1995). Developmental Psychology. In G.L. Maddox, *The Encyclopedia of Ageing* (2nd edition) (pp. 267–270). New York: Springer Publishing Company.

Baltes P.B. and Staudinger U.M. (1993). The search for a psychology of wisdom. *Current Directions* in Psychological Science, 2:1–6.

Baltes P.B., Smith J. and Staudinger, U.M. (1992). Wisdom and successful ageing. In T. Sonderegger (Ed.). *Nebraska Symposium on Motivation* (Vol. 39, pp. 123–167). Lincoln: University of Nebraska Press.

Bandura A. (1977). *Social learning theory*. Englewood Cliffs, NJ : Prentice-Hall.

Bengtson V.L., Cutler N.W., Mangen D.J. and Marshall V.W. (1985). Generations, cohorts, and relations between age groups. In R. Binstock and E. Shanas (Eds.). *Handbook of aging and the social sciences* (2nd ed., pp. 304–338). New York: van Nostrand Reinhold.

Bowlby J. (1988). *A secure base. Clinical applications of attachment theory*. London: Routledge.

Casper L.M. and Bryson K.R. (1998). Co-resident grandparents and their grandchildren, paper prepared for the 1998 annual meeting of the Population Association of America. Chicago.

Central Census Steering Committee (1999). *The 1999 Census of Vietnam at a Glance, Preliminary Results*. Hanoi Thé Gioi Publishers.

Csikszentmihalyi M. and Rathunde K. (1990). The psychology of wisdom: an evolutionary interpretation. In R.J. Sternberg (Ed.), *Wisdom: Its nature, origins, and development* (pp. 25–51). New York: Cambridge University Press.

Cutler S.J. (1995). Crime against and by the elderly. In G.L. Maddox, The encyclopedia of ageing (2nd edition) (pp. 243–244). New York: Springer Publishing Company.

Dallaire R. (2001). Transmitting Fundamental Values to Younger Generations Through the Healing of Painful Memories. Contribution to the Symposium convened by A. Stuckelberger and C. Taillon, Empowering Future Generations for Peace: The Elder's Role, World Congress of Gerontology, Vancouver, Canada, July 2001.

Demetriou A., Doise W., and van Lieshout C. (Eds.) (1999). *Life-span developmental psychology*. London: Wiley.

Diehl M., Coyle N. and Labouvie-Vief G. (1996). Age and sex differences in strategies of coping and defense across the life span. *Psychology and Aging*, 11: 127–139.

Eiguer A. (2001). *La famille de l'adolescent, le retour des ancêtres*. Paris: Editions in press.

Eitinger L. and Major E.F. (1993). Stress of the Holocaust. In L. Goldberger and S. Breznitz (Eds.), Handbook of stress (pp. 617–657). New York: Free Press.

Erikson E.H. (1959). Identity and the life cycle. *Psychological Issues*, 1:18–164.

Erikson E.H. (1963). *Childhood and society* (2nd ed.). New York: Norton.

Erikson e.H. (1982). *The life cycle completed*. New York: Norton.

Erikson E.H., Erikson J.M. and Kivnick H. (1986). *Vital involvement in old age: the experience of old age in our time*. London: Norton.

Farkas A.J., Distefan J.M., Choii W.S., Giulpin E.A. and Pierce J.P. (1999). Does parental smoking cessation discourage adolescent smoking, *Preeventive Medicine*, 28: 213–218.

Fuller-Thomson E. and Minkler M. (2001). American Grandparents providing extensive child care to their grandchildren: Prevalence and profile. *The Gerontologist*, Vol. 41(2): 201–209.

Gillion C., Turner J., Bailey C. and Latulippe D. (2000) (Eds). *Social Security Pensions, Development and Reform, Executive Summary*. Geneva: International Labour Organization.

Jung C.G. (1971). The stages of life. In J. Campbell (Ed.). *The portable Jung* (pp. 2–22). New York: Viking.

Kaës R-. Faimberg H., Enriquez M., Baranes J.-J. (1993). *Transmission de la vie psychique entre générations*. Dunod: Paris.

Kasl s.V. (1992). Stress and health among the elderly: overview of issues. In J.L. Wykle, E. Kahana and J. Kowal (Eds.), *Stress and health among the elderly* (pp. 5–34). New York: Springer.

Kinsella K. and Velkoff V.A. (2001). An Ageing world: 2001. International Population Reports. Washington DC: US Census Bureau.

Kohli M. (1998). Intergenerational transfers of assets. Conference Report, Expert Conference "Ageing in Europe: Intergenerational Solidarity – A Basis of Social Cohesion." Vienna, 16 November 1998.

Lawton P. (2001). Quality of life and end of life. In James E. Birren and Werner K. Shaie, *Handbook of the psychology of ageing*, (5th Edn. ch. 24: pp. 592–616). New York: Academic Press.

Lazarus R. and Folkman S. (1984). *Stress, appraisal, and coping*. New York: Springer.

Lehr, U. (1998). From the three-generation to the four-and five-generation family, Conference Report, Expert Conference "Ageing in Europe: Intergenerational Solidarity – A Basis of Social Cohesion." Vienna, 16 November 1998.

Lomranz J. (2001). Constructive Aging: Elders as Promoters of Humanistic Values. Contribution to the Symposium convened by A. Stuckelberger and C. Taillon, Empowering Future Generations for Peace: The Elder's Role, World Congress of Gerontology, Vancouver, Canada, July 2001.

Mead M. (1970). A study of the generations gap. New York: Doubleday.

Mead M. (1971). Le fossé des générations (A Study of the Generations Gap). Paris: Editions Denoël.

Media Awareness Network: Facts of Violence and Trauma - http://www.media-awareness.ca/english/index.cfm or http://www.wfmh.org/wmhday/wmhd2002/sec1fvt_media.htm

Mendel G. (1963). *Les conflits des générations*. Paris: Presses universitaires de France.

Mendel G. (2002). Une histoire de l'autorité, *Permanences et variations*. Paris: La Découverte.

Miller P. H. (1993). *Theories of developmental psychology* (3rd Edn.). New York: Freeman.

Myers G.C. (1992). Demographic aging and family support for older persons. In H.L. Kendig, A. Hashimoto and L.C. Coppard (Eds.) *Family support for the elderly* (pp. 31–68). Oxford: Oxford University Press.

Ofstad, H. (1972). Vart forakt for svaghet. Nauismens normer och varederingar – och vara egna (Our contempt for weakness. The Nazi values – and our own). Stokholm: Prisma.

Ogburn W.F. (1922). Social Change. New york: Huebsch.

Palmore, E. (1979). Predictors of successful ageing. Gerontologist, 19:427–431.

Pargament K.I. (1997). *The psychology of religion and coping, theory, research, practice*. New York: Guilford.

Parkes C.M., Stevenson, Hinde J. and Morris P. (1991). *Attachment across the life cycle*. London: Routledge.

Pearlin L.I. (1993). Environmental and Social sources, The social context of stress. In L. Goldberger and S. Breznitz (Eds.), *Handbook of stress* (pp. 303–332). New York: Free Press.

Pearlin L.I., Mullan J.T. Semple S.J. and Skaff M.M. (1990). Caregiving and the stress process: An overview of concepts and their measures. *The Gerontologist*, 30:583–594.

Perls, T.T. (1995, January). The oldest old. *Scientific American*, 272: 70–75.

Pynoos R.S., Sorenson S.B. and Steinberg A.M. (1993). Interpersonal violence and traumatic stress reactions. In L. Goldberger and S. Breznitz (Eds.), *Handbook of stress* (pp. 573–616). New York: Free Press.

Quinn K.M. and Tomita S.K. (1997). Elder abuse and neglect: Causes, diagnosis and intervention strategies (2nd ed.). New York: Springer.

Recovery Africa (January 2001). *Women central to peace-building*, p. 8–9.

Relations between generations (1998). 2nd meeting of the European experts for the international Year of old persons, Vienna

Roux, P.; Gobet, P., Clémence, A., Höpflinger, F. (1996) Generationenbeziehungen und Altersbilder. Ergebnisse einer empirischen Studie, Lausanne/Zürich (Switzerland): NFP 32.

Rowe J.W. and Kahn R.L. (1998). *Successful ageing: The MacArthur Foundation Study*. New York: Pantheon Books.

Ryle G. (1949). The concept of mind. London: Hutchinson.

Smith K. (2000). *Who's minding the kids? Child care arrangements:* Fall 1995, US Census Bureau Current Population Reports, Washington, DC. Government Printing Office.

Soldo B.J. (1996). Cross Pressures on Middle-Aged Adults: A broader view. *Journal of Gerontology*, 51B (6): S271–273.

Sperling M.B., and Berman W.H. (Eds.) (1994). Attachment in adults, on individual difference.

Sternberg R.J. (1998). A balance theory of wisdom. *Review of General Psychology*, 2: 347–365.

Sternberg R.J. (1999). Schools should nurture wisdom. In B.Z. Presseisen (Ed.), *Teaching for intelligences* (pp. 55–82). Arlington Heights, IL: Skylight.

Sternberg R.J. and Lubart T. (2001). Wisdom and creativity. In In James E. Birren and Werner K. Shaie, *Handbook of the psychology of ageing*, 5th Edition (ch. 20: pp. 500–522). New York: Academic Press.

Sternberg, R.J. (1990). *Wisdom: Its nature, origins, and development*. New York: Cambridge University Press.

Stuckelberger A. (2000). Vieillissement et état de santé subjectif: déterminants et mécanismes différentiels hommes femmes, Etude transversale de la population genevoise. Thèse de doctorat en psychologie, Université de Genève. Suisse.

Stuckelberger A. (July-August 1997). Men and women age differently, In World Health 'Active Ageing', 4:.8–9. WHO: Geneva.

Stuckelberger A. and Höpflinger F. (1998). Dynamics of ageing in Switzerland from a gender perspective, *Ageing International*: 62–84.

Stuckelberger A. et Höpflinger F. (1996). *Vieillissement différentiel: hommes et femmes*. Zürich: Editions Seismo.

Stuckelberger A. (2004). Mapping peace, a project endorsed by the NGO working group at the United Nations, Plan of action, "Women defending peace," ILO, Geneva, 2002.

Stuckelberger A. (2002). Population ageing and world peace. Empowering future generations. Older persons' role and responsibility. *Journal of Psycho-Social Intervention*, Contributions of the Psychology on Ageing: Towards a Society for all Ages. Special Issue for the 2nd United Nations World Assembly on Ageing in Madrid (pp. 29–75). Madrid, Spain.

Thornstam, L. (1989). Gero-transcendence; A Meta-theoretical reformulation of the disengagement theory, *ageing: Clinical and Experimental Research*, Vol. 1 (1): 55–63.

Tornstam L. (1992). The Quo Vadis of Gerontology, On the Gerontological Research Paradigm. *The Gerontologist*, 32(3). 318–326.

Toulemon L. (2001). *Combien d'enfants, combine de frères et sœurs depuis cent ans?*, Population et Sociétés, Bulletin mensuel d'information de l'Institut national d'études démographiques, no 374, Paris.

Tribune de Genève (7 March 2002). *De plus en plus de parents demandent qu'on leur retire la garde de leurs enfants*. ("More and more parents request that their custody right be withdrawn"), (p. 21). Geneva, Switzerland.

UN Press Release (6 March 2002). Secretary-General Urges Leaders to Act in Middle East. UN News: New York. http://www.un.org/News/ossg/sg/index.shtml

UNAIDS (December 2001). UNAIDS Annual Report. Geneva: UNAIDS.

UNFPA (1999). *A Time for Choices. The State of the World Population 1999*. New York: United Nations.

UNFPA (2001). *Population Issues. Briefing Kit 2001*. New York: United Nations Population Fund.

United Nations (1999). *Human Rights and Older Persons*. Document prepared for the UN International Year of Older Persons 1999. Geneva: United Nations.

United Nations (2001). We the peoples. *The role of the United Nations in the 21st Century. The Millennium Report*. New York: United Nations.

United Nations Population Division (2000). *World Population Prospects: The 2000 Revision*.

US Census Bureau (2001). An ageing world: 2001. Washington, D.C.: International Population Reports.

US Congressional Public Health Summit, 2000. Joint Statement on the Impact of Entertainment Violence on Children http://www.aap.org/advocacy/releases/jstmtevc.htm

Vaillant G. (1977). *Adaptation to life*. Boston, MA: Little Brown.

Vaillant G. and Milofsky E. (1989). Natural history of male psychological health: IX. Empirical evidence for Erikson's model of the life cycle. *American Journal of Psychiatry*, 137: 1348–1359.

Van Ijzendoorn M.H. (1995). Adult attachment representations, parental responsiveness, and infant attachment: A meta-analysis on the predictive validity of the adult attachment interview. *Psychological Bulletin*, 117, 387–403.

Vaupel J.W. and Jeune B (1995). The emergence and proliferation of centenarians. In B. Jeune and J.W. Vaupel (Eds.). *Exceptional Longevity: From prehistory to the present monograph on population aging*, No. 2, Odense: Odense University.

Whitbourne S.K., Zuschlag M.K., Elliot L.B. and Waterman A.S. (1992). Psychosocial development in adulthood: A 22-year sequential study. *Journal of Personality and Social Psychology*, 63: 260–271.

WHO (1999). *Suicide rates in the World*. Geneva: WHO.

Wilber K.H. and McNeilly D.P. (2001). Elder abuse and victimization. In James E. Birren and Werner K. Shaie, *Handbook of the psychology of ageing*, 5th Ed. (pp. 569–591). New York: Academic Press.

Chapter 9

Bullying and *Ijime* in Japanese Schools
A Sociocultural Perspective

Takashi Naito and Uwe P. Gielen

Japan's Public Debate on School Bullying

Since the middle of the 1980s, school bullying has received much attention as an emerging social problem in Japanese society. For example, in 1986, national newspapers and popular TV shows presented accounts and discussions of nine separate incidents where students reportedly committed suicide as a consequence of group bullying in school. In some cases, the public was presented with the students' suicide notes, which described their anguished cry for help. Since the early 1980s, numerous articles, reports, and books concerning bullying in schools have been published. According to Takatoku (1999), more than 1,200 papers and more than 400 books on this topic were published between 1985 and 1998.

A highly dramatic and widely publicized case of school bullying occurred in 1986 in a junior high school located in Tokyo: A 13-year-old student hanged himself and left a despairing suicide note accusing several boys of having created a living hell for him. In one instance when he came to school, he found that the *Ijime* group leaders had placed his desk in front of the class and arranged a mock funeral including burning incense, his photograph, flowers, and a condolence card that had been signed by most of his classmates, some other boys, his homeroom teacher, and three other teachers. Through this arrangement, he was made to understand that in the eyes of his classmates and some of his teachers he was somehow a failure as a human being.

This case demonstrates–in extreme form to be sure–some distinctive features of *Ijime*. Guns and knives are not in evidence. Instead, *Ijime* is in most cases a form of psychological intimidation or terror perpetrated by classmates and peers against mentally weaker, or merely different, victims. In the case of this 13-year-old boy, several of his teachers actually participated in the bullying, although this is unusual. When his father, after a series of prior nasty *Ijime* incidents directed against his son, contacted the homeroom teacher, the police, and the parents of the lead bully, he was merely advised that his son should change schools. Thus, many victims of *Ijime* feel themselves abandoned by their teachers who, in one way or the other, may merely counsel them to "endure." Other teachers and school principals remain ignorant of *Ijime* incidents or are inclined to hush them up in order to protect themselves and their school's reputation in the eyes of the public and their administrative superiors. *Ijime*, then, may be embedded in a school's culture and not merely represent individual acts of a group of students. Moreover, *Ijime* usually takes on less dramatic forms than those used in the case described earlier, such as name calling, relentless teasing, shunning, and other forms of social isolation.

In spite of Japan's extensive public discussion of school bullying and school avoidance, it should be kept in mind that Japanese schools remain much more peaceful places of group interaction and work than most American schools. Japanese homicide rates, including homicide rates for teenagers, remain among the lowest of any industrialized society, although rates for juvenile crime and school violence have been increasing since 1995 (Ministry of Education, Culture, Sports, Science, and Technology, 1999). Students do not have access to guns; at Japanese schools hard drugs are only very rarely in evidence, discipline remains strict in most cases, school regulations are extensive, and drop-out rates remain relatively low in comparison to most other industrialized countries. The teachers are well trained, well paid, and enjoy relatively high status although their position has become more controversial in recent years.[1] The students spend numerous hours together in a work-oriented environment. Thus, Japanese society became extremely concerned about school bullying in the 1980s *not* because Japanese schools were especially violent in nature, but precisely because the more extreme bullying incidents stood out in an otherwise achievement-driven, highly structured, conformist, demanding, and often stressful environment.

As a matter of fact, bullying began to increase at an alarming rate even as school violence in general decreased in the early 1980s. From 1982 to 1986, acts of school violence decreased from 4,315 to 2,801 incidents, although they have increased considerably in recent years (*The Japan Times Online*, 2001; The Ministry of Education, Culture, Sports, Science, and Technology, 1999, 2000). Bullying in schools was recognized by scholars and others as a distinct category of problematic behaviors, which needed to be distinguished from other types of school violence. In 1994, the powerful Ministry of Education, Science, Sports, and Culture (then called Monbushō and now known under the name of Monbukagakushyo) formed the Council for Research on Children and Students' Problematic Behaviors in order to cope with the problem of school bullying. The Council's public announcements about bullying, in turn, raised the schools' awareness of the problem and how to deal with it.

The Council introduced many suggestions about how to reduce school bullying in the context of family and community life, school functioning, collaboration between the police and the schools, and so on. The recommendations have stressed the importance of communication and a warm atmosphere in the family, more flexibility in helping victims of bullying to change classes and schools, greater openness of the schools vis-à-vis the surrounding community, improved counseling skills of teachers, and the importance of sickrooms in schools where the victims can open their hearts to others. Several of the suggestions are specifically intended to open otherwise tightly "sealed" classes, which tend to function as closed groups encouraging the more hidden forms of social manipulation. Nevertheless, school bullying continues to exist as a nationally recognized social problem. In addition, a growing number of anguished students refuse to go to school since they are unable or unwilling to survive in a pressured environment. Many of them display psychosomatic symptoms and a fear of being bullied while others are merely truant. Together, the twin problems of *Ijime* (bullying) and *Futoukou* (school refusal) suggest that Japan's bureaucratically-controlled educational system has lost some of its luster.

In 1996, an international symposium on school bullying was held by the Ministry of Education and Science and the National Institute for Educational Policy Research in Tokyo. Different scenarios of school bullying were discussed by scholars from Norway, Great Britain, the Netherlands, Australia, and Japan. Until that time, many Japanese believed that school bullying–and especially group bullying–represented a specifically Japanese manifestation of classroom tensions. When Ogi (1997), for instance, emphasized that "There are serious problems of bullying in foreign countries," he usually received the following response: "But, it is not so devious or 'dark' as the Japanese cases, isn't it?"

Such an argument may have appeared plausible to many because they understood the concept of group bullying in terms of their somewhat stereotyped images of Japanese society. These were influenced by Japanese social science literature that has traditionally emphasized the collectivist nature of Japanese society and the importance of striving for group harmony (e.g., Reischauer, 1988). Furthermore, a whole book industry labeled *Nihonjinron* ("Theory of the Japanese") has claimed that Japanese society and culture are unique and even characterized by a mysterious "essence" not to be found in other societies. In this context, group bullying of hapless victims in Japanese schools may be understood as the dark underside of a usually more benign emphasis on the individual's conformity to, and integration into, the group.

Given the collectivistic nature of Japanese society, groups often bully persons who deviate from explicit or implicit social standards and break the harmony of the group. For example, some Japanese newspapers have described several cruel and highly manipulative cases of group bullying in schools, in which the targets of the group were called "germs" and other members of classes were forbidden to interact with them. However, Japanese social scientists soon learned that Norwegian victims of school bullying have been referred to as "bacterias" in a quite similar way. Given such cross-cultural parallels, the 1996 conference succeeded in demonstrating that bullying is not unique to Japanese society, although the cultural aspects of school bullying need further analysis. Today, many Japanese teachers and scholars understand that school bullying is a widespread international phenomenon. In addition, as a direct consequence of the conference, various educational anti-bullying programs of other countries, such as Norway and Sweden, have been introduced in Japan (e.g., Morita, 1999).

This paper discusses research on school bullying from a cross-cultural point of view. It includes a discussion of the nature of Japanese classrooms, general definitions of bullying and of *Ijime*, reports on the frequency and nature of school bullying in Japan, and a selective review of some cross-cultural findings on school bullying, providing a broader perspective on Japanese discussions of the problem. The following brief discussion of Japanese classrooms is intended to supply some background information for the non-Japanese reader.

JAPANESE CLASSROOMS

Japan's educational system is highly centralized and tightly controlled from the top, resembling in this respect the French rather than the American system. The Monbukagakushyo prescribes national curricula and recommends textbooks to be used. Compulsory education includes elementary schools (six grades) and lower secondary schools (three grades). Most of these schools are public schools established by municipalities. The public and private senior high schools include three grades and are voluntary in nature. Nevertheless, an astonishing 96%–97% of all junior high school students advance to the status of senior high school student. In addition, most high school students attend tutorial cramming schools (*juku*) in order to prepare themselves for the very difficult entrance examinations to the better universities.

Altogether, Japan has been highly successful in upholding demanding educational standards. In addition, both parents and students know that in Japan's meritocratic system, school failure tends to destroy a student's chances to lead an economically successful life. Japan is truly a "school society" for its children, adolescents, and families.

Japanese schools place a major emphasis on group activities and the sharing of major responsibilities such as cleaning one's classroom and the school's hallways. Many of the students' activities are centered around their "homeroom"—the place where, according to Japanese studies, a major proportion of bullying activities take place, especially during class breaks. In comparison to other countries, such as England and Norway, fewer bullying incidents occur outside the school precincts, although a good many acts of *Ijime* also happen after school and on the students' way home.

One striking characteristic of Japanese schools concerns the extremely detailed list of rules and regulations that students are expected to follow (White, 1993). These typically include regulations for school uniforms, hairstyles, grooming, acceptable places in town for the students to visit, and even the precise routes that students must take on their way home. The numerous rules are designed by the authorities to increase school discipline and render the students more pliable, although the students may resent some of the more irksome demands made upon them. The purpose of schools is not so much to further the students' self-actualization and sense of individuality, but to help them function successfully in a demanding society within the context of group dynamics. Japanese students, in turn, often describe themselves as "ordinary" persons rather than as individuals having unusual personalities. Consequently, when incidents of bullying and *Ijime* occur, they frequently take place in a stifling atmosphere favoring the priority of group interests over individual interests.

Traditionally, both the social status and the general influence of Japanese teachers (*sensei*) in schools and vis-à-vis parents have been high, although in recent years there have been indications that more teachers find it difficult to control their classrooms. In addition, there have been government reports that rates of mental illness among teachers have been increasing since 1995 (The Ministry of Education, Culture, Sports, Science, and Technology, 2001). Partially due to the implicit influence of Confucian norms, many teachers continue to comport themselves in a somewhat paternalistic manner and are frequently seen by their students as somewhat distant, though more or less respected, authority figures. Furthermore, some students report that their teachers employ corporal punishment as a means of discipline although this is against the law. This practice is bound to alienate some of the children and adolescents even though many parents condone it at least in some educational situations. Moreover, because rapid social change has led to important attitudinal differences between generations, many teachers and other adults apparently find it difficult to fully understand the changing ways of their students. Seen in this context, opportunities for communication with teachers at a personal level are often limited in Japanese high schools.

Japanese students are placed under great pressure to achieve academically in an atmosphere that has been characterized as "examination hell." To gain acceptance to a leading university is extremely competitive, yet one's future career prospects depend to a large extent on such an achievement. Feeling pressured and tired, hedged in by numerous petty rules, lacking close contact with their teachers, and facing uncertain prospects for their future, a good many Japanese students suffer from feelings of unhappiness and even despair. For instance, in an international survey of general happiness with school life, only 26.3% of Japanese 10-year-olds reported feeling "very happy" placing them last among students from six countries (Nihon keizai shinbun,1997). This and other findings suggest that many Japanese students feel frustrated about their experiences in school thereby making the schools potential breeding grounds for acts of *Ijime*. These may enable some troubled students to take out their unhappy feelings on peers to are serve as convenient scapegoats.

Attempts to deal with one's stresses and strains may also occur because Japan is a "school-society" where to be a "good child" tends to be equated with being a docile, well-mannered, responsive, and cooperative "good student." By necessity, however, many students will be unsuccessful in their educational strivings and consequently feel frustrated. Some of these students end up refusing to go to school, while others may be tempted to bully a peer. To understand these actions better, it should prove useful to discuss in some detail what kinds of bullying occur in Japanese schools and the best way to define and investigate such actions.

DEFINITIONS OF BULLYING

A well-known definition of bullying by the pioneering Scandinavian researcher Olweus (1999) is as follows: "A student is being bullied or victimized when he or she is exposed repeatedly and over time to negative actions on the part of one or more other students" (1999, p. 10). The actions may be direct or indirect and of a more physical or a more psychological nature. In addition, there should be real or perceived asymmetric power relationships between the bully and his or her victims. Thus, quarrels or fights among equals are excluded from this definition.

It should be noted that this standard definition of bullying is a behavioral one that emphasizes social context. However, seemingly similar acts of bullying may have quite different causes and underlying psychological processes, just as the same act of stealing does not necessarily depend on the same underlying psychological processes or causes in different cultural settings. For instance, a definition of bullying emphasizing physical rather than psychological violence would lead to misleading research results in the case of Japan. From a methodological point of view, it should prove useful to provide situational school scenarios to the respondents of interviews and questionnaires.

Many scholars around the world (Smith, Morita, Junger-Tos, Olweus, Catalano, & Slee, 1999) have accepted Olweus' definition, including several Japanese investigators reporting nationwide surveys (e.g., Morita, Soeda, Soeda, & Taki, 1999; the Ministry of Education, Culture, Sports, Science, and Technology, 1999, 2000). In this context, the Ministry of Education, Culture, Sports, Science, and Technology (1999) defined bullying as repeated negative behavior that dehumanizes other(s) either physically or psychologically. However, several Japanese researchers have expressed some dissatisfaction in relation to Olweus' general framework (Ogi, 1997; Taki, 2001b). This dissatisfaction stems, in part, from sociocultural differences in the nature of school bullying and how participants and onlookers perceive and define it.

Defining Bullying from a Japanese Perspective

The corresponding Japanese word for bullying is *Ijime*. It is a term rather frequently used in everyday speech both for certain school situations and for other forms of "mobbing" in work situations or elsewhere. According to *Kojien*, one of the reliable Japanese dictionaries, the Japanese word, *ijimeru* (verb of *Ijime*) is defined as "to treat a weak person(s) harshly." Other dictionaries translate the term as "to be cruel to, to tease, to annoy, to bully."

The prototype of *Ijime* involves bullying in order to gain some sort of advantage over others who are handicapped and stigmatized in terms of their physical characteristics, social class background, meek personality, and so on. The prototype of *Ijime*, especially when this word is applied to situations involving adults, may be as follows. If B bullies A in the way of C, this situation implies that a) the way of C is an insidious one though probably not against explicit rules or laws, b) A is in some way disadvantaged when compared to B. This "mental" prototype of *Ijime* differs from the prototype of bullying in which a physically superior person hurts a weaker peer physically (Morita et al., 1999; Taki, 2001b).

It should be added that the term *Ijime* tends to have a feminine ring to many Japanese ears, pointing as it does to the more indirect styles of aggression. These include strategies designed to isolate a person socially, teasing the person in a destructive way, spreading rumors and slandering victims, whispering behind a person's back, introducing subtle innuendoes, ganging up on a person, and in general, the not so gentle arts of social manipulation and intimidation. In American psychology literature, such strategies are often referred to as relational rather than physical aggression. The term *Ijime* is also used for cases of hazing. However, the term would not be employed in cases where money is extorted as long as the main purpose of the extortion is financial in nature rather than trying to hurt the victim psychologically.

Furthermore, when the frequency of school violence incidents decreased in the beginning of the 1980s, the term *Ijime* came to be used as a label for a new and special type of violence in schools. This word was employed in a broad and vague way in those days, but, through discussions among teachers and scholars, it has been elaborated and more sharply defined in order to focus on a group of problematic behaviors distinguished from other types of school violence. As a result of this scholarly discussion, certain characteristics of *Ijime* have been disproportionately emphasized in Japanese literature on school bullying. For example, Japanese researchers have tended to focus on long-term bullying in same-age groups that can take on an especially insidious character.

We have discussed the concept of bullying as various researchers analyze it. However, students have their own conceptions of bullying or *Ijime*, which, in turn, will influence their behavior as well as their understanding of others' behavior in school. Furthermore, the students' conceptions include many ambiguities. In this regard, the Council for Research on Children and Students' Problematic Behaviors (1996b) reported that about 60% of students ranging from the second grade of primary school students to sophomore high school students indicated that they found it difficult to distinguish bullying from joking situations. Clearly, a gray zone exists ranging from jokes intended to be readily enjoyed by everybody, to jokes implicitly putting somebody down, to jokes intended to derogate a victim and to turn him or her into a target of future jokes and group contempt.

Ogi (1997) explored the concept of bullying held by 282 second-grade junior high school students in Tokyo. In this context, he presented thirty items that describe acts or situations in school and asked whether each act or situation constituted "bullying" or "not bullying but just joking." In response, only four behavioral items were identified as "bullying" by more than 75% of the respondents: Other class members have not spoken with him/her this week, even if he/she greeted them (91.1%); writing

"Drop dead," "Idiot" or "Get out" on a note to him/her (89.7%); shouting words such as "germ," "eczema," and so on at him/her (83.0%); stripping him/her of clothes or molesting him/her (75.9%). In contrast, only 5% of the students regarded "arguments that turned into a fistfight" as "bullying." These findings suggest that the students seem to share at least a few basic conceptions of bullying having to do with social isolation and derogation of a victim, but they also point to disagreements about such act items as "Going to the toilet with her/him even if I do not want to go," "Wearing his/her gym suit without permission," etc. These disagreements depend, in part, on the ambiguity of the described acts and situations. For example, the item "All students of a class sneer at him/her when the teacher appoints him/her" [to a classroom leadership position] was identified by only 36.2% as bullying, 38.7% concluded that it was not bullying, and 23% responded "don't know" to the item.

It is often unclear whether the students hold different concepts of bullying or whether there exists ambiguous or insufficient information about the situations presented. It is likely that at least in some research situations, the responding students needed additional information about the situation depicted, for example, how the protagonists felt about it. The fuzzy contours of the concept of *Ijime* make it difficult for social scientists to conduct reliable and valid research on the nature and frequency of bullying and mobbing in Japanese schools and to compare the results of their research with the results of studies conducted in other societies and cultures.

FREQUENCY OF BULLYING

The Monbukagakushyo has administered surveys on school bullying to public primary, junior high, and senior high schools every year since 1985. Reports from these surveys indicate that school bullying has gradually decreased from 60,096 cases in 1995 to 31,359 cases in 1999.

However, these numbers are misleading since they are far lower than those reported in surveys of students. For instance, the Council for Research on Children and Students' Problematic Behaviors (1996a) administered a nationwide survey on school bullying among 2,048 primary school students, 4,694 junior high students, and 2,648 senior high school students. In addition, 557 teachers and 9,420 parents/guardians were asked to respond to a questionnaire on school bullying. According to the results, 22% of primary school students (fourth to sixth graders), 13% of junior high school students, and 4% of senior high school students indicated that they had been bullied during the school year (the survey was conducted in December and January and the school year begins in April). A second survey among 16,824 students indicated that 5.3% of primary school students and 3.5% of junior high school students were bullied by someone at the time of the study (Management and Coordination Agency, 1998). These percentages may be compared to the results of a recent American study, which employed a representative sample of 6th through 10th graders. In the study, 29.9% of the students reported moderate or frequent involvement in bullying, either as a bully (13%), or as one who was bullied (10.6%), or both (6.3%) (Nansel et al., 2001).

Surveys of Japanese teachers and principals about the frequency of bullying incidents in schools are unreliable for a number of reasons. First of all, there is the aforementioned difficulty of defining the term bullying. Moreover, most Japanese students (especially those attending high schools) do not wish to report cases of bullying to their teachers. Furthermore, in the questionnaires used before 1994, the instruction "the acts of which the contents have been [clearly] identified" was included, but these words were omitted beginning in 1994 (Ministry of Education, Culture, Sports, Science, and Technology, 1999). In fact, 56,601 school bullying acts were reported in 1994, which is more than double the 21,598 cases reported in 1993. It is almost certain that the difference in reported cases between the two years does not reflect a dramatic increase in incidents, but mostly the different instructions of the Ministry.

In addition, there are problems of identifying bullying among similar acts occurring in schools. Yomiuri (1995), a newspaper publishing company, summarized the interview results of forty-seven chiefs of the Board of Education in Japan. Twenty-seven chiefs readily admitted that they found it difficult to distinguish school bullying from seemingly similar acts such as joking, mock teasing, chaffing, and so on.

In this context, Taki (1992) reviewed a number of school studies on bullying and determined that the frequencies outlined in those reports varied according to 1) the time period in which bullying occurred; 2) whether the respondents were instructed to report their subjective experiences of bullying others, witnessing bullying, or being targeted by the bullies themselves; 3) which negative behaviors were specified in the questionnaires. According to his results, Taki categorized cases of school violence as a) continuous group violence, b) one-on-one incidents occurring within one day, and c) other cases. Based on these distinctions, Taki conducted a four-year longitudinal study of junior high school students in a suburban area from 1985 to 1990. He found that long-term cases of group bullying (as reported either by the bullies or by the victims) did not decrease. In contrast, the other and more common forms of short-term and one-on-one violence decreased in the investigated period.

Concerning students' experiences as witnesses, he found that the frequency of long-term and many-against-one cases of violence observed by the students did decrease from 1985 to 1990; however, the frequency of being exposed to this type of bullying as reported by the students did not decrease during that period. This and other evidence suggests that some of the more serious forms of bullying tend to go underground during the later school years while the more direct, impulsive, and short lived forms may be readily observed in the earlier school years.

FINDINGS OF A CROSS-CULTURAL SURVEY AND SOME ADDITIONAL DATA ON BULLYING

As mentioned above, cultural differences influence how researchers conceive of bullying, and which of its aspects they wish to investigate. Such differences make it more difficult to arrive at valid cross-cultural comparisons. Nevertheless, cross-cultural research on bullying has been helpful in assessing bullying in different countries from a broad range of perspectives. In addition, cross-cultural findings point to the importance of developing effective intervention programs. In this context, Morita (2001a, 2001b) conducted a large-scale comparative study on bullying in Japan (N = 6,906), Norway (N = 2,308), the Netherlands (N = 1,993), and England (N = 5,825). He asked students from primary, junior, and senior high schools about their experiences during the second school semester.

In the study, bullying was defined as 1) abusing or poking fun at somebody, 2) ignoring or shutting someone out from one's circle, 3) hitting, kicking or threatening, 4) starting a rumor in order to induce others to dislike the victim, 5) giving him/her a sheet of paper with offensive words written on it, 6) other similar acts (Olweus, 1999). It was also explained that joking is distinguishable from bullying by the response of the victim: while joking is readily appreciated together, bullying is not. Finally, it was stated that quarreling or struggling with somebody of equal power should not be considered bullying.

The findings revealed both common features and differences in regards to bullying among the students from the four countries. Here we will list some characteristics of school bullying in Japan from a comparative point of view.

1. *Types of Bullying:* Bullying was perceived in a consistent manner across the four countries. The most agreed-upon form was saying bad things about someone or teasing him/her. However, as Taki (2001b) suggested, seemingly similar acts in different countries may in reality have different meanings. For instance, "calling someone names" may be done

openly in the western countries but the names will be whispered behind the victim's back in Japan.

2. *Frequency of Bullying:* 13.9% of the Japanese students, 39.4% of the English students, 27% of the Dutch students, and 20.8% of the Norwegian students answered that they were bullied during the present semester (Morita, 2001b). While some of these cross-national differences may be due to different educational systems (Japanese schools follow a three-semester system and the western schools a two-semester system), most of the cross-national differences between Japan and the other countries are too large to be accounted for merely by the different semester system. Bullying, then, seems to be especially observable in England, but is less common in Japan.

3. *Frequency of Long-Term Bullying:* Among the bullied students, 17.7% (Japan), 12.4% (England), 11.7% (the Netherlands), and 17.1% (Norway) were bullied more than once per week during the semester (Morita, 2001b).

4. *Number of Bullying Students:* While most of the bullying was done by two to three students at a time, 5.2% of the bullied students in Japan, 1.3% in England, 2.2% in the Netherlands, and 1.3% in Norway were bullied by more than ten students during the semester (Hoshino, 2001). To reinforce the Japanese finding, The Council for Research on Children and Students' Problematic Behaviors (1996a) reported that about 20% of the bullied female junior high and senior high school students were bullied by more than ten students. Thus, bullying by large and often female groups of students is disproportionately common in Japanese schools.

5. *Relations between Bully and Victim:* In the case of Japanese students, 80% of the victims were bullied by students of the same school year, as was also the case in the Netherlands (Hoshino, 2001). In contrast, Olweus (1999) suggests that Norwegian students, especially those at younger ages, tend to be bullied by older students: More than 50% of the second or third graders in elementary school indicated that older students bullied them. Japanese school bullying, according to these and other data, occurs above all among classmates, suggesting that it is a phenomenon based on group dynamics among same-age peers.

6. *Responses to Bullying:* 61.6% (Japan), 67.1% (England), 3% (Norway), and 66.5% (the Netherlands) of the bullied students answered that they ignored bullying. In addition, 33.9% (Japan), 29.5% (England), 21.7% (the Netherlands), and 25% (Norway) of the bullied students did not report being bullied to anybody (Matsuura, 2001). Fifty-three percent of the bullied students in Japan did not want it to be known that they were bullied, and this was true especially in the case of parents/guardians (48%), siblings (31.6%), and friends (17.4%) (Matsuura, 2001). Thus, the Japanese students

were especially likely to hide that they were victims of bullying. This observation is in agreement with other research findings and tends to hold true especially for the older students.

Sixty percent of the Japanese parents/guardians of those primary or junior high school students who were bullied more than once during the school year indicated that their children were not bullied or that they did not know whether they were bullied. As for the teachers' awareness of the situation, 30% (primary schools), 40% (junior high schools), and 70% (senior high schools) of the teachers stated that there was no bullying even in those cases when students reported bullying in their classes (The Council for Research on Children and Students' Problematic Behaviors, 1996a). It appears that both the parents and the teachers in Japanese senior high schools are frequently oblivious to the bullying that goes on in the classrooms.

As in other societies, Japanese researchers of school bullying have identified a number of important sex differences. Whereas boys are more apt to engage in physical kinds of bullying, Japanese girls are more likely to perform psychological acts of *Ijime* against others. This is especially true for efforts to isolate a victim socially (Morita et al., 1999). Similar sex differences have also been obtained in North American and European studies.

Hoshino (2001) and his research associates reported that 64.2% of the bullied female students were bullied by female students, and 82% of the bullied male students were the victims of male students. These data suggest that bullying tends to be a within-the-same-sex phenomenon, with male students being especially unlikely to be bullied by female students.

The most common acts of *Ijime* (87% for both sexes) involved saying negative things about the victim and/or teasing him/her. Male victims were much more likely to be hit and kicked than female victims (54% vs. 20.9%). Group bullying was especially prevalent among the girls: 40.9% of the female victims were bullied by four to nine students, and 9.2% by ten or more students. In contrast, the corresponding percentages for male victims were 29.7% (4–9 bullies) and 4.5% (10 or more bullies).

Many of the aforementioned sex differences are consistent with the feminine, group-oriented prototype of *Ijime* with its emphasis on psychological manipulation and isolation. In addition, the findings suggest that further research on group dynamics in girls' groups and on "mean girls" would be fruitful, just as American researchers and the American public are now becoming more aware of the powerful negative impact of relational aggression among girls (Crick et al., 2001; Talbot, 2002).

The likelihood of *Ijime* occurring is also related to the students' age and the type of school they are attending. According to the national

"Monbushō Survey" of *Ijime* administered during 1994–1995, 21.9% of elementary school students reported they are currently victims or "were victims in the year but not now." The corresponding percentages were 13.2% for lower-secondary school students and 3.9% for upper-secondary school students. These data show a rapid decline of *Ijime* incidents among the older students although it is also likely that they were less inclined than the younger students to report being the victims of bullying.

These research results point to the following characteristics of school bullying in Japanese schools: The frequency of bullying is relatively low in comparison to the other three countries, but the long-lasting forms of bullying and the bullying by many students are disproportionately common in Japan. Bullying is especially prevalent among younger students. Some boys are attracted to the more physical ways of bullying another person whereas groups of girls prefer to isolate the victim through nasty forms of social manipulation. Most of the school bullying episodes occur between same-age students who are part of the same class. It is clear that many of the victims keep quiet and refuse to admit their traumatic experiences to their parents, siblings, and friends. An element of secrecy surrounds many cases of bullying so that teachers and parents are frequently unaware how much some of their charges suffer. In fact, victims are often forced to act as if they were well integrated into their group when, in fact, they are subject to various acts of degradation and humiliation.

SOME DETERMINANTS OF BULLYING IN JAPANESE CLASSROOMS

Several Japanese studies have shown that school bullies are oriented toward breaking school rules and committing deviant acts against other students (e.g., Benesse Educational Institute, 1996; The Council for Research on Children and Students' Problematic Behaviors, 1996a). It appears that school bullies do not sufficiently internalize general social or cultural norms about not hurting others. When interviewed, many bullies state that they are "having fun" victimizing another classmate in an otherwise dull school environment while others merely go along with the group and feel uneasy and guilty about their behavior.

At the same time, bullying may depend on other factors: Even if the students recognize the social norms as those that should be followed, they may act against them in several ways. When a social norm, for instance, is described or interpreted in ambiguous or situational ways, they disregard it because of their own interpretation of the situation that deviates from that of most other students. Thus, they may perceive some bullying situations as ambiguous or harmless, because they are disguised as forms of joking, mild teasing, and so on. In this context, Morita and Kiyonaga (1994) argued that although more than 90% of all students denied "teasing someone" or "hiding someone's things," there was nevertheless bullying in their classes in a context where many bullies tended to ignore the serious implications of their actions.

In addition, the researchers asserted that many of today's students prefer to function in a "play mode." This encourages them to engage in or accept bullying more easily, because they misinterpret acts of bullying as normal and acceptable forms of joking and kidding. Such misinterpretations may make their lives easier, less constrained, less dull, and more "fun" in the short run, but they may also serve to hide unconscious aggressive impulses. Furthermore, Morita and Kiyonaga point to the current tendency of many adolescents to avoid profound commitments to their groups and to think seriously (see also Naito, 1990). This trend especially encourages bystander and audience behavior together with a lack of concern for the victims' suffering.

Several studies have suggested that bullying is more frequent in those classes that students perceive as having a poor moral atmosphere (e.g., The Council for Research on Children and Students' Problematic Behaviors, 1996a). According to Hoshino's (2001) investigation, the students in these classes state that many of their peers are not in tune with their classes, ignore others' distress, demonstrate negative attitudes toward those students who are praised by teachers, do wrong things because it is fun, and so on. Hoshino's research results suggest that 1) these classes do not accept or are not controlled by formal norms acceptable to the school authorities, 2) the students have little concern for each other, 3) the students conform to their somewhat deviant peer group, and 4) the students do not establish positive peer norms.

According to Morita and Kiyonaga (1994), classes with frequent bullying are made up of bullies, bullied students, an audience, and bystanders. In this context, "audience" refers to students who are amused by the bullying incidents and "bystanders" are those students who act as if they do not know the victims. According to the authors' multivariate analysis, the victims display a tendency to "conform to power" and adopt a positive "orientation to central or formal school values." In contrast, the bullies seek to gain "independence from school authorities' power" and adopt a "negative attitude toward formal school values." They argue that current Japanese school discipline supports students' conformity to adult expectations without developing their independence.

It should be added that a general explanation of bullying in Japanese schools needs to take into account the collectivistic nature of Japanese society. According to Triandis, "collectivists either make no distinctions between personal and collective goals, or if they do make such distinctions, they subordinate their personal to the collective goals" (Triandis,

1995, p. 5). Assuming that this is true, school bullying in Japan can then be understood as an educational and group oriented problem occurring in a collectivistic society.

Several common characteristics of *Ijime* are consistent with such an interpretation. These include the many incidents of group bullying especially among female students, the "enmeshment" of many perpetrators and victims, the secrecy surrounding *Ijime*, the inability of many victims to withstand the psychological pressures created by their peers, and so on. When Tai (2001) analyzed Japanese data as part of the previously mentioned cross-cultural study on bullying, he found that bullying occurred more readily in those school classes where some forms of group competition and collective punishment had been introduced. In such a context, anybody seen as interfering with collective goals is in danger of being ostracized from the group.

The collectivistic nature of *Ijime* should not induce us to believe that bullying per se is more common in collectivistic societies than in individualistic societies, especially since this is not supported by cross-cultural data. Instead, by drawing a distinction between collectivistic and individualistic societies we can better understand the specific forms that bullying assumes in Japanese schools. *Ijime* appears to be most common in those schools and classes where teachers lack moral authority, students display a certain lack of collective justice, and the same students lack intrinsic commitment to their groups (Naito, 1990; Shimuzu, 1987). In such circumstances, many students act as noncommital bystanders in bullying situations (Masataka, 1998). In contrast, when teachers do assume moral authority and are respected by their students, the students are also less likely to get involved in bullying activities. We may thus state that in a well integrated collectivistic society school bullying will rarely manifest itself, but that in a poorly integrated collectivistic society oriented toward collective punishment and relentless group competition, bullying will be common.

These considerations suggest that researchers need to pay more attention to the bystanders and the audience of bullying incidents. As an example, Masataka (1998) asked junior high school second and third graders (in schools where *Ijime* either occurred or did not occur) to respond to four hypothetical bullying situations. The percentage of students from bullying schools who selected playing the role of bystander as their own likely behavior was greater than the corresponding percentage in the other schools, although the percentage of students who said they would become bullies in the depicted situations differed little between the two groups. In addition, Masataka asked the students whether their mothers and their fathers would select the same behaviors that they did. The bystanders-to-be predicted more concordance with their mothers' behaviors but less with their fathers' behaviors when compared to the other students. In addition, the bystanders tended to come from nuclear families in which their mothers were unemployed.

The latter findings should be seen in the context of changing Japanese family constellations (Naito & Gielen, 2005) together with the diminishing ability of schools and communities to socialize children and adolescents successfully. Many modern Japanese fathers are "psychologically absent" from their families, a tendency that reinforces exclusive mother-child bonds. In such a situation, some of the mothers indulge their children too much in their desire to ensure the child's happiness, but they may thereby also further egocentric and "mother-child centric" attitudes. These, in turn, may induce the child to engage in egocentric acts of bullying together with a concomitant lack of empathy for the victim. Many Japanese psychologists and psychiatrists believe that the commonly encountered emotional enmeshment of Japanese mothers and their children, together with poor guidance by weak fathers, produces a disproportionate number of children who are unable to function well in competitive school situations. While some of them refuse to go to school, others become participants, bystanders, or the audience to various acts of bullying while developing somewhat passive, yet irritable and conflictual, personalities.

However, a psychological analysis such as this should not induce us to overlook the failings of an over-organized educational system relying on hierarchically organized forms of regimentation, the creation of "examination wars," the suppression of individual strivings, and efforts to thwart the emergence of an autonomous self. *Ijime* is embedded in children's peer cultures that tend to reproduce some of the more autocratic, regimented, stressful, and punishing aspects of their school environment. No matter what family-induced psychological predispositions children bring to school, it is the school environment itself that typically triggers and supports acts of *Ijime* and *Futoukou*. This process is further facilitated by teachers' loss of moral authority in recent years. As they now operate in a more stressful environment, teachers are finding it more difficult to control their classes, to integrate them in a moral and prosocial level, and to serve as models of moral rectitude and integrity.

CONCLUDING REMARKS

We have reviewed some research on school bullying and *Ijime* in Japan from a cross-cultural perspective. We focused on definitional problems and suggested that the prototypical *Ijime* incident is different from that of bullying as understood in the more individualistic Western countries, although both terms cover the same behaviors at times. The typical case of

Ijime refers to behaviors that are intended to psychologically rather than physically harm weaker, same-age classmates in insidious ways.

The prototype of *Ijime* has influenced Japanese investigators of bullying to focus mostly on group structures and functions rather than on the students' morality. The authors of most *Ijime* studies share an underlying belief that bullying occurs mainly because of various group factors rather than because of the bully's moral incompetence or inherent aggressiveness.

In a related vein, Japanese researchers are less likely to investigate whether school bullies have a tendency to later commit crimes in their adulthood, because it is difficult for them to believe that bullies have, or are likely to develop, stable aggressive and immoral personalities. This holds true although numerous Western studies have shown that those boys systematically bullying others from elementary school on are far more likely to grow into later delinquents than their less-aggressive peers (Olweus, 1993). However, as members of a collectivistic society, both the Japanese researchers and the public tend to hold situational rather than dispositional views of human behavior (Masataka, 1998), and they therefore tend to conclude that bullying is predominantly caused by the effects of intricate group dynamics. In contrast, American and West European researchers come from more individualistic cultures, and they, therefore, tend to pay more attention to personality dispositions.

Ijime is a conspicuous and widely discussed phenomenon although Japanese schools are not generally violent places. At the same time, discussions of *Ijime* strike a special nerve among many Japanese commentators because they readily recognize it as a difficult-to-avoid and "dark" collectivistic phenomenon frequently shrouded in secrecy. It represents the unattractive underside of a group-oriented, pressured, conformity-demanding, highly regulated but also rapidly changing society. In contrast to the Japanese situation, in the United States the more general forms of school violence, including shootings and knifings, have been the focus of national debate, with discussions of bullying taking second place because it results in deaths and serious injuries only rarely. In international comparisons, Japanese rates of bullying and *Ijime* are on the low side. Nevertheless, a disproportionate number of *Ijime* cases involve insidious and frequently silent forms of group bullying, with girls at least as likely to practice the more psychologically oriented arts of social isolation as boys.

Many victims remain quiet about their difficult lives, and neither parents, teachers, nor school principals are likely to understand the full extent of bullying in schools. The victims may believe that bullying is their own responsibility and they should endure it, they should not "bother" others with their problems, their teachers are unable or unwilling to help them, and telling authority figures about the bullying situation may only lead to further bullying incidents rather than their disappearance. In other words, some victims may fear acts of revenge by their classmates and so-called friends.

Because incidents of *Ijime* are frequently hidden, they are not easily controlled. In addition, the authority structures of Japanese schools tend to make it difficult to reduce *Ijime*; many teachers are not in tune with their students and it is uncertain whether introducing additional school rules and regulations will be all that successful in reducing the insidiousness of *Ijime*. It will be interesting to see whether current changes in the school curriculum, including a reduction of hours of instruction, the introduction of school counselors, and other measures will be successful in reducing incidents of *Ijime* and *Futoukou*.

Until recently, Western observers of Japanese schools and adolescents have presented us with predominantly positive descriptions of Japan's educational system and pointed to the excellent scores that Japanese students have achieved in international educational comparisons (e.g., LeTendre, 2002; Reischauer, 1988; Stevenson & Stigler, 1992; White, 1987, 1993). White (1987), for instance, held up Japanese society as a model educational society profoundly committed to its children and to educational excellence. In contrast to these works, our more somber analysis points to some of the hidden psychological costs of the Japanese educational system which, however, have become more visible in recent years. *Ijime* and *Futoukou* have proven difficult-to-solve problems whose roots reach deeply into the foundations of Japan's national culture, educational institutions, family life, attitudinal differences between the generations, and changing social conditions.

If Japanese society is indeed committed to its children and adolescents as the harbingers of its future, it needs to look more closely at the structural reasons responsible for the present crisis of its educational institutions. While many Japanese educators, commentators, and the public have clearly recognized that the prevalence of *Ijime* and *Futoukou* points to some important flaws in its school system, it remains unclear whether the political will exists to reform it in a thorough manner.

NOTE

1. Some Japanese readers will probably be surprised about the preceding comments since they may believe that the Japanese educational system is undergoing a severe crisis. When making such a judgment, they implicitly or explicitly compare Japan's school conditions during the last decade to those prevailing in the 1970s and 1980s. In addition, Japanese observers may be influenced by their perceptions of, and comparisons to, the educational systems of other East Asian and neo-Confucian societies such as China, Korea, Singapore, and Taiwan. However, when compared to schools in the United States and various European countries,

Japanese schools still function in a more efficient, less disorganized, and less violent way. It would, for instance, be difficult to find a single Japanese school that resembles one of the more dysfunctional inner-city schools in the United States.

REFERENCES

Benesse Educational Institute (1996). *Chyugakusei nau* [Junior high school students, now]. No. 54.

Council for Research of Children and Students' Problematic Behaviors (1996a). *Jidou seito no Ijime ni kansuru ankeitochyousakekka* [Results of questionnaire survey on bullying of children and students]. Government Report.

Council for Research of Children and Students' Problematic Behaviors (1996b). *Jidou seito no mondaiikoudoutou ni kansuru chyousa kaigi houkoku* [Report of Council for Research of Children and Students' Problematic Behaviors]. Government Report.

Crick, N.R., Nelson, D.A., Morales, J.R., Cullerton-Sen, C., Casas, J.F. & Hickman, S. (2001). Relational victimization in childhood and adolescence: I hurt you through the grapevine. In J. Juvonen & S. Graham (Eds.), *School-based harassment: The plight of the vulnerable and victimized* (pp. 196–214). New York: Guilford Press.

Hoshino, K. (2001). Higaishya to Kagaishyatono Kankei [Relations between bully and victim]. In Y. Morita (Ed.), *Ijime no kokusai hikaku kenkyu* [Cross-national study of bullying] (pp. 73–92). Tokyo: Kaneko shyobou.

LeTendre, G.K. (2000). *Learning to be adolescent: Growing up in U. S. and Japanese middle schools.* New Haven, CT: Yale University Press.

Management and Coordination Agency (1998). *Ijime , toukoukyohi, rounaibouryokumondai ni kansuru ankeito chyousakekka* [The results of a survey on school bullying, refusal to attend schools, and school violence]. Government Report.

Masataka, N. (1998). *Ijime o yurusu shinri* [Psychology of allowing bullying]. Tokyo: Iwanami shyoten.

Matsuura,Y. (2001). Higaisha no ningenkankei [Relation between bullied students and bullies]. In Y. Morita (Ed.), *Ijime no kokusai hikaku kenkyu* [Cross-national study of bullying] (pp. 113–112). Tokyo: Kaneko shyobou.

Ministry of Education, Culture, Sports, Science, and Technology (1999). *Seito shidojyono shyomondai no genjyonitsite* [Current problems of student counseling and guidance]. Government Report.

Ministry of Education, Culture, Sports, Science, and Technology (2000a). *Seito shidojyono shyomondai no genjyonitsite* [Current problems of student counseling and guidance]. Government Report.

Ministry of Education, Culture, Sports, Science, and Technology (2000b). *Japanese government politics in education, science, sports, and culture.* Printing Bureau, Ministry of Finance.

Ministry of Education, Culture, Sports, Science, and Technology (2001). *Kyoikushokuin ni kakawaru chyokaishobuntou nitsuite* [Concerning disciplinary punishment and other situations of teachers]. Government Report.

Morita, Y. (Ed.). (2001). *Sekai no Ijime* [Bullying in the world]. Tokyo: Kaneko shyobou.

Morita, Y. (2001a). Kokusai hikakuchousa no shyomondai [Problems of cross-national studies]. In Y. Morita (Ed.), *Ijime no kokusai hikaku kenkyu* [Cross-national study of bullying] (pp. 1–12). Tokyo: Kaneko shyobou.

Morita, Y. (2001b). Ijimehigai no Jittai [Facts about victims of bullying]. In Y. Morita (Ed.), *Ijime no kokusai hikaku* kenkyu [Cross-national study of bullying] (pp. 31–54). Tokyo: Kaneko shyobou.

Morita, Y. & Kiyonaga, K. (1994). *Ijime : Kyositsu no yamai* [Bullying: The classroom crisis]. Tokyo: Kaneko shyobou.

Morita, Y., Soeda, H., Soeda, K. & Taki, M. (1999). Japan. In P.K. Smith, Y. Morita, J., Junger-Tos, D. Olweus, R. Catalano, & P. Slee (Eds.), *The nature of school bullying: A cross-national perspective* (pp. 309–323). London: Routledge.

Naito, T. (1990). Moral education in Japanese public schools. *Moral Education Forum, 15(2),* 27–36.

Naito, T. & Gielen, U.P. (in press). The changing Japanese family: A psychological portrait. In J.P. Roopnarine & U. P. Gielen (Eds.), *Families in global perspective.* Boston: Allyn & Bacon.

Nansel, T. R., Overpeck, M., Pilla, R. S., Ruan, W. J., Simons-Morton, B. & Scheidt, P. (2001). Bullying behaviors among US youth: Prevalence and association with psychological adjustment. *Journal of the American Medical Association, 285(16),* 2094–2100.

Nihon keizai shinbun (1997). *2020 nen kara no keishō* [An alarm bell from the year 2020]. Tokyo: Nihon keizai shinbun.

Ogi, N. (1997). *Ijime boushi jissen puroguram* [Program for preventing bullying]. Tokyo: Gakuyo shobou.

Olweus, D. (1993). *Bullying at school: What we know and what we can do.* Oxford, UK: Blackwell.

Olweus, D. (1999). Norway. In P. K. Smith, Y. Morita, J. Junger-Tos, D. Olweus, R. Catalano, & P. Slee (Eds.), *The nature of school bullying: A cross-national perspective* (pp. 7–27). London, UK: Routledge.

Reischauer, E.O. (1988). *The Japanese today* (2nd ed.). Tokyo: Charles E. Tuttle.

Shimizu, Y. (1983). *Kodomo no shitsuke to Gakkouseikatsu* [The discipline of children and school life]. Tokyo: Tokyo University Press.

Shinmura, I. (1998). *Koujien* (5th ed.). Tokyo: Iwanami Shyoten.

Smith, P.K., Y. Morita,Y., Junger-Tos, J., Olweus, D., Catalano, R. & Slee, P. (Eds.). (1999). *The nature of school bullying: A cross-national perspective.* London: Routledge.

Stevenson, H. W. & Stigler, J. W. (1992). *The learning gap: Why our schools are failing and what we can learn from Japanese and Chinese education.* New York: Summit Books.

Tai, M. (2001). *Ijime* taiou to sonokouka [Treatments for bullying and their effects]. In Y. Morita (Ed.), *Ijime no kokosai hikaku kenkyu* (pp. 123–144). Tokyo: Kaneko shyobou.

Takemura, K. (2001). *Ijime* raretatoki no kimochi [Acts and feelings in being bullied]. In Y. Morita (Ed.), *Ijime no kokusai hikaku kenkyu* [Cross-national study of bullying] (pp. 95–112). Tokyo: Kaneko shyobou.

Taki, M. (1992). *Ijime* koui no hassei jyokyo ni kansuru jishoytekikenkyu-*Ijime* koui no koujoka to kagai, higaikeiken no ippanka [Empirical study of "*Ijime*" behavior]. *Japanese Journal of Educational Research, 52,* 113–123.

Taki, M. (2001a). *Ijime* no houhou, basho [Ways and locations of bullying]. In Y. Morita (Ed.), *Ijime no kokusai hikaku kenkyu* [Cross-national study of bullying] (pp. 55–72). Tokyo: Kaneko shyobou.

Taki, M. (2001b). Kokusaihikakuchyousakenkyu no igi to kongono kadai [Significance of cross-national studies and future tasks]. In Y. Morita (Ed.), *Ijime no kokusai hikaku kenkyu* [Cross-national study of bullying] (pp. 192–203). Tokyo: Kaneko shyobou.

Takatoku, S. (1999). *Ijime mondai handobukku* [Handbook of bullying problems]. Tokyo: Tsugeshyoboushinshya.

Talbot, M. (2002). Mean girls and the new movement to tame them. *The New York Times Magazine,* February 24, Section 6, pp. 24–29, 40, 58, 64–65.

The Japan Times Online (2001). Japan's public schools grow more violent. August 25, 2001.
    http://www.japantimes.cajp/cgi-bin/getarticle.pl5?nn20010825a2.htm.   Downloaded
    May 16, 2002.
Triandis, H.C. (1995). *Individualism and collectivism*. Boulder, CO: Westview.
White, M. (1987). *The Japanese educational challenge: Commitment to children*. New York: The
    Free Press.
White, M. (1993). *The material child: Coming of age in Japan and America*. New York: Free Press.
Yomiuri (1995). *Ijime tsukamenu jittai* [Bullying: Uncovering the real situation]. Dec. 15.

Chapter **10**

A Perspective on Child Abuse in the Philippines
Looking at Institutional Factors

Richard Velayo

In many Third World countries, violence against children continues to be a pressing problem. Such violence is often manifested in the form of abuse. The Philippines is similar to many other Asian countries in the way Western culture has greatly influenced its development and way of life. The Philippines' historical roots began with Spanish colonization four centuries ago. This colonization contributed to the development of a culture in which the church and the school usually emerge as the most influential institutions influencing the way children are brought up. Cases of physical and sexual abuse, as well as those considered "abuses of neglect," continue to be of major societal concern. Thus, violence in schools as well as other institutional sectors of society that play a role in a child's development is a problem of global proportions faced by most developed and developing countries.

Despite the increasing global awareness of children's rights, there continues to be numerous documented cases of child abuse in many countries. In the Philippines, there are approximately 33 million children under the age of eighteen and authorities estimate that in 1999 alone, there were roughly 12,000 cases of child abuse (Yacat & Ong, 2002). The Department of Social Welfare and Development (DSWD) documented an increase in cases of child abuse and neglect from 1991 to 1997 (Yacat & Ong, 2002). Of these cases 44.5% were classified as sexual abuse, 21.67% as physical abuse, and 15.07% as neglect. The Philippine General Hospital Child Protection Unit (PGH-CPU) (1998) also reported a similar trend during the same year in which 67.7% of the cases they handled were documented as child abuse cases. Physical abuse constituted only 10% of these cases. While the statistics suggest that the majority of alleged perpetrators of abuse are familiar to the victims of child abuse, 66% of abusers are family members, the statistics fail to reflect the abuse occurring in the Philippine institutions of the school and the church. Abuse in these institutions is difficult to measure for many reasons. Because of the esteem schools and the church hold in Philippine society, cultural factors prevent child abuse authorities from recognizing and addressing abuse occurring in the schools and church. This paper will illustrate a perspective on the problem of child abuse in Philippine society and will analyze institutional influences that have contributed to this problem.

The view of the child in Philippine society causes institutions and authorities to overlook and oftentimes encourage child abuse. Philippine authorities and institutions lack a clearly defined definition of abuse, especially in regards to verbal and psychological abuse. In conjunction with the Filipino view of the child, institutions remain focused on violence committed by children, as opposed to the violence committed by educators and clergy members. Much attention has been paid to child abuse occurring in families; however, with the considerable power and trust afforded to schools and the church, abuse often remains overlooked or under-examined. Research indicates that physical abuse cases may be underreported, and, therefore, the statistics fail to depict the actual incidences of abuse in communities. This underreporting may reflect a belief that only the most extreme forms of abuse necessitate intervention by the authorities. Thus, the home becomes overemphasized as the location where most abuse occurs. Numerous studies, articles, and books explore and validate the dominance of the family situation in the experience of abuse. A study conducted by the Psychosocial Trauma and Human Rights Program of the University of the Philippines Center for Integrative and Development Studies (UP-CIDS) stated that while both parent and child groups generally situated abuse in the context of parental discipline, some important differences existed. First, parents held more normative views of abuse and described it as a deviation from appropriate discipline. These parents perceived abuse as a manifestation of the abuse of parental authority and the taking advantage of the child's relatively inferior position in the family. Children viewed abuse less in terms of power, but rather as a betrayal of trust (Yacat & Ong, 2002). Children believed disciplinary measures became abusive when the discipline became excessive, intentional, and unreasonable. The characteristics of child abuse, the misuse of trust and power, are not exclusive to the family and can occur in any adult-child relationship which is based on trust and power.

BRIEF HISTORY OF EDUCATION IN THE PHILIPPINES

Education in the Philippines originates from the merging of the secular with the spiritual realms (Yacat & Ong, 2002). The school's primary task remains education; however, the church also retains the right and responsibility to look after children's moral and spiritual needs, creating a school-like atmosphere. The high number of private sectarian schools in the country demonstrate the church's continuing mandate to teach children religion and morality.

Prior to the Spanish colonization period (1521–1898), child socialization and instruction occurred mainly in the home rather than as part of any single institution. The colonization of the Philippines by Spain transferred the responsibility of the administration of education to the Catholic Church. The Spanish sought to indoctrinate the children with religion as a means to reach parents (Bennagen, Villones, & Eco, 1994). Along with the introduction of religion, Spanish culture, and formal schooling into Filipino society, the Spanish colonizers also introduced a separate curriculum for men and women (Vernon, 1962). Education for women rested on the assumption that women remained intellectually inferior; therefore, their curriculum focused less on academic subjects and more on domestic and social skills. In addition, education remained a benefit for only the *penisulares* (Spain-born Spaniards), *insulares* (Spaniards born in the Philippines) and the *mestizos* (half Spanish/Filipino) (Valeriano, 2003). The purpose of the church-administered education remained to keep the Philippine people subservient to the reigning Spanish colonists.

The Revolutionary government, established in 1898, attempted to sever the relationship between church and state by removing religion from the curriculum of government-supported schools while bringing education to the masses. However, the separation only commenced during the American period, in particular during the 1940s. During this period, American teachers used English as the medium of instruction as they focused on industrial skills (Tiongson, 1986). The separation of church and state created two institutions focused on the instruction of children. Despite their separation, the educational principles of each institution remain along with the adult-child relationship based on trust, power, and reliance.

The historical impact of the formation of a formal school system and the introduction of the Catholic Church developed trusted and culturally important institutions in which close adult-child relationships were important. Formal institutions such as the church and school define adult-child relationships very clearly as authoritative and hierarchical (Yacat & Ong, 2002). The adult holds the power over the child in both institutions. In the classroom, the students are expected to follow the teacher's instruction. The church retains the same power structure, in which young boys serve as assistants and alter boys. In fact, communities often gain spiritual guidance through apprenticing their young people to the parish priest. In the home, school, and church, the adult holds the position of authority. Children lack the position to ask questions or challenge adult authority; rather, they recognize the need to succumb to authority.

The beliefs and attitudes held by parents, students, teachers, and the clergy toward discipline contribute to the under-reporting of abuse in the churches and schools. Parents, teachers, and the clergy believe that children deserve appropriate discipline. In accordance with the view of children as "tabula rasa," discipline plays a large role in shaping unruly children into model citizens. With teachers and clergy entrusted with shaping the behavior and knowledge of children, child abuse often is overlooked or is perceived as necessary in shaping the child.

Teachers perceive discipline as necessary in imparting knowledge to young people (Nepomuceno, 1981). Schoolteachers often believe that punishment (as a form of discipline) maintains a quiet and orderly learning environment, promotes self-discipline, serves as a deterrent to potential offenders, and prevents offenders from becoming repeat offenders. During the period when the church took responsibility for education, two types of teaching styles became prevalent: the dogmatic and the liberal.

The dogmatic teaching style is authoritarian and reflects the values of the feudalistic system. This type of teaching became prominent in disciplining students in elementary schools, secondary schools, and universities, and the discipline took the form of corporal punishment. The liberal teaching style, on the other hand, is based on the principles of science and competition, and it consists of subtracting time from desirable activities or adding additional academic work. The American period (1889–1941) marked a change from the dogmatic teaching style to a consistently liberal style of teaching.

The change to liberalism brought with it more insidious styles of discipline. Under this liberal style, teachers use strategies such as hitting, slapping, and verbally abusing students in order to embarrass them. While there exist an order in the Teacher Service Manual which prohibits the use of physical, emotional, and verbal punishment at present, the above forms of embarrassment comprise the most frequent used forms of reprimand (Tan, 1982; Yacat & Ong, 2002). Despite the role of the school in protecting children from abuse at home, children suffer from all kinds of abuses in school, including the shouting invectives at them, embarrassing them, requiring them to complete work unrelated to school, and physically and even sexually abusing them. Teachers have become trained to identify and report failings of the home, to nurture children, and to care for them. The church remains the primary provider of assistance to abuse victims, but suffers the same pitfalls as the school.

SCHOOL AND CHURCH: INSTITUTIONAL POWERS IN THE PHILIPPINES

The perceived legitimacy of authority allows the school and church to obtain and exert power over their respective domains. Therefore, the representatives of these two institutions have been considered experts in their respective fields. Church representatives preside over matters that are considered divine, moral, or supernatural, while schoolteachers are the authority in secular matters such as knowledge acquisition. These functions earn educators and church workers high regard in Philippine society which regards these careers as very noble professions (Yacat & Ong, 2002).

The school and the church maintain significant importance in Philippine society in affording children education, morality, and future opportunities in society, thereby affording the school and the church the primary antecedents of abuse: trust and power. Schools maintain high-esteem in Philippine society due to the view that education is necessary for a successful and meaningful future. Filipino families regard education as the highest priority and a lasting legacy to their children. The primary role of the school is to provide a place for learning, for gathering information and skills that are essential to a child's integration into the adult world. In elementary and high school, students learn basic proficiency for living and the background needed for higher education (the latter perceived to be the ticket to a well-paying job and a stable career). In this regard, the school is greatly valued as a valid means of social mobility, especially when education is seen largely as a privilege, rather than a right, in a poverty-stricken country.

THE SCHOOL AND THE FILIPINO CHILD

Those children whose families fail to secure a proper education face bleak prospects. Filipino children who experience conflicts with the law tend to represent the most disadvantaged and marginalized sectors of society. Many of the children who are raised in poverty and who receive little or no education become suspected of committing minor crimes (Amnesty International, 2003). Those children who lack education, family, or community support are most likely to become delinquent or join gangs. A joint study conducted by non-governmental organizations (NGOs) in the Philippines in 2000 reported that 90 percent of children in conflict with the law experienced abuse at home. Many of these children who flee their homes join the Philippines' large population of street children, estimated to number at least 200,000 (Amnesty International, 2003). Despite the introduction of laws and safeguards designed to protect children in custody, grave defects in the juvenile justice system still exist and has led to widespread abuses within the law enforcement establishment. Nevertheless, the Philippine government and has ratified the UN Convention on the Rights of the Child (CRC). Amnesty International has identified many serious problems in the treatment of children in detention, including: 1) torture or ill-treatment following arrest and in detention: including beatings, sexual assault, electric shock, being threatened with death; 2) detention with adults in overcrowded facilities which fail to meet minimum international standards for treatment of prisoners; 3) denial of prompt access to social workers, lawyers, and relatives following arrest; 4) lengthy delays in being brought before a judge, and delays of many months before trial which sometimes result in children serving longer than the maximum sentence for their alleged offense; and 5) inappropriate sentencing and treatment due to the absence of any requirement to establish the age of the child on arrest. At least eight juveniles are under sentence of death (Amnesty International, 2003). Therefore, those children unable to secure the proper education face poverty, street life, and the possibility of abuse in other institutional systems.

As a result of the view of education as a privilege, and in light of the terrible possibilities occurring without education, parents inadvertently transfer the responsibility of teaching almost entirely to the school, while also entrusting to it their children's future as flourishing members of society. Families, therefore, spend large amounts of effort, time, and money in securing their children's education. Due to the transfer of power from families to educators, the school becomes an extension of the home where socialization occurs, in which children imbibe the culture, learn the norms of society, and explore the limits of proper behavior through their interactions with their teachers and peers. What children learn regarding right, wrong, and justice comes from both the school and the home. Metaphorically, teachers become referred to as "second parents" of the child.

The school's view of the child also contributes to the style of teaching espoused by the Philippine school. Filipino adults view children as born "tabula rasa;" therefore, adults must constantly correct and instruct children regarding appropriate behavior. This in turn creates a learning environment that encourages children to act and think in a passive manner, making them vulnerable to disciplinary actions designed to shape them into model citizens. Thus, the same pattern emerges in both the school and the home: the adults maintain absolute power over children. This imposing power becomes hypothetically justified by the noble responsibility of molding ignorant, passive, amoral, disorderly children into smart, active, compassionate, and obedient adults (Yacat & Ong, 2002).

THE CHURCH AND THE FILIPINO CHILD

The population of the Philippines is approximately 83% Roman Catholic, 9% Protestant, 5% Muslim, 3% Buddhist or other. The Catholic Church in the country draws its power from the historical and traditional role religion plays in the history of the Philippines and in Filipino life. Mabunga (1997) outlined two functions of the church: as a *buttress*, providing support, reconciliation, and consolation to individuals experiencing personal and social crisis while addressing their spiritual and emotional needs. The church also plays the role of the *prophetic*, a social critic answering the need for direction and vocalizing opinions regarding certain "secular" issues such as family planning, abortion, divorce and capital punishment (Yacat & Ong, 2002).

CHURCH AND SCHOOL AS CULTURALLY INTERTWINED INSTITUTIONS OF POWER

With the power bestowed on teachers and clergy members, the adult-child relationships within the institutions of the school and church closely mirror the Filipino family structure in regard to power and trust. The power and trust involved in these relationships remain primarily hierarchical in nature, where the individual holding the power maintains authority over a group or a unit of society. In the Filipino family, members become classified and ordered according to the power hierarchy. The father, the family's foundation, claims the upper-most rank in the hierarchy (this attitude originated during the Spanish occupation, due to the patriarchal nature of Spanish society); the mother occupies the next rank, followed by the eldest son or daughter, and continuing with children occupying ranks according to their birth order. The individual possessing the power retains complete control over all the subordinates and the subordinates surrender unconditionally. Therefore, the individual holding the power by virtue of the authority attributed to them in the dynamic of the power-trust relationship maintains the ability to manipulate, control and maneuver those beneath him (Valeriano, 2003). In turn, the child or subordinate remains obligated to submit to the power holder's commands and manipulation, while trusting that the powerful individual will protect his or her well-being.

With the power afforded to schoolteachers and clergy as the "second parents" of children, this power hierarchy exists outside the bounds of the family.

While abuse occurs within the adult-child dynamic in both the church and the school, abuse remains a largely invisible and silenced phenomenon. A preliminary survey conducted by Yacat and Ong (2002) of newspaper articles, interviews with staff and disclosure reports from the Center for the Prevention and Treatment of Child Sexual Abuse (CPTCSA), and disclosures from the roundtable discussion revealed that among reported abuse cases regarding the church and schools only the extreme forms of abuse merited attention and that the perpetrators rarely faced punishment. The extreme forms of abuse meriting attention include rape, molestation, sexual harassment, and extreme physical violence. CPTCSA received forty five disclosures of abuse in the years of 1997 and 1998. Teachers represented the perpetrators in six of these cases. The demographics of the cases consisted of five male victims, 10–13 years of age, and a lone female victim of 16 years of age. These cases involved fondling, the touching of private parts, and molestation. Another example involved a teacher who banged the heads of two boisterous students together, resulting to the death of one.

While these examples demonstrate the most drastic forms of abuse, the authorities consider some behaviors or circumstances less serious and therefore not abusive. For example, a mother who filed a complaint against a teacher for allegedly slapping her daughter in the face was instructed by the school principle to forget about the whole thing. However, she brought it to the attention of the Parent and Teacher Association and rather than receiving sympathy, she faced reprimand from the PTA for blowing the situation out of proportion. In frustration, she transferred her daughter to another school halfway though the school year (Yacat & Ong, 2002). This case illustrates the difficulties faced in accurately assessing the extent of abuse in the school. Only the most egregious forms of abuse become reported, and parents and children become discouraged from reporting less severe forms of abuse due to the threat of public embarrassment.

In addition to the under-reporting of lesser forms of abuse, teachers and clergy reported to engage in the more extreme forms of abuse are rarely punished. The church remains inclined to conceal incidents of abuse in order to protect its gracious image instead opting to settle cases, violating Republic act 7610 (Child Abuse Law) through extra-legal means. For example:

> The very first case handled by CPTCSA involved a priest who had a sexual relationship with his 15-year-old niece. It was found that, at age 12, the girl had come to live with her uncle to escape her father who had sexually abused her since she was eight years old. A neighbor who belonged to a non-governmental

organization occasionally saw the girl crying outside her uncle's house, and was convinced that she had been exhibiting symptoms of sexual abuse. The neighbor sought assistance from CPTCSA. After an investigation, it was determined that the girl should be separated from the priest and her parents needed to be informed. After her parents were found, a series of negotiations took place. The parents succeeded in covincing their daughter to drop the charges against the priest. He was never prosecuted in any judicial court. CPTCSA filed a report regarding the incident to the church authorities. They later learned that the priest, who was up for candidacy as bishop, was neither promoted nor given any pastoral assignment after the abuse complaint was known (Yacat & Ong, 2002)

Another case reported to the CPTCSA concerned a priest from a prestigious and exclusive school accused of molesting several high school boys during the students' spiritual retreat. From among a batch of 40 students, only one boy revealed his painful story. However, no legal action against the priest was taken and the school authorities transferred the priest to another school under their order (Yacat & Ong, 2002). The scarcity of reports regarding abuses within the church and school does not demonstrate that such abuses remain isolated cases. Rather, the lack of reports signifies the problems regarding identifying and reporting abuse. The two predominant reasons for the lack of reporting and documentation of abuses cases remains the difficulty in identifying abuse and the problems inherent in the system for reporting abuse.

CULTURAL VAGUENESS IN DEFINING ABUSE

The varying definitions of abuse cause difficulties in delineating abuse and discipline (de la Cruz, Protacio, Balanon, Yacat, & Francisco, 2000). Teachers' belief in the necessity of discipline in molding young students often obscures the line between abuse and discipline. For example, many parents feel that if a teacher uses inadvertently embarrassing tactics in order to encourage the child to behave more appropriately, then those tactics do not reflect abuse. Due to the parental stamp of approval of these tactics teachers use hitting, humiliation, slapping, and throwing things in the name of discipline. Therefore, many children experience these types of abuses every day of their school lives. Some parents accept this behavior as occurring for their child's own good; however, other parents view this abuse as a failure to respect children's rights. For those parents who object to this sort of discipline, abuse occurs anytime an individual hurts a child in any way, regardless of intention or consciousness, which consequently affects the child's development as a human being. One parent key-informant in the study conducted by Yacat and Ong (2002) explained why teachers' actions towards children sometimes lead to abuse: "We may know children's rights, but then the reality is that teachers are tasked to discipline children, and they are overloaded and underpaid. How does one keep from hurting a child (whether verbally, emotionally or physically) when he or she is under chronic stress?" Schoolteachers gain considerable attention for their lower pay. One Filipino politician stated that, "The overworked but underpaid teachers have always been extolled as the unsung heroes of our generation, and rightly so. On the hands of the teachers who mold young minds lies the future of the nation. Such being the case, the state I believe owes it to our educators to provide for their health and physical well-being" (Drilon, 1998). Teachers receive a great deal of understanding despite their treatment of children, due to their status as heroes and as builders of the future.

Of all the various definitions of abuse, only one response given in the Yacat and Ong (2002) study adhered strictly to all of the principles of the UN-CRC. The definition specified by the children, the teachers, and one parent reflects the Filipino cultural reality: Our children have grown up and are growing up accepting the fact that discipline and punishment (whether corporal, verbal, or any other type) go hand in hand. Children understand the necessity of these kinds of punishment and are willing to bear them as long as they are given love and justice. Due to the prevalence of abuse, it becomes difficult for people, especially children, to discern whether abuse is occurring or has occurred. The line, therefore, becomes blurred regardless of any experience of abuse. Parents may dismiss abusive actions committed by teachers because they either practice this kind of discipline at home or they may justify the teacher's behavior by deducing that the child's misbehavior merits the treatment.

Several issues create barriers to the reporting of abuse. First, children become afraid of ridicule or questions regarding their credibility by family, friends, and authorities. The close relationship between abuse and discipline also contributes to children's confusion in that some children begin to believe that they deserve the abuse. Therefore, victimized children hesitate to reveal abuse due to the fear that the community will side with the highly respected individual. This reluctance could also stem from the powerful role these institutions play in the community, which considers the church and school sacred institutions whose sanctity might become tainted by allegations of abuse. Due to these institutional roles in the community, the community would also face the blame for the abuse. Any abuse committed by an agent of a school or church is perceived as disrespectful to the community in which it exists. Due to the conjoined nature of the church, school and community, child victims and their families face a lack of support in reporting abuse. These institutions assume a protective stance regarding the perpetrators' welfare, rather than providing assistance and services to the victim, often to an extant that "victim blaming" occurs.

As the school and the church play an important and noble function in Philippine society, the possibility that some of the members of these institutions are abusers violates the general schema. Therefore, reports of abuse face a violent reception from members of the church, school and parent organizations in an attempt to preserve the righteous image of these institutions. In fact, the lack of support for any reports of abuse and the opposition against the very idea that abusive practices occur within the confines of the school or church, serves this purpose. In the case of the church, people find incredible difficulty in imagining, let alone accepting, that God's representatives would commit such atrocities. Due to the denial or opposition of the community regarding abuse, cases many go unnoticed, unreported, stagnate once reported, or become silenced.

The definition of abuse as occurring within the context of interpersonal encounters between children and adult authority figures limits the focus of abuse as an extreme infraction on interpersonal relationships. This limited view allows certain abuses to masquerade as disciplining practices and directly affect the developing child's view of the world and acceptance of abuse. Even organizations designed to develop policies, regulations, and sanctions remain ineffective when confronted with disciplining practices that border on abuse and become unsupportive or simply exist to pay lip-service to children's rights. As one youth participant shared:

> When it comes to participation in schools, yes, there is a student government but it is a token structure because it doesn't have any real power. And even if it were told to hold meetings, what would it organize? The president of the student government might be asked to speak in the program, or the students might be asked to prepare a song or dance number, but that's about the only participation that they get from children. (Yacat & Ong, 2002, p. 12)

Other examples include implementation of student fees, forced attendance at parties, mandatory sale of tickets in school-sponsored projects and programs, and the repression of sexual knowledge both in school and in the church. Schools fail to empower students to improve their quality of their lives when the authorities exert power and manipulation over student created organizations. In effect, these practices reflect the prevailing notions of children perpetuated by these institutions. As Philippine society widely accepts the need for discipline and the role of authority figures empowered by institutions to administer and instill such discipline, the roles that this view produces lend themselves to abuses.

Lack of a common definition contributes to difficulties in maintaining an accurate estimate of the problem and the creation of viable solutions. The examination of the perpetrators in the context of a network, not as an error confined to a single person, helps refine the analysis of the phenomenon of child abuse. This perspective suggests that a vast, complex, and organized network of abusers exists with each one reinforcing each other's interests, thus perpetuating the cycle of abuse. In an effort to better understand child abuse as a distinct social phenomenon and thus determine the parameters of further intervention design, Protacio-Marcelino, de la Cruz, Balanon, Camacho, & Yacat (1998) identify six elements that constitute child abuse. They present the six elements as, 1) the type of abuse, 2) circumstance of abuse, 3) degree and duration of the abuse, 4) age, 5) gender, and 6) the perpetrator. The theories, methods, and approaches used in interventions are primarily based on western models with a distinct dearth of local theorizing from the Philippine perspective. Existing interventions directed towards child abuse cases remains basically eclectic. These intervention initiatives remain in an experimental stage in which the most effective method remains unidentified and largely unexplored. For intervention work on child abuse in the Philippines to elevate to the next level, what's needed is proper documentation and impact evaluation, as well as the development of localized theories and methodologies for assisting the victims and survivors of child abuse (Protacio-Marcelino, de la Cruz, Balanon, Camacho, & Yacat, 2002).

PREVENTION EFFORTS AND OTHER RECOMMENDATIONS

Many programs designed to prevent violence in schools focus on the children as the source of violence. This may occur in response to concerns in the United States regarding childhood aggression. One Philippine preschool quoted the Children's Hospital of Pittsburgh with a list of adult tasks to reduce childhood aggression (School Violence: What Parents Can Do). Other community-oriented programs attempt to decrease youth violence through the integration of community, school, and church initiatives. For example, following his appointment, the Philippine National Police (PNP) Chief, Police Director General Leandro R. Mendoza, established two community-based initiatives aimed at creating lasting deterrents to crime. The first program involved schools in partnership with the PNP in which teachers organized school community coordinating councils. These councils planned, implemented, supervised, and monitored crimes occurring on school campuses and in the surrounding vicinities. The councils were charged with increasing student awareness of the dangers of illegal drugs, criminality, campus violence, and similar potentials for crime in schools. In addition, the councils established networks with local officials, civic leaders, and other non-government organizations. Part of their program initiative involved sports activities and other physical education programs. A majority of the crime prevention activities fell under the council's jurisdiction while the police maintained a visible presence on the campuses to ward off criminal elements. The second program sought the involvement of the church in the prevention of the sale and use of illegal drugs at the community level. This program remained similar to the school-based councils, but it maintained a wider area of coverage. The newly formed church community coordinating councils conducted forums, seminars, conferences, and other public gatherings with the goal of enlightening members against the use of illicit drugs and to warn against the effects of public apathy. The twin programs aimed to empower the community to play active roles in crime prevention, especially in preventing the proliferation of drugs within the areas that are producing positive effects (anti-crime programs as effective antidotes to violence and crime). The programs initiated by Philippine authorities and institutions support the view that crime and violence in schools and communities originates from children's misbehavior and serves to reinforce the view of children as being in need of discipline. These programs fail to address the aggressive actions children in schools and churches experience on a daily basis and the aggression and acceptance of aggression they learn through the experience.

Due to the lack of information regarding child abuse in school and church, there exists a need for refining the identification and documentation process for abuse cases. Future strategies and initiatives should encompass the nature of both institutions (hierarchical, authoritative) and incorporate these features into any proposed action. First, students, teachers, and the clergy are in need of better education regarding the United Nations Convention on the Rights of the Child (UN-CRC) in order to appreciate and develop positive attitudes toward the importance of children's rights and to understand the respect and protection children deserve. Second, the increased involvement of parents in their children's education would lead to an increase in the detection, reporting, and documentation of abuse. Third, the institutionalization of abuse reporting to authorities along with educational campaigns regarding children's rights and abuse would lead to an increase in the number of reported child abuse events. Fourth, research on the various contexts of discipline, its different definitions, practices, and reasons would help solidify the definition of appropriate discipline. Fifth, venues for the facilitation of discussion regarding moral and ethical issues arising from the support of children's rights should be provided. Sixth, the policies regarding children's complaints regarding teacher- or administrator-inflicted abuse need review. In order to help protect children's rights schools should be encouraged to develop school policies which allow children to report complaints against their teachers, school staff, and administrators, create mechanisms for investigating the complaints, and penalize the offenders if investigation reveals the complaints to have merit. Seventh, a review of the notions regarding childhood and children as reflected in the school curriculum thereby necessitating revision of administrative policies. The perspective towards children and childhood requires investigation in regard to church doctrines, teachings, and practices in order to discern the extent to which the church promotes and accommodates abuses by the clergy. In summary, prevention efforts aimed at reducing the incidence of child abuse in Philippine institutions must encompass the systemic factors leading to abuse, namely, identification and reporting practices, as well as the general attitudes held by the institutions which contribute to the abuse.

While child abuse in the home remains widely studied and reported in the Philippines, child abuse in the church and school receive drastically less attention. The same adult-child relationship dynamic in regards to trust and power occurs in these institutions as it does in the home. The lack of a solid and universal definition of abuse, as well as a system for reporting abuse, necessitates initiating programs that prevent abuse. In addition, situations of child abuse within the church and school require that authorities examine the systemic issues inherent in these institutions that encourage and produce abuse instead of merely directing their attention toward childhood aggression and violence. While current prevention programs aimed at decreasing youth violence remain impressive, the concern originates from western attention to the issue of school violence. In order to confront the problem of abuse in church and school, policy makers must design intervention programs directed at the sources of abuse. By creating a more open atmosphere for reporting abuse and improving the documentation system, the dimensions underlying abuse in the church and the school might come to light and more effective programs for confronting the problem can then be developed.

REFERENCES

Amnesty International. (April 14, 2003). Philippines: A different childhood – the apprehension and detention of child suspects and offenders. Featured Paper (May, 2003). http://www.childprotection.org.ph/monthlyfeatures/jun2k3b.doc

Bennagen, P., Villones, B. & Eco, R. 1994. *A Historical Study of the Child in Philippine Society*. Quezon City: Salinlahi Foundation, Inc.

de la Cruz, T.; Protacio, E.; Balanon, F.; Yacat, J. & Francisco, C. 2000. *Trust and Power: Child Abuse in the Eyes of the Child and Parent*. Philippines: United Nations Children's Fund and Save the Children Fund.

Drilon, F.M. (October 5, 1998). Speech of Senator Franklin M. Drilon before the Centennial School Health and Nutrition Congress. Senator Franklin M. Drilon web site, Speeches, http://www.sendrilon.org.ph/speech19981005.html.

Mabunga, R. (1997) Values reflected in and the laity's response to the pastoral letters of the Catholic Bishops' Conference of the Philippines. In S. Diokno (ed.), *Democracy and Citizenship in Filipino Political Culture*, p. 175–190.

Nepomuceno, L.C. (1981). *Behavior Modification as an Approach to Problem Behaviors Encountered Among Elementary School Children*. Unpublished MA Thesis, UP College of Social Sciences and Philosophy, Dept. of Psychology.

Philippine General Hospital Child Protection Unit. (1998). *Annual Report*. Manila: Advisory Board Foundation.

Protacio-Marcelino, E., de la Cruz, M.T.C., Balanon, F.A.G., Camacho, A.Z.V. & Yacat, J. (1998). Child abuse in the Philippines: An integrated literature review and annotated bibliography. Reprinted from *UP-CIDS Chronicle*, January–June 1998, http://www.childprotection. org.ph/monthlyfeatures/archives/archive01.html

Protacio-Marcelino, E., dela Cruz, T., Balanon, F., Camacho, A. & Yacat, J. (2002). *Child Abuse in the Philippines: An Integrated Literature Review and Annotated Bibliography*. Quezon City: University of the Philippines Center for Integrative and Development Studies.

STI Prep School, STI Education Services Group. *School violence: What parents can do*. From Children's Hospital of Pittsburg. http://www.sti.edu.ph/prepschool/html/schlviolence.html

Tan, F.L. (1982). *Punishment: a Form of Social Control among Pangasinan Rural School Children*. Unpublished PhD Dissertation. Quezon City: UP College of Education.

Tiongson, N. (1986). *Kasaysayan ng Edukasyon sa Pilipinas (1863–1935)*. Education Resource Enter Occasional Paper, Aug–Sept, 1986.

Valeriano, A. (2003). *Within the premises: Child abuse in schools*. Featured Paper, http://www.childprotection.org.ph/monthlyfeatures/archives/feb2k3b.html

Vernon, G.M. (1962). *Sociology of Religion*. New York: McGraw Hill, Inc. p. 174.

Yacat, J.A. & Ong, M.G. (2002). *Beyond the home: Child abuse in the church and school*. Featured Paper, http://www.childprotection.org.ph/monthlyfeatures/archives/ag2k2a.html

Chapter 11

Manifestations of Violence in Arab Schools and Procedures for Reducing it

Ramadan A. Ahmed

The Arab World, Land, and People: An Overview

The Arab world consists of 22 countries in which live more than 300 million people. Including countries as geographically spread out as Morocco, Iran, Turkey, and Somalia, the Muslim world stretches from the Atlantic Ocean to Central Asia, from the Black to the Mediterranean Seas, and to the Horn of Africa. This territory is a vast realm of enormous historical and cultural complexity. It lies at the crossroads where Europe, Asia, and Africa meet, and it is part of all three. Throughout history, its influences have radiated to these continents and to practically every other part of the world as well. On the Mesopotamian Plain between the Tigris and Euphrates rivers and on the banks of the Egyptian Nile arose the very earliest civilizations. In this territory walked prophets whose religious teachings are still followed by hundreds of millions of people. In this territory, in the twentieth- and twenty-first centuries, the most bitter and dangerous conflicts on earth have occurred, conflicts that could still provoke far reaching, armed confrontations (Ahmed, in press c).

Violence and aggressive behavior are very old phenomenon, which started with the early beginnings of the human history. Many writers consider violence as one of the main attributes of human beings. Forms or manifestations of violence change according to the social, economic, political, and cultural circumstances (Berkowitz, 1993; Gelles, 1999; Ohlin & Tonry, 1989). Currently, the most common forms of violence are (1) domestic violence (such as marital violence, violence against women, child sexual and physical abuse, violence against adolescents, and the violence against elderly); (2) violence among school students; (3) demonstrations; (4) strikes; (5) riots; (6) mutiny events; (7) assassinations and assassination attempts; and (8) coup de l'etat or attempts of coup de l'etat (Ismail, 1988; 1996; Helmy, 1999; Hagezy, 1986; Ibrahim, 1999; Seiam, 1994; El-Matewally, 1995; O'Donoghue, 1995).

In the Arab world, as in other parts of the world, violence has become a common phenomenon due to many social, economic, political and cultural factors (Jalabi, 1998). For example, Egyptian society has witnessed, especially during the last twenty-five years, a marked increase in violent events which has caused much psychological, social, physical and economic damage. Since 1981, Egyptian society has become the subject of a great number of political and religious violent accidents, which have resulted in more than a thousand deaths and thousands of wounded (Ahmed & Khalil, 1998). In Algeria, the picture is even worse. Since the early 1990s, the violent political events continue daily and have caused more than one hundred thousand deaths and an equal number of wounded (Al-Otaibia, 2000; Sidaoui, 2000).

The executive director of the National School Safety Center (NSSC) in the United States, R.D. Stephens, wrote in 1994 that there are two types of school in the U. S., those that just had a crisis and those that are about to have one. Further, Stephens said that if a crisis can be defined as an incident which causes emotional disequilibrium in which one's natural coping and defense mechanisms are not available, and where there is no perceivable solution, then it would be rare to find a school campus that has not experienced a crisis in the form of violence. It seems that Stephen's statement is applicable for the Arab countries in which violence among school students has been markedly increased in the last three decades.

Arab researchers have showed an early (and continuous) interest in investigating the aggressive violent behavior and its correlates with a particular focus on delinquent behavior. Examples of these studies are the studies of Soueif, 1958, 1968; Farag, 1975; Sabry, 1989; and El-Dousseki, 1998 in Egypt; El-Kadem, 1995, in Qatar; Awad, 2002, in Saudi Arabia; and Naceur, 2001, in Algeria. The last three decades have witnessed a gradual increase in the number of violent actions among Arab school students. Arab school students' violent behavior has many manifestations such as violence against classmates, tyranny, bullying, attacking school teachers and principals, and violence against school and governmental property. Some Arab studies have pointed out this violent behavior and its manifestations among school students. Examples of these studies are the studies of

Hussein (1994); Ibrahim (1996); Kamel (2002); Lutfy (1992); and Rizk (1992) in Egypt; Hasan (1998) in Iraq; El-Kadem (1995) in Qatar; Al-Garni (2001) in Saudi Arabia; and Naceur (2001) in Algeria.

In response to the gradual increase of violence and aggressive behavior among school and university students, a number of Arab research studies have been conducted over the last two decades to determine reasons and the correlated variables of this phenomenon. Examples of these studies are the studies of Abdel-Hamid (1990); Al-Kamel and Soliman (1990); Awad (1994); Gabrial (1994); Hussein (1994); Abou-el-Kheir (1995); Saleh (1995); Faied (1996); Ibrahim (1996); Hedia (1998); and Saleh (1998) in Egypt; Al-Naser (2000) in Kuwait; and Al-Garni (2001) in Saudi Arabia. In the following sections, some of these research studies will be briefly reviewed.

VARIABLES ASSOCIATED WITH VIOLENCE AMONG SCHOOL STUDENTS

In the following sections some variables will be discussed with respect to violence among school students in Arab countries as reported in several Arab research studies, which have been conducted during the last three decades.

Age: The Development of Aggressive Behavior

As for the development of aggressive behavior among school children, Al-Fakherani, 1989 (cited in Nasr, 1994) applied Eysenck and Wilson's scale for assessing aggressive behavior in a sample of male and female nursery and primary school children in Egypt. Results showed that, in general, aggressive behavior correlated negatively with the increase of age, and nursery school children ranked significantly higher in instrumental (functional) or actual aggressive behavior, while primary school children ranked significantly higher in verbal aggression.

An Egyptian cross-sectional study (Hasan, 1993) investigated the development of the ability to understand convertive (changing) aggressive behavior in three samples of primary school male and female children, aged 6.6; 8.2; and 10.2 years, respectively. Results showed that children's ability to understand convertive aggressive behavior increases by increasing in age.

Sex (Gender)

Some Arab research studies, mainly Egyptian, have focused on the relationship between gender (sex) and aggression in different age samples of school students and showed that in general males have shown higher levels of aggressive behavior than have females. Examples of these studies are the studies of Hafez and Kasem (1993a); Shehata, 1990 (cited in Faied, 1996); Elian (1993); Moussa (1993); El-Seka (2000); Kamel and Al-Fakherani; (2002); and Omar (2001). Shehata 1990 (cited in Faied, 1996) studied the relationship between aggression and gender in a sample of secondary school male and female students in Egypt and found that aggression was higher among males compared with females.

Males clearly showed more manifestations of direct aggression and, to a lesser extent, manifestations of verbal aggression, while females have showed more manifestations of indirect aggression, and, to a lesser extent, manifestations of verbal aggression. In their study on 10 year old primary school Egyptian children, Hafez and Kasem (1993a) found that male children ranked significantly higher on a locally devised scale for assessing aggressive behavior than their female counterparts. In another Egyptian study (Elian, 1993) male school students aged between 13–17 years old ranked significantly higher on aggression scales compared with their female counterparts. Elian explained this result as a reflection of the dominance of masculine behavior in Arab societies. In the same vein, Omar (2001) investigated the impact of some demographic and social variables on violence in a sample of male and female Egyptian secondary school students. Results showed that male students, and also students with a higher socioeconomic status student, ranked significantly higher on the scale for assessing violence than female students, and students with a lower economic status. Moreover, Sheban (1996) found that the improvements in the levels of aggressive behavior, as a result of the introduction of a program for the development social skills in Egyptian primary school children, were significantly greater in the case of girls than in the case of boys. In the same context, Moussa (1993) compared the manifestations of aggressive behavior in two samples of deaf-mute and normal male and female adolescents, and found that while deaf-mute and normal males tended more to express explicit aggressive behavior, deaf-mute and normal females tended more to show implicit aggressive behavior. A recent Egyptian study (Kamel and Al-Fakherani, 2002) found that while 19–20 year old males ranked higher in the total score of hostility and overt hostility, female counterparts ranked unexpectedly higher on hostility toward others. In addition, El-Seka (2000) in Syria found that preschool boys have shown higher aggressive behavior levels and different manifestations or forms of aggression, as compared with girls.

Parental Behavior, Family Size, and Birth Order

Several Arab research studies have focused on the relationship between parental behavior and family size on the one hand and violence and aggression on the other hand. Examples of these studies are Nasr (1983); Hussein,

1986; Hashem, 1991 (cited in Safwet & El-Dousseki, 1993); El-Dematy (1997); Metwally (1981); Boanke, 1989 (cited in Nasr,1994); Al-Kamel and Soliman (1990); Elian (1993); Salama (1990); Hafez and Kasem (1993a); El-Deeb, 1995 (cited in El-Deeb,1996); Habib, 1995; Abdel-Aziz (1995); Gebril and Al-Mowafy (1985); Gebril (1989a); Helwa (1997); and Yussen, Al-Mosawy and Al-Zamel (1998). In the following sections examples of these studies' results will be briefly discussed.

One of the first studies on the relationship between family size, dependency, violence, and aggressive behavior in school students between 10–13 years old was conducted in Egypt by Salama (1990), who found positive correlations between levels of dependency, violence, aggressive behavior, and family size. Small families, (in comparison to large families) provide their children with a healthy atmosphere for sufficient communication between parents and children, especially in tense situations. Salama's results are in line with results of an Algerian study conducted by Boanke, 1989 (cited in Nasr, 1994) in which violence and aggressive behavior correlated positively with larger family size, lower educational level, and lower socio-economic status. Moreover, the studies of Hafez and Kasem (1993a) and Habib (1995) on a sample of primary school children, and Abdel-Aziz (1995) and Helwa's (1997) studies on the relationship between types of parental behavior and aggressive behavior in deaf-mute children (which reported in general that children's perception of parental behavior as more warm and more accepting) correlated negatively with aggressive behavior in children. However, children's perceptions of parental behavior as more neglectful and more indifferent correlated positively with children's levels of aggression. The study by El-Deeb, 1995 (cited in El-Deeb, 1996) on the relationship between violent/aggressive behavior and both family size and perceived parental behavior in samples of university students in Egypt and the Sultanate of Oman has obtained similar results. However, some earlier studies (Munier, 1983) did not report any affect of family size on the levels of aggression in children.

A recent Saudi study (Al-Garni, 2001) aimed to explore the relationship between deviant behaviors, school truancy, and academic performance and how both family structure and family function factors (e.g., family size, birth order, parenting, parent's work, educational levels, marital status, family type, sponsorship, and the parent-child attachment) could increase the likelihood of deviant behavior in 346 secondary school male students in Mecca City, Saudi Arabia. Results showed that only family size, parent-child attachment, sponsorship, and the parent's educational levels, were the most important predictors of deviant behaviors.

Another Egyptian study (Elian, 1993) focused on the relationship between perceptions of parental behavior (acceptance/rejection) and both self-assertiveness and aggression in a sample of male and female school students between 13–17 years of age. Results revealed significant positive correlations between perceptions of parental rejection and each of the following traits in children: aggression, negative self-evaluation, emotional instability, lack of personal efficiency, and negative view toward life.

A recent Egyptian study (Abou-el-Kheir, 1999) investigated the relationship between birth order, perceived maternal acceptance/rejection and some personality traits in a sample of Egyptian male and female adolescents with a mean age of 17.9 years, by using Rohner's Parental Acceptance/Rejection and Personality Assessment Questionnaires (PARQ and PAQ). Results showed a significant positive correlation between maternal rejection and adolescents' negative personality disposition, such as aggression, dependency, and emotional instability. No significant correlation has been found between both sex and birth order and maternal acceptance/rejection. As for the relationship between sex and birth order variables and the negative personality disposition, results showed that later-born females were more aggressive than their first-born counterparts, while the first-born males when compared with the later-born ones ranked higher on both dependency and negative self-evaluation. Abou-el-Kheir's results did not give support to the results of other previous Arab studies conducted by Munier (1983), and Hafez and Kasem (1993a) in which no relationship between birth order and children's aggressive behavior has been found.

In an early study conducted in Egypt on the relationships between mothers' aggression levels and levels of aggression in their children, and to also assess the effects of mothers' work on their behavior, Gebril and Al-Mowafy (1985) found a positive relationship between mothers' levels of aggression and authoritarianism with the levels of aggressive behavior in their children. No difference was found between working and nonworking mothers concerning their levels of authoritarianism and aggression.

El-Deeb (1990) studied 160 Kuwaiti boys and girls aged 3–5 and their mothers in order to assess the relationships between the mothers' aggressive behavior and their methods of socialization and child-rearing with the aggressive behavior in their children. Results showed that the mothers' unhealthy socialization practices (such as neglect, indifference, dominance, and aggression) have correlated positively with their children's aggressive behavior levels, and conversely, the mothers' healthy socialization practices (such as warmth, care, and kindness) have correlated negatively with their children's aggressive behavior levels. Results also revealed a positive relationship between the mothers' aggressive behavior levels and their children's aggression.

Gebril (1989a) investigated sex differences in both children's perceptions of parental behavior, the way boys and girls express aggression, and their relations within the family's social structure. The sample consisted of 459 13–23 year old male and female Egyptian students in intermediate schools, secondary schools, and university. Two locally devised questionnaires were developed for assessing both the children's perception of parental behavior and their expressions of aggressive behavior. Results showed that male children perceived their parents' behavior as more strict, dominant, authoritative, and neglectful, while female children perceived their parents' behavior as more forgiving, moderate, and protective. Larger size families, in contrast to smaller size families, tended to be more strict, inconsistent, authoritative, and neglectful in raising their children. Well-educated parents tended, more than less educated or un-educated parents, to be forgiving, consistent, use moderate means and types of parental control, and provide protection. No differences have been found between working and non-working mothers regarding socialization methods and practices they follow. Children of authoritative, inconsistent, and neglected families, and also children of larger-size families, showed higher levels of aggression when compared with the children of smaller-size families as well as children from families who use forgiveness, consistency, moderation and protection in raising their children. In comparison with male children, female children tended more to show both direct and indirect negative verbal aggression, whereas male children showed more direct and indirect, but active, verbal and physical aggression.

In a recent cross-cultural study of the effects of both family atmosphere and sociocultural backgrounds on children's personality, Yussen, et al. (1998) investigated the forms and manifestations of the abuse of preschool children and its psychological correlates, as seen by 150 Egyptian and 82 Kuwaiti mothers. The study used a locally devised questionnaire to assess the preferences of the following four dimensions: acceptance, hostility, neglect, and rejection. Results showed that forms and manifestations of the abuse of pre-school children by mothers differ due to the differences in the socio-cultural backgrounds of the mothers. More conservative mothers in both Egypt and Kuwait, mainly those with lower socio-economic status, tended to use hostile abuse (such as blaming, yelling, shouting, and threatening, etc.), while the more liberal mothers (mainly those with higher socio-economic status) tended more to use other forms of child abuse (such as neglect, rejection, and avoidance). The differences in forms of preschool child abuse in both Egyptian and Kuwaiti mothers showed that Egyptian mothers, in general, tended more to use rejection while Kuwaiti mothers, in general, tended more to use neglect as a dominant form of preschool child abuse. It was also reported that while Egyptian mothers have perceived their children as having more independence and a greater tendency to withdraw, Kuwaiti mothers have perceived their children as having a stronger self-image and higher aggressive tendencies. Yussen et al. (1998)

explained the last results as a reflection of the political, economic and social circumstances in both Egypt and Kuwait. As for the relationship between pre-school child abuse and demographic variables (e.g., child's age, sex, mother's educational and socioeconomic level and family's place of residence), results showed that preschool child abuse, as seen by Egyptian and Kuwaiti mothers, was more common in the case of elder and male children, than in the case of younger and female ones, Pre-school child abuse was also more common in the less educated or non-educated and poorer mothers than in the case of more highly educated and well to do mothers.

Absence of Father

Several Arab research studies (Abdalla, 1992; El-Sayed, 1996; and the studies which have been summarized by Ahmed, in press, a and b) have shown that factors such as the absence of fathers are associated with an increase in children's tendencies for violent and aggressive behavior or delinquency. Fathers might be absent from the home for several reasons (death, divorce, separation, prison, work in other country), and the absence leads to increased responsibility on the mother and may weaken the influence of the family on the children.

Family Milieu

Some earlier Arab research studies have investigated the effects of the cultural and family milieu on the children's behavior (Diab, 1965; Meleikan, 1965; Hasan, 1990; Mahmoud, 1990). It was claimed that families in Arab societies are generally characterized with high levels of authoritarianism which could lead later to submissiveness and other behaviors (such as aggression) in their children.

Some Arab research studies have dealt with the effect of family atmosphere and family education on children's behavior, and especially aggressive and violent behavior (Debais, 1977; Metwally, 1981; El-Dematy, 1997; El-Deba, 1999; Al-Mussallam, 2001; El-Omeran & Ebada, 1993). Some other Arab studies have tended to focus on the effects of conflicts between mothers and fathers or the effects of marital maladjustment on the behavior of their children (Hedia, 1998; El-Dousseki, 1998; El-Shebini, 1985; Al-Mazroui, 1990; Thabet, 1987 [cited in Abdel-Rahman, 1989]). In the following section, results of these studies will be briefly discussed.

In a study conducted by Thabet, 1987, on antisocial behavior in childhood and adolescence in Egypt (cited in Abdel-Rahman, 1989), it was shown that children's and adolescents' aggressive behavior is an outcome of the following interactive factors: 1.) biological factors (chromosomes, genes), 2.) unhealthy socialization practices and ineffective education, 3.)

lack of intelligence, in which aggressive behavior could be considered as a defensive behavior, and 4.) broken homes and especially children of divorced parents, in which children were found to be significantly higher on the aggressive behavior scale than were the children of married women.

In Egypt also, Hedia (1998) investigated the relationship between marital maladjustment between parents and both aggression and self-perception among parents and in their children, by using 107 well-educated couples between 35 and 50 years old and their male and female children (between age 10–12) who were enrolled in private language schools in Cairo, Egypt. Results revealed a significant positive correlation between both marital maladjustment and hostility among husbands and wives and both the higher levels of aggression and the negative self-perception in their children on the other side. However, male children in the maladjusted families were significantly higher in aggression compared with their female counterparts. Hedia's results agreed with results of some other previous studies such as El-Shebini's (1985) in Egypt, which showed that maladjustment among husbands and wives could lead to problematic behavior in their children, and Al-Mazroui (1990) in Kuwait, in which maladjusted families' children tended more to be emotionally unstable and have lower self-esteem.

An Egyptian study (Lutfy, 1992) sought the reasons for violent behavior among primary school children, as perceived by their parents. Parents reported that weak religiosity, mal- or insufficient education and socialization, poverty, feelings of physical and emotional deprivation, parents' unequal treatment of their children, and the insufficient activity (or the abuse) of leisure time, in that order, were the reasons for violent behavior among primary school children. A recent Egyptian study of 400 12–15 year-old intermediate and secondary school male students in Cairo, Egypt (Al-Meghrabi, 2000), reached similar results.

Instigators of the Aggressive Behavior

Few Arab studies have investigated the instigators of aggressive behavior. Among the studies that have been done are Hasan (1998) in Iraq; Refeay (1983); and Aly (2000) in Egypt, and Al-Taher and Al-Mosowy (1997) in Kuwait. In 1976, the National Center for Sociological and Criminal Research in Cairo, conducted a study on the relationship between violence, rebel against authority and violent actions on one hand and some demographic variables on the other hand (cited in Safwat & El-Dousseki, 1993). Results showed that the lower socioeconomic status accompanied with awareness of deprivation was the influential factor in the adolescents' and adults' tendency toward violent actions in Egypt.

Hasan (1998) studied instigators of aggressive behavior in 31, 18–30 years old Iraqi male convicted murders and found that murders used to live in slums and suburban areas, suffering from lack of necessary life's requirements or insufficient income, having low or no education, and having a lower self-image.

Aly (2000) investigated the influence of normal and deviant peer groups aged between 14–19 years, on secondary school male students in Egypt, and found that deviant peer group could lead other students who belong to or participate in such group, to acquire later behavior and mood problems. In an early Egyptian study, Refeay (1983) found that blind girls, compared with non blind ones, were higher in hostility and it was explained that blindness could increase hostility among female adolescents.

Some other Arab research studies have dealt with the effects of stressful life events on aggressive behavior among school students. In this context, Al-Taher and Al-Mosowy (1997) reported that the levels of aggressive behavior among school students in Kuwait have been increased due to the Iraqi invasion on Kuwait 1990/1991.

Place of Residence

To test the impact of the place of residence on violent and aggressive behavior among school students some Arab research studies have been conducted, among them the studies of Abou-Hein, 1985 (cited in Abdel-Rahman, 1989) on the Gaza Strip in Palestine; Al-Fangery (1987) El-Deba (1999); Saleh (1998) on Egypt; Naceur (2001) on Algeria; and Debais (1997) on Saudi Arabia.

In the Gaza Strip, Palestine, Abou-Hein, 1985 (cited in Abdel-Rahman, 1989) investigated the manifestations of aggressive behavior in a sample of 6–12 year old children from a Palestinian refugee camp Palestinian by using the TAT and an index to assess the physical and verbal manifestations of children's aggressive behavior in school and in streets. A case study method was also used to collect demographic information. It was hypothesized that Palestinian children in the Gaza Strip, due to the daily violent actions they witness, compared with children in other countries reported in earlier studies, show higher aggressive tendencies and behaviors on the one hand, and, on the other hand, that Palestinian children will manifest more positive and negative aggression compared with the children of other countries. Results showed that Palestinian children were significantly higher on positive aggression (physical and verbal aggression), than the children of other countries, who were higher on negative aggression. Analyses of the TAT children's responses revealed a lack of security and a threat to the child's existence. Also, children's TAT responses showed marked self- defense and self-protection tendencies and sympathy with the scary models. Palestinian children's TAT responses also showed a fear of authority and a tendency to depend on other people. Finally,

TAT responses revealed a significant illusive aggression and an increasing tendency for withdrawal and isolation among Palestinian children.

Al-Fangery (1987) carried out a study by using a local scale for assessing aggressive behavior manifestations in a sample of urban and rural Egyptian school children. Results showed that rural children were found to be more aggressive than their urban counterparts. Urban male children, compared with females, were significantly higher on aggressive behavior manifestations. Yet such differences have not been found in rural children. Another study which investigated the aggressive behavior in urban and rural children has been conducted by Hasan, 1987 (cited in Abdel-Rahman, 1989) who compared the manifestations of aggressive behavior in samples of urban and rural boys and girls between 6–12 years. Results showed that male children were found to be significantly higher than their female counterparts on the aggressive behavior scale. Rural children in general, compared with urban children, scored significantly higher on the aggressive behavior scale, especially positive aggression (physical and verbal aggression); and urban children, compared with rural children, were significantly higher on negative aggression, including nightmares, acute anxiety, illusions and hallucinations, and daydreaming. Results of a later study (Gebrial, 1994) give support to Al-Fangery's results. Some other Egyptian and Arab studies (Abdel-Hamid, 1990; El-Sheribini, 1991; Lutfy, 1992; Abou-el-Kheir, 1995; Abdel-Kader, 2000), however, found that urban subjects, compared with rural ones, were significantly higher in their tendencies toward violence and aggression.

In Saudi Arabia, Debais (1997) examined the differences of the age and place of residence on dimensions of aggressive behavior in 503 mildly retarded children who have been institutionalized for 7–16 years and those non-institutionalized by using a scale of teachers' ratings of aggressive behavior of children with mild mental retardation (MMR). Subjects were classified according to three age groups (7–9; 9–12; and 12–16 years, respectively) into two groups: children who reside in institutions for the mentally retarded and children who reside with their families. While no significant differences in aggressive dimensions among the three age groups have been found, children who resided in institutes were significantly higher on the aggressive behavior dimensions than the children who resided with their families.

El-Deba (1999) investigated the effect of staying (and not staying) with the family on behaviors of an sample of Egyptian school children between 9 and 12 years old by using scales for assessing personality traits, motivation, and creative thinking. El-Deba also developed a counseling program to modify the antisocial behavior observed in children who did not reside with their families. Children who resided with their families scored higher in both psychological adjustment and motivation. Results also showed a significant improvement in the behavior of the children who did not reside with their families after they were enrolled in the suggested counseling program.

It was hypothesized that spatial layout of their surroundings may affect people's ability to establish any form of control behavior. To test this hypothesis, Naceur (2001) examined the rates of vandalism and design variations in two residential quarters in Batna City, Algeria. Findings suggested that the physical characteristics of quarters were particularly relevant to the patterns of the anti-social behavior observed in different sectors of the Algerian population, among them school students. Naceur's (2001) results supported the results of an earlier Egyptian study (Hafez and Kasem, 1993a) in which a significant and positive relationship between class crowdedness (e.g., number of students in a class) and the level of aggressive behavior in 10-year-old primary school children had been reported. Results of Hafez and Kasem (1993a) and Naceur (2001) showed an important impact of the level of crowdedness in the class and housing as physical environments on the level of aggressive behavior among school students, especially the younger ones. A more recent Egyptian study (Kamel and Al-Fakherani, 2002) of 19–20 year-old males and females reported that increased crowdedness as an environmental variable has led to high hostility and low assertiveness.

In Kuwait, Al-Naser (2000) investigated aspects of violent behavior and violent actions toward self and others and the influences of age, sex, and place of residence in 2385, 14–18 year-old secondary school male and female students by using a locally devised scale to measure antisocial behavior. Results revealed that violent behavior and violent actions did exist among male and female students. However, male and older subjects, compared with female and younger subjects, ranked significantly higher on violence behavior and violent actions. No significant differences have been found concerning the influence of place of residence on violent behavior and violent actions.

In another study, Saliem 1985 (cited in Abdel-Hamid, 1990) was reported that religion, along with habits and social customs plays an important role in the socialization process, especially in rural and suburban areas. Abdel-Hamid's (1990) study on Egyptian rural and urban school students showed that school systems are responsible for producing social differentiations.

In another study, Helmy, 1986 (cited in Abdel-Hamid, 1990), the focus was on the order of violent deviations in a sample of Egyptian youth, among them secondary school students. It was found that alcoholism, stealing, robbery, gambling, and drug abuse, in that order, were the most common violent deviations.

In Egypt, Al-Fakherani (1993) focused on assessing psychological conflicts, stress, pressure, neurotic disturbances, and illusions which accompanied violent actions and behaviors by using a case study method to investigate an 18-year-old male member of one of the phantic groups. Results showed that the subject was suffering acute anxiety, neurotic depression, hysteria, social introversion, guilt and homosexual feelings. In the same context, a recent study was carried out in Mecca, Saudi Arabia (Awad, 2002), and compared personality traits in samples of secondary school female juvenile delinquents, who were serving a punishment period in an institution for rehabilitation at the time of the study, with their non-delinquent peers. Results showed that the delinquent subjects ranked significantly higher on neurosis and extroversion but lower on self-esteem than their non-delinquent peers.

Physical Environment of the Classroom and Students' Personality Traits and Learning Levels

Although it is important to investigate the influence of the physical environment of the classroom on students' personality traits and learning levels, only one Arab study has been conducted that focused on the relationship between classroom environment and students' behavior (Meleikan and El-Deerni, 1984; Awad, 1994). Results showed that the less comfortable classroom environment was associated with higher levels of aggression and academic carelessness. Meleikan and El-Deerni (1984) reported also that students with higher levels of aggressive behavior ranked lower in academic achievement, while loss aggressive students ranked higher in academic achievement.

Socio-Economic Status (SES): Parents' Educational and Vocational Levels

Saleh (1998) observed and interviewed two samples of secondary school students in Cairo, Egypt, between 16–19 years old to assess the impact of the family's socio-economic status (SES) level (parents' educational and vocational levels and family income) and place of residence on children's violent behavior in school. Results revealed a significant negative correlation among a family's SES and the place of residence and children's violent behavior in school.

Mass Media and Violence among School Students

Studies of Saad, 1980 (cited in Abdel-Hamid, 1990); Day and Ghandour (1984); El-Gamil (1988); and Abdel-Mokhtar (1998) on the influence of watching action- and sex- movies and violent television programs, reported positive correlations between watching aggressive models, including those in movies and television programs and the increase of violent attitudes among youth. This result was repeatedly noticed in many other studies (*Al-Ahram*, September 11, 2000).

Factorial Analytical Studies on Violence among School Students

Some Arab research studies have focused on determining factors that determine violent behavior. Among these were the studies of Hafez and Kasem (1993c); Hussein, 1983 (cited in Nasr, 1994) in Egypt; Abdalla and Abou-Abaa (1995) in Saudi Arabia; and Al-Naser (2000) in Kuwait. Hafez and Kasem (1993c) administered a locally developed scale for assessing aggressive behavior among Egyptian children (Hafez and Kasem, 1993b) to 450 10-year fifth grade boys and girls. A general factor for aggressive behavior (a response to frustration) and four sub factors (e.g., physical aggression, verbal aggression; negative aggression, and normal behavior) have emerged.

Hussein, 1983 (cited in Nasr, 1994) assessed aggressive behavior in a sample of Egyptian female students by using a local scale for assessing the aggressive behavior. Five factors have emerged, namely, general aggression; overt active aggression/covert negative aggression; direct aggression/indirect aggression; aggressive tension; and verbal aggression/physical aggression.

Abdalla and Abou-Abaa (1995) conducted a study to investigate the inter-correlations between the four dimensions of aggression–anger, hostility, verbal aggression, and physical aggression–by applying Buss and Pery's scale for aggressive behavior to 573 Saudi male intermediate, secondary school, and university students aged 15, 17, and 22 years, respectively. Results supported the main hypothesis, that aggressive behavior is a general domain which contains the following four factors- anger, hostility, verbal aggression, and physical aggression. Abdalla and Aou-Abaa's results showed also that Buss and Pery's scale could assess successfully aggressive behavior among the Saudis.

In another study in Kuwait (Al-Naser, 2000) on violent behaviors and actions among secondary school male and female students 14 to 18 year-old, eight factors have emerged as the components of violent behaviors and actions, namely, stealing and destructiveness, rejection of the social context, hostility, self-assertiveness, self-destruction, rudeness, avoiding the elderly, and academic carelessness.

MEASURES AND SCALES FOR ASSESSING VIOLENT/AGGRESSIVE BEHAVIOR

Some Arab researchers have been interested in developing measures and scales to assess violent/aggressive behaviors especially among children and adolescents. For example, Hafez and Kasem (1993b and c) developed Ain Shams Scale for Aggressive Behavior Forms in Children. Gebril (1989b) developed a scale for assessing the types of aggressive behavior. In Kuwait, Al-Huessani (1997) has developed a scale for assessing the practical instinct impulsiveness. Other Arab researchers have tended to use some projective techniques to assess violent/aggressive behavior, and especially the differences in aggressive behavior among samples of male and female normal and deaf-mute adolescents, by using the Hand test (Moussa, 1989) which revealed that deaf-mute adolescents scored significantly higher on aggression and were more likely to act out aggression than their normal counterparts. In addition, some Arab researchers have shown interest in assessing aggressive behavior in mentally retarded children. An example of these efforts is the scale for rating aggressive behavior among mild mentally retarded Saudi children, which was developed by Debais (1997; 1999) and which aims at assessing four aspects of aggressive behavior: 1) explicit aggressive behavior, 2) general aggressive behavior, 3) choastic behavior, and 4) the lack (or the inability) of self-control.

BEHAVIOR MODIFICATION PROGRAMS, THERAPEUTIC AND COUNSELING STUDIES

Several Arab studies have tried to find ways to modify or reduce violent/aggressive behavior especially among children and adolescents. One of the earliest Arab studies in the field of modification of violent/aggressive behavior was conducted by Farghli (1979) in Egypt. The study reported that competitive athletic activity has a positive impact on modifying aggressive behavior in adolescents. Sheban (1996) has applied a program for developing the social skills aims at reducing aggressive behavior in a sample of primary school Egyptian boys and girls between 9–12 years old. Children's levels of aggressive behavior (in the following four aspects–aggression toward the self, aggression toward others, aggression toward public and private belongings, and aggression toward the societal norms) have been significantly decreased as a result of the application of the program. Improvements in aggressive behavior among girls were significantly greater than in the case of boys.

Some Arab studies have been conducted, especially in Egypt, Kuwait, Jordan, and the Sudan, to assess the efficiency of using therapeutic approaches in reducing violence/aggression and extreme behavior (Al-Fakherani, 1993; Nasr, 1998; Gaber, 1989; Mahmoud, 1995; Saigh & Omar, 1983; Al-Khatib & Hamdy, 1997, Abdel-Khalek, 2002; and Azab, 2002). Moreover, a small number of Arab research studies have investigated the efficacy of remedial behavior programs in reducing psychological and negative stress in male and female secondary school students (Awad, 2000).

In the following sections, results of some of these studies will be briefly reviewed.

In a more recent Egyptian study, Nasr (1998) developed a program based on modeling, role taking, and reinforcement aimed at modifying social behavior among a sample of abused mentally retarded children between the ages of 9–12, whose IQ's ranged between 4 and 7 years, and who showed some aspects of social maladjustment such as, aggression, withdrawal, and antisocial behavior. Results showed a significant improvement in children's social behavior due to the application of the suggested program. Results also revealed a positive correlation between children is maladjustment and parental abuse.

Al-Fakherani (1993) used the Rational-Emotive approach to reduce the extreme behavior of one of the phantic group members. Results showed a marked decline in the subject's clinically violent symptoms. In this direction, Gebrial (1994) found, in a sample of Egyptian school students, that Gestalt therapy approach had a positive impact in reducing hostility levels.

Some Arab research studies have tried to investigate the effects or the efficiency of using play to reduce violence and aggressive behavior in children (El-Sheribini, 1987; Gaber, 1989; Mahmoud, 1995), other Arab studies have focused on the effects of using the Good Behavior Game technique in reducing disruptive and aggressive behaviors among primary school children and intermediate and secondary school students (Saigh & Omar, 1983; Al-Khatib & Hamdy, 1997). In addition, some Arab researchers have shown an interest in developing therapeutic and/or counseling programs to overcome or to reduce violent/aggressive behaviors (Abdel-Khalek, 2002; Azab, 2002). In the following, results of these studies will be briefly reviewed.

El-Sheribini (1987) used the children's program the Dummy Show as a means for reducing aggressive behavior in a sample of kindergarten children in Egypt. Results showed that watching the Dummy Show program has had a positive affected on aggression and behavior disorders in children.

Mahmoud (1995) developed a program based on group play and aimed at reducing the aggressive behavior of preschool children. The sample consisted of 75 4–7-year-olds (45 boys and 30 girls). The subjects were classified into three age groups (4–5, 5–6, and 6–7 years, respectively) and were chosen from the same socioeconomic status and the intellectual levels of the children were controlled. The following measures and techniques were used:

1. Goodenoug and Harris's Draw-A-Man Test
2. A local devised scale for assessing aggressive behavior among preschool children

3. An index for assessing the child's daily activities
4. A suggested program based on group play to reduce the preschool children's aggressive behavior. The program includes providing children with motor activities and art
5. Case studies

Results revealed that 1) aggressive behavior increases by increasing age in both boys and girls and particularly those who between the ages of 5 and 6; 2) Boys in general scored significantly higher on the aggressive behavior scale than girls; 3) Children of working mothers were found to be higher on the aggressive behavior scale, compared with the children of non-working mothers; 4) Children who are more active scored significantly higher on the aggressive behavior scale than less active children; and 5) Aggressive behavior been decreased markedly as the result of the group play program.

In Kuwait, Gaber (1989) developed a counseling program based on play to reduce psychological disturbances (such as hostility, aggression, anxiety, and introversion) and to improve self confidence, social participation and interaction, and intellectual levels for a sample of Kuwaiti school boys and girls between 6 and 12 years of age who have shown such disruptive behavior and who have learning difficulties. The children were diagnosed by their teachers as being trouble makers and having learning difficulties, and they were tested before and after the suggested counseling program. By using discriminant analysis, results showed that due to the counseling program there was a significant decrease in the following aspects of the children's behavior–social and physical aggressive behavior, introversion, and anxiety. Another study on effect of play on reducing aggressive behavior in preschool children was conducted in Syria by El-Seka (2000), who reported a significant improvement in the levels of aggressive behavior in preschool children as a result of exposing children to a program based on play. It was also shown that social participation and interaction and self-confidence have been markedly improved due to the application of the counseling program. Yet, results revealed no significant improvement in the intellectual levels in the children after they were exposed to the counseling program.

In Sudan, Saigh and Omar (1983) investigated the effects of using a Good Behavior Game technique for reducing the disruptive behavior in a sample of second grade boys and girls (7–8 years old) in a Sudanese rural setting. Observations have been collected by trained school teachers and the researchers themselves. A 5-week program for a good behavior game has been developed. This program is based on Western studies and consists of five stages: a) preliminary stage, in which the disruptive behaviors have been shown and read to the children by the classroom teacher, (b) second stage, included blaming and punishing children who continued to show aspects of disruptive behaviors, (c) initiative remedial stage by using a good behavior game played by two groups of children for one week in which it was announced that any child who breaks the rules will negatively affect the whole group, and that the group which obeys and follows the regulations will be well rewarded, (d) the basic stage, in which the game was completely stopped, and (e) the second remedial stage, in which the game of good behavior is repeated by the children and supervised and controlled by the teacher. Analysis of the observations collected during the 5-week period showed a great improvement in the good behavior of the Sudanese children.

In Jordan, Al-Khatib and Hamdy (1997) investigated the efficiency of the Good Behavior Game in reducing inappropriate behavior, disruptive behavior, and aggressive behavior in two separate samples of Jordanian school students. The first sample consisted of 95 fourth and sixth grade male and female students between the ages of 10 and 12, while the second sample was consisted of 1077 students (male and female) from the second through the tenth grade, between the ages of 7 and 16. Observations have been collected and analyzed; results of the analyses showed significant decrease in both inappropriate motor and verbal behavior as well as aggressive behavior in students. The decrease was more significant in the case of the older students. Moreover, results suggested that using the Good Behavior Game technique as a procedure for reducing inappropriate and aggressive behaviors for a short period of time is not effective; rather, the study showed the necessity of using this technique for a long period of time in order to achieve an effective and long lasting change in children's behavior. It was also suggested that using the Good Behavior Game with children should not be stopped suddenly. It should be stopped gradually, step by step.

Some Arab studies have investigated the influences and effects of using both psychodrama techniques and school theatre to modify aggressive behavior among school students in general and among deaf-mute primary school children in particular. The findings of these studies indicate the efficiency of using psychodrama and school theater in reducing aggressive behavior. Examples of these studies are the studies of Abdel-Gawad (1990); El-Sheribini (1987); El-Mohamady (1998); Ghreeb (1994); Mater (1986); and Negela (1997). In the following section, results of these studies will be briefly discussed.

Mater (1986) investigated the efficiency of a program using psychodrama and developing reading skills to reduce aggressive behavior in a sample of 14–16 year old intermediate school male students in Egypt. Results showed that both using psychodrama and developing reading skills have positively influenced aggressive behavior in students; however, results showed that psychodrama techniques have greater influence on reducing aggressive behavior compared with developing reading skills. Concerning the psychodrama techniques used in the study, results also revealed that asking students to play double roles (e.g., once as son, and once as father) and asking students to play positive, instead of negative, roles has a great positive influence on aggressive behavior.

Abdel-Gawad (1990) used psychodrama techniques in treating behavioral problems and reducing aggressive behavior in a sample of Egyptian preschool boys and girls, between the ages of 3–6. Results revealed a significant reduction in the levels of anxiety, avoidance, and also in aggressive behavior after children have been exposed to the psychodrama techniques.

Another Egyptian study (El-Sheribini, 1987) exposed a group of kindergarten children to The Dummy Show, and reported a significant reduction in the levels of aggressive behavior after they watched this show. Ghreeb (1994) also tested the effects of using psychodrama techniques in reducing the emotional disturbances of Egyptian school students, and reported a significant improvement in emotional disturbances, giving support to Abdel-Gawad's (1990); and El-Sheribini's (1987) results.

In another Egyptian study Negela (1997) found that school theatre has contributed positively in reducing aggressive behavior in a sample of 9–11 year old primary school boys and girls. In Egypt also, El-Mohamady (1998) studied the influences of both psychodrama techniques and school theatre for modifying aggressive behavior among 9–12 year old deaf-mute children. Results showed a significant improvement in the levels of aggressive behavior due to exposing the children to both psychodrama techniques and school theatre. In addition to the above mentioned studies, few other Arab studies have studied the effectiveness of using strategies based on reward-punishment reinforcement and peer pressure (Saleh, 1995) or on reinforcement-punishment (Abdel-Naser, 1997) for modifying aggressive behavior in normal and deaf-mute preschool and primary school children. Results showed significant improvements in the children's aggressive behavior when these strategies have been used.

Some Arab studies have tried to develop therapeutic and/or counseling programs to overcome or to reduce violent and aggressive behaviors among siblings. Examples of these studies are Abdel-Aziz (1986); Aboud (1991); Saleh (1998); Ghreeb (2000); Azab (2002) and Abdel-Khalek (2002). Aboud (1991) developed a counseling program aimed at reducing aggressive behavior in a sample of intermediate school students in Egypt. Results indicated the efficiency of such a program for reducing aggression levels. In another Egyptian study, Saleh (1998) developed a counseling strategy for eradication of violence among secondary school students. Saleh's (1998) results were in line with Aboud's (1991). Azab (2002) devised an integrative, negative and therapeutic program to overcome violent behaviors (directed at parents, siblings, class mates, school teachers, and principals) in a sample of secondary Egyptian students. The program, which lasted two months and had 16 sessions, was based on psychoanalytic techniques, cognitive and behavioral techniques, and group techniques, such as psychodrama, relaxation, modeling, lectures and group discussions, and a training course aimed at providing students with negotiation skills. Students' violent behaviors were assessed before and after the application of the suggested program. Results revealed that the levels of violence had been decreased significantly as a result of the application of the therapeutic program. Ghreeb's (2000) study showed that developing children's communication skills within the family could lead to positive improvements in children's aggressive and violent behavior levels.

Abdel-Khalek (2002) has developed a counseling program aimed at reducing verbal and physical aggressions in a sample of Egyptian siblings. Siblings' verbal and physical aggression was assessed before and after the application of the suggested counseling program. Results revealed a significant improvement in the levels of verbal and physical aggression among siblings due to the counseling program.

A few Arab researchers, mainly in Egypt, developed programs for modifying social behavior and aggressive behavior among mentally retarded children. Examples of these studies are Nasr (1998) and Shelby (1999). Nasr (1998) assessed the efficiency of a locally developed program for modifying social behavior in abused mentally retarded children between the ages of 12–13, with mental ages ranging among years 4–7. Nasr reported significant improvements in children's social behavior and adjustment due to the application of the program. Shelby (1999) studied the efficiency of behavioral programs for reducing violence in a sample of mentally retarded children, and had results similar to Nasr's (1998).

Some Arab research studies have focused on reducing violent and aggressive behavior in children by using special techniques such as school theatre or watching television movies (El-Sheribini, 1987; Negela, 1997), while other Arab research studies tended to use psychodrama techniques to reduce violent/aggressive behavior (Abdel-Gawad, 1990; Aboud, 1991; Ghreeb, 1994; Mater, 1986). In addition, other Arab research studies have focused on psychological techniques to reduce violent/aggressive behavior in deaf-mute children and adolescents (Abdel-Gewad & Abdel-Fattah, 1999; Abdel-Naser, 1997; El-Mohamady, 1998) and in autistic children (Mohammed, 1999).

EFFORTS, MEASURES, AND PROCEDURES TO REDUCE SCHOOL STUDENTS' VIOLENT BEHAVIOR

Many efforts, measures, and procedures have been used in schools in many Arab countries, especially in Egypt and the oil-producing Arab Gulf states. These efforts have been aimed at improving the school milieu and overcoming, or at least, reducing violent or aggressive behavior among school students at different grade levels. One recent effort has been to issue laws and regulations that are aimed at strengthening school authority and enabling school administrators to deal, in an effective way, with students' problematic behaviors, such as violence, tyranny, bullying, and absenteeism. Improving the school physical milieu and reducing the student's cowardliness were also considered in several Arab countries, and which positively contributed to reduce the violent behavior among school students.

Enhancing the value system and religious orientation among school students could lead to a reduction in aggressive/violent behavior. Some Arab research studies (Ghalab & El-Dousseki, 1994) have shown that intrinsic religious orientation has correlated positively with negative attitudes toward violence.

Proper qualification of teachers and principals was, and still is, an effective method to provide school administration with healthy ways of dealing with violent behavior among school students (Kamel, 2002), and for providing students with a proper model (Ghanem, 2000). Last but not least, in several Arab countries, and especially Egypt, and the oil-producing Arab Gulf states, ministries of education have during the past twenty years assigned school psychologists and social workers to work mainly in intermediate and secondary schools in order to help school administrators and teachers solve students' problematic behavior, and to improve the school milieu. The number of school psychologists working in intermediate and secondary schools in Egypt at present could be estimated as more than one thousand. In Kuwait, the Department of Psychological Services of the Ministry of Education, which was established in 1972, continues to employ many psychology graduates to provide a variety of services, such as provided by counselors and school psychologists. Through its support a number of research studies on students' behavior have been conducted. A good example of school psychologists' efforts in developing countries is found in De Jong's (2000) study in South Africa, which could be adapted by Arab countries to develop a health- promoting school.

The way in which the public sees school violence should be changed dramatically. Public still considers violence among school students to not be as serious an issue as it is in reality (Abdel-Quei, 1994; Ghanam, 1998, 2000). Investigations of violent/aggressive behavior among school students in Arab countries should go much deeper, and this violent/aggressive behavior should be seen in a panoramic view, which should include searching for the roots of violence and aggression in the entire society and trying to interpret it in an integrative way (Ewis, 1968).

The Arab education system, in general, is in need of urgent reform. "Do more with less" is the central theme of educational reform in Arab countries. Most of the Arab countries are suffering economic, social, and political hardships which have hindered any educational reform. This reform or challenge takes on daunting magnitude when considered against the present reality that many schools in Arab countries are adverse environments. They are often characterized by low educator morale and insufficient ideals (Ghanem, 2000), poor resources and facilities, mismanagement, social problems such as gangsterism and substance abuse, and disillusioned learners (Kamel, 2002; Rizk, 1992). Arab schools desperately need to be better. "Learner friendly" promotion of quality education for all is a central challenge that faces the Arab educational system as a whole to develop an inclusive learning environment which promotes the full personal, academic, and professional development of all learners irrespective of race, class, gender, disability, religion, socio-cultural background, sexual preference, learning styles, and language.

FINAL COMMENTS

1. Arab research studies on violence among school students that have been conducted during the last two decades mainly in Egypt, Kuwait, Saudi Arabia, and, to a lesser extent, in Algeria, Jordan, Qatar, Syria, and the Sudan, lack the proper theoretical framework which could guide Arab researchers to establish proper hypotheses, to obtain appropriate tools and samples, and to use suitable statistical methods.

2. There is no continuity in Arab research studies on violence among school students.

3. There is no clear plan to guide conducting research on violence among school students in Arab countries. Most of the Arab research studies on violence among school students have been carried out for academic purposes such as obtaining M.A. and/or Ph.D. degrees or being promoted to higher academic ranks.

4. It was also noted that Arab research studies on violence among school students are suffering from the great ambiguity concerning psychological terms used in these studies. Most of the studies have mixed terms such as violence, aggression, hostility, and extreme behavior. This ambiguity could lead to negative and/or invalid explanations and interpretations of the results obtained.

5. Goldstein and Conoley (1997) focused on youth violence and stated that "school violence is complexly caused, and its optimal remediation must be of similar complexity" (Goldstein & Conoley, 1997, p. 16). The complicated characteristics of school violence, however, were not apparent from the Arab research studies on violence among school students. Most of the Arab research studies tended to concentrate on the relationship between violence and personality traits, and, to a lesser extent, parental

behavior, leaving some other important aspects, such as school systems, and socioeconomic and cultural contexts. Violence among school students cannot be investigated without considering society's structure (e.g., social, economic, political, cultural and religious history or particularity) as Hasan (1990) and Bayyumi (1992) have observed.

6. Until now, no Arab research study on violence among school students has investigated this phenomenon developmentally.

Also, it was noticed that Arab research studies on violence among school students have been conducted by either psychologists or, less frequently, sociologists or educators, and that no study has been carried out yet by a team of researchers belong to disciplines such as education, medicine, law, etc.

7. A great number of Arab research studies on violence among school students have focused on either the correlations (relationships) between violence and some other variables (such as the personality traits of parents and children and children's perception of parental behavior), or the influence of some demographic variables (such as age, sex, educational and vocational levels, family's socio-economic status, and family size and birth order), or the diagnosis of violence. In our opinion, Arab research studies on violence among school students should move a step forward and develop and design programs and techniques aimed at predicting and preventing violent behavior, especially among children and adolescents.

8. Last, but not least, schools in Arab countries have to transform themselves from an adverse learning environment which is typical of many Arab schools (and most likely schools elsewhere) to a safe, supporting, caring, mutually respectful, and generally well organized educational environment.

References

Abdalla, J. (1992). Hostility as a function of father absence. *Psychological Studies*, (Egypt), 2(2), 351–369.

Abdalla, M.S. and Abou-Abaa, S.A. (1995). Dimensions of aggressive behavior: A comparative factor analytic study. *Psychological Studies* (Egypt) 5(3), 521–580 (in Arabic).

Abdel-Aziz, E. (1986). *Psychological variables related with aggressive behavior in adolescents and the impact of a psychological counseling in reducing it.* Unpublished Ph.D. thesis: Faculty of Education, Sohag, Assuit University (Egypt) (in Arabic).

Abdel-Aziz, I. (1995). *The relationship between types of parental behavior and aggressive behavior among deaf-mute children.* Unpublished M.A. thesis, Faculty of Education, Zagazig University (Egypt) (in Arabic).

Abdel-Gawad, A.M. (1990). *Using the psychodrama techniques in treating psychological disturbances in preschool children.* Unpublished M.A. thesis, the Institute for Higher Studies on Childhood, Ain Shams University (Egypt) (in Arabic).

Abdel-Gawad, E. and Abdel-Fattah, A.K. (1999). Efficiency of using a program based on play for reducing aggressive behavior in deaf-mute children. *Journal of Psychology* (Egypt), 13(50), 88–113 (in Arabic).

Abdel-Hamid, T. (1990). *Producing compelling: A study in education and social control*. Cairo: Sinai for Publishing (in Arabic).

Abdel-Kader, A.A. (2000). Assertiveness between submission and hostility (aggression) toward authority: A comparative study of adolescents in rural and urban areas. Proceedings of the *7th International Conference of the Center of the Psychological Counseling, Ain Shams University, Cairo, Egypt*, (pp. 313–348) (in Arabic).

Abdel-Khalek, S.A. (2002). The efficiency of using a counseling program in reducing aggression among siblings. Paper presented at the *9th Annual Conference of the Psychological Counseling Center*. Ain Shams University, Cairo, Egypt, December, 21–23, 2002 (in Arabic).

Abdel-Mokhtar, M.Kh. (1998). *Alienation and extremeness toward violence: A psychological study*. Cairo: Dar Ghreeb for Printing, Publishing and Distribution (in Arabic).

Abdel-Naser, G.M. (1997). *The effects of some types of reinforcement and punishment on modifying the aggressive behavior among deaf-mute children*. Unpublished M.A. thesis, Faculty of Education, Menoufia University (Egypt) (in Arabic).

Abdel-Rahman, S.M. (1989). Children and the tendency for aggression. In M.G. Rada (Ed.), *Children, prejudice and education; The 6th Annual Book of the Kuwait Foundation for Advancing the Arab Childhood* (KFAAC) (pp. 71–120), Kuwait: KFAAC (in Arabic).

Abdel-Quei, S. (1994). Terrorism in the eye of youth: A psychological pilot study. *Journal of Psychology* (Egypt), 8(31), 48–77 (in Arabic).

Aboud, S. (1991). *Efficiency of counseling program in reducing aggressive behavior among intermediate school students*. Unpublished M.A. thesis, Faculty of Education, Aswan, Assuit University (Egypt) (in Arabic).

Abou-el-Kheir, M.M.S. (1995). *Physical punishment and patterns of parental control and their relation with psychological characteristics in children and adolescents*. Unpublished Ph.D. thesis, Faculty of Arts, Zagazig University (Egypt)(in Arabic).

Abou-el-Kheir, M.M.S. (1999). Birth order and its relation to maternal acceptance/rejection, and personality traits in sample of adolescents. *Psychological Studies* (Egypt), 9(3), 445–473 (in Arabic).

Ahmed, R.A. (in press, a). Egyptian immigrations. In L.L. Adler and U.P. Gielen (Eds.), *Migration: Immigration and emigration in international perspective*. New York: Greenwood Press.

Ahmed, R.A. (in press, b). Egyptian families. In Roopnarine, J. and U.P. Gielen (Eds.). *Families in global perspective*. Boston: Allyn & Bacon.

Ahmed R.A. (in press, c). A critical review of Arab research studies on violence/aggression and extreme behavior. In L. Adler and F.L. Denmark (Eds.), *Violence around the world*. New York: Greenwood Press.

Ahmed, R.A. and Khalil, E.A. (1998). A critical review on the Arab research studies on aggression/violence and extremeness with particular emphasis on the Egyptian research. *Proceedings of the International Conference on Social Sciences and their Roles in Eradication of Violence and Extremeness Crimes in Islamic Societies*. Saleh Kamel Center for Islamic Economy, Al-Azhar University (Egypt), June 28–30, 1998, Vol. 4, 61–105 (in Arabic).

Al-Ahram (2000). An Egyptian daily newspaper (in Arabic). Mon. Sept., 7.

Al-Fakherani, Kh. I. (1993). Efficacy of the rational emotive therapy in facing some psychological disturbances among extremism: A case study. *Journal of Counseling* (Egypt) 1(1), 257–281(in Arabic).

Al-Fangery, H.A.H. (1987). *Aggression among rural and urban children: A comparative study*. Unpublished M.A. thesis, The Institute for Higher Studies on Childhood, Ain Shams University (Egypt) (in Arabic).

Al-Garni, M.M. (2001). The impact of family structure and family function factors on the deviant behaviors of high school students in Mecca City, Saudi Arabia. Paper presented at *The First International Conference on Social Sciences & the Development of Society*, College of the Social Sciences, Kuwait University, Kuwait, April 10–12, 2001.

Al-Huessani, H.M.S. (1997). Divide and standardization of a scale for practical instinct impulsiveness. *Proceedings of the Conference on Psychological Services in the State of Kuwait.* Kuwait University, Vol. 2 (pp. 576–655), April 6–8, 1997 (in Arabic).

Al-Kamel, H.M. and Soliman, A.E. (1990). Aggressive behavior and students' perception of parental attitudes toward socialization: A predictive study. *Proceedings of the 6th Annual Convention on Psychology in Egypt.* Part II, (pp. 763–788), The Egyptian Association for Psychological Studies, Cairo Egypt, January 22–24, 1990 (in Arabic).

Al-Khatib, G. and Hamdy, N. (1997). The efficiency of the Good Behavior Game in reducing antisocial behavior in the classroom. *The Educational Journal* (Kuwait), *11*(42), 255–276(in Arabic).

Al-Mazroui, S.S. (1990). *Marital adjustment and its relation with children's personality traits.* Unpublished M.A. thesis, Faculty of Arts, Ain Shams University (Egypt) (in Arabic).

Al-Meghrabi, A.M.M. (2000). *The psychological and psychosocial determinants of aggressive behavior in early adolescents: A study of the interaction relationships.* Unpublished M.A. thesis, Faculty of Arts, Cairo University (Egypt) (in Arabic).

Al-Mussallam, B.Kh. (2001). The effects of parents-child relationship on juvenile delinquency: A comparative study. *Journal of the Social Sciences* (Kuwait), *29*(1), 71–107 (in Arabic).

Al-Naser, F.A. (2000). Aspects of violent behavior among secondary school students. *Annals of Arts and Social Sciences*, Kuwait University, Kuwait, Monograph 146, Vol. XX (in Arabic).

Al-Otaibi, S.D. (2000). Political violence in Algeria: A comparative and analytical study 1976-1998. *Journal of the Social Sciences* (Kuwait), *28*(4), 7-57 (in Arabic).

Al-Taher, H. and Al-Mosowy, M.S. (1997). Aggressive behavior in Kuwaiti school students after the Iraqi invasion to the State of Kuwait. *Proceedings of the Conference on Psychological Services in the State of Kuwait*, Vol. 2 (pp. 439–490), Department of Psychology, Faculty of Arts, Kuwait University, Kuwait 6–8 April, 1997 (in Arabic).

Aly, A.A. (2000). The peer group and its relation with behavioral and moral problems in secondary school students. *Psychological Studies* (Egypt), *10*(3), 443-474 (in Arabic).

Awad, R.A. (1994). *Interaction between parental attitudes and school environment and its impact on aggression and self-actualization among intermediate school students.* Unpublished M.A. thesis, Faculty of Education, Menoufia University (Egypt) (in Arabic).

Awad, R.R. (2000). *Efficacy of a remedial behavior program in reducing psychological and negative stress in male and female adolescents.* Unpublished Ph.D. thesis, Faculty of Education, Tanta University, Kefr el-Sheikh Branch (Egypt) (in Arabic).

Awad, S.M. (2002). A comparative study of personality traits in juvenile delinquent and non-juvenile delinquent females students in Mecca, Saudi Arabia . Paper presented at the *9th Annual Conference of the Psychlogical Counseling Center, Ain Shams University*, Cairo, Egypt, December, 21–23, 2002 (in Arabic).

Azab, H.M. (2002). The efficiency of an integrative, neogative and therapeutic program to overcome violent behaviors in adolescents. Paper presented at the *9th Annual Conference of the Psychological Counseling Center, Ain Shams University*, Cairo, Egypt, December 21–23, 2002 (in Arabic).

Bayyumi, M.A. (1992). *Violence phenomenon: Reasons and treatment.* Alexandria (Egypt): Dar el-Maarefa al-Gamiaa (in Arabic).

Berkowitz, L. (1993). *Aggression: Its causes, consequences, and control.* Philadelphia: Temple University Press.

Day, R.C. & Ghandour, M. (1984). Te effect of Television-mediated aggression and real-life aggression on the behavior of Lebanese children *Journal of Experimental Child Psychology*, 1038, 1, 7–18.

Debais, S.A. (1997). Dimensions of aggressive behavior for children with mild mental retardation in terms of age and place of residence. *Psychological Studies* (Egypt), 7(3), 353–385 (in Arabic).

Debais, S.A. (1999). A scale for rating aggressive behavior of children with mild mental retardation. *The ERC Journal* (Qatar) 8(15), 61–85 (in Arabic).

De Jong, T. (2000). The role of the school psychologist in developing a health-promoting school: Some lessons from the South African context. *School Psychology International*. 21(4), 339–357.

Diab, L. (1965). Authoritarianism and submission in two different cultural groups. In. L.K. Meleika (Ed.). *Readings in social psychology in he Arab countries*. Vol. 1 (pp. 137–180), Cairo: The National House for Printing and Publishing (in Arabic).

El-Deba, N.R.S. (1999). *The effect of staying with the family on children's personality traits and the effect of a suggested counseling program to modify children's antisocial behavior.* Unpublished Ph.D. thesis, The Institute for Higher Studies on Childhood, Ain Shams University (Egypt) (in Arabic).

El-Deeb, A.A. (1990). Styles of reward and punishment in the light of Islam and the modern trends and their effects on the preschool (Kindergarten) children's aggressive behavior. *Proceedings of the International Conference on Childhood in Islam, Al-Azhar University*, Cairo Egypt, October 9–12, 1990 (pp. 803–826) (in Arabic).

El-Deeb, A.M. (1996). The relationship between violently/aggressive behavior and both family size and perceived parental behavior in samples of university students in Egypt and Sultanate of Oman. In A. M. El-Deeb (Ed.), *Research in psychology*. Part 1 (pp. 68–120), Cairo: The Egyptian General Book Organization (in Arabic).

El-Dematy, M.A.S. (1997). *Parenthood and its relation with drugs addiction in children.* Unpublished Ph.D. thesis, Faculty of Arts, Ain Shams University (Egypt) (in Arabic).

El-Dousseki, M.M. (1998). Psychological conflict and its relation with psycho-pathological symptoms in samples of male and female delinquents and non-delinquents *Proceedings of the 5th International Conference of the Center of Psychological Counseling: Psychological Counseling and Development*, Ain Shams University (Egypt), December 1–3, 1998, (pp. 535–638), (in Arabic).

El-Gamil, S.S. (1988). *Watching violence in TV programs and their relation to some aspects of aggressive behavior among watching children.* Unpublished M.A. thesis, Faculty of Arts, Zagazig University (Egypt) (in Arabic).

Elian, I. A.E. (1993). *A study of the relationship between parental acceptance/rejection and self-assertiveness and aggression among adolescents.* Unpublished M.A. thesis, Faculty of Arts, Zagazig University (Egypt) (in Arabic).

El-Kadem, A.A. (1995). Juvenile delinquency in Qatari society: A pilot study of the manifestations and factors. *Annals of the Faculty of Humanities and Social Sciences, University of Qatar* (Qatar), 18, 109–141 (in Arabic).

El-Matewally, M. (1995). *Violence and legality in Egypt: A legal study.* Cairo: The General Egyptian Book Organization (in Arabic).

El-Mohamady, A.A. (1998). *Efficiency range of both psychodrama and school theatre on modifying the aggressive behavior among the deaf-mute primary school children.* Unpublished M.A. thesis, the Institute for Educational Studies and Research, Cairo University (Egypt) (in Arabic).

El-Omeran, G.A. and Ebada, A.A. (1993). Common psychological problems among nursery children (3-6 years) in the light of some family variables in Bahrain. *Journal of Counseling* (Egypt), 1(1), 37–108 (in Arabic).

El-Sayed, A.A. (1996). *Father image in addicts.* Unpublished Ph.D. thesis, Faculty of Arts, Ain Shams University (Egypt) (in Arabic).

El-Seka, S.M.F. (2000). *An experimental study on the effect of play on aggressive behavior in preschool children.* Unpublished M.A. thesis, Faculty of Education, University of Damascus (Syria) (in Arabic).

El-Shebini, H.I.A. (1985). *Problematic behavior in pre-school children and its relation with some family variables.* Unpublished M.A. thesis, the Institute for Higher Studies on Childhood, Ain Shams University (Egypt) (in Arabic).

El-Sheribini, E.K. (1991). *A comparative study in attitude towards violence in rural and urban settings.* Unpublished M.A. thesis, Faculty of Arts, Ain Shams University (Egypt) (in Arabic).

El-Sheribini, H.A. (1987). *Using dummy show in modifying some behavior disorders in kindergarten children.* Unpublished M.A. thesis, College of Girls, Ain Shams University (Egypt) (in Arabic).

Ewies, S. (1968). *A study in the interpretation of hostile feelings.* Cairo: Dar el-Kitab el-Arabi for Printing and Publishing (in Arabic).

Faied, H.A. (1996). Dimensions of the aggressive behavior among university students. *Proceedings of the 3rd International Conference of the Center of the Psychological Counseling, Ain Shams University,* Cairo, Egypt (pp. 135–182) (in Arabic).

Farag, M.F. (1975). Response sets among delinquents and non-delinquents. In S. Fahmy (Ed.), *Yearbook on Psychology,* Vol. 3 (pp. 149–161), Cairo: The General Egyptian Book Organization (in Arabic).

Farghli, M.M. (1979). *Psychological variables related to aggression and the impact of the competitive athletic activity in modifying aggression: An experimental study.* Unpublished Ph.D. thesis, Faculty of Education, Al-Azhar University (Egypt) (in Arabic).

Gaber, E.A. (1989). *Developing a counseling program based on play for treating psychologically disturbed children: A field study.* Unpublished Ph.D. thesis, Institute for Higher Studies on Childhood, Ain Shams University (Egypt) (in Arabic).

Gebrial, Th. (1994). Hostility (aggression) among university students and the impact of Gestalt therapy in reducing it. *Proceeding of the First International Conference of the Center of Psychological Counseling, Ain Shams University* (Egypt) November 28-December 2, 1994 (pp. 615–655) (in Arabic).

Gebril, F.A. (1989a). Family's social structure and its relation with parental behavior types and aggressive behavior in children. *Journal of the Faculty of Education, Mansoura University* (Egypt), 2(12), 47–136 (in Arabic).

Gebril, F.A. (1989b). *The scale for aggressive behavior expression types.* Cairo: The Anglo-Egyptian Bookshop (in Arabic).

Gebril, F.A. and Al-Mowafy, F. (1985). Mother's levels of aggressive and authoritarian and their relationship with children's aggression and family's demographic variables. *Journal of the Faculty of Education, Mansoura University* (Egypt), 2(7), 181–220 (in Arabic).

Gelles, R.J. (1999). Family violence. In R.L. Hampton (Ed.), *Family Violence: Prevention and treatment, Vol. 1: Issues in children's and families' lives,* 2nd ed. (pp. 1–32), Thousand Oaks: Sage Publications.

Ghalab, M.A. and El-Dousseki, M.I. (1994). A comparative psychological study between extrinsic religious orientations and intrinsic religious orientations in attitudes toward violence and some personality traits. *Psychological Studies* (Egypt), 4(15), 327–374 (in Arabic).

Ghanam, M.H. (1998). Violence phenomenon in the eyes of a sample of Egyptian intellectuals. *Journal of Psychology* (Egypt), 12(45), 80–90 (in Arabic).

Ghanam, M.H. (2000). Ideal and good example for the secondary school students: A psychological pilot study. *Journal of Psychology* (Egypt), 14(56), 132–149 (in Arabic).

Ghreeb, A.A. (1994). *Using psychodrama technique to reduce the emotional disturbances in children.* Unpublished Ph.D. thesis, College of Girls, Ain Shams University (Egypt) (in Arabic).

Ghreeb, Z.A. (2000). *Assessment of efficacy of a program for developing communication skills in the family atmosphere: An experimental study.* Unpublished Ph.D. thesis, College of Girls, Ain Shams University (Egypt)(in Arabic).

Goldstein, A.P. and Conoley, J.C. (1997) (Editors). *School violence Intervention: A practical handbook.* New York: Guilford Press.

Habib, M. A. (1995). Types of parental behavior (Socialization) and family size as early determinants for children's extreme behavior. *Journal of Psychology* (Egypt), *9*(33) 98–127 (in Arabic).

Hafez, N. and Kasem, N.F. (1993a). A suggestive counseling program for reducing aggressive behavior among children in the light of some variables. *Journal of Counseling* (Egypt), *1*(1), 143–177 (in Arabic).

Hafez, N. and Kasem, N.F. (1993b). *Ain Shams Scale for Aggressive Behavior Forms in Children.* Cairo: The Anglo-Egyptian Bookshop (in Arabic).

Hafez, N. and Kasem, N.F. (1993c). Frustration and aggression. *Egyptian Journal of Psychological Studies* (Egypt), *2*(6), 75–84 (in Arabic).

Hagezy, E. (1986). Mass violence: A preliminary observations. In F.A. Abou-Hatab (Ed.) *Yearbook in Psychology,* Vol. 5 (pp. 279–296), Cairo: The Anglo-Egyptian Bookshop (in Arabic).

Hasan, B. H. (1993). The development of the ability to understand convertive aggressive behavior in primary school children. *Journal of Psychology* (Egypt), *7*(27), 26–35 (in Arabic).

Hasan, H.A. (1990). Conformity and nonconformity to norms of Egyptian society. *Journal of the Social Sciences* (Kuwait), *18*(2), 109–128 (in Arabic).

Hasan, M.S. (1998). Instigators of the aggressive behavior. *Journal of Social Affairs* (U.A.E.), *15*(59), 123–136 (in Arabic).

Hedia, F.M.A. (1998). Differences between marital adjusted and maladjusted couples' children in aggression and self-concept. *Journal of Psychology* (Egypt), *12*(47), 6–20 (in Arabic).

Helmy, I.I. (1999). *Familial (marital) violence.* Cairo: Dar Kabaa for Printing, Publishing and Distribution (in Arabic).

Helwa, M.A.M. (1997). *The relationship between perceptions of parental acceptance and rejection and the aggressive behavior in deaf-mute male and female children aged between 14-18 years.* Unpublished M. A. thesis, the Institute for Higher Studies on Childhood, Ain Shams University (Egypt) (in Arabic).

Hussein, M.H. (1994). *Aggressive behavior and its relation to class environment variables as perceived by fourth grade pupils.* Unpublished M.A. thesis, Faculty of Education, Alexandria University (Egypt) (in Arabic).

Ibrahim, M.A.M. (1996). The societal factors lead to violence in some schools in Greater Cairo. *Educational and Social Studies, Faculty of Education, Helwan University* (Egypt), *2*(3,4), 1–35 (in Arabic).

Ibrahim, M.M. (1999). *Psychology of frustration (compelling) and creativity.* Beirut (Lebanon): Dar al-Farabi (in Arabic).

Ismail, E.S. (1988). *Psychology of terrorism and violent crime.* Kuwait: That el-Selasal (in Arabic).

Ismail, E.S. (1996). The psychology of extremism and terrorism. *Annals of the Faculty of Arts, Kuwait University* (Kuwait). Monograph 110, Vol. XVI (in Arabic).

Jalabi, Kh. (1998). *Violence psychology and peace process strategy.* Beirut (Lebanon): Dar al-Fikr (in Arabic).

Kamel, A.M. (2002). Expectational education for prevention school crisis and disaster: A pilot study. In A. M. Kamel (Ed.), *Research in psychology: Field and experimental studies.* (pp. 193–207), Cairo: El-Nahada el-Mesaria Bookshop (in Arabic).

Kamel, A.M. and Al-Fakherani, Kh.I. (2002). The effect of crowding [high density population] as [an] environmental variable on hostility and assertiveness. In A.M. Kamel (ed.), *Research in Psychology: Field and experimental studies* (pp. 209–246), Cairo: El-Nahad el-Mesaria Bookshop (in Arabic).

Lutfy, T.I. (1992). Socialization and violent behavior in children: A field study of a sample of primary school children in Beni Soueif, Egypt. In A. Shukry (Ed.), *Family and Childhood* (pp. 177-231), Alexandria (Egypt): Dar el-Maarefa al-Gamiaa (in Arabic).

Mahmoud, F.H. (1995). Developing a program based on group play to reduce aggressive behavior among preschool children. In A.M. El-Sayed (Ed.), *Studies and research in psychology* (pp. 295-331), Cairo: Dar el-Fikr al-Arabi (in Arabic).

Mahmoud. M.M. (1990). The effect of authority on aggression and its relationship with personality. *Journal of the Social Sciences (Kuwait)* 83–107 (in Arabic).

Mater, A.M. (1986). *A study of the relationship between aggression and some variables and the efficiency of a counseling program in reducing aggression.* Unpublished Ph.D. thesis, Faculty of Education, Suez Canal University (Egypt)(in Arabic).

Meleikan, L.H. (1965). Authoritarian and some related variables in two different cultural groups. In. L.K. Meleika (Ed.), *Readings in social psychology in the Arab countries.* Vol. 1 (pp. 572–589), Cairo: The National House for Printing and Publishing (in Arabic).

Meleikan, L.H. and El-Deerni, H.A. (1984). Some manifestations of aggressive behavior among intermediate and secondary school students: A pilot study on interests and psychological attitudes. *Center for Educational Research, Qatar University* (Qatar), 7(2), 389–439 (in Arabic).

Metwally, L.A. (1981). *Aggressive behavior and its relationship with some types of family education (Socialization). Unpublished M.A. thesis, Faculty of Education, Mansoura University (Egypt)* (in Arabic).

Mohammed, A.A. (1999). The efficiency of a behavioral training program based on a diversity of group activities in reducing aggressive behavior among autistic children. *Journal of Faculty of Arts, Menoufia University* (Egypt), 20(38), 41–67 (in Arabic).

Moussa, R.A. (1989). The differences in aggressive responses among deaf-mute and normal adolescents: A psychodynamic study by using the Hand Test. *Proceedings of the 2nd Annual Conference on Egyptian Child, The Center for Studies on Childhood,* Ain Shams University (Egypt), Vol. 1, pp. 52–78 (in Arabic).

Moussa, R.A. (1993). Antisocial behavior of handicapped children: A comparative study. *Journal of the Faculty of Education. Al-Azhar University* (Egypt), 31, 38–62 (in Arabic).

Munier, D. (1983). *The relationship between aggressive behavior and some personality and social variables among primary school children.* Unpublished M.A. thesis, Faculty of Education, Mansoura University (Egypt) (in Arabic).

Naceur, Farida (2001). Built environment and antisocial behavior: Case study of Batna City: Algeria. Paper presented at the *First International Conference on Social Sciences and the Development of Society,* College of the Social Science, Kuwait University, Kuwait, April 10–12, 2001, Kuwait.

Nasr, S. (1983). *Aggressive personality and its relation with socialization.* Unpublished M.A. thesis, Faculty of Arts, Ain Shams University (Egypt) (in Arabic).

Nasr, S. (1994). *Violence in Egyptian society: A Bibliography of Arab studies on violence.* Vol. 1. Cairo: National Center for Sociological and Criminal Research (in Arabic).

Nasr, S.A.A. (1998). *The efficiency of a program to modify the social behavior in a sample of abused mentally retarded children, and its relation with the children's social adjustment.* Unpublished M.A. thesis, the Institute for Higher Studies on Childhood, Ain Shams University (Egypt) (in Arabic).

Negela, A.M. (1997). *The impact of school theatre on reducing aggressive behavior in primary school children.* Unpublished Ph.D. thesis, Faculty of Education, Zagazig University (Egypt) (in Arabic).

O'Donoghue, J. (1995). Violence in the schools. In L.L. Adler and F.L. Denmark (Eds.), *Violence and the prevention of violence* (pp. 101–108), Westport, CT: Praeger.

Ohlin, L. and Tonry, M. (1989). Family violence in perspective. In L. Ohlin and M. Tonry (Eds.), *Family violence* (p. 1–18), Chicago: The University of Chicago Press.

Omar, A.R. (2001). The relationship between students' violence and some social variables in a sample of secondary school students. Paper presented at the *8th Annual Conference of the Psychological Counseling Center, Ain Shams University*, Cairo, Egypt, November 4–6, 2001 (in Arabic).

Refeay, N.M. (1983). *A study on the level of hostility in blind and non-blind girls*. Unpublished M.A. thesis, Faculty of Education, Tanta University (Egypt) (in Arabic).

Rizk, K. (1992). On the dynamics of attacking school teachers. *Proceedings of the 8th Annual Convention on Psychology in Egypt*. The Egyptian Association for Psychological Studies, the Institute for Higher Studies on Childhood, Ain Shams University (Egypt) (in Arabic).

Sabry, Y.E. (1989). Risk behavior among juvenile delinquents and its relation to intelligence. *Contemporary Education* (Egypt), 13, 133–149 (in Arabic).

Safwet, A. and El-Dousseki, M. (1993). The contributions of Egyptian Psychological research studies in investigating prejudice. *Psychological Studies* (Egypt), 3(4), 429–477 (in Arabic).

Saigh, P.A. and Omar, A.M. (1983). The effects of a good behavior game on the disruptive behavior of Sudanese elementary school students. *Journal of Applied Behavior Analysis*. 16, 329–344.

Salama, M.M. (1990). The relationship between family size and children's dependency and aggression. *Journal of Psychology* (Egypt), 4(14), 34–42 (in Arabic).

Saleh, A. M.H. (1995). Efficiency of reward-punishment reinforcement package and peers' pressure in modifying the aggressive behavior in preschool children: An experimental study. *Educational Studies* (Egypt), 10(78), 17–56 (in Arabic).

Saleh, S. Kh. (1998). *A strategy for eradication violence among secondary school students: A critical view and field study*. Cairo: Dar Ghreeb for Printing, Publishing and Distribution (in Arabic).

Seiam, S. (1994). *Violence and religious speech in Egypt*. 2nd ed. Cairo: Sinai for Publishing (in Arabic).

Shelby, A.M. (1999). *Efficiency of a behavioral program in reducing violence level in a sample of mentally retarded*. Unpublished M.A. thesis, Faculty of Arts, Ain Shams University (Egypt) (in Arabic).

Sidaoui, R. (2000). Sociology of violence: Discourse and action. *Arab Studies* (Lebanon), 36(4), 75–92 (in Arabic).

Sheban, A.G.M. (1996). *The efficiency of a program for social skills in reducing aggressive behavior among primary school children*. Unpublished M. A. thesis, the Institute for Higher Studies on Childhood, Ain Shams University (Egypt) (in Arabic).

Soueif, M.I. (1958). Extreme response sets and delinquency. *The National Review of Criminal Science* (Egypt), 1(3), 24–38 (in Arabic).

Soueif, M.I. (1968). *Extremeness as a response style*. 3rd ed. Cairo: Anglo-Egyptians Bookshop (in Arabic).

Stephens, R.D. (1994). Planning for safer and better school: School violence prevention and intervention strategies. *School Psychology Review*, 23, 204–216.

Yassen, H. M., Al-Mosowy, H. and Al-Zamel, M. (1998). Abuse of preschool child and its psychological correlates: A cross-cultural study in Kuwaiti and Egyptian societies. *Proceedings of the First International Conference on: The Kindergarten Child at the State of Kuwait*. Part I (pp. 477–509), Department of Psychology, College of Basic Education, Public Authority for Applied Education and Training, Kuwait 13–15 April, 1998 (in Arabic).

Chapter 12

Violence in Schools
Australia

Judith E. Papházy

In June 2003 a young woman from Victoria, Australia, was awarded $76,000 for what was referred to in court as "sustained bullying during her high school years." John Bertrand, the six-foot, two-inch tall skipper of Australia 2, winner of the 1983 America's Cup, recalled his fears when at the age of 14 years he was bullied in high school. Now, some 40 years later, he can still feel the same fear when he is cornered! And, in December 2003 a Victorian family petitioned the Children's Court for an intervention order to create a 5 meter exclusion shield around their son to keep two bullies aged 14 years away from him.

These examples illustrate what many surveys and studies have found, namely, that bullying is perceived as a significant problem in many Australian schools. In fact, the incidence of bullying in Australian schools has been estimated as high as one-in-five students in any given year (Rigby, 1996). In New South Wales, Australia's most populous state, a 1999 study found that 23.7% of students in grades six to eight reported they had bullied other students. A further 12.7% said they were bullied while 21.5% indicated that they were both bullied and also had bullied others. At a co-educational high school in Tasmania (Australia's smallest state), students between the ages of 12 and 16 reported that 32% of the girls were bullied (Rigby, 1995). However, of even greater concern was their conclusion: "that school was not a safe place."

Examining the effects of bullying on their final two school years, Rigby (1999) found that peer victimization resulted in relatively poor mental and physical health for these students. There are numerous studies linking childhood bullying to subsequent adolescent and adult depression. Salmon, James, and Smith (1998) as well as Rigby (1998) found that bullied secondary student victims reported anxiety, depression, and low self-esteem. A further effect was an impaired ability to form appropriate peer, and later adult, relationships (Olwens, 1992). These are the ongoing tragedies for victims. However, bullies, too, often suffer long-term consequences. Studies have shown that students who bully have a 25% greater chance of committing juvenile and adult offences (Olwens, 1989).

Many elementary and secondary school students find their school years hell because bullying is not dealt with effectively by their schools. These young people do not benefit from school. They lose out scholastically. They lose out socially. They feel the need to escape from their intolerable school world. They abuse alcohol and other drugs as a ways of anesthetizing themselves from the threat of violence at school. Truancy and feigned illness are other avenues of escape. Moreover, some of these bullied youngsters do become ill. Migraines, stomach disorders, and other stress induced symptoms, such as panic attacks and phobias are not uncommon (Salmon et al., 1998; Boulton et al., 1994; and Rigby, 1993).

Another important factor in school violence relates to teacher-student bullying. Very preliminary work by Eslea, Stepanova and Cameron-Young from the University of Central Lancashire (see <www.uclan.ac.uk/facs/science/psychol/bully/files/montreal.pdf>) indicates that out of 200 university students 76% (n = 152) were the recipients of some form of teacher aggression; 53% were ridiculed or humiliated; 51% had their academic work picked on; 46% felt they were unfairly punished; 33% were verbally abused; and 22% were physically abused. Another 45% of victims indicated that teacher aggression happened "sometimes," while 96% indicated it happened during class, especially math, which scored in the top 40%; followed by English, 32%; and physical education, 28%. In addition, 36% indicated bullying by teachers also happened in their elementary school years.

In the Australian context this aspect of school violence is not well researched. Many students perceive some of their teachers' behaviors as bullying. This of course raises the question – what is teacher bullying? Rigby & Slee (1993) provide an Australian definition. They state, "bullying is a repeated oppression, psychological or physical, of a less powerful person by a more powerful individual or group of persons." Bullying can be verbal, physical, or psychological. It can be abuse, threat, intimidation, or assault. Thus, teachers who are negatively critical, sarcastic, intimidating, threatening or abusive in their language are bullies. Teachers who use their position of power to tease or put down students are bullies. Teachers who belittle students' academic or athletic ability are bullies. And of course teachers who hit or force students to perform excessive or physical tasks are bullies. In discussion with teachers as to their views about teacher bullying, a number considered what students felt was bullying to be merely "disciplining" or "correcting" the student.

The final part of the school violence triangle is student-to-teacher bullying. Some Australian states have passed legislation, for example, to forbid a former problem student from coming onto school property. This is a result of physical assaults on teachers on school grounds. Teachers, usually those in the secondary school years, have reported incidents of intimidation by students. These students have challenged the teacher's authority, have used abusive language, have threatened physical harm, or have made threatening phone calls or left threatening SMS text messages and e-mails. And, very occasionally, weapons, such as knives, have been brought into schools.

What makes one human being or a group of human beings bully another? The answer points to many factors. Starting at the beginning, the family has a great, perhaps the greatest, influence on how children develop their social and interpersonal skills. Also, the interaction between genetics and the environment helps shape personality, problem- solving skills, learning styles, and emotional intelligence. It is, however, the school environment which, after the family, plays the most significant role in socializing children and adolescents. Children in Australia attend school for thirteen years, from Prep to Year 12. Legally they must attend from the ages of six to fifteen. They spend most of their waking hours at school. As their focus changes from family to peers, their social, emotional, intellectual, and physical experiences at school develop their sense of competence and self-worth. Research indicates that successful school adjustment increases self-esteem and an array of healthy behaviors (Williams, Chambers, Logan, & Robinson, 1996). Conversely, children and adolescents who fail to adjust well to school and who fail to form healthy behaviors are more likely to turn to deviant peer groups, use drugs, or engage in other delinquent behaviors. They are more likely to be anti-social, aggressive, depressed, and sometimes suicidal (Williams et al., 1996; Rigby & Slee, 1993). Thus, schools are places where pro-social skills must be taught and practiced. Teachers must be positively involved with their students. Bullying in any form must be seen as totally unacceptable. Schools that promote a sense of community, where students and teachers have a strong sense of belonging, are places where bullying, delinquency, violence, and alienation are unlikely to exist.

PROGRAMS AGAINST SCHOOL VIOLENCE

All Australian schools have anti-bullying policies but not necessarily actual anti-bullying programs. When they exist they are rather ad-hoc and therefore often not effective. Professor Prior of Melbourne University reports that anti-bullying programs are only mildly effective, reducing bullying by 15%. So, what is the role of the school in stopping bullying? First and foremost, each school must decide that there is zero tolerance for violence. It has to be a whole school approach that involves an active partnership between the school as an organization, i.e., teachers and students, and the parents. Studies conducted in a number of countries show that the way to significantly reduce, if not eliminate, school violence is by the whole school approach (Olwens, 1994). Anti-bullying programs such as "Healthy Relationships" make use of health, legal, and educational experts to give children and adolescents skills in, among other things, learning how to deal with bullying. "Peer support groups" and "Cross-age tutoring" are ways of connecting students with each other to help prevent bullying. "Building Better Buddies" is an anti-bullying program which John Bertrand espouses. It is used in a number of Australian schools and focuses on changing the attitudes of bystanders as well as the culture of the school.

RESILIENCE PROMOTION IN SCHOOLS

I would now like to outline a program we have been running in a number of Victorian pre-schools, elementary schools, and junior secondary schools. The program is based on Grotberg's (1995 & 1999) Resilience Promotion model – the I HAVE, external supports; the I AM, internal strengths; and the I CAN, social/interpersonal and problem solving skills. Grotberg, after conducting research in 27 countries, finalized the definition of resilience as "the human capacity to face, overcome, be strengthened by, and even transformed by adversity." Resilience gives children and adolescents the strengths and skills to overcome adversities such as bullying.

Grotberg's model is based on fifteen elements of resilience:

I HAVE

- people around me I trust and who love me, no matter what.
- people who set limits for me so I know when to stop before there is danger or trouble.
- people who show me how to do things right by the way they do things.
- people who want me to learn to do things on my own.
- people who help me when I am sick, in danger, or need to learn.

I AM

- a person people can like and love.
- glad to do nice things for others and show my concern.

- respectful of myself and others.
- willing to be responsible for what I do.
- sure things will be all right.

I CAN

- talk to others about things that frighten me or bother me.
- find ways to solve problems that I face.
- control myself when I feel like doing something not right or dangerous.
- figure out when it is a good time to talk to someone or take action.
- find someone to help me when I need it.

(Grotberg, 1995)

Teachers are crucial in the promotion of resilience; they are the I HAVE people who provide the climate that allows students to feel comfortable enough to express their thoughts, and to discuss and negotiate solutions to problems even when there are differing views. In fact, such a school climate allows and encourages different points of view so that tolerance develops. Students who can negotiate, problem-solve, and accept differences are unlikely to either bully or to be victims. Obviously, teachers' I AM resilience factors need to be well developed. They need be respectful of others and generally calm. They need to be people who show empathy and behave responsibly. They need to be confident, optimistic, forward-looking, and able to plan for the future. Their I CAN resilience factors, their interpersonal and problem solving skills need to be very evident. Are they the type of people who generate new ideas, and do they encourage this in their students? Do they use humor effectively, for example, a tension breaker? Do they communicate appropriately with their students? Do they demonstrate a range of problem-solving skills and encourage students to explore different ways to problem solve? Do they seek help when they need it and thus show their students that it is sensible to ask for help at times?

To assist teachers to evaluate honestly their own resilience-promoting language and behavior, a personal checklist of necessary I HAVE factors is presented below.

As the teacher do I

1. show my trustworthiness to *every* student by the positive and fair way I speak and interact with each student?   A   U   S   N
2. set and enforce rules/limits/consequences in a consistently fair way – i.e., without criticism or negative attitudes?
                                                                                        A   U   S   N

3. consistently model appropriate behaviors and speech in my interactions with every student?   A   U   S   N
4. encourage every student to develop independence by my words,
behaviors, lesson plans, and, if necessary for the student, by manip-
ulating the environment?*   A   U   S   N
5. help every student to persist with his/her tasks until finished? However, I accept that the level of accomplishment will/may vary because of physical/academic differences in students.

                                                 A   U   S   N
6. help in a positive manner as and when necessary without impa-
tience?   A   U   S   N
7. praise students' efforts and attempts, as well as their successes?

                                                 A   U   S   N
8. regularly remind and discuss with students what **fair** means in the
classroom and playground?   A   U   S   N
9. lead discussions and activities on optimism and sense of community in the classroom and school?   A   U   S   N
10. practice the resilience factors which are not yet well developed in
me?   A   U   S   N

> Scoring: A = Always
>   U = Usually
>   S = Sometimes
>   N = Not yet

*Putting the student into a group/pairing with another, etc., as necessary for the
student.

With any program that addresses changing language, behavior and
attitudes, the earlier one starts the better. Hence, this resilience program
is best commenced in the early school years. Then, as children begin to
master the dual skills of academic work and social interaction with peers,
their teachers model and promote resilience. When teachers model I HAVE
resilience behaviors, they provide a safe environment in which students'
internal strengths (I AM), coupled with problem solving and social skills
(I CAN), further develop. Grotberg's research indicates that students can
promote their I HAVE resilience factors around the age of nine. Until then,
they rely on teachers and other adults as their I HAVE models. Thus teachers who show young students how to talk and listen, how to take turns and
share, how to show concern and care, how to allow and value others' differences, and how to problem solve, actively demonstrate resilience. Further,
they help students to resolve personal and learning problems. Take this

example from a Grade 2 class in which two boys are teasing a little girl who cannot balance on a wooden beam in physical education.

TEACHER Tom and Tyson, I see you are good at balancing. That's great. I also see some other people are not so good; well that just shows how we can't all be good at balancing. Now, could you help by holding Sandra's hands, one on each side, to make sure she can safely walk along the beam? And, by the way, it would be nice if you could tell Sandra you're sorry you laughed at her.

When the students return to the classroom the teacher can build on this incident and talk about difference (e.g., How we differ in height, in hair and eye color; how we differ in skills – sports, art, music, etc.; how we differ in academic skills – math, reading, writing, etc.).

TEACHER So, as your teacher, one of my jobs is to help you all to learn how to be fair to each other. When we see someone is not very good at something we can help them get better at it, okay?

In this example the teacher used the following resilience factors:

From the I HAVE–shows me how to do things right, wants me to learn.
From the I AM–respectful of self and others responsible for what I do.
From the I CAN–problem solve, control self.

The next example is the result of work we did to help resolve a series of bullying problems with nine- and ten-year-olds in a country school. We started by asking these children, "Why do games have rules?" Their answers, condensed after brainstorming were:

- so people can't cheat
- so it's fair to everyone
- so it can be played
- so people get turns
- so no-one gets hurt

Our next question was, "Why are there rules about driving cars?" Their answers were:

- so there are no crashes
- to keep us safe
- so we can get where we're going
- so we know what to do
- so there's order

Finally, we asked, "Why do you think schools have rules?" Their answers were:

- to stop people getting hurt
- for safety
- because things would be out of control
- to help us learn
- to keep us quiet
- to keep the school tidy

Much discussion of these reasons for rules followed. Thus it was rather easy to ask the children which of these reasons they thought were really important and why they thought them important. Their final selection comprised three reasons:

- so its fair to everyone
- to be safe
- so no-one gets hurt

(I HAVE – I AM – I CAN)

These three reasons led to three additional questions:

- Is bullying fair?
- Is it safe (especially for the victim)?
- Does anyone get hurt?

The children agreed that bullying wasn't fair, that it was not safe for the victims, and that people got hurt when bullied.

Our next task was to remind them of earlier discussions about the I HAVE elements and ask them to list some of the I HAVE people in their lives. Many children listed parents, grandparents, teachers, sports coaches, club leaders, relatives, and peers. This led to asking them if they were, or could be, an I HAVE person for anyone (e.g., a friend, a younger brother or sister, a little student at the school, etc.).

Having established that they could be I HAVE people in a variety of ways, we asked if they could be I HAVE people to bullies and victims. Needless to say, this caused heated discussion. After some time, when the need to be punitive was exhausted, many practical ways of being an I HAVE person emerged.

- being trustworthy
- stopping people from being hurt

- showing people how to behave sensibly
- helping people to feel safe

Now we came to crunch time' our question was: "Is it possible to be fair to both bullies and their victims?" Again, a rather natural tendency to deny fairness to the bully had to be worked through. However, this was much easier as the children were seriously trying to use I HAVE factors. Agreement was reached that if we really meant "being fair to everyone" it had to include bullies.

The task the children set themselves was to come up with "ways of being fair so no-one gets hurt" ideas. They brainstormed and filled sheets of paper with suggestions. We worked through these with them. Their final result was:

- Everyone is responsible to keep things fair and safe.
- Everyone needs to stop bullies.
- Everyone needs to help the kids being bullied.

Actually, their three points utilized many I HAVE – I AM – I CAN factors. From the I HAVE factors:

- people I can trust who help me
- people who set limits to stop dangerous things/behaviors
- people who show me how to do things right.

From the I AM factors:

- respectful of myself and others
- willing to be responsible for what I do
- sure things will turn out okay.

From the I CAN factors:

- talk to others about things that bother me
- find ways to solve problems
- find someone to help me when I need it.

Our view of these children was that they were serious in dealing with bullying and wanted practical ways to achieve a good outcome. Once more we brainstormed about ways to get involved, and everyone was responsible and helped out.

As is often the case, if young people are given the direction and opportunity to problem-solve, the results are amazing. These wonderfully inventive and well-intentioned children came up with the following:

- That anyone who sees bullying is to gather a group of peers (because bullies can be tough and a bit frightening) larger than that of the bully or bullies, and go up to the bully (or bullies) and say, "Stop, that's not fair."
- This is to happen every time bullying is seen.
- The victim is to be invited to come away with the group. (And after a time one of the children suggested that maybe the bully should be invited to join the group also.)

(I HAVE – I AM – I CAN)

We conducted regular sessions with these nine- and ten-year-olds over a period of six weeks. A follow up some three months later found that bullying among the nine- and ten-year-olds was almost non-existent. That bullies were now more regular class members who, if they did a bit of teasing, were quickly reminded to be fair, and that was the end of it. Other classes noticed the changes and asked what was going on, so these children showed other children in their school what could be done. Teachers reported better co-operation and classroom behavior.

The children said they were learning better, and those who had been frightened now felt safer. The final reporting came from parents. They said their children seemed happier at home and at school, and that aggression between siblings was much less.

The outcome for the groups at this school was an overall improvement in the lives of all concerned. Resilience, we found, improved not only their skills, attitudes and behaviors, but it also built a sense of community. In consciously promoting resilience these children and adults worked together and learned to overcome a challenging problem.

In the junior secondary years it is important to develop problem solving skills in academic, athletic, creative, social, and community settings. Young people need practice in and success with a great variety of tasks. They need good communication skills to ensure they can listen and speak appropriately. They need self-confidence and self-control, the ability to stand up for themselves, to be assertive but not aggressive. They need to be able to relate to peers, to be generally friendly and good-natured. And, they need to know when and from whom to ask for help.

We know that the quest for identity is the major task of adolescence. The "who am I?" questions occupy much of adolescents' time. This can make young people vulnerable if they feel alienated, humiliated, or laughed at. It can also result in victim behaviors. Young people are likely to feel frustration and anger as a result of not being accepted by peers. Take the case of Jillian, a fourteen-year-old who can't control the anger she feels at being excluded by a group of girls she wants to be a part of. Her response is to shout obscenities at them. In fact, she throws objects, anything at hand – books, chairs, etc., at them. As a result, Jillian is suspended for "dangerous behavior." Jillian's secondary school has just commenced the Resilience Promotion program and the Grades 7 and 8 teachers are working on designing lunch-time activities to keep these thirteen- and fourteen-year-olds busy. The teachers have been discussing the I HAVE, I AM, I CAN factors with the senior grades and have a group of the prestige students – those perceived "winners" because of their social and/or athletic skills. These senior students will run the recess and lunch-time activities. The aim is to involve all Grade 7 and 8 students so that everyone will have the opportunity to play either a sport or a game or join an activity (e.g., target-throwing, chess or other board games, music, horticulture, designing herb/kitchen/flower gardens, etc.). The younger students will be encouraged to find something that suits them or something they would like to try. The older students provide the I HAVE factors. Hopefully, as a result of these efforts, the Jillians of this world will develop and learn some of the I AM and I CAN factors and so become more self-controlled and more acceptable to peers. In addition, those young people who practiced exclusion might learn the skill of sharing.

There is no doubt that teachers, schools, and parents must work together to help children and adolescents to grow into competent, caring people with a sense of commitment to their community. The Australian Financial Review (17 October, 2003) cited the cost of bullying to Australian businesses at "up to $21 billion a year." In a country with a population just touching 20 million that is an astronomical cost, one which the country cannot afford. The answer to this problem lies in the education and socialization of children. Modeling, teaching and practicing resilience promotion through the I HAVE, I AM, and I CAN factors may well prove to be a significant part of the answer. An outline of how to introduce the program into schools follows.

RESILIENCE PROGRAMS IN SCHOOLS

To introduce any program into schools involves a number of steps and stages. First, approval from the local education authority or school principal is necessary. This best achieved by face–to-face meetings. The person responsible for giving such approval needs to hear and see not only the value of resilience promotion but also your passion and commitment. At this meeting, the Resilience Promotion Information needs to be covered and the two resilience diagrams presented and explained.

What Is Resilience?

Resilience is the human capacity to face, overcome, and even to be strengthened and transformed by the effects of adversity.

How Does It Work in Schools?

- With resilience children can triumph over adversities (small and large problems as well as crises and traumas).
- How teachers respond to situations and how they help children to respond separates those teachers who promote resilience in their students from those who destroy resilience.
- The three sources which promote resilience are I HAVE – I AM – I CAN (Grotberg, 1995).

I HAVE: (external supports)

- teachers I trust, who like and respect me.
- teachers who set limits for me, explain rules and apply appropriate consequences.
- teachers who encourage me to do things on my own.
- teachers who help me when I am sick, in danger, or in need to learn.

I AM: (internal strengths)

- a person who can like and love, and generally be good natured.
- a person who can show pleasure and concern for others, and has empathy.
- a person who can be self-respecting and respect others.
- a person who can accept personal responsibility.
- a person who can have faith and optimism about the future.

I CAN: (problem solving and social/interpersonal skills)

- share my thoughts and feelings and problems with others.
- work out problems for myself and persist with tasks.
- control myself when I feel like doing something dangerous or wrong.
- know when to talk or when to act.
- find help when I need it.

WHY IS IT IMPORTANT?

Children and adolescents need resilience to face many common problems (e.g., teasing, bullying, self-doubt, no friends, etc.), academic problems (e.g., reading/writing/comprehension problems, memory or cognitive processing problems, other learning difficulties), and common crises (e.g., death, divorce, drugs, illness, accident, etc.). Children and adolescents often feel lonely, fearful, and vulnerable. These feelings are less overwhelming for those who have the resources of resilience.

WHAT ARE THE OUTCOMES?

Teachers who promote resilience encourage their students to become more autonomous, independent, responsible, problem-solving and caring. As a result, students can become more active in promoting their own resilience. Building resilience safeguards them against depression and runaway behaviors. It gives them optimism and the ability to move forward confidently. In the school environment the whole school culture improves. Strengthening resilience has a positive impact on all facets of school functioning; it helps produce better behavior, better cooperation, better work and curriculum outcome. Resilience-promoting schools develop a culture that promotes belonging that in turn promotes a sense of community.

How Can It Be Promoted—By Whom?

Resilience is a basic human capacity nascent in all students. Initially parents but later and, often more importantly, teachers can awaken and form this human capacity in students into an active, coping resource. Teachers promote resilience in students through their words, actions, and with the environments they provide. They learn to use the resilience set of tools. Able to use the language of resilience, teachers help students to identify resilient behaviors in themselves and others. The more teachers understand resilience the greater their opportunities for acting and speaking in ways which guide their own and their students' behaviors. This helps students meet and often resolve their problems and crises with strength and hope.

What Does the Program Contain?

1. Resilience Promotion for each stage:

   a. Prep to Grade 2   d. Grades 7 and 8
   b. Grades 3 and 4   e. Grades 9 and 10
   c. Grades 5 and 6

2. Each stage will have the following five steps plus reference material.

1. *Tasks of the age*: description of where the student is in developmental terms, what tasks are being mastered and how these relate to resilience
2. *What teachers can do*: actions teachers need to take and language they need to use to enhance resilience at student's different stages
3. *Examples of resilience responses*: how positive/negative responses foster/fail resilience in students at each developmental stage
4. *Results*: What happens when resilience has been promoted? What skills have students learned? How do they feel about themselves?
5. *Checklist*: for perceptions of resilience in students

This overview process should be repeated twice, first to the senior staff and senior administrators, and then to the whole school staff. The next step is to break the teaching staff up into the appropriate developmental years. In our Australian experience that is the preparatory year and Grades 1 and 2 (five- to seven-year olds); Grades 3 and 4 (eight- to ten-year olds); and, finally, Grades 5 and 6 (eleven-year-olds). The secondary school divisions are Grades 7 and 8 (twelve- to fourteen-year-olds) and Grades 9 and 10 (fourteen- to sixteen-year-olds).

REFERENCES

Boulton, M.J. & Smith, P.K., Bully/victim problems among middle school children: stability, self perceived competence, and peer acceptance. *Br. J. Dev. Psychol*; 12: 315–329

Eslea, M., Stepanova, E. & Cameron-Young, B. Department of Psychology, University of Central Lancashire, Preston. U.K. *Aggressive Classroom Management: Do Teachers Bully Pupils? Outline*. Access: <www.uclan.ac.uk/facs/science/psychol/bully/files/montreal.pdf>

Forero, R., McLellan, L., Rissel, C. & Bauman, A. (1999). Bullying behaviour and psychosocial health among school students in N.S.W. Australia: Cross sectional survey. BMJ; 344–348 (7 August).

Grotberg, E.H. (1995). *A Guide to Promoting Resilience in Children*. The Hague: The Bernard van Leer Foundation.

Grotberg, E.H. (1999). *Tapping your Inner Strength: How to Find the Resilience to Deal with Anything New*. New Harbinger Publications.

Olwens, D. (1989). Bullying/victim problems among school children; basic facts and effects of school based intervention program. In K Rabin & D Peper (eds.), The Development and Treatment of Childhood Aggression. Hillsdale NJ: Erlbaum.

Olwens, D. (1992) Victimisation by peers: antecendents and long-term outcomes. In K.H. Rabin & J.B. Asendorf (eds.). *Social Withdrawal, Inhibition and Shyness in Children*. Hillsdale NJ: Erlbaum.

Olwens, D. (1994) Bullying at school: basic facts and an effective intervention programme. *J. Child. Psychol Psychiatry Allied Disciplines;* 35: 1171–1190.

Paphazy, J.E. (1993). *The Troublesome Years: Adolescence. Melbourne, Australia: Flactem Pty Ltd.*

Paphazy, J.E. (1994). *Coping with Children: from 3 to 12. Melbourne, Australia: Flactem Pty Ltd.*

Prior, M. (2003) Are our schools doing enough? *The Age—education Oct 20,* access: <education.the age.com.au>

Rigby, K. & Slee, P. (1993) Children's attitudes towards Victims. In D.Tattum, (ed.). *Understanding and Managing Bullying,* Oxford, UK: Heinemann.

Rigby, K. (1995). The motivation of Australian adolescent schoolchildren to engage in group discussion about bullying. *The Journal of Social Psychology* 1354(6): 773–775.

Rigby, K. (1996) Bullying in Australian schools—and what to do about it. Melbourne: Australian Council for Educational Research.

Rigby, K. (1998) Peer relations at school and the health of adolescents. Youth Stud. Aust., 17: 13–17.

Rigby, K. (1999). Peer victimisation at school and the health of secondary school students. *The British Journal of Educational Psychology,* 69, P. 1: 95–105.

Salmon, G., James, A. & Smith, D.M. (1998). Bullying in schools. Self-reported anxiety, depression, and self esteem in secondary school children. BMJ; 317: 924–925.

The Australian Financial Review (October 17, 2003). Access: <www.afr.com>

Williams, K., Chambers, M., Logan, S. & Robinson, D. Association of common health symptoms with bullying in primary school children. BMJ, 313: 17–19.

Chapter 13

Predicting School Violence

DANIEL A KRAUSS

INTRODUCTION

It has been over five years since the fateful day in April of 1999 when Dylan Klebold and Eric Harris began a shooting rampage at Columbine High School in Colorado that led to the deaths of 15 students and teachers, including themselves, and injuries to another 23 students. Recently, the release of a videotape showing both Dylan and Eric laughing and shooting trees with automatic weapons and shotguns six weeks before the incident has reinvigorated discussions of how such tragedies could be prevented (Associated Press, 2003). The echoes of this gruesome event have also continued to engage the attention of researchers, the public, and policy-makers and have led to whole scale changes in the security surrounding our schools. In the wake of this event and other high profile cases of school violence, school administrators have implemented myriad policies aimed at reducing the likelihood of these events re-occurring, including any number of safe school and zero tolerance initiatives (e.g., automatic suspensions or expulsions: 1) for weapons brought to school;[1] 2) for threats made against students or administrators; or 3) for violating school drug policies) (Mulvey & Cauffman 2001). In some cities millions of dollars have been spent post-Columbine on the installation of metal detectors and the hiring of additional security guards for their schools (Vossekuil, Fein, Reddy, Borum, & Modzelski, 2002). Yet, these policy attempts to make schools more secure environments have some scholars suggesting that the measures will have the opposite effect by further alienating students from the school administrators, making it less likely that students will convey possible threats to the faculty (Mulvey & Cauffman, 2001).[2]

In addition to securing the physical environs of the school, post-Columbine policy has also sought to be proactive in assessing the risk of violence within the student body. School administrators and policy-makers have become fixated on the idea of identifying students or "profiling" those who are more likely to engage in these violent acts in order to avoid future tragedies. Such policies have called on mental health professionals as well as students and faculty to name troubled students. In fact, the principal at Columbine High School circulated a memorandum after the tragic events requesting that students report other students who were acting in an unusual manner (Aronson, 2000). While such attempts to identify and predict school violence are clearly heartfelt, at present a vast number of problems inherent in the prediction of school violence suggest that these attempts will be less than adequate in achieving their stated purpose.

This chapter will first examine rates of school violence with special emphasis placed on "targeted" school violence. Targeted violence is a term first used by the United States Secret Service in another context; it was utilized to define the prediction of whether certain individuals would engage in serious attempts and attacks on public or prominent officials (Fein & Vossekuil, 1998). Most recently, targeted school violence has been adopted by the Department of Education and the United States Secret Service joint task force of the Safe School Initiative to describe "school shootings and other school-based attacks where the school was deliberately selected as the location for the attack and was not simply a random site of opportunity" (Vossekuil et al., 2002, p. 4). As such, targeted school violence will be used in this chapter to describe incidents of school violence like the Columbine shootings, in which the school and its surrounding area were specifically chosen by the perpetrators as the setting for their violent acts.[3] Second, recent advances in risk prediction and assessment by mental health professionals will be examined, and the specific limitations of these techniques in predicting targeted school violence will be explored. Finally, several new directions for research and policy-making in this newly emerging subfield will be advanced.

SCHOOL VIOLENCE

Although media portrayal of the Columbine incident (one reporter noted that the three major networks—i.e., ABC, NBC, CBS—aired over 296 news reports on Columbine [Stossel, 1999 as reported in Reddy et al., 2001]) and other school violence issues might have the public believing that such incidents happen frequently,[4] schools remain one of the safest environments for today's youth for both general school violence as well as targeted school violence (DeVoe et al., 2003). Research has found that high-risk youth from the most impoverished neighborhoods are much more likely to be the victims of crime outside rather than inside their school (Snyder & Sickmund, 1999). In fact, for non-fatal violent crimes (i.e., rape, sexual assault, robbery and aggravated assault) generally in 2001, school-aged children were about twice as likely to experience these events away from school as they were to suffer from them at school (DeVoe et al., 2003). From 1995 to 2000, the percentage of students victimized at schools has even dropped from 10 percent to 6 percent, and this trend is true for both violent and non-violent victimization (DeVoe et al., 2003). With the exception of bullying, which has evidenced a slight increase, all other forms of less serious violence in schools, such as physical aggression and petty theft, appear to be on the decline in recent years (DeVoe et al., 2003).

Researchers examining the relationship between the most serious forms of violence and the school setting found that for 1992–1994 and 1997–1998 less than one percent of school-age children's homicides and suicides occurred in or around schools (Dwyer, Osher, & Wagner, 1998; Kachur et al., 1996). Moreover, for every year from 1995 to 2000, children between the ages of 5 and 19 were 70 times more likely to be murdered away from school than at school (DeVoe et al., 2003). Current estimates of the probability that a child will die at school indicate that this likelihood is extremely remote, with probabilities ranging between one in a million or one in two million (Reddy et al., 2001).

The fact that research amply demonstrates that schools overall are relatively safe environments for children does not, however, suggest that our society should be unconcerned with the recent rash of targeted school violence tragedies nor does it suggest we should be unconcerned with preventing such incidents. A joint task force between the United States Department of Education and the United States Secret Service has catalogued 37 targeted school violence events perpetrated by 41 individuals over a 25-year period, 1974–2000. The number of these incidents, unlike other areas of school violence, has remained fairly constant between 1994 and 1999, with three to five events occurring each year. Two thirds of these incidents resulted in the deaths of the perpetrators or other students, faculty, and school administrators (Vossekuil et al., 2002). Although these targeted events represent a very small proportion of an already small number of school crimes, the loss of life associated with them, the destruction these events caused to the community in which they occurred, and the horror they hold for the general public all suggest that additional policy steps need to be undertaken to prevent future incidents. While hindsight is twenty-twenty, facts, such as that the vast majority of these attacks were pre-meditated and often others knew well in advance specific details of the perpetrators' plan, indicate that at least some of these tragedies may have been preventable (Dwyer et al., 1998). Other key findings identified by the joint United States Secret Service and Department of Education task force relating to incidents of targeted school violence suggest that: 1) attacks were rarely sudden and impulsive; 2) most attackers did not directly threaten their targets; 3) attackers often engaged in some behavior over the period prior to the attacks that indicated that they needed help; 4) attackers often evidenced difficulty dealing with significant loses; 5) attackers were often subject to being bullied, persecuted, or injured; 6) attackers often possessed access to weapons and used weapons prior to the attack; 7) no accurate or useful profile of attackers exists; 8) attackers were often stopped by means other than law enforcement (Vossekuil et al., 2002). The common belief that mental health professionals will be able to predict which individuals are most likely to engage in targeted school violence, however, is not a scientific or policy-making avenue that is likely to lead to success.

RISK PREDICTION AND ASSESSMENT

There are a number of different techniques that mental health professionals could utilize in attempting to categorize and predict which students are most likely to engage in targeted school violence. These include: 1) a prediction based on the assessor's intuition and years of clinical experience (i.e., "pure" clinical prediction); 2) a prediction based on an actuarial assessment instrument designed to assess such violence (i.e., an actuarial prediction); 3) a prediction based on a combination of clinical judgment and actuarial factors (i.e., a guided clinical prediction); 4) a prediction based on the profiles of past perpetrators, (i.e., prospective profiling); 5) a prediction based on techniques designed by the Secret Service to "identify, assess, and manage individuals who pose a risk of violence to an identified or identifiable target" (Reddy et al., 2001) (i.e., a threat assessment approach). Yet, all of these techniques suffer from significant weaknesses in predicting violence in general, and therefore suffer from significant weaknesses that suggest their application to the prediction of targeted school violence would be problematic. Moreover, the prediction of targeted school violence also presents a number of unique issues that renders these techniques less useful (Mulvey & Cauffman, 2001; Verlinden et al., 2000). Similar to, and expanding on, the framework suggested by Reddy et al., (2001), each of the general problems of these prediction techniques will be discussed in turn with specific difficulties that targeted school violence present for these methods highlighted.

Pure Clinical Predictions

A large body of empirical literature suggests that mental health professionals relying solely on their clinical hunches are incorrect a majority of times in their predictions of future violence (Faust & Ziskin, 1988; Grisso & Appelbaum, 1992; Hart, Webster, & Menzies, 1993; Lidz, Mulvey, & Gardner, 1993; Melton et al., 1997; Monahan, 1981; Monahan & Steadman, 1994; Otto, 1992; Showalter, 1990). However, more recent research suggests that mental health professionals may not be as inaccurate as was originally believed for long-term predictions of violence (e.g., Mossman [1994] finds in his meta-analysis on this topic that clinical predictions were appreciably better than chance), and they may be even more accurate for short-term predictions of violence (Mossman, 1994; McNeil, Sanders, & Binder, 1998). Yet, a variety of other prediction techniques have demonstrated superiority to pure clinical predictions in various contexts (see e.g., Gardner, Lidz, Mulvey, & Shaw 1996; Harris, Rice, & Cormier, 2002).

Perhaps, the greatest weakness with mental health professionals relying on their judgment and clinical experience in making predictions of violence is that they often ignore the base rates associated with the event being studied. A base rate refers to the frequency of the event among the chosen population. Events with low base rates of occurrence, such as violent behavior generally and targeted school violence predictions in particular, tend to be over-predicted by clinical decision-makers, with these errors in judgment tending to increase as the base rates of the predicted event decreases (Grove & Meehl, 1996). As a result, clinical decision-makers often make false positive errors, predicting an individual will commit violent acts when he/she will in actuality not commit such an act (See Figure 1 for a 2 × 2 depiction of the types of errors a clinician can make).

With regard to targeted school violence, this suggests a substantial problem with a pure clinical prediction because the base rate associated

		Actual Outcomes	
		School Violence Act	No School Violence
Predicted Outcomes	School Violence Act	True Positives	False Alarms or False Positives
	No School Violence	Misses or False Negatives	True Negatives

Figure 1. Different possible outcomes of predictions of targeted school violence.

Actual Outcomes

		School Violence Act	No School Violence
Predicted Outcomes	School Violence Act	6 True Hits	4 False Negatives
	No School Violence	399,996 False Positives	599,994 True Negatives

Figure 2. 2 × 2 table of clinical predictions when the base rate is 1 in a 1,000,000 and the predictive accuracy is 60%.

with such incidents is extremely low. For example, assume the base rate for committing a targeted violent act is ten in a million (it is actually closer to one in a million) and clinical accuracy in predicting such an event is 60 percent (which is far higher than any clinical method is likely to achieve).

As highlighted in Figure 2, of the million students in the sample, six would be correctly identified as likely to be violent, but 399,996 students would be misidentified as violent when they were not actually violent (i.e., 399,996 false positives). These false positive students would be subject to the stigmatization associated with being highlighted as high risk for violence, social service resources would be misused by focusing on counseling and treatment for these identified individuals, and these individuals would likely suffer additional restrictions on their freedom and behavior (Verlinden et al., 2000). Such attempts at labeling will harm a large number of students because these identified students, while still potentially benefiting from any treatment provided, are more likely to be injured by existing policies that suspend them or expel them from school. Even when these misidentified students are allowed to return to school (if they are ever allowed to return) the stigma associated with the label of being high risk for targeted school violence is likely to color others' (i.e., friends, families, and school officials) perceptions as well as their own perceptions of themselves for years to come. Moreover, four actual perpetrators of future targeted school violence would have gone undetected (i.e., false negatives), and four school tragedies would have resulted. Given the low likelihood of an individual actually committing an act of targeted school violence, the costs associated with misidentifying such a large number of students as violent when they are not, and the likelihood that a substantial number of events would still occur, it appears that pure clinical predictions are extremely ill-suited for predictions of targeted school violence.

It might, however, be possible for mental health professionals using such a technique to limit the pool of individuals (i.e., decrease the number of likely individuals from 1 million to a 100 or fewer) that might engage in an act of targeted school violence. This assumes that the mental health professional understands the factors that lead to such violence, and that they could use them in an optimal way in their decision-making. A limited amount of research in this area suggests the former is an incorrect assumption (Furlough & Morrison, 2000; Reddy et al., 2001), and a vast body of empirical literature indicates that even if the former were true the latter would still not be a fair assumption (e.g., Grove & Meehl, 1996). Research on mental health professionals' risk assessment decisions demonstrates that clinicians engage in a number of cognitive errors that inhibit them from being accurate decision-makers in this context, including: 1) often relying on risk factors that they believe are related to violence risk which the empirical literature demonstrates that they are not (i.e., a diagnosis of a mental illness); 2) placing excessive weight on one or a couple of risk factors (i.e., the perpetrators employment instability) to the detriment of other more predictive factors; and 3) placing excessive weight on easily retrievable or salient factors (i.e., the heinousness of a previous violent act). Many of these problems in decision-making have also been demonstrated to exist even if the clinician is warned of these biasing tendencies (Grove & Meehl, 1996). In the end, it is unlikely that pure clinical predictions of targeted school violence will be accurate, and it is likely that such prediction will lead to a large number of students being misidentified as violent when in fact they are not.

Actuarial Predictions

Actuarial based predictions of general violence have demonstrated superiority over pure clinical predictions in several head to head comparisons (Gardner et al., 1996; Harris et al., 2002), but significant problems with this method are also unlikely to make them appropriate for the predictions of targeted school violence. Actuarial instruments are created from empirically verified risk factors (i.e., past history of violence, psychopathic personality, prior arrests, etc.), which have been demonstrated to predict the appropriate outcome for the population being studied (Monahan & Steadman, 1994). These factors are subsequently statistically combined in a manner that maximizes their ability to predict the intended outcome (Harris & Rice, 1999). In the area of violence risk assessment among those suffering from a significant mental illness, actuarial instruments have been developed, such as the Violence Risk Appraisal Guide (VRAG), which predicts such violence at a relatively high rate (Quinsey, Harris, Rice, & Cormier, 1998). This 12-factor instrument normed on a large sub-sample of Canadians has demonstrated in a number of studies to possess a classification accuracy close to 75% for violent offenders (Harris et al., 2002). An iterative decision tree developed by Monahan et al. (2001) on a diverse U.S. sample of civilly committed individuals has even demonstrated a substantially higher classification accuracy.

Yet, while generally superior to clinical predictions of violence, actuarial instruments suffer from a number of flaws generally, and have more additional specific problems that detract from their applicability to targeted school violence prediction and assessment. Researchers have questioned the utility of actuarial prediction instruments for general violence prediction on a number of grounds (e.g., Melton et al., 1997; Monahan et al., 2001). Scholars have criticized: 1) the generalizability of these instruments beyond their original sample; 2) the failure of these instruments to incorporate very rare but important risk factors, for example, a risk factor that would not be relevant to a large population of offenders but might be especially significant to a particular case (i.e., a significant physical disability); and 3) the failure of these instruments to include protective factors, characteristics that lower an individual's risk (i.e., a supportive family) (Monahan, 2003).

As advances in risk prediction have occurred, investigators have also moved away from static (i.e., unchanging traits that predict violence like past criminal acts), dispositional (i.e., the person has a violent personality), and dichotomous (i.e., the person will either be or will not be violent) predictions of violence, and moved towards dynamic (i.e., predictor variables that may change over time, like employment stability), contextual (i.e., examining violent behavior as being controlled by a complex array of person-situation variables), and continuous risk assessments (i.e., people are either more likely or less likely to commit violent acts, and these acts can be prevented) (Borum, 1996; Borum, Fein, Vossekuil, & Berglund, 1999). Actuarial predictions to date, while allowing for more graded predictions of violence, do not often incorporate dynamic or contextual factors in their assessment (Monahan, 2003). As a result, they often fail to allow for changes in an individual's risk or place insufficient weight on the situational factors that might lead to greater violence for an individual.

Perhaps most troubling is the fact that no actuarial instruments currently exist for the prediction of school violence or targeted school violence, and there are a substantial number of reasons to believe that the existing instruments designed for prediction of serious violence among adults would not generalize well to this population (Mulvey & Cauffman, 2001; Reddy et al., 2001). First, with few exceptions, targeted school violence perpetrators have been adolescents.[5] Many personality characteristics and behaviors are in flux during this turbulent developmental time period and often little stability in traits exists (Oltmanns & Emery, 2003). This lack of stability in criminal behavior in particular, has been aptly demonstrated by empirical findings (e.g., Moffit, 1993), and has caused the Diagnostic and Statistical Manual of Mental Disorders, 4th edition Text Revision (DSM-IV TR) as well as earlier iterations to recognize the normality of adolescent limited criminal behavior. The volatility associated with characteristics during the adolescent years is likely to cause actuarial instruments based on adult predictors to be less accurate for adolescents. For example, half of the 12 variables contained in the VRAG are simply not applicable to adolescents (e.g., marital status, failure on a prior conditional release, diagnosis of psychopathy,[6] diagnosis of a personality disorder, number of previous non-violent offenses, diagnosis of schizophrenia). Furthermore, even if an actuarial instrument could be developed for this specific type of prediction for an adolescent population, its reliance on static, dispositional predictors would likely also cause its predictive accuracy to suffer (Mulvey & Cauffman, 2001).

Second, the type of prediction called for in a targeted school violence assessment is a far more specific outcome than the outcome called for by the commonly available actuarial prediction schemes. All the existing actuarial measures use serious violent incidents as their outcome measure. This outcome includes instances of assault, battery, and other serious behavior that would be of less interest to policy-makers interested in solely predicting targeted school violence incidents. Consequently, a prediction based on one of the existing measures might be generalizable to violent student acts in general but have limited utility in predicting specific targeted school violence events. Furthermore, the more general the prediction outcome becomes, the less likely the instrument will be able to predict the most serious and least common instances of violence (Mulvey & Cauffman, 2001). For example, if the broader outcome variable of bullying, physical aggression, and homicidal acts was used as the variable of interest in an actuarial scheme, the larger number of bullying instances and fights would make the instrument a better predictor of these outcomes rather than instances of homicidal acts.

Unfortunately, the limited existing research suggests that the risk factors for general adolescent school violence may be significantly different from those for targeted school violence. Verlinden et al. (2000) in their review of the available warning sign checklists[7] for both general school violence and targeted school violence found that over 1/3 of the variables contained in targeted school violence checklists were not included in the more general warning signs for adolescent violence. In particular, recognized general school violence warning signs, such as: 1) poor achievement in school, 2) low commitment to school, 3) a history of school discipline problems, 3) bringing a weapon to school, and 4) being a victim of abuse or neglect, have not been similarly determined to be important risk factors in targeted school violence incidents (Verlinden et al., 2000). As such, any actuarial instrument that focuses on broader school violence outcomes may be especially susceptible to failing to identify individuals who are the most likely to commit targeted school violence acts.

Third, actuarial instruments are not immune to problems associated with predicting low base rate events. Outcome variables with low base rates are more difficult to develop predictor variables for because insufficient data exists to find and test useful variables. Both the VRAG and Monahan et al.'s (2002) interative decisional tree relied on large population of high risk individuals (over 500) with a substantial plurality of them engaging in the specified outcome variable (over 30 percent). These large numbers of both future offenders and non-offenders allow researchers to narrow the field of appropriate predictor variables and develop the optimal manner for combining the relevant variables to predict the outcome of interest. Although the Secret Service and Department of Education's intensive review of 41 perpetrators of school violence is a start, researchers are far from having a means to identify a sufficient sample of high risk children for targeted school violence who will also attempt to commit the identified act at a sufficient base rate (i.e., a substantial portion will actually attempt to engage in targeted school violence). Without this sample, investigators cannot determine which potential variables are the most accurate predictors, nor can they determine the most optimal means to combine the existing variable for accurate future prediction.

Even if an actuarial prediction instrument could be developed that contained relevant variables that were sufficiently predictive of targeted school violence, however, the actuarial instrument would likely still suffer from the problems associated with high false positive error rates (see Figure 3).

To return to our 2 × 2 table and our previous example, it is likely that an actuarial prediction scheme would be a more accurate predictor

		Actual Outcomes	
		School Violence Act	No School Violence
Predicted Outcomes	School Violence Act	9 True Hits	1 False Negatives
	No School Violence	99,999 False Positives	899,991 True Negatives

Figure 3. 2 × 2 table of actuarial prediction when the base rate is 1 in a 1,000,000 and the predictive accuracy is 90%.

of school violence than a pure clinical prediction method. Yet, even if the predictive accuracy of such a device reached 90 percent (the points mentioned previously suggest that such an achievement is extremely unlikely), it would still produce a large number of false positives. If the number of actual incidents of school violence was again 10 and the number of potential perpetrators was again 1 million, then 99,999 false positives would still result from the use of the instrument. These 99,999 students would confront the problems and liberty restrictions associated with being classified as high risk for such a behavior. In addition, one non-predicted incident of targeted school violence would still occur and one community would have to face the devastation that such an event evokes. The development of appropriate predictor variables or research examining useful warning signs for a high risk adolescent might allow the pool of potential assailants to be substantially limited (i.e., developing initial factors such that a high risk population sample could be generated which evidence a one in one-hundred risk of committing an act of targeted violence rather than a one in one million), which could significantly decrease the false positives associated with an actuarial prediction. Yet, current research is a far from being able to successfully limit the field of potential assailants in this manner, and for all the reasons mentioned previously, it is unlikely that investigators will be able to achieve this goal in the near future.

To summarize, although actuarial risk assessment has shown considerable success in predicting serious adult violence for certain populations, no actuarial instruments currently exist for either general adolescent school violence or targeted school violence. It is also unlikely that useful actuarial predictors will be able to be created for targeted school violence because of the low base rates associated with these events, and actuarial instruments based on more general adolescence school violence are unlikely to generalize to this specific area. Finally, even if an actuarial instrument could be developed specifically for targeted school violence, it is likely that its accuracy would be such that a large number of false positives and significant number of false negatives would result from its use.

Guided Professional Judgments

Partially in reaction to problems inherent in actuarial schemes (i.e., poor generalizability, neglect of rare or protective risk factors, and neglect of dynamic or contextual variables), investigators have developed prediction methods that combine the flexibility of clinical judgments with the scientific accuracy of actuarial decision-making. These risk assessment methods utilize risk factors that have been empirically demonstrated to be linked to risk in the research literature, but they allow mental health professionals to determine how much weight to afford to each of the predictive factors in their final decision-making as well as afford them the opportunity to add additional factors into their calculus (Webster, Douglas, Eaves, & Hart, 1997). The HCR-20 represents one example of the guided clinical judgment approach, and it is designed to assess risk of future violence in adults. It consists of a checklist of twenty items, 10 assessing past or "Historical" factors related to risk, 5 assessing present risk "Clinical" risk factors, and 5 assessing future "Risk" factors. Each item is scored either 0 (absent), 1 (possibly or partially present), or 2 (definitely present). Based on the scoring of the twenty items, the practitioner is intended to offer a statement assessing whether the assessed individual is low, medium, or high risk (Webster et al., 1997).

The same criticisms that have been leveled against pure clinical predictions also have bearing on guided clinical judgments. In particular, the errors associated with assigning non-optimal weights to factors and combining factors in a manner that is subjectively appealing rather than empirically derived is still a significant problem for this method of assessment. This and other problems have led some scholars to suggest that guided clinical judgments are unlikely to be the equal of well-validated actuarial predictions of dangerousness in most contexts (Quinsey et al., 1998). The addition of clinicians being able to adjust assessments with outside factors (i.e., rare or protective factors) or their ability to use these factors in the risk assessment calculus, as allowed by most guided professional judgment instruments, is also controversial. While some commentators have argued it would be unethical for a mental health professional to rely exclusively on a guided professional judgment assessment or even an actuarial risk prediction scheme when a factor not represented in the instrument could be highly predictive in a specific case (Hart, 1997; Hanson, 1998; Monahan et al., 2001),[8] others have suggested that adjusting either an actuarial instrument or guided professional judgment assessment with an outside factor is likely to decrease predictive accuracy (Harris et al., 2002).

With regard to the specific prediction of targeted school violence, there are also a number of factors that caution against the use of guided professional judgments for these assessments. Similar to the discussion of actuarial instruments, there are currently no valid guided professional judgment instruments available for the prediction of targeted school violence, and it is unlikely that schemes developed for other risk prediction contexts would generalize appropriately in this area. As previously noted, the warning signs that have been created for general adolescent school violence are also ill-suited for transfer to the area of targeted school violence prediction. However, some of the factors highlighted in the Secret Service and Department of Justice report on targeted school violence[9] might one day be informative in fashioning a guided professional judgment instrument. It remains to be seen whether such as an instrument would still produce a significant quantity of false positives, but the low base rate associated with targeted school violence incidents indicates that this hypothetical instrument would likely be a significant problem for this approach as well.

Prospective Profiling

Popular media, the public, and even a number of administrators believe that "profiling" potential targeted school violence perpetrators is likely to be an effective means of preventing future Columbines. Unfortunately, the scientific community, with good reason, does not share the optimistic pronouncements that are sometimes voiced for this method of prediction (Borum, 1996). As opposed to general profiling, which uses elements of the crime to focus the investigation on particular suspects, prospective profiling utilizes a description or characteristics of past individuals as a means to describe the likely characteristics of a future perpetrator (Pinizzotto, 1984). Under this rubric, it is believed that a sufficiently small quantity of past assailants' personality characteristics or traits exist that can identify future perpetrators of similar acts with significant sensitivity so that the vast majority of individuals who will commit such crimes will be identified and that the profile or characteristics used to identify these assailants will be sufficiently specific so that they will not describe a large number of individuals who will not commit similar future acts. In a variety of areas, prospective profiling has not been found to be exceptionally accurate, often producing large numbers of both false positives and false negatives (Wrightsman, 2001). One has to go no further than the attempts of certain profilers to describe the likely characteristics of the Washington, D.C. area sniper of 2002 to find evidence of considerable problems with this methodology. At that time, these profiles suggested that it was likely that the Washington sniper was a white male, 20–30 years of age, who was working alone and was likely to engage in a police confrontation that would end in his death (Court TV, 2002). This profile clearly failed to describe the African-American, two-person team who were apprehended by police without either perpetrators' death. Similarly, it has been the conventional wisdom for years that three characteristics, bed-wetting, cruelty to animals, and fire setting, were predictive of the development of serial killers. This profile also has not garnered empirical support when it was further investigated (Reddy et al., 2001).

Given the low base rate associated with targeted school violence events, it is even more likely that any constructed profile of a school shooter will suggest a large number of false positives and a significant number of false negative results (Cooper, 2000; Morse, 2000; Reddy et al., 2001; Vossekuil et al., 2002; Sewell & Mendelson, 2000). Again, such a technique will likely result in a substantial number of students being identified as high risk for violence with all the concomitant detrimental effects such a label is likely to connote. That is not to say that "profiles" of the school shooter have not already entered popular culture as well as the policies of schools but only to highlight that such profiles are particularly likely to be inaccurate because they are often based on limited, insufficient, or no data (Reddy et al., 2001). A number of common profiles, including the "classroom avenger profile" and the "school shooter" profile, indicated that targeted school violence perpetrators were white males who were loners and social outcasts. Unfortunately, the existing evidence does not support these statements (Vossekuil et al., 2002). Such profiles have also been questioned because they could be used as a means to identify students based on existing societal prejudices, such as race, religion, or other distinguishing features of individuals (Morse, 2000).

Much like other risk assessment measures, profiles are also likely to offer school administrators, students, and the public a false sense of security in their schools. Results from the Secret Service's study demonstrate that there is no single set of criteria that describe most targeted school shooters (Vossekuil et al., 2002). In fact, the often-reported shooter profile characteristic, that is, as an individual who has been a school discipline problem, was not supported in the majority of 37 incidents nor was the commonly reported characteristic of the individual coming from a broken home (e.g., Vossekuil et al., 2002, found that two thirds of the perpetrators came from two parent families and two thirds had never been in trouble at school). In addition, while schools may devote all their counseling and treatment resources to students who meet their profile, other at-risk students who would benefit from such treatments are likely to be ignored, and they are just as likely to become the next perpetrator of a targeted school violence incident.

Threat Assessment Approach

Unlike the other risk assessment methods discussed, the threat assessment approach is explicitly a risk management strategy rather than simply a prediction scheme; that is, it is focused on both identifying individuals who are most likely to commit violent acts as well as investigating means to lessen these individuals' risk to commit these acts (Fein & Vossekuil, 1998). Three specific principles have been advanced as underlying the threat assessment approach: 1) targeted violence follows from a specific process of cognition and behaviors; 2) targeted violence is caused by an interaction among the perpetrator, past stressful events, the current set of circumstances, and the targets of the violence; and 3) successful prevention of incidents requires that assessors pay special attention to behaviors that have been found to precede violent acts (Borum et al., 1999).

Although the threat assessment approach has resulted in the collection, examination, and dissemination of the most useful information concerning incidents of targeted school violence, and has also led to the debunking of the myth of a uniform school shooter profile, there are still a number of significant difficulties with this approach that argue against its whole scale adoption. First, this time intensive investigative approach was developed by the Secret Service in their attempts to protect public officials from potential assassins. As such, even its advocates acknowledge that it is unclear how well this management strategy will generalize to targeted school violence incidents (Reddy et al., 2001). This generalizability issue is especially salient in the school violence context because the Secret Service is a specially designed organization whose primary purpose is to prevent future acts of violence against public officials. No similar organization exists in schools to undertake the intensive investigations necessitated by this approach. School officials are only likely to receive a minimal level of training in these techniques, and then they will be confronted with the problems of attempting to utilize this approach with limited resources, few or no trained investigators, and limited amounts of time. As a consequence, it is likely that school administrators and faculty will understand, utilize, and perform the threat assessment less ably than Secret Service agents whose primary job responsibility is to perform these assessments.

A second significant problem for the threat assessment approach is that it is not clear how individuals come to the attention of authorities using this approach. According to its advocates, a threat assessment may be initiated by any communication or concern for a student, but threats are not necessary for the first steps to be initiated. In fact, Vossekuil et al.'s (2002) own data suggests that it unlikely for a direct threat to precede an incident of school violence (83% of assailants in his sample did not offer direct threats).[10] Therefore, the question remains when using the threat assessment approach: how do you decide when to start to more actively investigating a youth? If there are no clear criteria when to implement the approach, then it is still very likely that a large number of false positives and a significant number of false negatives will result from well-meaning school administrators trying to prevent future violent incidents.

Moreover, this particular problem is likely to be exacerbated by the lack of training school officials have undergone in the threat assessment approach. A large body of psychological literature on decision-making suggests that when outcomes are ill-defined, less-trained evaluators (i.e., school officials) are more likely to revert to existing stereotypes and prejudices in making these decisions (Grove & Meehl, 1996). Therefore, school administrators are more likely to focus on factors irrelevant to risk in determining which students should be thoroughly assessed using the threat assessment approach, and a substantial number of false positives will result.

One possible indication for the implementation of a threat assessment approach by school officials would be evidence of one or any combination of several signs found in the Secret Service and Department of Education's intensive study. Several key findings from their study might serve as initial factors in determining which students need more intensive supervision, including evidence of a student 1) planning an attack (93% of the school shooting incidents examined were premeditated) and 2) telling another student of his plans (81% of perpetrators told another party about their planned attack and smaller portion even planned the attack with another party); 3) experiencing a major loss (98% of assailants examined in the study experience such a loss with 66% experiencing a loss of status and 51% loss of a loved one); 4) experiencing bullying or persecution by school peers (71% of school shooter examined in the study felt that they were bullied or persecuted by other students); and 5) having possession of or access to weapons (61% of perpetrators in the study had possession of or access to handguns before the attack) (Vossekuil et al., 2002).

Yet, while these factors offer insights into the characteristics of targeted school shooters who did carry out their plans, they offer less information concerning differentiating a "true" school shooter from a potential false positive. Without additional data examining how normative these risk factors or behaviors are among adolescents who do not engage in targeted school violence, it is not possible to determine how specific these attributes are to school shooters. For example, within a normal adolescent population 60% of students may have access to or possession of hand guns, in which case the Secret Service finding, that 61% of school shooters had access to or possession of a hand gun, would have no useful predictive accuracy in identifying a potential school shooter. Although many of these factors may still be predictive of targeted school violence when data on normative behavior of adolescent is collected, it still may be the case that using such indicators may cause a large number of students to be misidentified as potential school shooters (i.e., false positives). To carry this example further, the portion of the entire adolescent population that might engage in planning an attack on a school may be relatively small, but even a small percentage of the total number of adolescents, given the low base rate of targeted school violence events, would likely lead to many students being falsely highlighted as possible school shooters. Hypothetically, imagine that 1% of a sample of one million students have engaged in planning of an attack against their school. Such a finding only narrows the population of potential assailants to 10,000. Even if school administrators could accurately predict which students of these were most likely to engage in targeted school violence (which they likely cannot), there would still be a large number of misidentified students. Additionally, a large number of resources would have to be devoted to investigating these high-risk students, and these students would be stigmatized by the additional scrutiny they would face.

In the end, while the threat assessment approach may offer promise as means to collect and disseminate data concerning the attribute of school violence perpetrators as well as debunk myths concerning a typical school shooter profile, it is unlikely to lead to the prevention of significant number of targeted school violence incidents. The lack of clear criteria for school administrators to use in implementing this approach, the lack of training school administrators possess in the threat assessment approach, the lack of data available on the normative nature of the factors most common among targeted school violence incidents, and the low base rate associated with targeted school violence in general, all point to significant difficulties for the successful use of this approach.

CONCLUSIONS AND FUTURE DIRECTIONS

Given the innumerable problems inherent in predicting targeted school violence incidents, the question becomes, how can we prevent these tragedies if we cannot easily identify high risk students without inaccurately highlighting a large number of non-dangerous students? The answer may lay in the opposite direction of many of the high security measures and restrictive policies that have been implemented in schools following Columbine. The data collected by the Secret Service and Department of Justice clearly point out that the vast majority of these attacks are not impulsive and are clearly planned over a considerable period of time. (Vossekuil et al. [2002] found that over two thirds of the perpetrators had created plans at least two days before the tragic event). In addition, it is clear that over three quarters of assailants told another student or sibling about their plan. As such, rather than increasing the security around school or expelling students for bringing a weapon or drugs to school, it may be more useful to encourage greater communication among students and faculty and school administrators. Without schools in which students feel comfortable bringing information to the administration, it may be extremely difficult to prevent school shooting tragedies. Draconian penalties appear unlikely to encourage this type of open communication behavior in students, and they are likely to lead to greater levels of an "us" vs. "them" mentality among the students (Mulvey & Cauffman, 2001).

Researchers must also begin to investigate the factors identified by the Secret Service and Department of Justice within a normative adolescent population. Further knowledge regarding the prevalence of these behaviors within this group will lead to more useful data and greater potential discrimination between those students who will be more likely to engage in targeted acts of school violence and those who will not. However, it should be noted that this research when collected, while informative, is not likely to be a panacea to the problem of preventing such acts. Low base rates associated with these incidents will always be a major barrier to identifying high-risk children by using this methodology.

Finally, we should keep in mind that although targeted school violence events have been perceived by the public as an epidemic, these attacks are extremely rare. Overall, schools remain one of the safest environments for our children, and rates of violence other than bullying continue to decline within their halls. It would be a mistake to devote substantial resources to programs and policies designed specifically to prevent these events without considering what effects these policies will have on the larger school environment.

ACKNOWLEDGMENT: I would like to acknowledge the help of Courtney Carrell in researching and reviewing this chapter. All mistakes are solely the fault of the author, and not his talented research assistant.

NOTES

1. In the school year 1998–1999 for example, 3523 students were expelled for bringing a firearm to school (National Criminal Justice Reference Service, 2003, citing Report on State Implementation of the Gun-Free School Act: School Year 1998–99).
2. This is a point to which I will again return in the final section when I address new directions for research and policy.
3. For discussion of more general school violence see the initial section of chapters in this volume. The literature addressing adolescent risk factors for general school violence is also beyond the scope of this chapter; see Verlinden, Hersen, & Thomas (2000) for a review of this literature, and why it may be inappropriate to attempt to apply research on general adolescent risk factors to targeted school violence perpetrators.
4. A Time poll in 2000 indicated that 70% of teens and 59% of parents reported that they were afraid that such an incident could occur in their school (Morse, 2000).
5. Vossekuil et al.'s (2002) report sponsored by the U.S. Department of Education and U.S. Department of Justice indicated that the age range of the assailants in the 37 incidents examined was between 11–21 years of age.
6. Psychopaths are individuals who are superficially charming but lack normal emotional expressions of guilt, remorse, and shame. They also have a strong propensity to abridge the rights of others and to engage in multiple criminal acts. Psychopathy as measured by Hare Psychopathy Checklist (PCL-R), has often been found to be the best predictor of future violent criminal behavior and receives the largest factor weighting in the VRAG (Qunisey et al., 1998). Most

recently, a juvenile version of the checklist has been created (see Psychopathy Checklist Youth Version [PCL:YV; Forth, Kosson, & Hare, 2003], but it remains to be seen if this construct will be a reliable predictor of adolescent violence in general (see Forthe & Burke, 1998 for some preliminary data on this issue) and targeted school violence in particular.

7. The warning signs that are available for school violence also vary greatly in the degree to which the signs they espouse have been validated by empirical findings (Verlinden et al., 2000); for checklists that appear to contain a large number of researched risk factors, see the American Psychological Association (1999) as well as the National School Safety Center (1998) lists.

8. For example, these scholars suggest that a direct explicit statement by the individual being assessed for violence (i.e., a statement such as, "After I leave here, I will go kill my husband with the gun I have in my purse") represents a clear instance in which one should deviate from an actuarial scheme. The reasonableness of whether clinicians should deviate from an actuarial prediction based on such data or other less direct data, however, is an area of continuing controversy with proponents on both sides (Monahan, 2003).

9. These factors will be discussed in more detail in the section detailing threat assessment approaches to risk assessment.

10. It should be noted that this finding is in direct contrast to the threat assessment approach advocated by the FBI based on their intensive review of 18 cases of targeted school violence (NCAVC, 1998). Their report highlights 28 risk factors in four categories (personality traits, family situations, school interactions, and social interactions), and suggests graded risk should be specifically based on the directness of the threat voiced by the potential perpetrator (NCAVC, 1998).

REFERENCES

American Psychological Association. (1999). *Warning signs: A violence prevention guide for youth.* Retrieved October 28, 2003, from http://helping.apa.org/warningsigns/index.html

Aronson, E. (2000). *Nobody left to hate: Teach compassion after Columbine.* New York: Worth.

Associated Press (2003, October 22). Video shows Columbine gunmen. *MSNBC.com.* Retrieved October 22, 2003, from http://www.msnbc.com/news/983695.asp?0sl=-11.

Borum, R. (1996). Improving the clinical practice of violence risk assessment. *American Psychologist, 51*, 945–956.

Borum, R., Fein, R., Vossekuil, B. & Berglund, J. (1999). Threat assessment: Defining an approach for evaluating risk of targeted violence. *Behavioral Sciences and the Law, 17*, 323–337.

Cooper, K.J. (2000, April 19). Riley rejects schools' profiling of potentially violent students. *Washington Post*, p. A11.

CourtTv. Jay Salpeter (October12, 2002). NYC Detective speaks on the Sniper profile.

DeVoe, J.F., Peter, K., Kaufman, P., Ruddy, S.A., Miller, A.K., Planty, M., Snyder, T.D. & Rand, M.R. *Indicators of School Crime and Safety: 2003* (NCES Publication No. 2004–004). Washington, DC: U.S. Departments of Education and Justice, Bureau of Justice Statistics.

Dwyer, K., Osher, D. & Warger, C. (1998). *Early warning, timely response: A guide to safe schools.* Washington, DC: U.S. Department of Education.

Faust, D. & Ziskin, J. (1988). The expert witness in psychology and psychiatry. *Science, 241*, 31–35.

Fein, R. & Vossekuil, B. (1998). *Protective intelligence and threat assessment investigations: A guide for state and local law enforcement officials*. Washington, DC: U.S. Department of Justice.

Forth, A.E. & Burke, H.C. (1998). Psychopathy in adolescence: Assessment, violence, and developmental precursors. In D.J. Cooke, A.E. Forth & R.D. Hare (Eds.), *Psychopathy: Theory, Research, and Implications for Society* (pp. 205–229). Dordrecht, The Netherlands: Kluwer.

Forth, A., Kosson, D. & Hare, R. (2003). *The Hare Psycopathy Checklist: Youth Version*. Mental Health Services.

Furlong, M. & Morrison, G. (2000). The school in school violence: Definitions and facts. *Journal of Emotional and Behavioral Disorders, 8*, 71–82.

Gardner, W., Lidz, C., Mulvey, E. & Shaw, E. (1996). Clinical versus actuarial predictions of violence in patients with mental illness. *Journal of Consulting and Clinical Psychology, 64*, 602–609.

Grisso, T. & Appelbaum, P. (1992). Structuring the debate about ethical predictions of future violence. *Law and Human Behavior, 17*, 482–485.

Grove, W. & Meehl, P. (1996). Comparative efficiency if informal (subjective, impressionistic) and formal (mechanical, algorithmic) prediction procedures: The clinical-statistical controversy. *Psychology, Public Policy, & Law, 2*, 293–323.

Hanson, R. (1998). What do we know about sex offenders in risk assessment. *Psychology, Public Policy, & Law, 4*, 50–72.

Harris, G., Rice, M. & Cormier, C. (2002). Prospective replication of the Violence Risk Appraisal Guide in predicting violent recidivism among forensic patients. *Law & Human Behavior, 26*, 377–394.

Hart, S. (1998). The role of psychopathy in assessing risk of violence: Conceptual and methodological issues. *Legal and Criminological Psychology, 2*, 338–341.

Hart, S., Webster, C. & Menzies, R. (1993). A note on portraying the accuracy of violence predictions. *Law and Human Behavior, 17*, 695–700.

Kachur, S., Stennies, G. & Powell, K. (1996). School-associated violent deaths in the United States, 1992–1994. *Journal of the American Medical Association, 275*, 1729–1733.

Lidz, C, Mulvey, E. & Gardner, W. (1993). The accuracy of predictions violence to others. *Journal of the American Medical Association, 269*, 1007–1011.

McNeil, D., Sanders, D. & Binder, R. (1998). The relationship between confidence and accuracy in clinical predictions of psychiatric patients' potential for violence. *Law and Human Behavior, 25*, 655–671.

Melton, G., Petrila, J., Poythress, N. & Slobogin C. (1997). *Psychological evaluations for the courts: a handbook for mental health professionals and lawyers*. New York: Guildford Press.

Moffit, T. (1993). Adolescence-limited and life-course-persistent anti-social behavior: A developmental taxonomy, *Psychology Review, 100*, 674–701.

Monahan, J. (1981). *The clinical prediction of violent behavior*. Beverly Hills, Ca: Sage.

Monahan, J. (2003). Violence risk assessment. In I.B. Weiner (Series Ed.) & A. Goldstein (Vol. Ed.), *The Handbook of Psychology: Vol. 11. Forensic Psychology* (pp. 527–542). Hoboken, NJ: John Wiley & Sons, Inc.

Monahan, J. & Steadman, H. (1994). *Violence and mental disorder: Developments in risk assessment*. Chicago: University of Chicago Press.

Monahan, J., Steadman, H., Silver, E., Appelbaum, P., Robbins, P., Mulvey, E., Roth, L., Grisso, T. & Banks, S. (2001). *Rethinking risk assessment: The MacArthur study of mental disorders and violence*. New York: Oxford University Press.

Morse, J. (2000, April 24). Looking for trouble: More and more schools are trying to spot the potential killers in their midst. But what about the innocents? *Time*, pp. 50–54.

Mossman, D. (1994). Assessing predictions of violence: Being accurate about accuracy. *Journal of Consulting and Clinical Psychology, 62*, 783–792.

Mulvey, E. & Cauffman, E. (2001). The inherent limits of predicting school violence. *American Psychologist, 56,* 797–802.

National Center for the Analysis of Violent Crime. (2000). The school shooter: A threat assessment perspective. Washington DC: U.S. Department of Justice, Federal Bureau of Investigation.

National Criminal Justice Reference Service. (2003). *School safety resources – facts and figures.* Retrieved November 2, 2003, from http://www.ncjrs.org/school_safety/facts.html

National School Safety Center (1998). *Checklist of characteristics of youth who have school-associated violent deaths.* Retrieved 22 October, 2003, from http://www.nssc1.org/reporter/checklist.htm

Oltmanns, T. & Emery, Robert E. (2003). *Abnormal Psychology.* Upper Saddle River, NJ: Pearson Education, Inc.

Otto, R. (1992). Predictions of dangerous behavior: A review and analysis of second generation research. *Forensic Reports, 5,* 103–133.

PBS Frontline. (2000). The "classroom avenger." Retrieved November 9, 2003, from http://www.pbs.org/wgbh/pages/frontline/shows/kinkel/profile/avenger.html

Pinizzotto, A.J. (1984). Forensic psychology: Criminal personality profiling. *Journal of Police Science & Administration, 12,* 32–40.

Quinsey, V., Harris, G., Rice, M. & Cormier, C. (1998). *Violent offenders: Appraising and managing risk.* Washington, DC: American Psychological Association.

Rice, M. & Harris, G. (1995). Violent recidivism: Assessing predictive validity. *Journal of Consulting and Clinical Psychology, 63,* 737–748.

Reddy, M., Borum, R., Berglund, J., Vossekuil, B., Fein, R. & Modzeleski, W. (2001). Evaluating risk for targeted violence in schools: Comparing risk assessment, threat assessment and other approaches. *Psychology in Schools, 38,* 157–172.

Sewell, K.W. & Mendelsohn, M. (2000). Profiling potentially violent youth: Statistical and conceptual problems. *Children's Services: Social Policy, Research, and Practice, 3,* 147–169.

School shooter profile. (n.d.). Retrieved November 9, 2003, from http://knowgangs .com/school_resources/shooter/school_shooter_001.htm

Showalter, C. (1990). Psychiatric participation in capital sentencing procedures: Ethical considerations. *International Journal of Law and Psychiatry, 13,* 261–280.

Snyder, H.N. & Sickmund, M. (1999). Juvenile offenders and victims: 1999 national report. Washington, DC: U.S. Department of Justice, Office of Juvenile Justice and Delinquency Prevention.

Verlinden, S., Hersen, M. & Thomas, J. (2000). Risk factors in school shootings. *Clinical Psychology Review, 20,* 3–56.

Vossekuil, B., Reddy, M., Fein, R., Borum, R. & Modzeleski, W. (2002). The final report and findings of the safe school initiative: Implications for the prevention of school attacks in the United States. U.S. Department of Education, Office of Elementary and Secondary Education, Safe and Drug-Free Schools programs and U.S. Secret Service, National Threat Assessment Center, Washington, DC.

Webster, C., Douglas, K., Eaves, D. & Hart, S. (1997). *HCR-20: Assessing risk for violence.* Burnaby, British Columbia, Canada: Simon Fraser University, Mental Health, Law, and Policy Institute.

Wrightsman, L. (2001). *Forensic Psychology.* Belmont, CA: Wadsworth/Thompson Learning.

Chapter 14

Preventing Violence in Schools
Lessons from King and Gandhi

MARAM HALLAK, KATHRYN QUINA, AND
CHARLES COLLYER

The importance of nonviolent alternatives is evident in our society's ongoing struggle with the issue of violence as it invades our schools, workplaces, and streets.[1] The United Nations declared "nonviolence" to be the main theme for the first decade of the twenty-first century. The State of Rhode Island has undertaken an effort to become a "model" as the first nonviolent state in the nation, and the University of Rhode Island is acting as the laboratory for this experiment.

The Center for Nonviolence and Peace Studies was formed to promote nonviolence as a flexible approach to conflict resolution. Dr. Bernard Lafayette, a civil rights activist who worked closely with Martin Luther King, Jr. and the co-founder of the Student Nonviolent Coordinating Committee (SNCC), was hired to bring to the University of Rhode Island the

---

[1] My (MH) passion for this subject started long ago as I watched the devastating effects of violence on my beloved home country of Lebanon. Such experiences forced me to question the factors that lead to practicing violence, the psychological effects of violence, and how people respond to it differently—that some decide to adopt the methods of hate and revenge, while others learn to love even when surrounded by hatred. In particular it seems that people's behaviors are usually limited to the options they perceive as available to them. Thus one way to move away from violent conflicts might be to show people other, nonviolent behavioral choices.

teachings and theories of Kingian nonviolence and its applications. The Center's mission can be summarized as an ultimate goal to build a nonviolent society that promotes mutual understanding and peaceful processes in resolving conflicts. The Center seeks to accomplish this by providing training programs and education, by expanding its efforts to build additional centers nationally and internationally, and by cooperating with other peace-building organizations.

This chapter describes a nonviolence training program offered by the Center for Nonviolence and Peace Studies at the University of Rhode Island. The Center offers nonviolence training to University of Rhode Island students; in addition, it has been contracted by local school districts to provide training to high school students and teachers in Rhode Island. The training consists of a two-day seminar that focused on issues of conflict resolution within a multicultural medium. We also describe the results of an evaluation of the program, designed to find out if this particular training seminar is achieving its goals and objectives. To do so, we first defined those goals and objectives; next, we developed an appropriate nonviolence measure which we later used to assess changes among students and teachers who have participated in the program.

VIOLENCE

Early theorists thought that violence was innate (Freud, 1959) or followed an evolutionary pattern (Lorenz, 1976). Dollard, Doob, Miller, and Sears (1939) added an environmental "trigger" in their frustration-aggression hypothesis, later revised by Berkowitz (1978). Yet conceptualizing violence as either biologically caused or as a biological response to a context of frustration, does not leave much room for reversing or reducing violent behavior. In contrast to these essentialist positions, Bandura (1965) proposed that aggressive behavior is learned from watching and imitating others' behaviors. His social learning theory allows us to envision and develop preventive measures to help individuals unlearn their violent behavior: "if people are capable of violence, they could also be capable of conducting themselves nonviolently" (Nakhre, 1988, p. 6).

School shootings in particular and school violence in general have triggered the creation of various educational and preventive programs to balance the "quick fix" techniques that school administrators resorted to in their desperation, such as installing metal detectors, zero tolerance policies, etc. Teaching nonviolence and conflict resolution skills to both students and teachers is becoming increasingly essential for building a healthy school environment. Many of our young adult students admit to having difficult and at times traumatizing experiences throughout their high school years, without having any way to respond or change the violator's behaviors.

As teachers and psychologists, we understand the toll that a conflict-laden environment can take (Bonta, 1997; Holms, 1990). There is increasing evidence of the negative impact of this phenomenon even for school children as young as five and six years old. Snyder et al. (2003) argued that increased harassment is causing a rise in children's depression and antisocial tendencies. Aronson (1999) emphasized that if we succeed in teaching our children arts and sciences and other subjects but fail to provide them with the very important skills in conflict resolutions, then we will have failed miserably. Thus teaching those skills is just as important if we want our society to survive.

NONVIOLENCE

Nonviolence is not merely the absence of violence (King, 1958). Rather, it is a school of thought, a philosophy, and a way of life. In social science terms, it is based on the concept and strategies of conflict resolution that are built on certain moral principles (Pelton, 1974), such as doing no harm, holding to the truth, and accepting suffering and sacrifice. A very idealistic definition is given by Sharp (1979), "non injury in thought, words, or deeds to any form of life" (p. 134).

Nonviolence appears in various religions, philosophies and moral teachings. It surfaced first in the United States in the works and writings of the Quakers and Henry David Thoreau; then it appeared in Russia in the writings of Leo Tolstoy. Feminists employed nonviolence approaches throughout the early women's movement (Adams, 1990; Alonso, 1993; Brock-Utne, 1994). Its first academic appearance was in 1923, when the sociologist Clarence Case published *Nonviolent Coercion*. This book had a great impact on Mahatmas Gandhi, who drew from Case's much needed scientific orientation to promote the nonviolence strategies which ultimately led to India's independence (Bruyn & Rayman, 1979). Gandhi's successful nonviolence movement became a model for Martin Luther King, Jr. in the struggle for civil rights in the United States. A thorough historical review reveals countless important men and women who practiced, taught, and investigated nonviolence principles, including Gandhi himself, Thich Naht Hanh, Olive Schreiner, Barbara Deming, Jane Addams, Rosa Parks, and the Pankhurst sisters.

Of these, Gandhi's work is the most thoroughly analyzed (e.g., Bondurant, 1965). Gandhi spent 40 years building a theory of nonviolence based on three moral values: *Satyagraha*, which translates literally to holding to the truth or the truth force (Nakhre, 1982; Pelton, 1974); *Ahimsa*, which means doing no harm to any living thing nor allowing harm to exist (that is, to fight all injustices); and *Tapasia*, which means accepting suffering as self-sacrifice, without retaliation, for the sake of the cause and the well-being of others.

A powerful example of Ahisma is found in one of Olive Schreiner's letters to Adela Smith (December, 1916). A passionate peace activist, she wrote:

> I met a woman the other day whom I'd not seen long time and the first thing she said to me was: "Aren't you glad to hear that the Kaiser's got cancer?" Now what could I say? I've had much too much physical suffering to rejoice in the suffering of any sentient creature; if a lion had torn my arm off I wouldn't want it to have cancer. There would be its physical suffering added to my physical suffering, to make the terrible sum total of suffering bigger! I think I can understand most things in human nature; but delight in human (or animal) suffering I cannot understand. (Taken from the World Wide Web on March 17, 2000 at http://spartacus.schoolnet.co.uk/Uschreiner.htm).

KINGIAN NONVIOLENCE

Martin Luther King, Jr. adopted the philosophy of nonviolence during the U.S. Civil Rights Movement (1955–1968), and developed six principles around it:

1. Nonviolence is the way of life for courageous people. This means that one is to confront conflict with courage, not to avoid or run away from it. A nonviolent activist resides at the heart of the conflict and seeks to deal with it constructively.

2. The beloved community is the framework of the future. This means that the importance of the community's common welfare and goals, with no oppressed or oppressor, with no winner or loser, rather, with all parties living in harmony with good will for all is the goal and the way of the future.

3. Attack forces of evil, not people doing evil. This means that the nonviolent activist separates the person from her or his role. The nonviolent activist treats the adversary with respect and openness and honesty and wishes the adversary no harm, in fact, tries to protect the opponent from any harm.

4. Avoid internal violence of the spirit as well as external violence. This emphasizes the importance of matching our thoughts, words, and deeds to produce congruence in our spirit, so it cannot cause internal conflict, which could result in stress and negative energy.

5. Accept suffering for the sake of the cause, without retaliation. This shows the importance of practicing the principles of nonviolence at all times, even when violated. When people sacrifice for a superior cause, and

when they see evidence and are convinced that violence only leads to violence, breaking the cycle becomes vital. This doesn't mean that the nonviolent activist, just by being open and honest and trustful and accepting, will not be exploited: Gandhi was exploited, the women that fought throughout the years for women's rights and for human rights were exploited. Rather, the nonviolent activist practices both patience and tolerance, while continuing to resist oppression firmly.

6. The world is on the side of justice. This is best explained by Collyer and Zepp (2003):

> Imagine that events in the human universe can be sorted into five boxes: the intentionally good, the accidentally good, the neutral, the accidentally bad, and the intentionally bad. When asked to change the universe by throwing out one box, almost everyone chooses to discard the box containing intentionally bad events. (p. 111)

KINGIAN TRAINING

Kingian nonviolence training is built on strategies that stem from the heart of the teachings of Martin Luther King and Mahatma Gandhi as they relate to the theories of psychology in general and social psychology in particular. It consists of two days of training and covers various topics, such as historical movements and the meaning and the philosophical interpretations of nonviolence. Exercises and strategies allow the participants to demonstrate their own viewpoints about the topic while providing the participants with the applicable methods and tools.

The Kingian training suggests six steps for conflict reconciliation. The first one is "gathering information." During this step, the participant is encouraged to study the conflict from all its angles before jumping to a conclusive decision. Examples and readings are provided to show the importance of this step from the work of Dr. Lafayette (personal communication, July, 1999), who participated in the Civil Rights Movement. His research, investigating the problems in Selma, Alabama, showed the more likely reasons for the conflict was not hatred of Black people but were more general, namely, the poverty of the area which led to conflict over resources. Recognizing that, other options emerged for consideration.

The second step is "education," which simply means that the other party might not be aware of the problem or of its severity. Information must be shared and needs must become known. The third step in conflict reconciliation is personal commitment. Here, consistency, endurance, and self-sacrifice are vital. The fourth step is negotiation. In this step the two parties must be able to discuss the issues with open mindedness and flexibility. If negotiations do not lead to desired changes, then the fifth step, direct action, becomes important. Direct action is active and firm, at the same time it is nonviolent. It can have many forms such as noncooperation, peaceful demonstrations and vigils, boycotts, and civil disobedience. The literature on the women's movement is filled with examples of practicing these actions, as well as more extreme measures such as participating in hunger strikes.

The sixth and last step of problem-solving, according to the Kingian nonviolence training, is reconciliation. This is a very important step where both parties reach the desired outcome, both parties win, and the victory is over the problem rather than over each other. This is more powerful than resolution because it insures that both parties are satisfied and content. The emphasis here is on the structure of power, which is not coercive power. Winning a war only means that some people's violence was stronger than other people's violence. Nonviolence power, on the other hand, seeks to reach real change, not mere compliance. It is humane and empathetic.

EFFECTIVENESS OF NONVIOLENCE

There is evidence of the effectiveness of the nonviolence approach in historical movements around the world. The nonviolent movement lead by Gandhi in South Africa and India reshaped world history. The women's liberation movement over the past century succeeded in creating equal opportunities and similar rights of gender in the U.S. and Europe, and it is continuously expanding to the rest of the world (Denmark, Rabinowitz, & Sechzer, 2000). Martin Luther King (1968) pointed out that in 1960 the lunch counter sit-ins achieved desegregation in 150 cities within one year. In 1961, the freedom rides eliminated desegregation on interstate transportation. The Montgomery, Alabama, bus boycotts changed laws in all cities in the South through a Supreme Court ruling. The 1963 Birmingham movement produced the most important and extensive civil rights amendment in a century and the 1965 Selma movement made way for new, improved voting laws and rights.

All of those nonviolent protests, acts of civil disobedience, boycotts, and demonstrations were very effective in yielding results that wars and other violent movements failed to produce. Not only were accomplishments achieved with no bloodshed or the sacrifice of human life, nonviolence also was effective in improving morale. Some psychological investigations that show increased positive self-perception for participants include the work of Frazier (1968), who reported increased self-respect among Black college students who participated in civil rights demonstrations, compared to those who did not participate. These students perceived greater control over their lives as they showed that they felt there was something they could do. Another study by Pierce and West (1966) showed that Black children who participated in sit-ins in Oklahoma City still showed "magical" faith and self-respect after six years, compared to children who did not participate.

The notion of learned helplessness is very important here. When people feel they are locked in their uncontrollable bad events and can't make any changes, their perceived lack of control is paralyzing. In contrast, students who felt they were able to do something about oppression and injustice were rewarded emotionally and psychologically.

Some available evidence of effectiveness is found in the work of Katz (in Kool, 1990). His research team, from the Program for Nonviolence and Conflict and Change at Syracuse University, went in 1979 to Seabrook, New Hampshire, where the Clamshell Alliance was demonstrating against the construction of a nuclear power plant. The team interviewed 113 demonstrators and 144 residents to evaluate how the demonstrators and the third party, in this case the residents, were affected. The findings showed a great amount of support, both between the demonstrators and the way that the residents viewed them. Residents reported understanding and respect for the demonstrators' effort, underlining the importance of community education about the issues.

Feeney and Davidson (1996) studied the effectiveness of training for conflict resolution in a sample of 28 men and 20 women. Half were trained in conflict resolution and the other half were not. The researchers formed groups of dyads in three different conditions: trained/trained, trained/non-trained, non-trained/non-trained. Each group was given 10 minutes to negotiate a case of extreme importance that they didn't agree upon (shown in a previous questionnaire to result in different stands, for example, legalization of marijuana or abortion). The dyad groups that consisted of trained/trained showed the most cooperation, appropriate assertion, active listening and understanding, followed by the groups of trained/untrained and last by the untrained/untrained.

Baumgardner (in Kool, 1990) translated the "Nonviolence Test" (developed by Kool, 1975) from Hindi to English and administered it to college students, Quakers, Buddhist monks, and teenage delinquents. The results easily mapped on two quartiles, with the two end dimensions as violent/nonviolent. Participants were then selected from the two ends of the quartiles and asked to judge and attribute responsibility to four different rape scenarios. Findings showed that people classified as violent attributed causes in terms of singular causes (either the victim or the rapist were entirely at fault), whereas participants that were classified as nonviolent were able to see the rapist's and the victim's worldviews, an extreme example of empathy.

Do These Interventions Work? The URI Nonviolence Project Evaluation

We undertook an evaluation of a set of nonviolence training programs carried out in two high schools and one college in Rhode Island. First, however, we had to establish goals for the program. Extensive discussions with the individuals in charge of the training and with staff at the high schools identified five desired outcomes: an increase in content knowledge about the philosophy and principles of nonviolence; new skills for dealing with conflict in nonviolent ways; more positive attitudes towards nonviolence principles; greater intentions to practice nonviolence; and use of nonviolent strategies in future conflict situations. Thus in the evaluation, we examined whether participants in the intervention groups would show increases in knowledge, skills, positive attitudes towards nonviolence principles, and intentions to practice nonviolence, in comparison to participants in a control group (teachers in a high school serving juvenile detainees). It was hoped that these changes would then be seen in actual behavior once the training was put into practice and in a three-month followup.

An extensive review of the literature did not reveal any instrument that could be used to measure these particular outcomes. Therefore, the next step was to develop an instrument appropriate to the training goals. A total of 86 items, generated from the training manual and discussions with personnel, were administered to 247 university students. Principle Components Analyses were performed and 39 items were retained for the final instrument. The resulting Nonviolence Effectiveness Scale demonstrated excellent psychometric properties for five subscales measuring the defined outcomes. The Knowledge subscale consisted of six multiple choice questions. The other four Likert-type scales measured: Attitudes (alpha = .73), Behavioral Intentions (alpha = .81), Behavioral Management (alpha = .77), and Actual Behavior (alpha = .84).

For the actual nonviolence training, participants were drawn from four groups who participated in nonviolence training in three settings: high school students, high school teachers/staff, and university students. At T I, there were 114 participants (65 women, 24 men). This number dropped to 107 at T II and to 104 at T III. Most (91.2%) were white Americans, 2.6% were African American, less than 1% Hispanic and Native American, and 4% "other." Each group numbered between 17 and 32 (see Table 1). The majority (80.7%) had had less than one hour of previous participation in nonviolence training, although 4.4% had participated in such training for six or more hours. Control participants (11 women, 14 men) were comparable teachers and staff drawn from a school at a juvenile facility.

Table 1. Participant Demographics

Age/gender composition	Group 1: High school teachers and staff	Group 2: High school teachers and staff	Group 3: High school students, teachers	Group 4: University students	Group 5 (control): Training school teachers and staff
Under 18					
Female	0	1	15	5	0
Male	0	0	12	1	1
19–35 years					
Female	4	1	1	2	2
Male	1	0	0	0	4
36–45 years					
Female	6	4	0	2	4
Male	2	0	1	1	4
46–55 years					
Female	6	11	2	4	5
Male	3	0	0	2	5
Over 55					
Female	1	0	0	0	0
Male	0	0	1	0	0

Data collection for this project started in January, 1999, and was completed in November, 2000. The nonviolence training intervention was offered in three different forms: a 2-day core training, a 12-day trainer's training and a 2-day training with a booster session. All of these trainings are derived from a training manual written by Lafayette and Jehnsen (1995), and contain similar instructions, exercises, role-plays, feedback and reading assignments. Four teams of two or three trainers each delivered the training. Training sessions that were conducted by new trainers were monitored and supervised by a team of evaluators. Consent forms, approved by the Institutional Review Board, were signed by each participant prior to training. For minors, parental consent was also obtained.

Participants filled out the first questionnaire (TI) prior to training; the second (TII) immediately after training; and a third (TIII) was mailed to them three months later. Data were collected by the first author and a supervisor from the Center for Nonviolence and Peace Studies. Training was provided to insure consistency and similarity in this process. In order to minimize experimental bias, standardized instructions were written and followed. Missing data were minimal, which may perhaps be attributed to the clarity and consistency of the instructions that participants received or to the participants' own enthusiasm to fully participate in this project. Only 7 out of 114 participants did not complete the post-test and four did not complete follow up tests.

The primary evaluation measure was the Nonviolence Effectiveness Scale, with its five subscales. The questionnaire also included a social desirability scale (alpha = .84) used to assess whether participants were giving answers in a way that seemed socially agreeable to them. This issue is often a problem in attitude research when people are trying to "look good" (Edward, 1957) to the extent that participants might bias their responses. If this scale shows significant differences, it would have to be controlled for as a covariate.

The number of conflicts that occurred during the participants' last three months was also included as a control variable. It is important to know if the number of opportunities to practice nonviolent methods or the number of problem areas in the person's life varied systematically across groups or across time.

Finally, five items from the Internal-External Control Scale (Rotter, 1966) were also included, to assess whether individuals with an internal locus would be more responsive to the requirements of self-control inherent in nonviolence training. This scale showed reliability of $r = .70$.

Means and standard deviations for the four intervention groups and the control group are shown in Table 2. Due to the lack of randomization, and to see if the groups were comparable, a between-subjects MANOVA was conducted on the baseline (TI) data, comparing the five groups on the five outcome and three control measures. Only the Knowledge outcome was significant, $F (4, 105) = 3.059$, $p < .01$, eta squared $= .10$): the control group began the study with less knowledge about nonviolence philosophy than the intervention groups. Tukey follow up tests showed that the high school teachers and staff of Group 1 showed higher pretest knowledge than the high school students of Group 3 and the detention facility teachers of Group 5 (the control group). However, results for the remaining seven measures were non-significant, indicating that there were few problems with the lack of randomization.

A 3×2 repeated measures MANOVA for Time (pretest, post-test, and follow-up) and Gender was conducted on all dependent measures across groups to assess gender differences. The results on all outcomes were nonsignificant; consequently gender was excluded from further analyses. Three separate 3×5 repeated measure MANOVAS for Time (pretest, post-test, and follow-up) and Group were conducted on the control measures of social desirability, locus of control, and number of conflicts. None of the main effects or the interactions were significant, thus these variables were not incorporated as covariates in subsequent analyses.

Table 2. Means and Standard Deviations for All Variables Across Time

Variable	Time I Mean (sd)	Time II Mean (sd)	Time III Mean (sd)
Group 1			
Knowledge	3.48 (.901)	4.65 (1.61)	4.22 (1.62)
Attitude	22.5 (3.74)	24.7 (.902)	23.9 (1.94)
Behavioral intentions	8.39 (2.31)	7.50 (2.92)	8.89 (2.75)
Actual behavior	12.7 (4.79)	13.4 (4.82)	11.7 (4.28)
Behavioral management	14.5 (4.96)	15.6 (4.37)	14.2 (3.50)
Social desirability	5.78 (1.88)	5.43 (1.36)	6.00 (1.78)
Locus of control	13.5 (1.78)	12.9 (1.68)	13.4 (1.73)
Number of conflicts	7.13 (2.67)	7.71 (2.47)	7.00 (2.10)
Group 2			
Knowledge	2.88 (1.22)	4.53 (.940)	3.47 (1.46)
Attitude	20.9 (2.32)	22.8 (2.13)	21.4 (2.58)
Behavioral intentions	9.94 (3.13)	8.25 (2.49)	8.94 (2.23)
Actual behavior	12.1 (3.11)	11.0 (2.78)	11.3 (4.00)
Behavioral management	15.7 (3.29)	14.3 (3.37)	14.1 (5.50)
Social desirability	7.06 (1.88)	6.59 (1.73)	6.50 (1.75)
Locus of control	13.7 (1.69)	13.7 (1.50)	13.6 (1.41)
Number of conflicts	8.06 (2.89)	7.88 (2.34)	7.31 (2.96)
Group 3			
Knowledge	2.44 (1.16)	4.19 (1.06)	3.44 (1.44)
Attitude	20.9 (2.46)	21.1 (2.76)	21.1 (1.78)
Behavioral intentions	8.72 (2.34)	8.52 (2.40)	8.34 (3.40)
Actual behavior	14.4 (4.10)	14.9 (4.40)	14.4 (4.02)
Behavioral management	15.3 (3.39)	14.4 (4.13)	14.6 (4.01)
Social desirability	6.19 (1.54)	6.38 (2.12)	6.37 (1.78)
Locus of control	12.9 (1.89)	13.7 (1.76)	13.3 (1.76)
Number of conflicts	7.19 (2.26)	7.72 (2.50)	7.37 (2.37)
Group 4			
Knowledge	3.00 (1.58)	5.00 (1.97)	4.47 (2.24)
Attitude	20.5 (2.70)	23.3 (2.25)	21.1 (1.77)
Behavioral intentions	8.69 (2.56)	7.54 (2.40)	7.31 (2.02)
Actual behavior	11.6 (2.99)	10.9 (2.81)	11.9 (2.63)
Behavioral management	13.5 (3.91)	12.6 (3.92)	14.0 (3.87)
Social desirability	5.82 (1.24)	6.07 (1.75)	5.50 (1.40)
Locus of control	13.4 (1.73)	13.8 (2.04)	13.3 (2.16)
Number of conflicts	6.82 (1.85)	6.73 (2.60)	6.64 (2.68)
Group 5			
Knowledge	2.44 (1.12)	1.92 (1.22)	1.72 (1.28)
Attitude	21.0 (3.27)	19.2 (3.61)	19.8 (3.80)
Behavioral intentions	9.05 (3.42)	7.41 (2.92)	9.09 (2.89)
Actual behavior	13.0 (4.41)	13.4 (4.34)	13.0 (4.41)
Behavioral management	13.7 (3.37)	13.9 (3.93)	13.9 (4.40)
Social desirability	6.54 (2.19)	6.95 (2.94)	6.68 (2.57)
Locus of control	13.0 (1.79)	12.2 (2.33)	12.3 (2.75)
Number of conflicts	7.72 (2.69)	7.64 (2.40)	7.45 (2.58)

To examine the effect of the intervention on program outcome variables, separate 3 (Time) × 5 (Group) repeated measures MANOVAs were performed on each of the defined outcome variables. To insure that the Type I error rate was not inflated due to multiple tests, a Bonferroni correction was applied, so that $p < .01$. An effect size was also computed, to assist in determining appropriate power for future analysis (since there is no literature to date that has such information).

For the knowledge variable, both main effects and the interaction were significant: for Time, F (2, 108) = 25.39, $p < .01$, eta squared = .32; for Group, F (4, 109) = 21.25, $p < .001$, eta squared = .44; for the interaction, F (8, 216) = 4.21, $p < .01$, eta squared =.14. In addition to the pretest findings described above, at T II, all four intervention groups were significantly higher (at $p < .001$) on the Knowledge subscale than the control group. At follow-up (T III), all four intervention groups were again significantly higher than the control group, at $p < .006$ or better. Indeed, knowledge scores had increased for the four intervention groups but had decreased for the control group. Thus, participants in the intervention groups showed the anticipated effects of training, with greater knowledge than the control group at post-test and follow-up. Intervention participants had their highest knowledge immediately after training, and it went down slightly at the follow-up. This pattern fits the Learning Curve Theory described over a century ago by Ebbinghaus (1885). Over the same time period, the control group knowledge scores declined. Since their learning curve fit a typical pattern, this could not be attributed to test-retest effects. Furthermore, since scores for all intervention groups increased while scores for control group declined, the initial lower knowledge scores for the control group could not explain these effects. Although the pattern for the intervention groups showed the typical learning curve, T III scores were still quite high, showing a robust learning effect for knowledge.

For the Attitude outcome, a 3 × 5 repeated measures MANOVA for Time × Group showed significant differences for both main effects and for the interaction. For Time, F (2, 93) = 7.74, $p < .001$, eta squared = .14; for Group, F (4, 94) = 8.57, $p < .001$, eta squared = .27; for the interaction, F (8, 186) = 4.21, $p < .001$, eta squared = .15. As mentioned earlier, at T I, there were no significant differences between the groups. However, follow-up Tukey tests showed that at T II three of the four intervention groups (those involving university students and teachers) had significantly more positive attitudes towards nonviolence than the control group (all $p < .001$). The exception was the group of high school students only, whose scores were significantly lower than two of the other three intervention groups. At T III, two intervention groups (teachers/staff and college students) were again significantly higher than the control group, at $p < .001$, with the group consisting of only high school teachers and administrators significantly higher than other intervention groups ($p < .03$). Thus all the groups, except for high school students in Group 3, had more positive attitudes after training than the control group. This indicated that the intervention had an effect in changing adult participants' attitudes towards adopting the approach of nonviolence; however, it did not have the same effect on the group that consisted of high school students.

Three similar 3×5 repeated measure MANOVAs were conducted on the outcome variables Behavioral Intentions, Behavioral Management, and Actual Behavior. None of these analyses yielded statistical significance at the .01 level. Table 3 contains the MANOVA summary for all outcome variables. The means for all groups on the Behavioral Intentions scale were all near the end of the scale, suggesting a ceiling effect (Aron & Aron, 1999).

Two behavioral items were further reviewed: physical violence (item 39, "I used a physical response [hitting, shoving, etc.] on someone)" and resolving conflicts (item 44, "I reached a reconciliation with the person/group I had a conflict with"). Separate one way ANOVAs comparing the five groups were conducted on each of these items at each time point.

Table 3. MANOVA for Outcome Variables

Variable	df (Hypoth.)	df (Error)	F	eta2	p
Knowledge					
Main Effect T	2	108	25.389	.32	.000
Main Effect G	4	109	21.248	.43	.000
Interaction Effect T × G	8	216	4.207	.14	.000
Attitude					
Main Effect T	2	93	7.744	.14	.001
Main Effect G	4	94	8.571	.27	.000
Interaction Effect T × G	8	186	4.191	.15	.000
Behavioral Intentions					
Main Effect T	2	92	3.425	.07	.037
Main Effect G	4	93	1.000	.04	.412
Interaction Effect T × G	8	184	2.074	.08	.049
Actual Behavior					
Main Effect T	2	94	.417	.01	.660
Main Effect G	4	95	2.788	.11	.031
Interaction Effect T × G	8	188	1.283	.05	.255
Behavioral Management					
Main Effect T	2	91	.645	.01	.014
Main Effect G	4	92	.565	.02	.688
Interaction Effect T × G	8	182	1.157	.05	.048

Table 4. Items 39 and 44 Means and Standard Deviations

Variable Name	Time I Mean (sd)	Time II Mean (sd)	Time III Mean (sd)
Item 39: I used a physical response (hitting, shoving, etc.,) on someone.			
Group 1	1.09 (.29)	1.43 (.92)	1.19 (.51)
Group 2	1.06 (.24)	1.12 (.33)	1.13 (.50)
Group 3	1.81 (.93)	1.91 (.89)	1.70 (.84)
Group 4	1.18 (.39)	1.20 (.41)	1.14 (.63)
Group 5	1.48 (.82)	1.50 (.74)	1.45 (.74)
Item 44: I reached a reconciliation with the person/group I had a conflict with.			
Group 1	3.13 (1.3)	3.24 (1.1)	3.05 (1.0)
Group 2	3.06 (1.2)	2.94 (1.1)	3.00 (1.4)
Group 3	3.38 (1.1)	3.03 (1.1)	3.17 (1.1)
Group 4	3.18 (1.0)	2.87 (1.3)	2.93 (1.0)
Group 5	2.96 (1.5)	2.95 (1.3)	2.95 (1.3)

The results were significant for item 39 at all three time points: at T I, $F (4, 109) = 6.010$, $p < .01$; at T II, $F (4, 102) = 4.088$, $p < .004$; and at T III, $F (4, 98) = 3.333$, $p < .013$. Follow-up Tukey tests showed that at T I, Group 3 (high school students) had higher scores than Groups 1, 2, and 4; at T II, these high school students had higher scores than Groups 2 and 4; and at T III, they had higher scores than Group 2. In general, high school students showed less attitude change and more general physical violence.

Results for item 44 showed no significance at any time point. The means for this item were all at the end of the scale, evidence again of the "ceiling effect" (Aron & Aron, 1999). Table 4 contains means and standard deviations for these two items.

WHAT DO THE FINDINGS TELL US ABOUT NONVIOLENCE TRAINING?

The purpose of this project was to determine whether the nonviolence training intervention offered by the Center of Nonviolence and Peace Studies at the University of Rhode Island led to any changes in five main outcomes: knowledge, attitudes, behavioral intention, actual behavior, and behavior management. Each of these outcomes was clarified and agreed on by both providers and recipients of training and assessed with a psychometrically sound set of measures developed for this evaluation project.

Although there were four different group memberships, three variations in training, and four teams of trainers, the effects were consistent, with each intervention producing some significant improvements over the control group. This is an indication that the training was robust across presentations.

Overall findings show that there were changes in knowledge and attitudes due to the training. The first outcome, increased knowledge, is straightforward and simply implies that participants left the training with greater content about the history, philosophy, and strategies of nonviolence. The second outcome, more positive attitudes and its relationship to behavioral change, is much more complicated. While increased knowledge and more positive attitudes are desirable results of training, the lack of increased nonviolence on behavioral measures does not allow easy interpretation. If knowledge and attitudes change but not behaviors, can we conclude that the intervention will have an impact on an individual's future use of nonviolence or even her or his choice of actions in any specific situation?

There were no significant effects for three potentially confounding variables: social desirability, locus of control, and number of conflicts. However, each should be evaluated further in future research, particularly since scores on the social desirability measure appeared to have a ceiling effect. A fuller locus of control measure might also provide useful information; for example, locus of control might affect willingness to change to a nonviolent way of life, in accordance with the theory of planned behavior (Azjen & Fishbein, 1991). Furthermore, some have suggested that Locus of Control varies across ethnic groups (Moghaddam, 1998), an issue not examined here because of the lack of diversity.

High school students did not have a greater number of potential conflicts, yet they were more likely to act out with physical violence. One possibility is that teenagers have a greater acceptance of violence, which may explain this group's more aggressive behavior and weaker attitude changes. Contrary to stereotypical beliefs, including the effects discussed by Gilligan (1996) of being young and male in relation to violence, there were no significant differences found between males and females on the item assessing incidents of engaging in physical violence. Violence by girls and women is an interesting and controversial topic, not resolved in the current study which used only a single item. Further research exploring the types of violence and the level of intended or actual force or harm would help clarify this issue.

Additionally, the finding of greater teen violence underlines the importance of attending to the violence surrounding high school students in our society. Since the birth of this project, school shootings and teen violence have been major news topics.

Four problems are important to consider in this study. First, the sample is very small and not geographically or ethnically diverse. Second, the sample was a sample of convenience and the design was quasi-experimental (no random sampling and no random assignment), limiting comparisons, although pretest analyses revealed no differences which affected the outcomes. Third, we used volunteers, who may be biased towards the topic under study and thus change more than non-volunteers. In this instance, the teachers might be particularly highly motivated since participation was not part of their normal job expectations. Fourth, the control group included a higher proportion of adult males and scored lower on pre-test measures of knowledge, even though theis group was comparable on other measures and results suggested this did not matter in the long run. Finally, the study relied on self-reports; systematic observations would perhaps reveal more about behavioral changes, in particular. Feeney and Davidson's (1996) observations of dyadic interactions could provide a model for adding this behavioral dimension. Another interesting approach for future study might incorporate the person's readiness for change as well as the actual level of change (Prochaska et al., 1994).

In summary, the present study was a quasi-experimental longitudinal research design that assessed the effectiveness of the nonviolence training program that is offered by the Center for Nonviolence and Peace Studies at the University of Rhode Island. Findings showed significant gains on two program objectives, Knowledge and Attitude, after intervention, which were robust over time. Participants in the four intervention groups showed increased knowledge in comparison to the control group, and participants in three of the groups showed significantly more positive attitudes in comparison to the control group. However, behavioral outcomes were not observed, perhaps due to ceiling effects on the measures, low power, or measurement error in this newly developed scale. Furthermore, high school students behaved less consistently across time and showed more general violence than the other intervention groups.

Nonviolence training, particularly with the Kingian approach, provides positive skills for human survival. Providing nonviolent options to solving problems might be the solution for the survival of the human race. Precious lives could be spared and evil could be conquered if the philosophy and ideals of nonviolence were practiced.

ACKNOWLEDGMENTS: We express appreciation to the Center for Nonviolence and Peace Studies at the University of Rhode Island, in particular to Bernard Lafayette and Abu Bakr, for their assistance and support during this project. Correspondence can be addressed to the first author at mhallak@bmcc.cuny.edu.

REFERENCES

Adams, J. (1990). *Peacework, oral histories of women peace activists.* Boston, MA: Twayne.

Azjen, I. & Fishbein, M. (1991). The theory of planned behavior. *Organizational Behavior and Human Decision Processes, 50,* 179–211.

Alonso, H. (1993). *Peace as a woman's issue.* Syracuse, NY: Syracuse University Press.

Aron, A. & Aron, E. (1999). *Statistics for psychology.* Upper Saddle River, NJ: Prentice Hall, Inc.

Aronson, E. (1999). *The social animal.* New York: Worth Publishers, Inc.

Bandura, A. (1965). Influence of models' reinforcement contingencies on the acquisition of imitative responses. *Journal of Personality and Social Psychology, 1,* 589–595.

Berkowitz, L. (1978). Whatever happened to the frustration-aggression hypothesis? *American Behavioral Scientists, 21,* 698–708.

Bondurant, J.V. (1965). *Conquest of violence: The Gandhian philosophy of conflict.* Berkeley, CA: University of California Press.

Bonta, B.D. (1997). Cooperation and competition in peaceful societies. *Psychological Bulletin, 121,* 299–320.

Brock-Utne, B. (1989). *Feminist perspectives on peace and peace education.* Elmsford, NY: Pergamon Press, Inc.

Bruyn, S. & Rayman, P. (1979). *Nonviolent action and social change.* New York: Irvington Publishers, Inc.

Case, C. (1923). *Non-violent coercion.* New York: Century.

Collyer, C. & Zepp, I. (2003). *Nonviolence: Origins and outcomes.* Calcutta: Writers Workshop.

Denmark, F., Rabinowitz, V. & Sechzer, J. (2000). *Engendering psychology.* Needham Heights, MA: Allyn and Bacon.

Dollard, J., Doob, L., Miller, N., Mowrer, O. & Sears, R. (139). *Frustration and aggression.* New Haven, CO: Yale University Press.

Ebbinghaus, H. (1885/1913). *Memory: A contribution to experimental psychology.* (translated 1913, H.A. Ruger & C.E. Busserinus). New York: Teachers College, Columbia University.

Edward, A. (1957). *The social desirability variable in personality assessment and research.* New York: Holt, Rinehart and Winston, Inc.

Feeney, M.C. & Davidson, J.A. (1996). Bridging the gap between the practical and the theoretical: an evaluation of a conflict resolution model. *Journal of Peace and Conflict, 2*(3), 255–269.

Frazier, R.R. (1968). An analysis of nonviolent coercion as used by the sit-in movement. *Phylon, 29,* 27–40.

Freud, S. (1920/1959). *Beyond the pleasure principle: A study of the death instinct in human aggression.* (J. Strachey, trans.). New York, NY: Bantam Books (reprinted in 1959).

Gilligan, J. (1996). *Violence, reflections on a national epidemic.* New York: Vintage Books.

Holms, R. (1990). *Nonviolence in theory and practice.* Belmont, CA: Wadsworth Publishing Company.

King, M.L. (1958). *Stride toward freedom.* New York: Harper & Row.

King, M.L. (1968). *The trumpet of conscience.* New York: Harper & Row.

Kool, V.K. (Ed.). (1990). *Perspectives on nonviolence.* New York: Srpringer-Verlag New York, Inc.

Lafayette, B. & Jehnsen, D. (1995). *A structured guide and introduction to Kingian nonviolence: The philosophy and methodology.* Galina, OH: Institute for Human Rights and Responsibilities, Inc.

Moghaddam, F.M. (1998). *Social psychology: Exploring universals across cultures.* New York, NY: Freeman.

Nakhre, A.W. (1982). *Social psychology of nonviolent action, a study of three Satyagrahas.* Delhi, India: Chanakya Publication.

Pelton, L.H. (1974). *The psychology of nonviolence.* Elmsford, NY: Pergamon Press LTD.

Pierce, C.M. & West, L.J. (1966). Six years of sit-ins: Psychodynamic causes and effects. *International Journal of Social Psychiatry, 12,* 29–34.

Prochaska, J., Velicer, W., Rossi, J., Goldstein, G., Marcus, B., Rakowski, W., Fiore, C., Harlow, L., Redding, C., Rosenbloom, D. & Rossi, S. (1994). Stages of change and decisional balance for 12 problem behaviors. *Health Psychology, 13*(1), 39–46.

Rotter, J.B. (1966). Generalized expectancies for internal versus external control of reinforcement *Psychological Monographs, 80*(1), 609.

Sharp, G. (1979). *Gandhi as a political strategist.* Boston, MA: Porter Sargent.

Snyder, J., Brooker, M., Patrick, M.R., Snyder, A., Schrepferman, L. & Stoolmiller, M. (2003). Observed peer victimization during early elementary school: Continuity, growth, and relation to risk for child antisocial and depressive behavior. *Child Development, 74,* 1881–1898.

Chapter 15

What Can We Do About School Violence?

MELISSA LARACUENTA AND FLORENCE L. DENMARK

Even though research regarding the causes, correlates and warning signs of violent behaviors still needs more attention, we can use our current knowledge to inform intervention. For those school staff that work with students, addressing violent behaviors may be a daunting and confusing task. The purpose of this chapter is to bring together the current information regarding school violence in terms of the implications for intervention and give specific guidelines and examples of what schools, teachers, parents, and students can do about school violence.

Prevention and intervention are interrelated and should always be carried out together within a school and community. Ideally, interventions should target violent behaviors at three levels including: primary prevention, secondary intervention, and tertiary prevention and intervention (Keep Schools Safe website). Primary prevention is used to prevent violence within the school. Secondary intervention aims to treat those students who seem to be at risk or have already committed violent acts. Tertiary prevention and intervention is a global process that provides more continuous services extending the intervention efforts beyond the school by including the family and community (Keep Schools Safe website).

DEVELOPING A SAFE SCHOOL ENVIRONMENT

In order to prevent violence, schools can do several things to help instill a safe, violence free environment. Initially, the school administrators should aim to foster an environment that feels safe. The U.S. Department of Education (1998) outlines several characteristics of a school that is and feels safe for students. A school that is safe is responsive to children's needs, focuses on academic achievement, and places emphasis on positive relationships among students and school staff. All students are treated with respect. A safe school fosters family involvement and community links. Methods have been developed to help children to more effectively and comfortably express their concerns; safety issues should be openly discussed. A safe school also promotes good citizenship and is capable of identifying potential or current problems and of assessing progress toward solutions for these problems. The National Mental Health and Education Center (2000) states that a safe school also engages in specific actions such as intervening with aggressive students, implementing victim support programs, establishing school-wide violence prevention programs, and making efforts to improve the school climate by changing the conditions that indirectly or directly are conducive to violence.

The National School Safety Center (1999) suggests that a safe school can be developed through making school safety a priority on the educational agenda and by developing a "safe schools plan". This plan consists of an "ongoing process that encompasses the development of district-wide crime prevention policies, in-service training, crisis preparation, interagency cooperation and student/parent participation." This safe schools plan can help a school community to begin to address prevention of violence and other problematic behaviors on several levels. Hopefully, through this process, educators will take a more active role in initiating positive programs instead of solely reacting when negative events take place.

Nation, Crusto, Wandersman, Kumpfer, Seybolt, Morrissey-Kane, and Davino (2003) identified nine characteristics correlated with effective intervention programs. Such programs were "comprehensive, included varied teaching methods, provided sufficient dosage, were theory driven, provided opportunities for positive relationships, were appropriately timed, socioculturally relevant, included outcome evaluation, and involved well-trained staff." (p. 1). Austin (2003) states that prevention efforts can be organized into discrete categories including: using functional behavior analysis and behavior intervention plans effectively, screening for risk factors, teaching acceptance of diversity, building self-esteem and social skills, conflict resolution through peer mediation, involvement of the family and community, and focusing on the classroom as a community. As many of those components as possible should be included in a school violence prevention program. In a controlled study of an elementary school intervention to reduce violence, Twemlow, Fonagy, Sacco, Gies, Evans, and Ewbank (2001) concluded that an antiviolence intervention may improve the learning environment in a school if it does not focus on individual pathology or interfere with the educational process. In their program, the intervention consisted of four components: a zero tolerance policy for violent behaviors, a discipline plan for modeling appropriate behaviors, a physical education plan for teaching self-regulation skills, and a mentoring program for adults and children to assist students to avoid engaging in violent behaviors. This program attempted to address violence at multiple levels.

DEVELOPING A VIOLENCE RESPONSE PLAN

Secondary and tertiary school violence interventions should include several steps. An important part of violence intervention is to develop a specific plan for how to respond to violent behaviors or crisis when a particularly severe act of violence has occurred. An effective response plan includes specific descriptions of: warning signs of potentially violent behaviors, effective prevention programs the school has put into place, intervention strategies that the school can use to help students (i.e. early interventions for at-risk students and intensive individualized interventions for students exhibiting severe mental illness or behavioral issues), and a crisis intervention plan including immediate responses in the aftermath of a tragedy (U.S. Department of Education, 1998).

A school crisis plan for responding to violence, or any other crisis situation, should be specifically outlined to help school staffs deal with these situations rapidly, effectively, and smoothly. Waddell and Thomas (1998) describe the components of an effective plan for responding to a disaster. These include plans for immediate responses to the event (e.g. how information will be communicated to school staff, plans for school dismissal), intermediate steps for crisis control (e.g. support and counseling for students, how deaths or funerals will be addressed if appropriate), and long-term interventions (e.g. plans for on-going counseling support and additional resources for teachers who deal with students' daily reactions). A school crisis team should be identified, with specific roles and duties assigned to each person. Duties include internal communication, external communication to parents and others, medical aid, counseling/psychological support, and security maintenance. A distinct emergency signal that is understood by all staff should be put into place. A clear evacuation plan also should be outlined to specify how and where children will be organized and dismissed (Poland, 1999).

An essential component of violence interventions is to formulate specific guidelines and methods for identifying students who are at risk for either engaging in or becoming victims of violence. In general, anyone in contact with students, including parents, teachers, school staff, and other students themselves, should become aware of how to identify potential warning signs. There are several principles for identifying early warning signs of school violence. One is for individuals to understand that violence and aggression are contextual, in that they can be set off by certain environments or situations. Warning signs also should be viewed within a developmental context in that children express their needs and emotions differently depending on their social-emotional development. Most importantly, individuals should be aware that children usually exhibit multiple warning signs, repeatedly with increasing intensity over time (U.S. Department of Education, 1998). Examples of characteristics of students at risk for violence are: a history of violent behaviors (e.g. bullying), poor school achievement, exposure to violence at home or within the community, and difficulties controlling impulses and emotions (NASP Communiqué, 1999). Warning signs of a potentially violent student include: verbal or nonverbal threats, irrational beliefs or ideas, inability to take criticism, and fascination with weapons or acts of violence (NASP Communiqué, 1999).

INTERVENTION STRATEGIES

Warnings signs can be used to shape intervention responses. Once at-risk students or behaviors are identified, interventions must be provided. The U.S. Department of Education (1998) states that effective interventions are "culturally appropriate, family-supported, individualized, coordinated, and monitored." Interventions should be flexible over time and include input from the child, family, and others who interact with the child. Effective interventions are multifaceted, long-term and broad reaching. Other principles underlying violence intervention are sharing responsibility by establishing collaboration between the child, home, school, and community, developing the skills of staff, students, and families with interventions, and supporting students in becoming responsible for their actions. Interventions should be sustained over time, across settings, and coordinated in these settings. The context in which the violent behaviors may or has occurred should be analyzed by conducting a functional analysis of the antecedents of the student's behaviors.

Within the School

Intervention techniques for dealing with violent or potentially violent behaviors can be further individualized for specific members of the school community. Examples of what each person can do are helpful in order to provide more concrete guidelines for those who are the closest to the students. On a school wide level, many interventions are possible. Leffler and Snow (2001) state that school-wide programs usually involve an ongoing process of planning and staff development to create building-wide guidelines for consistently responding to violent behaviors. In discussing the problem of bullying and victimization, Miller, Ruben, and Carroll (1999) makes several suggestions that can also be applied to violence in general. The school administration should facilitate accurate and timely reports of violence. The safety of the actual physical setting can be improved through increasing lighting in dim areas, instituting surveillance measures, and having hall monitors in the building during the day. On-going staff development to increase sensitivity and knowledge of prevention and intervention strategies should be provided. The school should provide students with a safe forum to conduct mediation and conflict resolution in order to avoid violence. The National Mental Health and Education Center (2000) note that the school can also use discipline practices that emphasize restitution and positive behaviors instead of expulsion, and other negative outcomes. The school can also institute standardized prevention program, such as the Peace Builders Universal School-Based Violence Prevention Program. This program aims to alter the climate of a school by teaching the school community (i.e. students and staff) simple strategies to improve the students' social competence and reduce aggressive behaviors (Flannery, Liau, Powell, Vesterdal, Vazsonyi, Guo, Atha, and Embry, 2003; Shapiro, 2000). Other examples of school-wide initiatives are the Project ACHIEVE's School Safety and Effective Behavior Management Model, Effective Behavior Support (EBS), and Conflict Resolution/Peer Mediation Project (Leffler and Snow, 2001).

Within the classroom, teachers can implement very simple interventions to counteract violence. These interventions should target the entire classroom and be designed to improve the social climate. In addressing bullying, examples of interventions are to establish rules against bullying behaviors, create positive and negative consequences of bullying, hold regular classroom meetings to provide a forum for students and teachers to discuss the rules, and meet with parents to improve school-family communication and informed regarding anti-bullying, anti-violence efforts (Center for the Study and Prevention of Violence, 2001). To address violence within the classroom, the U.S. Department of Education (1998) suggests teaching social skills, such as social problem solving and social decision-making. Aber, Brown, and Jones (2003) found that children whose teachers taught many lessons in conflict resolution displayed positive changes in their social-emotional development and less likelihood of following a path toward violent and aggressive behaviors. If a persistent behavior problem

or poor academic achievement is noted, the teacher may consider referring the child for a special education evaluation to determine if the child
is disabled and eligible for services under the Individuals with Disabil-
ities Education Act (U.S. Department of Education, 1998). Fields (2004)
suggests a three-step plan for teachers to intervene with fighting amongst
students. School staff should familiarize themselves with school guidelines regarding their authority and role in the event of a violent act, seek
out training in verbal de-escalation, physical interventions, and physical
restraints, if necessary, and create a mental plan of action for what one will
do when violence occurs. If a physical fight occurs, Fields suggests that
the teacher, or other school staff member, should: give a loud, clear verbal
command, decide whether or not to physically intervene, quickly decide
how to get help from others, and physically intervene if it is safe. Examples of in-classroom curricula to teach children social and problem solving
skills are Second Step: A Violence Prevention Program for Children, and I
Can Problem Solve (ICPS) (Leffler and Snow, 2001).

Within the Home

Parents at home can also learn effective intervention methods to deal with
violent behaviors. In addressing bullying, parents can try to provide as
much positive feedback as possible for their child when warranted, avoid
physical punishment, and model appropriate behaviors with other adults
and children. If the parent sees their child engaging in violent behaviors,
he or she should immediately put a stop to the negative behavior and
then have the child practice a more appropriate behavior (National Mental
Health and Education Center, 2000).

Specific students who are engaging in or are victims of violence (e.g.
bullies) can be targeted in more tailored interventions. Intensive interventions that involve multiple settings (e.g. school, home, mental health clinic)
and intense family support should be used with children displaying dangerous patterns of behavior. Nontraditional schooling in an alternative
school or therapeutic facility may be a necessity when the safety of school
staff and students is at high risk. Effective alternative programs provide
anger and impulse control training, psychological counseling, academic
and remedial instruction, and vocational training (U.S. Department of Education, 1998). The Center for the Study and Prevention of Violence (2001)
suggest several individual interventions for bullying. For example, immediate discussions with the bullies should include: documenting the event,
the adult communicating that bullying is unacceptable, and warning the
bullies of the negative consequences that will occur if the behavior continues. Both the victim and the victim's parents should be contacted and
discussions should include: documenting the event, providing information

regarding the teacher's plan of action for dealing with bullying, and encouraging the victim to immediately report any future bullying behaviors to the teacher or other adults.

Students themselves should also be a part of violence intervention techniques. Peer mediation, as a part of a conflict resolution curriculum, is a way to involve students in the development of a nonviolent school atmosphere, as well as including the students in the larger school community. A peer mediator's role is to provide fair and impartial arbitration in a forum where both sides of a conflict are presented. Student-chaired mediation can facilitate an open meeting of the two disputants without fear of disciplinary action being taken by adults or other authority figures (Austin, 2003). Peer mediation can also help students learn to understand and respect other points of view, as well as learn problem solving, improve communication and critical thinking skills, and reduce adult intervention in student conflicts (Chittooran, 2000).

CONCLUSION

The current research regarding school violence addresses the range of issues from prevention and identification of at-risk students to intervention and what to do in the wake of a violent tragedy. With all of the information regarding violence in the literature, it may be overwhelming or confusing for those who work directly with the students to know what to do. This chapter attempts to clarify what people can do to reduce and address school violence. From the data presented in this chapter, several conclusions and implications can be made. School violence must be addressed on multiple levels, including the school, home, and community. All of these settings should collaborate in order to establish clear strategies for addressing violent behaviors. Within the school, all staff that interacts with students, as well as the students themselves, is an integral part of violence intervention. Together, hopefully violence can be reduced and the schools can become a safer place to foster children's development.

REFERENCES

Aber, J.L. Brown, J.L. & Jones, S.M. (2003). Developmental trajectories toward violence in middle childhood: Course, demographic differences, and response to school-based intervention. *Developmental Psychology, 39*(2), 324–348.

Austin, V.L. (2003). Fear and loathing in the classroom: A candid look at school violence and the policies and practices that address it. *Journal of Disability Policy Studies, 14*(1), 17–25.

Center for the Study and Prevention of violence. Retrieved on 31 March, 2002. Safe communities-safe schools: Bullying prevention-recommendations for schools. http://www.colorado.edu/cspv.factsheets/

Chittooran M.M. (2000). Conflict resolution and peer mediation: A guide for educators. *Behavioral Interventions: Creating A Safe Environment in Our Schools*, 23–24.

Fields, L. (2004). Handling student fights: Advice for teachers and administrators. *The Clearing House*, 77(3), 108–111.

Flannery, D.J., Liau, A.K., Powell, K.E., Vesterdal, W., Vazsonyi, A.T., Guo, S., Atha, H. & Embry, D. (2003). Initial behavior outcomes for the peace builders universal school-based violence prevention program. *Developmental Psychology*, 39(2), 292–308.

Keep Schools Safe. Retrieved 18 July, 2004. Violence and Aggression in Children and Youth: How to Intervene. http://www.keepschoolssafe.org/school/violence-aggression-5.htm

Leffler, S. & Snow, S.T. (2001). School-based programs that reduce violence. *Reclaiming Children and Youth*, 9(4), 234–238.

Miller, G.E., Rubin, K.A. & Carroll, S. (1999). Victimization of school-age children: safe schools strategies for parents and educators. *Communiqué*, 8–9.

Nation, M., Crusto, C., Wandersman, A., Kumpfer, K.L., Seybolt, D., Morrissey-Kane, E. & Davino, K. (2003). What works in prevention: Principles of effective prevention programs. *American Psychologist*, 58(6/7), 449–456.

National Mental Health and Education Center. (2000). Position statement: School Violence. *Behavioral Interventions: Creating A Safe Environment in Our Schools*, 13–14.

National School Safety Center. (1999). Working together to create safe schools. *Educated Public Relations: School Safety 101*. www.nssc1.org

Poland, S. (1999). School crisis planning: Questions answered. *NASP Communiqué*, 6–9.

Shapiro, J.P. (2000). The peacemakers program: Effective violence prevention for early Adolescent youth. *Behavioral Interventions: Creating A Safe Environment in Our Schools*, 18–20.

Twemlow, S.W., Fonagy, P., Sacco, F.C., Gies, M.L., Evans, R. & Ewbank, R. (2001). Creating a peaceful school learning environment: A controlled study of an elementary school intervention to reduce violence. *The American Journal of Psychiatry*, 158(5), 808–810.

U.S. Department of Education. (1998). Early warning, timely response: A guide to safe schools. Washington, D.C.

Waddell, D. & Thomas, A. (1998). Disasters: Developing a crisis response plan. *Helping Children at Home and School: Handouts from your School Psychologist*, National Association of School Psychologists.

Chapter 16

Summary and Conclusion

THE EDITORS

Violence within schools is a current concern that affects all of us—children, parents, teachers, and psychologists. During the 2003–2004 school year, a tally of 48 deaths attributed to school related violence was reported in the United States. This number is apparently higher than in any year in the past decade. A sudden increase in gang activity within schools also has been noted with apprehension (Toppo, 2004, June 28). These occurrences have led to questions such as: Why are these children engaging in violent behaviors? Is it learned? Is it biological? Are the school environment and experiences different in other countries? Can we prevent violence? How can we make schools safer? These questions led to considerable research, and in turn the compilation of this volume of data and analysis regarding school violence within the United States and throughout the world.

School violence is a phenomenon that occurs not only in the United States, but also within other parts of the world. It is not limited to any specific age, culture, ethnicity, or social group. This volume aims to bring together knowledge, research, and hopefully inspire important questions to be asked, within our societies. The authors of these chapters are all quite knowledgeable in their fields and they have presented historical facts, definitions and types of violence, related factors, and models of prevention and intervention in order to understand more of the complete picture of school violence.

Following a foreword by Laura Barbanel, an eminent school psychologist, which outlined some general issues related to school violence, Herbert H. Krauss provided a description of the current state of violence in our society in his paper "Violence in the Schools: An Introduction". A detailed description of violent behaviors within schools and institutions was provided, as well as an introduction describing how and why the Editors came together to work on this book. The goals of this volume include recognizing that violence is a problem around the world, making an effort to take into account all of the various factors which have contributed to it, and presenting current information that can be of use to those in various professions.

In "A History of Violence in the Schools", Elizabeth Midlarsky and Helen M. Klain reviewed the history and types of violence that have occurred through time, dating as far back as ancient Mesopotamia through medieval times in Europe. Then they described student violence in schools within the United States, ranging from the 17th century until today. The historical events occurring within society were discussed in terms of their relationships to school violence. They emphasized that even though the goal throughout history was to make American schools safe places, this has never been a reality. Midlarsky and Klain discussed factors and possible predictors of school violence, including corporal punishment, bullying, intrapersonal characteristics, the media, and availability of weapons.

Violence itself is a broad term. In "Conceptualizing Violence," Herbert H. Krauss aimed to provide a framework within which to study violence. Krauss described current perceptions of violence, in particular the World Health Organization's definition of violence. In addition, a dramatistic model of violence is presented; with an example to illustrate it's utility and relevance in being applied to the existence and experience of violence.

The impact of multiple environmental factors which interact with a child's development was discussed in "Developmental Aspects of School Violence: A Contextualist Approach" by Roseanne Flores. Flores used Brofenbrenner's ecological systems theory as a model that may explain how various factors within and outside of the child can interact and lead to the development of violent behavior. Developmental precursors to a child engaging in violent behaviors, such as a history of violence, childrearing practices, culture, and more specifically, the impact of the school environment on children were reviewed.

Similarly, in "Warning Signs: School Violence Prevention," June F. Chisholm and Alfred W. Ward reviewed violence prevention research in terms of both proximal and distal warning signs of violent behavior. They discussed environmental predictors stemming from the community, school, and the family, as well as individual characteristics such as peer relationships and social competency skills. Theories and empirical research related to primary, secondary, and tertiary prevention were presented. Examples of each approach as applied to the community at large and within schools were discussed. A primary prevention project, conducted in collaboration with the APA and MTV was described.

Other chapters focused on more specific factors related to how school violence impacts children based on individual differences, such as gender and ethnicity, and type of violence, such as relational aggression and sexual violence. Darlene C. DeFour discussed gender and ethnic differences in the types of violence experienced in schools in her paper "Gender and Ethnicity Issues in School Violence." The differential impact and experiences of boys and girls were described, as well as special focus on the phenomenon of relational aggression, which is a nonphysical form of violence. Ethnicity and school violence were discussed in terms of typical rates of exposure to violence and theoretical frameworks of taking culture and ethnicity into account when examining violence. Finally, implications for school violence interventions that incorporate knowledge of gender and ethnicity issues were highlighted. In "Sexual Violence in the Schools" Beatrice J. Krauss, Herbert H. Krauss, Joanne O'Day, and Kevin Rente defined the different types of sexual violence that students may experience within schools. Prevalence rates, research on the effects of these experiences on adolescents, and recent legislation that has "changed the school liability and school response landscape" were presented. Samples of school policies were presented, as well as personal perspectives of school nurses and students in terms of these issues.

Astrid Stuckelberger reviewed the role and influence of grandparents in the development of a peaceful, non-violent society in her paper "Transgenerational Perspective on Peace and Violence Prevention." The role of elders in the lives of the younger generations was highlighted at all levels of society. A developmental theory, "transgenerational developmental psychology," which includes consideration of social learning, attachment, and psychosocial theories, was posited as a way to understand the lives of older persons. This is related to the importance of transmission of adults' behaviors to their children. A "transgenerational model of violence" suggested that violent behaviors are learned within the family and transmitted from one generation to the next. Older persons are seen as "key to violence prevention" and an "Intergenerational Plan of Action for Conflict and Violence Prevention in Schools" was proposed.

Although the emphasis in this volume has been on school violence within the United States, it is clear from reviewing our authors' work that it is not solely an American problem. Authors from different parts of the world discussed the existence and experience of violence in the schools in their respective countries. Takashi Naito and Uwe P. Gielen examined patterns of school bullying in Japan in "Bullying and *Ijime* in Japanese Schools: A Sociocultural Perspective." Richard Velayo described the phenomenon of child abuse in the Philippines and how societal and institutional factors are related to this issue in "A Perspective on Child Abuse in the Philippines: Looking at Institutional Factors." Ramadan A. Ahmed presented empirical research examining many variables such as age, gender, and family atmosphere in terms of their relationship to the development of violent behaviors in Arabic children in "Manifestations of Violence in the Arab Schools and Procedures for Reducing It." Similarly, Judith E. Papházy discussed bullying within Australian schools in terms of incidence rates and definitions (e.g. bullied by other students vs. bullied by teachers), as well as violence prevention programs that have been implemented in "Violence in Schools-Australia."

In terms of intervention, the emphasis throughout all of the papers has been on prevention at all levels. Ideally, prevention of violence that affects our children and occurs within the school context is the goal. In "Predicting School Violence," Daniel Krauss presented different techniques that could be used to predict which students that are likely to engage in school violence. The strengths and weaknesses, which unfortunately were many, of each method were discussed. Suggestions for the future directions of predicting, and hopefully preventing, school violence were to encourage greater communication between students and school staff and to conduct further research investigating the relevance of risk factors amongst a normative adolescent population. A very detailed description of a specific nonviolence program is presented by Maram Hallak, Kathryn Quina, & Charles Collyer in "Predicting Violence in Schools: Lessons from King and Gandhi". These authors described nonviolence in terms of Gandhi's and Martin Luther King Jr.'s philosophies. A nonviolence-training program was described in terms of its goals, which ultimately include usage of nonviolent methods of conflict resolution, and the results of an evaluation of this program. Finally, in "What Can We Do About School Violence?", Melissa Laracuenta and Florence L. Denmark bring together specific information to clarify what people can do to address school violence within the school, classroom, and at home.

In sum, as is quite obvious, violence is a part of society and has been documented in schools throughout the world. However, in the wake of such serious mass incidents, such as the school shootings in Columbine, Colorado in the United States, it is clear that something should be done to address the violence. In reading this volume, several points are evident. Violence has unfortunately been a part of educational systems from history through today in the United States and in other parts of the world. Throughout these papers, authors have emphasized that there are many factors both within and outside the individuals, schools, institutions, and society related to the development of violent behaviors. Many methods of trying to predict and prevent school violence have been developed over the years, but clearly still there are strengths and weaknesses to each approach.

An overarching theme throughout this volume is that prevention efforts are key to addressing the problem of violence. Prevention should not only be encouraged within our schools, but also become an integral part of efforts to decrease violence in society at large. These efforts should include presenting knowledge, improving communication patterns between children and adults and teaching nonviolence. Ideally, prevention should be at many levels including within the individual, family, institutions and society. It is our hope that the information presented in this book can serve as a valuable resource. Examples of prevention efforts both within the United States and in other countries will hopefully serve as not only a resource, but as an inspiration to others to work on addressing violence in society.

REFERENCE

Toppo, G. (2004, June 28). Schools safe, but danger lurks. *USA Today*, pp. 6D, 1A.

About the Editors

Florence L. Denmark is an internationally recognized scholar and researcher. She received her Ph.D. from the University of Pennsylvania in social psychology. She is currently the Robert Scott Pace Distinguished Research Professor at Pace University in New York, where she served as chair of the Psychology Department for 13 years. Denmark has published extensively on the psychology of women and gender and has long been an energetic force in advancing psychology internationally.

Dr. Denmark served as the eighty-eighth president of the American Psychological Association and has been an active member of many boards and committees, including the Council of Representatives and Board of Directors. She served as president of APA Divisions 1, 35, and 52. In addition, she was president of the International Council of Psychologists, the Eastern Psychological Association, the New York State Psychological Association, and Psi Chi. She was also a vice president of the New York Academy of Sciences. She has four honorary doctorates and is the recipient of many awards, including APA's Distinguished Contributions to Education and Training, Public Interest, and the Advancement of International Psychology. Dr. Denmark is currently an APA/NGO representative to the United Nations. Recently, she was elected Chair of the United Nations NGO Committee on Aging. She is the recipient in 2004 of the American Psychological Foundation's Gold Medal for Lifetime Contributions to the Public Interest.

Uwe P. Gielen is professor of psychology and director of the Institute for International and Cross-Cultural Psychology at St. Francis College, New York City. He received his doctorate in social psychology from Harvard University. He is the past chair of the Psychology Section of the New York Academy of Sciences and has served as president of both the International

Council of Psychologists and the Society for Cross-Cultural Research. He
has served as organizer and co-organizer of several international psychology conferences and has been editor of *World Psychology* and of the *International Journal of Group Tensions*. His areas of interest include moral development, international and cross-cultural psychology, and family studies.
He is co-editor/co-author of 13 books, including *The Kohlberg Legacy for
the Helping Professions, Cross-Cultural Topics in Psychology, Handbook of Culture, Therapy, and Healing,* and *Childhood and Adolescence in Cross-Cultural
Perspective*.

Herbert H. Krauss is professor of psychology and Chair of the Department
of Psychology, Pace University, New York City. He earned his B.S. (Experimental Psychology) and M.S. (Clinical Psychology) from The Pennsylvania
State University and his Ph.D. (Clinical Psychology) from Northwestern
University. His internship was in the Department of Medical Psychology
of the University of Oregon Medical School. In addition to his appointment
at Pace, he currently serves as Adjunct Associate Professor of Psychiatry
(Psychology) at Weill Cornell Medical College and Adjunct Associate Attending Psychologist at the Payne-Whitney Clinic. In the past he has been
a consultant to New York City's Commission on the Education of the Disabled and to a number of school districts both in New York and elsewhere.
The author of approximately 100 scholarly works, his primary intellectual
commitment is to understanding the relationship between social institutions and personal development and action. In addition he has published
in such diverse areas as personality development, psychopathology and
its treatment, and rehabilitation psychology.

Elizabeth Midlarsky is professor and director of the Master's program in
the Department of Counseling and Clinical Psychology at Columbia University, Teachers College, and is professor in the Graduate School of Arts
and Sciences of Columbia University. She obtained her Ph.D. in clinical psychology from Northwestern University, Evanston, where she was also a lec-
turer in psychology and a Northwestern University scholarship recipient.
Her major research interests include the development of personal control
and responsibility, altruism and helping in people of diverse ages, helping
within families, and help seeking. Her national activities have included
appointments to review boards of the *National Institute of Mental Health,*
and the *National Institutes of Health,* where she reviewed for the *Human
Development Study Section* and the *National Heart, Lung, and Blood Institute*.
She has been in the *National Reviewers Reserve,* and was on the *National
Bone Marrow Registry Evaluation Panel,* which had direct input to the Sen-
ate Appropriations Committee. She was Editor of the *Academic Psychology
Bulletin,* and is on the editorial board of the *Journal of Traumatic Stress*. Her

articles are in journals which include *Journal of Personality and Social Psychology, Developmental Psychology, Journal of Research on Adolescence, Child Development, American Journal of Mental Retardation, Journal of Personality, Journal of Clinical Psychology, Journal of Traumatic Stress, Sex roles, Social Justice Research,* and the *Journal of Nervous and Mental Disease.* Midlarsky is a member of Phi Beta Kappa, Sigma Xi, and Psi Chi, and is a Fellow of the American Psychological Association, American Psychological Society, and the American Orthopsychiatric Association.

Robert W. Wesner has been a scientific and academic publisher his entire career since leaving graduate school. He was the program director in Math and Science at Scott, Foresman & Co.; he was one of two publishers at Aldine Publishing Co, specializing in psychology and economics; he was a senior executive editor at Random House specializing in developing new corporate ventures; and was the CEO of Psychological Dimensions, Inc. In all of these positions, Bob Wesner, as he likes to be called, made the final decisions on what was and what was not going to be published. Of the nearly one thousand books that Bob has published, approximately sixty percent were commissioned by him. During his career he was very active in the field of gamed simulations. He designed five gamed simulations, gave courses in gamed simulations, made countless presentations, and consulted extensively in the field. Now in retirement, Bob is still active in the field of gamed simulations. He is also doing extensive pro bono work for the United Nations in his capacity as an NGO representative. Bob is on the Advisory Committee in Psychology for the New York Academy of Sciences; on the Advisory Committee of the Publishing Program at Pace University; on the Working Committee on Education for UNICEF and is a vice president of the International Organization for the Study of Group Tensions; where is also director of publications.

About the Contributors

Ramadan A. Ahmed has degrees in both psychology and law and received his Ph.D. in cognitive psychology—specifically in the development of concepts in cross-cultural perspective—from the University of Leipzig, Germany in 1981, and has since taught in Egypt, Sudan, and Kuwait. Dr. Ahmed is a professor of psychology at Menoufia University, Egypt. At present, he is on leave at Kuwait University, Kuwait.

Laura Barbanel, Ed.D., ABPP, Professor Emerita Brooklyn College, CUNY, has served as program head of the graduate program in School Psychology for many years. She is currently in private practice in Brooklyn, New York. Dr. Barbanel is a Fellow of the American Psychological Association and a Diplomate of the American Board of Professional Psychology in psychoanalysis. She has served in a number of elected and appointed positions in the American Psychological Association, including the Board of Educational Affairs, The Policy and Planning Board, the Finance Committee, the Council of Representatives, and the Board of Directors of APA. She is recognized for her publications and presentations on school violence.

June F. Chisholm is professor of psychology at Pace University and adjunct professor at New York University Medical Center, and an adjunct clinical supervisor at St. John's University. She is a clinical psychologist who worked for many years as a senior psychologist in the outpatient psychiatric department at Harlem Hospital Center, providing psychological services to an ethnically diverse, primarily poor, urban population. She has a small, part-time private practice in Manhattan. Her clinical and research interests include issues in the psychological treatment of Women of Color, psychological assessment of children and adults, parenting, community psychology, violence, and prejudice in the theory and practice in psychology.

Charles Collyer received his doctorate in psychology from Princeton University in 1976. He is professor of psychology and a former Chair of his department at the University of Rhode Island. He was a cofounder of the Center for Nonviolence and Peace Studies at URI, and serves as its Associate Director. His current research examines individual differences in attitudes toward violence. He codirects the Ira and Mary Zepp Center for Nonviolence and Peace Education in Westminster, Maryland. Charles Collyer received his doctorate in Psychology from Princeton University in 1976. He is Professor of Psychology, and a former Chair of his department, at the University of Rhode Island. He was a co-founder of the Center for Nonviolence and Peace Studies at URI, and serves as its Associate Director. His current research examines individual differences in attitudes toward violence.

Darlene C. DeFour, Ph.D. is a social psychologist/community psychologist. She is a graduate of Fisk University and received her doctorate from the University of Illinois at Urbana–Champaign. She is currently an associate professor of psychology at Hunter College of the City University of New York; where she teaches classes including "Social Psychology," "Personal Adjustment," "Psychology of Women," "Theories of Ethnic Identity Development," and "Issues in Black Psychology." She is a currently a member of the Board of Directors of the New York Association of Black Psychologists and has served on the Board of Directors of the National Association. Dr. DeFour is also active in several divisions of the American Psychological Association. The theme of her current research is the exploration of the various ways that violence in the form of racism and sexism as well as physical violence affects the everyday lives of adolescent and adult black females.

Roseanne L. Flores is currently an assistant professor in the Department of Psychology at Hunter College of the City University of New York. She obtained her B.S. in psychology from Fordham University, M.A. in psychology from the New School for Social Research, and her Ph.D. in psychology, specializing in Developmental Psychology, from the Graduate Center of the City University of New York. Her research focuses on the effects of poverty on young children's cognitive development. She is currently looking at the relationship between teacher's reading practices and children's se of temporal language during story-book reading. Professor Flores has recently begun a research project in which she and her students will be examining the perceptions of early adolescents' perceptions of violence, peer pressure and other risk behavior.

Maram Hallak is an assistant professor of psychology at the Borough of Manhattan Community College at the City University of New York. She received her Master's degree in Counseling Psychology from the University for Massachusetts and her Ph.D. from the University of Rhode Island in Experimental Psychology. Her work and research interests emerge from Nonviolence and Peace Studies, Psychology of Women, and Multicultural Psychology. She is a member of the Implementation Collective of the Association of Women in Psychology, and the co-chair of Feminism, Gender, and Peace Working Group of the Society for the Study of Peace, Conflict and Violence (Division 48 of the American Psychological Association). Additionally, she is the representative of the Association of Women in Psychology to the United Nations.

H. Marie Klain is a research assistant in the Department of Neuroscience at the New York State Psychiatric Institute. She obtained her M.A. in the Department of Counseling and Clinical Psychology at Teachers College, Columbia University, and her B.A. in psychology and criminal behavior from the University of South Florida. Her major research interests include the etiology of school violence, adolescent development and psychopathology, and forensic psychology. She is a member of the Golden Key International Honor Society, Pi Gamma Mu (Social Science Honor Society), Psi Chi (Psychology Honor Society), and the American Psychological Association.

Beatrice J. Krauss received her doctorate in Social Personality Psychology from The Graduate Center, City University of New York, and an M.A. in Clinical Psychology from the University of Kansas. Since 1989, Dr. Krauss has directed more than 20 NYS, national, and international HIV-related research projects, nearly all concerned with the development and evaluation of interventions. Formerly with Memorial Sloan Kettering and National Development and Research Institutes, Inc., Dr. Krauss is currently Executive Director of the Center for AIDS, Drugs and Community Health at Hunter College and Professor of Urban Public Health. Her current work focuses on adolescent sexuality and HIV prevention. She has co-designed and is evaluating a program to empower parents to be HIV/STI/hepatitis health educators of their preadolescent and adolescent children (PATH, NIMH). PATH has been replicated in Miami, Mexico City and India. An ongoing investigation (NIMH) examines the social settings within which adolescents enact their romantic and sexual relationships.

Daniel A. Krauss is an assistant professor in the Psychology and Legal Studies departments at Claremont McKenna College. He holds a B.A. in Psychology from The Johns Hopkins University, and M.A., J.D. and Ph.D. (clinical and psychology, policy, and law dual major) degrees from the University of Arizona. Prior to joining the faculty, Dr. Krauss served as a Clinical Psychology Intern at the Federal Bureau of Prisons in Butner, North Carolina and at the University of North Carolina Medical School–Chapel Hill. Dr. Krauss also served as the Supreme Court Fellow to the United States Sentencing Commission for 2002–2003. His research and clinical experience has focused primarily on the intersection of law and psychology. Dr. Krauss's recent publications have appeared in the journals *Psychology, Public Policy & Law* (an APA journal and law review) and *The International Journal of Law & Psychiatry*. He has contributed book chapters with Bruce Sales to the *Handbook of Psychology* and the *Handbook of Forensic Psychology*. He is a member of the American Bar Association, the American Psychological Association, the American Psychological Society, Arizona Bar, and the Supreme Court Bar.

Melissa Laracuenta received her B.A. in Psychology from Marist College. She has completed her MS.Ed in School Psychology from Pace University in New York City. She is pursuing her Psy.D. in School-Clinical Child Psychology at Pace University. Her research interests include the effects of parental mental illness on children's depression, anxiety, and expression of violent behaviors.

Takashi Naito is a professor of psychology at Ochanomizu University in Japan. He received his Ph.D. from Keio University in 1998. He is the current director of the Japanese Association of Educational Psychology. His interests lie in moral development, group tensions, and international psychology. He is the author of Kodomo, Shakai, Bunka (Children, Society, and Culture: Development of Morality) Sajensusha: Japan. He has published articles in the *International Journal of Group Tensions* and *Psychologia*.

Joanne O'Day currently works for the Hunter College Center on AIDS, Drugs and Community Health where she is the Project Director for the NIMH funded Study of Adolescents in Social Settings (SASS) Project.

Judith E. Papházy is a consulting psychologist in private practice. Her background covers a broad spectrum of professional skills and community interests. They range from education, working with children and families, national radio broadcasting, newspaper writing and television appearances to assisting organizations, corporations and industries with diverse human resource management programs. She consults to kindergartens, primary and secondary schools in a number of areas. Through her membership of the International Council of Psychologists, she and a colleague have a program called Resilience Promotion and Optimism, as well as co-authored a book on this subject. Her work in resilience promotion is used by many schools to underpin their student welfare programs.

Kathryn Quina, professor of psychology and women's studies at the University of Rhode Island and APA Fellow, has studied the sequelae of childhood trauma in community and incarcerated women, leading naturally to a concern about nonviolent alternatives. Her most recent contributions are Arming Athena: Survival strategies for women in academe (Sage, 1999), Childhood Trauma and HIV: Women at Risk (Taylor & Francis, 1998), and Teaching Gender and Multicultural Psychology (American Psychological Association, 2003).

Kevin Rente is currently a research interviewer for the Hunter College Center on AIDS, Drugs, and Community Health. He has a Master's degree in Sociology from the New School for Social Research.

Astrid Stuckelberger holds a Master's degree and a doctorate in psychology from the University of Geneva. She has published more than 100 books, articles, and reports. Dr. Stuckelberger currently teaches in the Master's of Public Health program at the Faculty of Medicine, University of Geneva. She is also an international consultant for the United Nations as well as for governmental and nongovernmental agencies. Dr. Stuckelberger is recognized as an expert after twenty years of conducting research on ageing within a social and human development perspective and codirecting the Swiss National Research Programme on Ageing.

Richard Velayo obtained his Ph.D. in Psychology and Education from the University of Michigan in Ann Arbor, specializing in Cognitive Psychology and Educational Technology. He obtained his M.A. in Applied Behavioral Analysis from the University of the Pacific, B.A. in Psychology and B.A. in Sociology–Anthropology from De La Salle University (magna cum laude), Manila, Philippines. His scholarly interests focus on multimedia technology as pedagogical tools for classroom instruction. He is also looking into pedagogical strategies that foster a multicultural approach towards effective teaching and learning. He has published in peer-reviewed journals and his works have been presented in various regional and national conferences. Dr. Velayo is currently a full-time faculty member of the Psychology Department at Pace University. He was the 2004 President of the Division of International Psychology (Division 52) of the American Psychological Association in which he also served as the organization's Membership Chair and Program Chair. He is also the International Council of Psychologists' Representative to the United Nations and is the Vice-Chair and an Advisory Board Member of the Psychology Section of the New York Academy of Sciences.

Alfred W. Ward is an associate professor of psychology at Pace University in New York. His research has ranged from the evaluation of lie detection via the polygraph to management assessment. He is involved in test development and has developed norm-referenced achievement test assessing Basic Skills in Spanish and Arithmetic (BASIS-A) for ESL grade school students. Dr. Ward, along with graduate students and another colleague, is currently engaged in an ongoing research project examining risk and protective factors that moderate the relationship between exposure to community violence and symptomology associated with Post-Traumatic Stress Disorder among inner-city youth. In addition, he is conducting research on the assessment of cultural values, as well as the role of spirituality on bereavement responses.

Index

of truth, the others' needs have taken a back seat to their own. Other men have had only a fleeting commitment to change. They are motivated from time to time, but seemingly never at the time when change is called for. It is fair to say of these men that they do not truly want to change. There are, however, a number of men who have backed away from intimacy not because they lack desire but rather because they lack direction.

"WHEN AND WHERE DO I START?"

"Maybe I'm making this whole thing harder than it really has to be, but for the life of me I honestly can't figure out how to get started on getting close. I can't very well just sit down with my wife after dinner and say, 'Let's get close.' The times when she demands some feeling from me, I'm really not ready to give it. I absolutely won't start on my relationship with the kids, because I might really screw them up. My friends are another thing entirely. I'm afraid they would be completely blown away if we sat down around the card table and I opened up with, 'I bet a quarter. By the way, do any of you guys have the problem with impotence that I do?' I know I need to be more intimate, and I really do want to be. I just don't know when and where to start."

The timing of intimate behavior is all-important. It is especially so in the early stages of a man's efforts to be more disclosing and loving. The wrong revelation to the wrong person at the wrong time will be rebuked, perhaps even ridiculed. The negative reaction of others is likely to reinforce all of a men's preconceptions about self-disclosure and cause him to withdraw further from relationships.

Some men shy away from intimacy even though they want to be close, because they imagine that being intimate means being completely open with everyone, all the time. They argue, correctly, that a man should keep some things to himself. There may be a time and a place for intimate behavior, but it's not all the time, every place. Uncertain as to when and where to be disclosing, these men choose not to disclose at all. There is a simple rule for disclosure: *Where and when a man should be disclosing is in those relationships and at those times in which his behavior with or toward another emanates from dimensions of himself that he has not revealed to the other.* This is usually private or personal information he possesses that he has not shared with the other: feelings he has about himself, about the other, or about the relationship. We learned from our research that, more often than not, a man does not share these dimensions of himself in his relationships. He provides no context for his behavior; those closest to him do not have the information they need to understand why he behaves as he does, what his behavior means.

This is not to suggest that a man needs to be or should be intimate with everyone. In many of a man's casual relationships—for example, those with his buddies—the basis for his behavior is public and known to all. In such relationships, it is only when the man would like to move the exchange to a deeper, more personal interaction that he needs to disclose enough of himself to help others understand his behavior. The low disclosure level that characterizes male relationships may be quite appropriate for what men want or need from their casual friendships. Such is not the case for a man's relationships with his wife and family.

The evidence from relationships with spouses and families suggests that there is a need for men to be much more revealing of the information they have about themselves that they use as a basis for behavior in the relationship. Women have said time and again, "I just don't know where he is coming from":

■ "For the longest time I was guilty of using home as a dumping ground for whatever emotional garbage I had collected during the day. I would come home and rant and rave about everything, from what we were having for dinner to why the kids hadn't done their homework to the dog's bad breath. I was an ogre to be around. None of that behavior was really directed at my family, but they had no way of knowing that, because I wasn't telling them anything about what was really bugging me. They thought I was angry with them when I was really angry at my boss or the customers, or even at myself. Now when I come home, my wife and I sit down over a drink and go over the day before we deal with anything else. I completely unload before I talk to the kids or do any household stuff. We've become a lot closer as a result. The things at work don't eat away at me like they used to, and I've become a lot more fun for the kids to be around. It's working out just great."

- "I guess I always expected people to know how I felt, so I never bothered to explain myself. That all began to change when I finally realized what it was doing to my relationship with the kids. My wife was always able to figure out pretty much what was going on with me from how I was behaving. She's a very intuitive person, plus she's had years of living with me. It was different with the kids. They had only my behavior toward them to go on. I thought that they would see my caring for them behind my grousing at them, my love behind all the rules and punishments. It didn't work out that way. We had some real problems with the oldest girl, drugs and worse. Working through those problems with her helped me see that I had to share some of *me* if I wanted my message to get through to them. Now I work harder on explaining to them how I feel than on setting rules for them to follow. I think for the first time they really understand that I do love them. Amazingly enough, I don't feel the need to set so many rules anymore."

- "There was a time when I couldn't have sex for almost a year. As you can imagine, it was a pretty hellish time for me and my wife, but one great thing came out of it: I discovered all the different ways there are to show how much you love someone without making love. Like most men, I had pretty much limited my expressions of affection to sex. I thought that sex was *the* way to show love. When my accident happened, I was really afraid that since I couldn't make love to my wife, she might stop loving me. I think if the tables had been turned, that might have been my reaction. Thank God she knew there was a lot more to showing love than screwing. I never knew that talking could be loving until she talked to me about her love. I didn't change overnight, but gradually I found myself showing her some of the same love she was showing me. Now we have sex again, and it's better than ever. Not because we missed it for so long, but because there's so much love to go with it now that I never knew before and never showed her."

A man need not be self-disclosing in all of his relationships all of the time. As much as the question of *when* to disclose stands in the way of men being more intimate, many have questions about *what* to disclose as well. The disclosures required to relate effectively to a spouse or children are much greater than those needed between casual friends.

"WHAT DO I DO?"

"I don't want to have to bare my soul every time I want to get close to somebody. What if it doesn't work? It seems to me like this is an all-or-nothing proposition. You lay yourself totally open and either you get close or you get clobbered. Can't you sort of ease into intimacy? What exactly do you have to do?"

When men ask what they have to do to be loving, the question is often accompanied by an implicit concern: "I don't have to be *completely* open, do I?" Men often back away from intimacy at the moment of truth because they fear that self-disclosure is an all-or-nothing proposition. Just as when and where to be intimate are defined by need, so too is *what* to be open about. A man need not disclose his sexual desire (personal self) if his behavior in a particular relationship and situation is rooted in his feelings about work (private self). It also means that he should not attempt to pass off public-self disclosures as substitutes for needed personal disclosures. This is particularly the case where a disclosure of feeling is required. Here the tendency of men is to fall back on mystery-mastery behavior.

"HOW DO I FEEL?"

"I get all geared up to be intimate. I really believe I need to do it. I think I can sense when, where, and even what I need to do. Then the moment comes when my wife says to me, 'How do you feel?' That's when all the resolve I have to be close starts to wilt. I can't answer her because I honestly don't know how I feel. How can I find out how I feel?"

As much as men use ignorance of their own feelings as an excuse for not being intimate, it is nonetheless true that many men do not know how they feel. Years of suppressing their feelings and hiding them from others have resulted in men being cut off from their own emotional responses. When they do get in touch with how they feel, so unfamiliar are these feelings that men tend to discount them as irrelevant or not actionable. For these men, the desire to be intimate and a plan for how to become intimate are frustrated by the fact that they honestly do not know how they feel.

There are several levels at which we can experience ourselves and the world. There is the external world, which we experience largely by observing events and the behavior of others. There is our own behavior; here, the focus of our attention is on our own actions, what we are doing. Finally, there is our own internal cognitive-emotional structure, what we think and feel. Most men experience the world at the first level, as observers of others. Some men are skilled at self-observation. A very few men are in touch with their own thoughts and feelings. To be intimate, a man needs to learn how to experience himself and the world at the feeling level. Several issues confront a man as he attempts to tune in to his own feelings and express them to others.

Most men respond to situations and people from the mystery-mastery mode. Their immediate reaction is to hide themselves or, if that is not possible, to intellectualize so as to avoid a feeling response. Feelings are seldom at the forefront of a man's consciousness. To learn how he feels, a man may need to restrain his habitual, automatic responses and give time for his feelings to emerge:

- "One of the first things I had to learn was to shut off thinking. There's such a difference between feeling and thinking. Thinking is what we men are good at; the rational, logical approach is how we go at things. When a problem comes up, my first response used to be, 'What makes sense here?' Now I'm trying to hold off on what makes sense and ask instead, 'What do I sense here?' There's a big difference."

Because the behavior of men is so conditioned by "shoulds"—what a man *should* be, how a man *should* behave—they often look for the "feeling" shoulds. This behavior is frequently encouraged by women, who expect that men should feel as they themselves do. When confronted by a situation, a man may struggle so hard over how he should feel that he doesn't attend to how he *does* feel. Feelings are neither positive nor negative, neither right nor wrong; feelings simply *are*:

- "I think that whenever you're learning something new, you naturally want to know how you're doing. The more unsure you are, the more you want some indication that you are on the right track. As far as expressing feelings went, the hardest thing for me to get used to was that there was no way I *should* feel. There is just the way I *do* feel. I used to wait until somebody else, like my wife, said how she felt. If I didn't feel the same thing, I didn't share my feelings because I thought they were wrong. It was as if I wanted to know how I should feel before I checked to see how I did feel. I'm over that now, and now that I'm not concerned with how I should feel, I find it a lot easier to know how I do feel."

It is the parts of our behavior that don't fit that often provide the best clues to our feelings. The tendency to do first one thing and then another, our avoidance of certain types of behavior, our masking of others—all may signal certain feelings that are being suppressed. These forms of behavior are very evident to others. Seeing ourselves as others see us often shows us our own feelings:

- "You have to pay attention to what other people tell you about yourself, even when you don't especially want to hear it. Make that *especially* when you don't want to hear it. That's when there is the most to learn. I mean, when other people tell you about your own inconsistencies, you're forced to look at yourself. If you look close enough, you'll learn something about yourself."

Men avoid intimacy as a means of protecting their own self-images. They avoid feelings for the same reason. One way men can get in touch with feelings is to explore those dimensions of a situation or encounter that make them uncomfortable because they challenge a man's self-image.

Feelings are not a man's strong suit. If he is to know his feelings and express them in a relationship, he must be prepared to work from a position of weakness for a time. Others, particularly women, will know their own feelings better and more quickly, and be more accustomed to acting upon them. This may place a man at a disadvantage in his interactions with women. This cannot be avoided, but the effects can be ameliorated by working on feelings in those relationships where there is the greatest caring and trust:

- "The most difficult thing of all is that it all feels so awkward. That's the incredible paradox: when you get closest to what you really are, it doesn't feel like it's you because it's so strange. When you get to where you are dealing with your feelings, it feels uncomfortable because you're in strange territory. Add to that the sense of vulnerability, really feeling defenseless, and it takes a lot of guts to hang in there and change. I truly feel that it is the most courageous thing I have ever done in my life."

Gil Ackerman is one man who has made the transition from distant and detached to close and caring. His comments on his change in behavior at mid-life underscore the importance of the steps outlined above: "I'd be the last person to tell you that it was easy. But there was a time when I would have been the last person to say that getting close to others was worth it. Maybe it's harder if you're not sure it's something that you really want to do. Even after I made up my mind to try to show the people I cared about just how much I did care, it still wasn't an overnight thing. In some ways it's a lot like learning anything else. At the beginning, you're self-conscious and unsure. You make simple mistakes and think that everyone else is watching. There were plenty of times when I felt like a fool. That's probably the hardest thing for any man, to be unsure and look foolish. Every time it happened, I wanted to cash it all in and go back to my old ways. Except I couldn't go back. If I did, I would have lost the people I love most, my wife and kids. My wife made me change and she helped me change. I wouldn't have wanted to do it if she hadn't forced me, and I couldn't have done it if she hadn't helped."

Where men have made the change to more loving behavior, they have been quick to credit the women in their lives not only for helping them to see the need to change, but for helping them to change, as well. Sometimes the credit is grudgingly given, but it is invariably given:

▪ "I simply could not have done it without her. She was right there all the way. I'm glad that now I can show her just how much she means to me."

▪ "God, she was such a bitch about it. She never gave up on me, even when I gave up on myself. She nagged me into it, shamed me into it, and dragged me into it. Thank God she did. I never would have done it otherwise."

■ "I don't know where she gets the patience. I don't have it with myself, but she has it with me. It has taken me much longer than I ever thought it would, but now, thanks mainly to her, even I can see the difference in me."

■ "She didn't do it alone, she got the kids working with her on me. When your kids are involved in changing you, let me tell you, the pressure is really on. I feel like it's not just something that I am doing for myself, I'm becoming more loving for all of us. And like they all tell me, 'It's about time!'"

In the pursuit of greater intimacy in their relationships, many men have encountered barriers erected by others, usually by women, usually in the guise of help. It behooves men and women to be conscious of these barriers as they work at getting closer. Perhaps the barrier most frequently mentioned by men is the demand for intimacy. Demanding intimacy invariably arouses a man's defenses and leads to his withdrawal. In addition to demanding intimacy, women often confound a man's efforts to be more loving by trying to do it for him. The role of emotional interpreter is all too comfortable for all too many women. When a woman supplies a man's emotional responses for him, or interprets his responses for the children, she effectively protects him from the discomfort that must accompany his learning to be intimate. It is difficult to remain quiet while he struggles to talk about his feelings; it is difficult to refuse sex when he wants to use it as a surrogate for sharing; it is difficult to see him falter in his attempts to relate to the children; but without these difficulties a man will never experience firsthand the need to know himself and to share himself with others.

No two of us experience a given event in quite the same way. Even though we may both have seen the same thing or done the same thing, your reaction to it will be quite different from mine. There is no right feeling; there are only your feelings and mine. Feelings are not to be judged, yet many men feel that women judge their feelings. Their response in the face of judgment is to retreat to more familiar, less intimate ground.

One thing rings clear from the stories of men who have tried intimacy: in every case it was necessary for them first to unlearn their old ways before they could learn new ones. Loving is not a quickly acquired skill. It takes time and requires patience. There will be backsliding. It is important to keep a sense of perspective. Both parties in a relationship must keep in mind what is really most important. It may be less important that a man share every detail of his workday than that he openly express his love for his children. Neither men nor women should settle for less intimacy than they need from a man, but both should look carefully at the line between their needs and their wants in a relationship.

It is also clear from the reports of men that regardless of the personal benefits of increased intimacy, a man is unlikely to persist in his efforts unless he experiences some affirmation from others. His spouse, family, and friends can provide needed reinforcement for his new behavior. Without rewards for his effort, a man is likely to return to his habitual ways. He will lose touch with his feelings, and those close to him will lose his loving.

For some women, this may seem to be simply too much. To get the loving behavior she wants, it appears that a woman must be confidante, confronter, consoler. As if that were not enough, she must reward *him* for the effort *he* makes! What of *her* rewards? Her reward is in his love.

Gil Ackerman's wife knows about her reward: "Sometimes Gil and I will be together talking, really talking now about important personal things, and I will think about how different things are for us now that he is so much more caring, and my eyes will fill with tears. Gil asks why I am crying and I tell him it's because I feel that he loves me so much, and he smiles and starts crying too. You can't know what it means to me to see my husband cry because of the love we have. I can truly say that his tears are my reward for whatever part I had in helping him open up."

"HOW WILL I KNOW WHEN I'M THERE?"

"I don't want to set out to do something unless I know what it's going to be like when I accomplish it. If you don't know what the finish line looks like, how will you know when you get there? How will I know when I am close enough to other people?"

Curiously, this final question is one that those men who have become more loving have the greatest difficulty answering. It is not that they don't know the answer, but rather that their answers are universally vague. Even with their new-found expressiveness, these men find that some things are still difficult to put into words:

- "You'll just know, that's all."
- "When you get there, you'll realize that question isn't important."
- "It's a feeling that you'll have."
- "You won't feel different, but people will feel different about you, and you'll feel that. I can't describe it any other way."
- "When you're there, you don't need to ask, 'Is this it?' You know what it is."
- "It's the sort of question I would have asked before, but not now."

What would it be like if men were more loving? For their wives and families, it would mean that they would feel loved where today they are only told they are loved. For families and friends, it would mean that they could understand why men behave as they do, and they could offer help and solace to men. For men themselves, if they were more loving, it would mean that they could rely upon their close relationships with others to help them deal with the stresses of their lives, enable them to act more effectively in their lives, and lead them to know themselves better. Most of all, it would mean that men would know love.

The goal of intimacy for any one man and for all men is beautifully captured in the words of an elderly respondent who had come to be intimate with others very late in life. He wrote, "I never knew how much I was loved until I loved."

This has been written in hope that we may all love and, through our loving, know how much we are loved.

Appendix

INTIMACY QUESTIONNAIRE

This list of twenty-five questions asks the extent to which you have revealed information about yourself, your actions, and your feelings to others whom you are with in a variety of relationships. You can be assured that your anonymity will be protected, as there is nothing in the questionnaire to identify individuals. We are interested only in groups of respondents.

Instructions: You are to indicate the extent to which you have disclosed the information in the question to each of the individuals in the relationships identified.

Write an 0 in the space if you know you have never talked about the item to that person.

Write a 1 in the space if you have discussed almost nothing about the item with that person, if they know very little about you with respect to this item.

Write a 2 in the space if you have talked about this item in general terms with that person, but have left out most of the specific details.

Write a 3 in the space if you have discussed the item in general and also disclosed some specific details to the person.

Write a 4 in the space if you have talked about most of

the important details in regard to this item, if the other knows a great deal about you in relation to this item.

Write a 5 in the space if you have brought the other completely up to date in detail on this item, if they know all there is to know about you in relation to this item.

Write MR in the space if you have purposely misrepresented yourself to the other on this item or allowed them to make assumptions about you without correcting them.

Once again, the scale you will be using is:

0 = Never Disclosed
1 = Disclosed Almost Nothing
2 = Disclosed in General
3 = Disclosed Some Specific Details
_ = Disclosed Most Details
5 = Disclosed All There Is to Know About You
MR = Misrepresented Yourself

Spouse or Intimate Other (Check One)	Mother	Father	Son Daughter (Check One)	Brother Sister (Check One)	Male Friend	Female Friend	Male Work Associate	Female Work Associate

SAMPLE: The last movie you saw and how you felt about it.

5	1	1	3	2	3	4	2	2

QUESTIONS:

I. 1. What are your views on the way a husband and wife should live their marriage?

2. What are your usual ways of dealing with depression, anxiety, and anger?

285

	Spouse or Intimate Other (Check One)	Mother	Father	Son Daughter (Check One)	Brother Sister (Check One)	Male Friend	Female Friend	Male Work Associate	Female Work Associate
3. How you feel about the choice of career you have made, whether or not you are satisfied with it?	___	___	___	___	___	___	___	___	___
4. What are the actions you have most regretted doing in your life and why?	___	___	___	___	___	___	___	___	___
5. What are your personal religious views and the nature of your religious participation?	___	___	___	___	___	___	___	___	___
6. What are the ways in which you feel you are most maladjusted or immature?	___	___	___	___	___	___	___	___	___
7. What are your guiltiest secrets?	___	___	___	___	___	___	___	___	___
8. What are your personal views on politics, the Presidency, foreign and domestic policy?	___	___	___	___	___	___	___	___	___

	Spouse or Intimate Other (Check One)	Mother	Father	Son Daughter (Check One)	Brother Sister (Check One)	Male Friend	Female Friend	Male Work Associate	Female Work Associate
9. What are the habits and reactions of yours that bother you at present?	——	——	——	——	——	——	——	——	——
10. How much money you make?	——	——	——	——	——	——	——	——	——
11. What are the sources of strain and dissatisfaction in your marriage (or your relationships with the opposite sex)?	——	——	——	——	——	——	——	——	——
12. What are your favorite forms of erotic play and sexual lovemaking?	——	——	——	——	——	——	——	——	——
13. What are your hobbies, how do you like best to spend your spare time?	——	——	——	——	——	——	——	——	——
14. What were the occasions in your life in which you were the happiest?	——	——	——	——	——	——	——	——	——

	Spouse or Intimate Other (Check One)	Mother	Father	Son Daughter (Check One)	Brother Sister (Check One)	Male Friend	Female Friend	Male Work Associate	Female Work Associate
15. What are the aspects of your daily work that most satisfy you?									
16. What characteristics of yourself give you cause for pride and satisfaction?									
17. Who are the persons in your life whom you most resent? Why?									
18. How do you budget your money, the proportion that goes to necessities, luxuries, etc.?									
19. Who are the people with whom you have been sexually intimate? What were the circumstances of your relationship with them?									
20. What are the unhappiest moments in your life; why?									

	Spouse or Intimate Other (Check One)	Mother	Father	Son Daughter (Check One)	Brother Sister (Check One)	Male Friend	Female Friend	Male Work Associate	Female Work Associate
21. What are your preferences and dislikes in music?	___	___	___	___	___	___	___	___	___
22. What are the sources of strain and dissatisfaction in your work?	___	___	___	___	___	___	___	___	___
23. What are your personal goals for the next 5 to 10 years?	___	___	___	___	___	___	___	___	___
24. What are the circumstances under which you become depressed and when you are hurt?	___	___	___	___	___	___	___	___	___
25. What are your most common sexual fantasies?	___	___	___	___	___	___	___	___	___
II. 1. Indicate the number of years you have been involved in each of these relationships.	___	___	___	___	___	___	___	___	___

	Spouse or Intimate Other (Check One)	Mother	Father	Son Daughter (Check One)	Brother Sister (Check One)	Male Friend	Female Friend	Male Work Associate	Female Work Associate
2. Rank these relationships in terms of the value you receive from them. 1 = highest 9 = lowest	___	___	___	___	___	___	___	___	___
3. How frequently do you encounter these people? D = Daily W = Weekly M = Monthly A = Annually or Less Frequently	___	___	___	___	___	___	___	___	___

III.

1. What is your age? ___
   The ages of these people? ___

2. What is your sex? M ___ F ___

3. What is your income? Less than $15,000 ___; $15,000–$25,000 ___; $26,000–$40,000 ___; $41,000–$60,000 ___; over $60,000 ___

DESIGN

The methodology used is patterned after work pioneered by Dr. Sidney Jourard. The Intimacy Questionnaire is in three parts. Part 1 consists of twenty-five statements, each of which is information about an individual's tastes and interests (four items), attitudes and opinions (three items), work and money views and behaviors (five items), personality and self-esteem (ten items), and sexual views and behaviors (three items).

Questionnaire items were drawn from a pool of 671 items generated by D. A. Taylor and I. Altman to tap verbal-informational aspects of social penetration, titled "Intimacy Scaled Stimuli for Use in Research on Interpersonal Exchange" (Bethesda, Maryland: Naval Medical Research Institute Technical Report No. 9, MF022.01.03-1022, May 1966); from Sidney M. Jourard, *Self-Disclosure: An Experimental Analysis of the Transparent Self* (Wiley-Interscience, New York, 1971); and from items generated by the author. The items have face validity in that they have generally accepted connotations, but they also were submitted to validation by twenty judges for evaluations of depth and grouping of items into topical categories. For example, in the category of Attitudes and Opinions, "religious views" was judged to be somewhat superficial (2.4) on a five-point scale and was grouped with items of similar intimacy-scale value. The resultant ranking of categories from least to most intimate corresponds with findings from other studies (Taylor and Altman, Jourard): Tastes and Interests (2.2), Attitudes and Opinions (2.9), Work and Money (3.5), Personality, Self-Esteem (3.7), Sex (4.5).

Respondents were asked to indicate the extent to which they have revealed this information to the other in specified relationships—Spouse or Intimate Other, Mother, Father, Son or Daughter, Brother or Sister, Male Friend, Female Friend, Male Work Associate, Female Work Associate. Responses are made on a six-point scale, ranging from

"Never Disclosed" (0) to "Disclosed All There Is to Know About You" (5). There is also a response (MR) for "Misrepresented."

For any one reported relationship there are six scores on Part 1 of the questionnaire, five subset scores, one for each category of information represented, and a Total Disclosure Score. A respondent who was fully disclosing of information about himself or herself to any one other person would have a score of 429. Fully disclosing subset scores are: Tastes and Interests = 44, Attitudes and Opinions = 44, Work and Money = 88, Personality and Self-Esteem = 185, Sex = 68.

Questionnaire responses were graded and coded onto the Statistical Package for the Social Sciences (SPSS). T-Tests were performed to test for significant differences in the disclosure patterns of men and women based on the depth and breadth of disclosure.

In Part 2 of the Disclosure Questionnaire, respondents were asked to indicate the length of relationships and frequency of interaction and to rank their relationships in terms of the value they attach to them, 1 = most valuable to least valuable. Pearson Correlations were performed to examine relationships between disclosure and duration of relationships, disclosure and frequency, and disclosure and value.

Demographic data regarding sex, age, and income were requested in Part 3. Anonymity of all responses was assured.

ADMINISTRATION AND SAMPLING

The questionnaire was administered in forty-three different cluster samples over an eighteen-month period from 1982 to 1983. These cluster samples were selected because of availability and are not represented as random samplings. The cluster samples consist of members of national professional, social, and fraternal associations and organizations, as well as their spouses and families, in attendance at national meetings. These groups included professional and nonprofessional respondents, male and female, in a broad age range. The forms were administered to groups of respondents by myself or an assistant. With some groups, respondents returned the forms by mail. Only fully completed forms were used in the research. A total of 3,500 questionnaires were administered. Of these, a total of 1,383, or 39.5 percent, were usable (complete) responses. Of this number, 737 respondents were male and 646 were female. The range in ages was 18–73; the average age of male respondents was 38, the average age of female respondents was 34. Income was reported in ranges with the following distribution: Less than $15,000 = 8 percent; $15,000–25,000 = 39 percent; $26,000–40,000 = 33 percent; $41,000–60,000 = 17 percent; and over $60,000 = 3 percent.

INTERVIEWS

In addition to the questionnaire, respondents were asked to indicate whether or not they would be willing to be interviewed for one hour about their intimate relationships. Four hundred twenty-seven agreed to be interviewed; of this number, seventy men, seventy women, and twenty man-and-woman couples were selected for one-hour, open-ended, responsive interviews. Interviewees were selected with an eye toward ages and incomes representative of distributions in the larger sample. Each interview began with three standard questions: With whom are you intimate? Why are you close to these people? How would you describe your behavior in these relationships? Subsequent questions probed for more detailed information on the subjects' responses.

Some questionnaire respondents not interviewed wrote letters telling of their experiences with intimacy. Excerpts from these letters were used in the book to illustrate points in the data.

Index

Darek snorted. Then, as he watched Zantor playing with Rowena, a strange thing began to happen. Happy little thoughts started pushing into Darek's head. They seemed to swell and pop, one after another, like bubbles. For a moment, Darek swore he could smell the perfume of Rowena's hair. He could almost feel the touch of her hands. Then, just as quickly as the funny feelings had come, they were gone. Confused, Darek shook his head.

"What's wrong?" Pola asked.

"I . . . It's weird," Darek said. "I felt like I was inside Zantor's head for a minute."

Pola looked over at Zantor and Rowena and laughed out loud. "Sounds like wishful thinking to me," he said. Then he gave Darek another poke.

Darek's frown returned. If he *had* been inside

Zantor's head, he didn't like what he had felt there. Zantor was growing way too fond of Rowena. "Zantor!" he shouted. "Get back over here."

Rowena wound her arms tightly around the dragon. Zantor glanced over at Darek but didn't try to break free.

"Now!" Darek boomed.

With a sudden jerk Zantor broke away from Rowena. He scuffled over to Darek as fast as his little legs would carry him. Darek looked at Rowena and grinned, as if to say, "See, he's all mine." Rowena glared back, tossing her head.

"I was just petting him," she called. "You don't have to be so mean about it."

"Zantor's not a pet," Darek snapped. "He and I have work to do. If you want to pet something, go pet a yuke."

Rowena glared a moment longer, then turned and stormed away.

Pola looked at Darek and shook his head.

"What's wrong with you?" Darek asked.

"You have a funny way of showing a girl that you like her," Pola said.

"I *don't* like her," Darek insisted. "She's nothing but a pest."

"Oh, yeah?" Pola said. He laughed and pointed to Zantor. The dragonling was still gazing, dreamy-eyed, after Rowena. "Doesn't look like Zantor agrees with you."

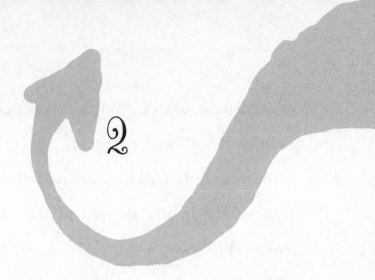

2

"YOU SHOULD HAVE SEEN ZANTOR today," Darek said to his mother and father and his brother, Clep, over dinner. "He's learning so fast! He takes off and lands on command. He can fly a circle and a figure eight. . . ."

Hearing his name, Zantor uncurled himself from the hearth. He shuffled over and nuzzled Darek's arm. *"Thrrummm,"* he sang happily at

Darek's elbow. Darek smiled and slipped him a spoonful of barliberry pudding.

Darek's mother, Alayah, attempted to frown.

"No feeding the dragon at the table," she reminded her son.

Darek's father ate quietly. He listened but did not respond to Darek's chatter. Yanek had come to accept Zantor. He even loved the little dragon, but at the same time he had doubts about Darek's dream. A future where people and dragons lived peacefully, side by side, helping each other?

"It's a nice idea," Yanek would say when Darek pressed him about it. "But such things are not always as simple as they seem."

It was true that such things *weren't* simple. Darek had learned that the hard way. When his father had allowed Darek to bring Zantor back to Zoriak, the villagers had been very angry. They had almost burned Yanek at the stake! But Darek and Zantor had proved to the villagers that they were wrong about dragons. One day, Darek was sure, he and Zantor would prove his father wrong about the future, too.

Darek turned toward his big brother. "Hurry and finish eating, Clep," he said. "I want to show you everything Zantor learned today."

Clep was just swallowing his last spoonful of pudding when someone rapped on the door.

"I'll get it," Darek said, jumping up.

He pulled the door open, then stepped back in surprise. "Excellency," he said, bowing low. The Chief Elder himself stood on their doorstep.

Darek's parents and Clep quickly rose to their feet.

His mother rushed forward. "Enter, Sire," she said. "Please take some supper with us."

"I have already supped, Alayah," the Elder said. He nodded stiffly to them all. "I have come to have a word with Yanek."

"Of course." Darek's father bowed and led the way to the front parlor.

Darek and Clep glanced uneasily at each other.

Alayah twisted her apron in her hands. "I hope this visit does not bode ill," she whispered to her sons.

"As you know," they overheard the Chief Elder say, "my daughter's Decanum approaches."

Darek sighed with relief. So that was all. The Chief Elder had come to talk over the arrangements for Rowena's Decanum. The whole village was soon to celebrate her tenth birthday. There would be a full parade, a banquet, and a formal ball. Darek's father, as Chief Marksman and Captain of the Guard, would have much to do to prepare.

Darek's mother seemed relieved too. She went back to the table to finish her pudding.

"You know, Darek," she said with a teasing smile, "there has been much talk in the village. Everyone is wondering who Rowena will choose to be her escort for the Decanum Ball."

Darek's face reddened. Rowena's escort? What was his mother getting at?

"Have *you* any idea who her escort will be?" she asked.

"Not at all," Darek answered shortly.

Clep grinned. "I've heard some names mentioned, Mother," he said. "One very familiar name, in fact." He shot a teasing glance at Darek. "Perhaps that explains the Chief Elder's visit, eh?"

Darek gave Clep such a look of dismay that Clep had to laugh out loud. "It's not the end of the world, little brother," he said. "I can think of fates worse than having to dance with the lovely Rowena."

"Why don't *you* escort her if you think she's so lovely?" Darek snapped. "I think she's a spoiled brat."

"Hush, you two!" Alayah whispered. "Have you forgotten who speaks with your father in the next room?"

Zantor bounced over and butted Darek in the arm. Glad of the interruption, Darek went to the cupboard. He took out the dragonling's bowl and began to prepare his supper.

"It makes no difference what you think,

Darek," Clep said in a more serious voice. "You will, of course, accept if you are asked."

Darek didn't answer. He filled Zantor's bowl with fallow meal and barliberries. Then he ladled warm water over all and stirred it into a mash. The smell of it suddenly made his stomach growl

hungrily. He raised the bowl to his lips and took a big gulp.

"Blaah!" It tasted awful. Darek spit the mash back into the bowl and stared at it. What on Zoriak had possessed him to eat Zantor's food? He'd just finished eating his own dinner! And even if he was hungry, he would never eat fallow meal mash! He looked up and saw Clep and his mother staring at him strangely.

"What *are* you doing?" his mother asked.

Zantor butted Darek's arm again, nearly upsetting the bowl. Darek lowered it slowly to the floor. The dragonling dived eagerly for the food, gulping and gulping. Slowly the hunger pangs in Darek's stomach began to subside.

"I know what he's doing, Mother," Clep said. "He's trying to change the subject."

"What subject?" Darek mumbled, still staring at Zantor. The dish was nearly empty now, and Darek was feeling quite full. A bubble swelled and swelled in his stomach. It wiggled its way up through his chest and burst from his mouth. "Bu-urp!"

"Darek!" his mother exclaimed.

Darek clapped a hand over his mouth. "Sorry," he muttered. What was happening to him?

Clep frowned and shook his head. "Why would anyone want to go to the ball with a dragon-wit like you, anyway?" he asked.

"I'm sure Rowena *doesn't* want to go with me," Darek retorted. "Why do you even listen to those stupid rumors?"

"*Ahem.*"

Darek looked up at the sound of the deep voice. His father's broad frame filled the doorway. He was staring at Darek with a serious look on his face.

"You had better come in here, son," he said. "The Chief Elder's mission today concerns you."

Darek swallowed hard and stared at his father.

"Go on with you," Clep said, grinning broadly and giving Darek a little push toward the parlor. Darek stumbled a few steps, then recovered and followed his father in silence. The Chief Elder stood waiting, tall and stern.

"I've a question to put to you, boy," he said as Darek approached.

Darek's heart sank. He lowered his eyes and nodded. "I . . . I would be honored, Sire," he mumbled.

"Honored?" the Elder repeated. "Honored to do what?"

Darek glanced up at his father and then back at the Elder.

"Why . . . to escort Rowena to the ball, Sire," he said. "Isn't that why you're here?"

The Elder's lips twitched. A glint of humor sparkled in his eyes. "You flatter yourself, son," he said. "My daughter sent me on no such mission."

Darek wanted to faint with relief. The Chief Elder's mission had nothing to do with the Decanum Ball! He wouldn't have to dance with Rowena after all. But then a warm flush of embarrassment crept up his neck. What a fool he had made of himself!

"I'm sorry, Sire," he mumbled. "What is it that you wished to discuss with me?"

The Elder folded his arms across his chest, and his long robes gathered around him. "I want your dragon," he said. "I came to buy Zantor."

3

DAREK'S EYES OPENED WIDE. COULD he have heard right?

"Y-you want to *buy* Zantor?" he stammered.

"Yes." The Chief Elder began to pace. His mood seemed suddenly to turn sour. "I never dreamed I'd allow one of the nasty creatures into my household," he said. "But Rowena has taken a fancy to the beast and will have nothing else. I wouldn't give the matter a second thought if it weren't her

Decanum. One must . . . make allowances at such a time." He rolled his eyes at Darek's father. "You are a father too, Yanek," he said. "I'm sure you can understand."

"Well I do, Sire," Yanek said, nodding.

The Elder stopped pacing and turned to Darek. "Name your price, boy," he said. "And mind you, be fair about it."

Darek's mouth dropped open. "But I *can't* sell Zantor," he said. "I mean, he's not for sale."

The Elder's brows crashed together. "Not for sale?" he boomed. "What do you mean, not for sale? Everything is for sale. Don't be trying to cheat me, boy—driving the price up. I'll have you in the stocks!"

"No, Sire," Darek blurted. "I'm not. It's just that . . . Zantor isn't a *thing*; he's my friend. I can't sell him. I . . . I don't own him. Dragons can't be *owned*."

"Barli rot!" the Elder bellowed. "Your father said I must speak to you. Now, name your price and be quick about it!"

Darek glanced at his father and swallowed hard. Then he took a deep breath and bravely returned the Elder's stare. "I . . . I don't own him," he repeated. "He followed me home from the Valley of the Dragons of his own free will. He stays with me because he wants to. He's my friend. That's all."

The Chief Elder's eyes blazed. "Yanek," he said, turning to Darek's father, "I grow weary of your son's impertinence. Name me a price for the beast, and let me be on my way. I've more important matters to attend to."

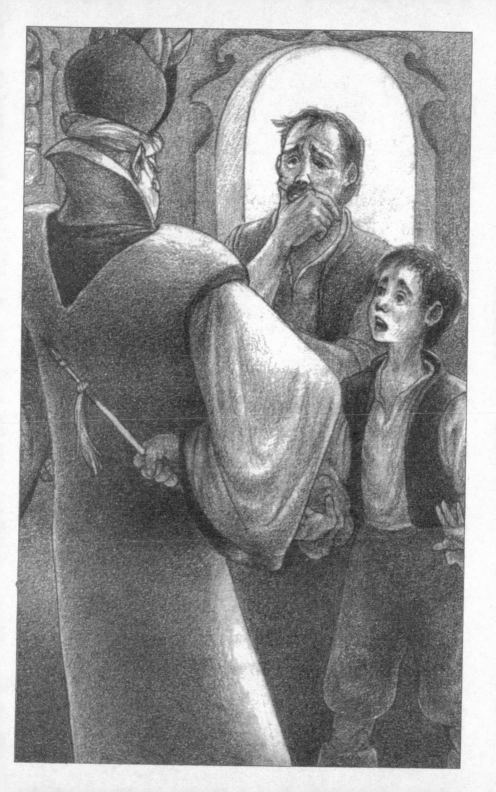

Yanek glanced at Darek. Darek pleaded with his eyes, begging his father to understand. Inside, he could feel himself trembling. He remembered all too well what had happened the last time his father had defied the Chief Elder.

At last, Yanek drew in a deep breath and bowed to the Elder. "My apologies, Sire," he said. "But if my son says the beast is not for sale, I fear it is not for sale."

The Chief Elder's eyes widened, then narrowed down to angry slits. His nostrils flared. "Fine, then," he spat. "In that case, Yanek, you will ready your men for a dragonquest on the morrow. Be prepared to leave at dawn for the Valley of the Dragons. There you will stay until you have captured a dragonling for my daughter's Decanum." He leaned forward and pressed a finger hard into Yanek's chest. "And it had better be a Great Blue!"

With that, the Elder turned and strode from the room, his royal robes billowing out behind him.

4

DAREK RAN ACROSS THE PADDOCK
after his father, tugging at the sleeve of his jerkin.
"Please, Father," he begged. "You can't do this. It
isn't right."

"Darek," his father said, "I am weary of discussing this with you. The Council of Elders decides
what is right and wrong. I am Captain of the Guard.
I must follow the orders of the Council."

"But you're an elder yourself," Darek argued.

"With one vote," his father reminded him.

"But you can convince the others. . . ."

Darek's father stopped and stared down at Darek. "Convince them of what? That my son should have a dragon and the Chief Elder's daughter should not?"

"But Zantor chose to be with me. No one *captured* him. It isn't the same," Darek argued.

Yanek shook his head. "I'll do my best to try and prevent bloodshed," he said quietly. "That's all I can promise."

Darek saw the expression in his father's eyes and realized that it was senseless to argue further. Yanek did not approve of this mission either. But nothing would keep him from doing his duty. Darek sighed and nodded. "Can I go along, at least?" he asked.

"I'm sorry," Yanek said. "You're to stay here, with your mother." Then he strode over to where Clep and the others stood waiting in the early morning light.

Yanek gave the order to mount, and the dragon-quest party rode out. Throngs of villagers followed them to the edge of town, cheering and wishing them well. *Just like the old days*, Darek thought, *when the men used to hunt dragons*. Darek had hoped those days were gone forever. Zantor shuffled over to him.

"*Rrronk,*" he cried.

Darek stared sadly at the little dragon. Zantor's own mother had been killed brutally, needlessly, on just such a dragonquest. "I'm sorry, my friend," Darek said quietly.

Suddenly from across the paddock there came a soft call. "Zantor . . . Zantor, come here, fella!"

Zantor's ears pricked up, and Darek whirled around.

Rowena! How dare she come here now?

"Stay," Darek commanded in a low growl, but it was too late. Zantor was already half running, half flying toward the girl. Darek ran after him, but by the time he reached Rowena and the dragon, they were already snuggling together.

"Zantor!" Darek shouted, stomping his foot. "Come here!"

Zantor glanced at Darek but did not pull away. Rowena twined her arms around the little dragon's neck and kissed him on the nose. Zantor looked up at her, his green eyes shining.

"Soon we'll have a new friend!" she told him excitedly. "Another little dragon to play with."

"Thrummmm," Zantor sang happily.

Darek was so angry at Rowena he felt like he could breathe fire.

"A friend!" he spat. "Do you steal a *friend* from its mother, Rowena? Do you tear it from its family? Force it to leave its home? Is that how you treat your *friends*, Rowena?"

Rowena glared at him. "That's what *you* did, isn't it?" she asked innocently.

"You know full well it's not," Darek snapped. "Zantor's mother was dead when I found him. She was killed on a dragonquest. He came with me because he chose to."

Rowena tossed her head. "And my dragon will choose to be with me," she said. Then she hugged Zantor tighter and narrowed her eyes. "Just like Zantor would, if you'd *let* him. Wouldn't you, Zantor?"

Zantor stared at her with adoring eyes. *Thwip!* Out flicked his tongue, planting a kiss on her cheek.

Suddenly all Darek's anger melted, and he felt a rush of tenderness toward Rowena. She seemed to be the sweetest, loveliest creature he had ever seen. Before he knew it, *he* was kissing Rowena on the cheek too!

"What are you *doing,* you dragon-wit!" she shrieked. She gave Darek a shove, and he sprawled on his back in the dirt. He lay there staring at the sky, his head spinning. Did he . . . ? Had he just . . . ? No. He couldn't have. It must have been a dream. He turned and looked. Rowena was gone.

Yeah, that's what it was, he told himself. A terrible, horrible dream. That's all. But . . . then . . . if it *was* just a dream, why did he feel like thrumming?

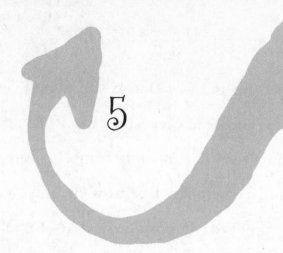

5

DAREK COULDN'T SLEEP. HE WAS TOO
confused. And too angry with that . . . girl! She
had no idea how much trouble she was causing.
She had never been to the Valley of the Dragons.
She didn't know how beautiful it was, how majes-
tic the dragons were at peace.

A dragonquest! Darek shuddered at the
thought. What did Rowena know of the horrors
of battle? Had she ever ached over the loss of a

dear one the way Darek still ached over Yoran? Yoran had been Clep's best friend. He'd been like a third brother in their house as long as Darek could remember. But now he was dead. Killed on the last dragonquest, like so many other young men before him. Killed fighting a dragon that only wished to be left alone. Yoran had died fighting Zantor's mother. And she had died too, defending her baby, Zantor. Now other dragons might die. And men, too, maybe even his father or Clep. All for the foolish whim of a spoiled, selfish girl.

Darek sat up and threw his covers aside. At the foot of the bed, Zantor stirred, instantly alert. Darek couldn't stand it any longer—doing nothing. Even now a battle might be raging. He had stopped a battle once. Maybe he could do so

again. His father would be angry with him if he disobeyed, but Darek had to follow his heart. He had always followed his heart, and it had not yet led him astray. He dressed quickly and pushed his bedroom window open. Then he motioned for Zantor to come to him.

"Hush," he whispered, pressing a finger to his lips. He stared directly into the little dragon's eyes. How could he explain to Zantor what he wanted him to do? He touched Zantor's chest, then his own, then pointed to the ground, two stories below. "I want you to fly me down there," he said.

Zantor looked out the window and then back at Darek. Goose bumps broke out on Darek's skin as he saw a light dawn in the dragon's eyes. Zantor understood! They were communicating somehow, mind to mind. Darek had little time to ponder this

wonder, for Zantor quickly sprang into action. He leaped to the window ledge and fluttered out into the night. Slowly he began to circle, then picked up speed. Darek climbed out and crouched on the windowsill, waiting. He had no doubt that Zantor could do what he'd asked. Small as the dragon was, he was capable of enormous, if brief, bursts of power. Darek had seen him carry things many times his own weight.

Zantor circled twice more, then somehow Darek knew the time was right. Just as Zantor swooped by, Darek leaned forward, and the dragonling plucked him neatly from the ledge. Together they fluttered toward the ground. Zantor's wings pumped mightily as his claws gently grasped Darek's arms.

"You did it!" Darek praised him when they touched down safely. "Good boy."

"Thrummmm, thrummmm," Zantor sang, glowing with pride.

Motioning the dragonling to follow, Darek crept around to the stables. He chose two strong, young yukes and led them outside. They began to fret in the darkness, but he calmed them with sugar cubes and saddled them. He climbed up on one and grabbed the other's reins.

"C'mon, Zantor," he whispered. "Let's go get Pola."

Zantor took to the air and followed at close range.

Pola's bedroom was on the ground floor of his family's home. A light rap on his window quickly

woke him. It took no more than a word from Darek to persuade him to come along. Pola never was one to resist an adventure. He was dressed in an instant, and they were off.

The going was slow at first because of the darkness, but once the sun rose, Darek, Pola, and

Zantor made better time. By midday they had reached the Black Mountains of Krad.

"We're about halfway to the Valley of the Dragons," Darek announced. He eyed the Black Mountains warily as they skirted the smoke-shrouded crags. The trees and grasses on the mountainsides had died long ago. Nothing was visible through the haze but twisted stumps and jagged rocks. "Lord Eternal, those mountains are creepy," Darek said.

Pola nodded, shivering in the shadows of the peaks. "I get the feeling that something—or *someone*—is up there watching," he said. "Don't you?"

Darek laughed. "Kradens?" he asked.

Pola laughed too. Zorian legends told of Kradens, fierce, hairy men who had supposedly driven the Zorians' ancestors out of Krad long ago.

"You don't believe those old myths, do you?" Pola asked.

Darek snorted. "What do you take me for, a nurseling? Of course I don't believe those old wives' tales."

"It's supposed to be true that our ancestors came out of those mountains in the Beginning, though," Pola said.

Darek shrugged. "It's hard to believe anything alive could come out of there," he said.

"They weren't always black and dead," Pola reminded him. "It is said that in the Beginning, they were just as beautiful as the Yellow Mountains of Orr."

Darek stared hard at the forbidding peaks. "If that's true," he wondered aloud, "then what caused them to die?"

"I don't know," Pola said. "But I'd sure like to go up there and try to find out."

Darek whirled to look at his friend. "Are you joking?" he asked. "You know it's forbidden to go up there."

Pola laughed. "Oh, and you never do *anything* forbidden, do you?" he teased. "Might I remind you that we're on a forbidden quest right now?"

"That's different," Darek said.

"Different how?"

Darek turned serious. "People used to go into the Black Mountains in the Long Ago," he said quietly, "but no one ever came back alive. That's why it's forbidden, Pola. Have you forgotten?"

"But nobody's gone in generations," Pola argued. "Maybe things have changed."

"Yeah." Darek nodded toward the mountains.

"For the worse. Only a fool would go up there, Pola."

Pola was quiet for a while. There was no sound but the *clip-clop* of yuke hooves and the rush of wings as Zantor soared overhead. An acrid smell hung in the air, though, a smell like death.

"What if . . . What if the ones who went didn't come back because it's so nice there?" Pola said at last. "What if they didn't come back because they didn't *want* to come back?"

Darek laughed out loud. "Nice?" he said. "Does anything about those mountains look *nice* to you? Besides, if it was so nice, don't you think *someone* would come back and tell the rest of us?"

Pola smiled. "Yeah, I guess you're right," he said. Then he gazed back over his shoulder. "Sure would be a great adventure, though, wouldn't it?"

6

DAREK, POLA, AND ZANTOR REACHED
the Yellow Mountains of Orr by night. The camp-
fires of the Zorian hunting party flickered on a
ridge about halfway up the slopes. Darek and Pola
made their own camp well below. To be sure they
wouldn't be seen, they went without a campfire.
At dawn they skirted the main path and found
another way up the peaks, leaving the yukes tied

below. Darek looped a halter around Zantor's neck to keep him close.

"Easy, now, easy," he whispered. "This is just to keep you safe, my friend." Zantor did not object. He seemed to sense the danger and put his trust in Darek. Carefully, quietly, the three climbed the last few hundred feet.

"Wow!" Pola exclaimed when they finally reached the top.

"*Thrummmm,*" Zantor sang softly as he gazed once again upon the valley of his birth.

"I told you it was beautiful," Darek whispered.

"I've never seen anything so beautiful in all my life," Pola agreed in a hushed voice.

Everything was peaceful in the valley. Although they had a day's head start, the hunting party had apparently made no move as yet. Darek was not

surprised. His father had promised to try to avoid bloodshed. To do so, the hunters would have to lie low and watch the dragons' movements for some time. They would have to wait for just the right moment to sneak in and do their dirty work. Only then would they stand a chance of escaping. Even so, it would not be easy.

The mountains around the valley sparkled. The soft violet rays of the morning sun bathed them in pale hues of blue and rose. Dragons perched on the crags like great colorful blossoms. Others soared in graceful circles through the air. Still others grazed peacefully on the valley floor. Darek saw Yellow Crested dragons, and Green Horned, and also a few small Purple Spotted. The dreaded Red Fanged and Purple Spiked that once struck terror into the hearts of all Zorians were completely

gone. Zorians had hunted them to extinction. It was the Red Fanged and Purple Spiked that had long ago given dragons a bad name, Darek was certain.

"Where are the Blues?" Pola asked.

Darek searched the valley, troubled by this question. "I don't know," he said. "I saw only one female and her three dragonlings when last I came. She lived in that cave high up on the mountainside there." Darek pointed. "I'd hoped there were others, off hunting or something, but I see no Blues again today."

"The Great Blues have been the favored game of the dragonquests ever since the Red Fanged and Purple Spiked disappeared," Pola said. "Can it be that they are nearly extinct now too?"

Darek looked at Zantor and swallowed hard. He had not thought of this before. "I pray not," he said quietly.

Pola gazed thoughtfully out over the valley. "Two males were taken in the dragonquest before last," he said. "They could have been the fathers of Zantor and the other three."

Darek felt a sinking in his heart as he recognized

the likely truth of Pola's words. "Yes," he said quietly. "They could, indeed."

"The other three young ones . . . ," Pola said. "Are they males or females?"

Darek thought back to his earlier trip to the valley. He had spent time in the Great Blue's cave, trying to get her to adopt Zantor. He remembered that the Great Blue's dragonlings had pouches like their mother. "They are females all," he said.

Zantor suddenly sprang upright and started thrumming wildly. Darek tightened his halter and pulled him close.

"*Rrronk! Rrronk!*" Zantor cried, struggling to get free.

"Shush, shush, Zantor, no!" Darek cried in Zantor's ear. "You have to stay still."

The dragonling quieted, but Darek sensed

his longing as he stared out across the valley.

"Look!" Pola whispered.

So that was what Zantor was so excited about. The Great Blue was emerging from her cave! She unfurled her silvery wings and stretched them out full-length. She stepped to the edge of the cliff and sprang off as lightly as a bird. Out against the sky she soared, blue on blue. The sun glinted and danced on her wings as she circled nearly over their heads.

"She's magnificent," Pola said.

"*Thrummmm,*" Zantor sang, looking up.

"Yes." Darek smiled and rubbed the little dragon's head. "One day you will be just as magnificent, my friend."

One by one, the three smaller Blues appeared at the cave mouth and fluttered out after their

mother. Darek smiled, happy to see that they were all still there and healthy. Then, like a cloud across the sun, a new thought came to him.

"Pola," he whispered, "if what you say is true, then Zantor is the last male Blue alive."

Pola nodded somberly. "And if he doesn't grow up and mate with one of those three," he added, "they will be the last Blues . . . *ever.*"

As if he clearly understood Darek and Pola's words, Zantor looked up at them with mournful eyes. *"Rrronk,"* he cried softly.

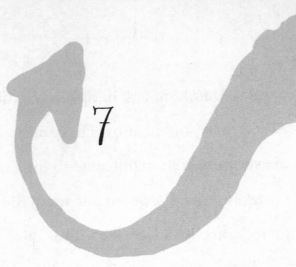

7

NOTHING MOVED ON THE RIDGE
through all the long, hot day. Pola went back to
the yukes to get the waterskins, then took Zantor
with him in search of food and fresh water. He
returned with an assortment of nuts and berries
and the two bulging skins. Darek drank deeply
and squirted a little of the refreshing liquid over
his sun-scorched head. Zantor curled up to sleep
in the shade of an outcropping of rock. As the

afternoon dragged on, Darek and Pola dozed too.

"Do you think the hunting party will try anything today?" Pola asked when they woke.

Darek stretched and looked at the sky. "I don't know," he said. "If they do, it should be soon. The dragons will be waking from their afternoon naps shortly."

"Why is that a good time?" Pola asked.

"The adults wake first," Darek explained. "They go off to forage for dinner while their little ones are still asleep."

"But how will our men capture a dragonling without causing a ruckus?" Pola asked.

Darek shook his head. That he didn't know. He feared to think what might happen if things went wrong. Dragons were peaceful if left alone, but they were fierce and dangerous when threatened.

Their fiery breath and razor-sharp claws had sent many a Zorian to an early death. Darek prayed to Lord Eternal that his father had a plan.

True to Darek's words, the adult dragons soon began emerging from their caves and drifting down into the valley. Before long, the Great Blue appeared. She flew to the valley's far end and disappeared into the thick forest. Sadly Darek watched her go. She had no idea of the danger threatening her young ones.

Darek still clearly remembered his first meeting with her. She had been ready to defend her babies with her very life. She was a mother, after all, as loving as any human mother. He didn't like to think of the pain and loss she must suffer now because of Rowena. New anger at the girl flared inside him as he watched the mouth of the cave.

The little ones were in there, probably still sleeping, just as Zantor still snored beneath his rock. If the hunting party planned to act today, now would be the time.

"Look!" Pola whispered. He pointed to the ridge above the cave.

For a moment Darek couldn't believe what he saw there. Another Great Blue had appeared! It was a male, small for a Blue, but definitely full-grown. The shape of the head and the color of the scales were unmistakable. As Darek and Pola watched, the new dragon started to move down the mountain face. But something was wrong. It didn't have an adult dragon's strong, high-stepping gait. Instead it moved in a sluggish, awkward fashion, almost as if it were dragging itself.

"Lord Eternal!" Darek whispered. "It's a decoy!"

He and Pola stared at each other in astonishment. "They must have made it from one of the dragon-skin hangings in Elder Hall," Pola said.

Darek smiled and shook his head in wonderment. What a wise man his father was!

"Do you think it could possibly work?" Pola asked.

Darek felt torn as he watched the awkward creature lurch into the mouth of the cave. He'd been against the whole quest from the start, and his heart wanted it to fail. But his head knew that lives were on the line, including his father's and Clep's. If this plan didn't work, there would surely be bloodshed and death before the day was over. He grabbed Pola's arm and squeezed tight. "Pray," he whispered.

✳ ✳ ✳

Not one, but all three little dragons followed the strange new Blue out of their cave and up over the ridge. Darek and Pola moved around the mountain, closer to the hunting party's encampment, to get a better look. Zantor had awakened, and Darek was having trouble controlling him.

"Easy, fella, easy," Darek whispered. "I know you want to go to them, but you can't just now."

"*Rrronk,*" the dragonling replied.

The odd procession was coming closer and closer, making its way down the back side of the mountain. Strange emotions tumbled through Darek's mind as Zantor thrummed and tugged on his halter.

"Easy," Darek repeated, but he now felt drawn to the procession too. The need to be with the other dragons was becoming an ache inside him.

He found himself itching to let Zantor go.

"Here," he said, handing the halter to Pola. "You'd better hold him. I'm not sure I can trust myself."

Pola looked at him strangely. "Trust yourself to do what?"

"I feel like I'm inside Zantor's head again," Darek said.

Pola arched an eyebrow. "What are you talking about?"

Darek shook his head. "I'll explain later," he said. "Just hold him—tight."

Pola took the tether and wrapped it tightly around his wrist. Zantor's head sagged, and Darek felt the dragonling's disappointment as keenly as if it were his own. He turned away and tried to concentrate on the procession.

"Do you think they're going to take all three?" Pola asked.

"I'm afraid they'll have to now," Darek said. "If they try to separate them, there'll be a ruckus for sure. And that would bring the mother in no time."

"Won't she follow anyway?" Pola asked.

"Not for a while," Darek said. "The dragonlings are old enough to forage for themselves. She probably won't miss them until nightfall when they don't return to the cave." A picture of the distressed mother dragon flashed into Darek's mind. She would be so worried about her young ones. If only there were some way to stop this cruel quest.

"But nightfall is only four or five hours away," Pola said.

Darek shrugged. "That's all the head start the hunting party can hope for," he said. "That, and the chance that it will take her a while to pick up the trail. It's all rock up on the mountain, so there won't be footprints, and dragons don't have much sense of smell."

"Maybe she *won't* pick up the trail," Pola said hopefully. "Maybe she'll think they're lost in the valley somewhere."

"Maybe," Darek said, but he was doubtful.

Suddenly Zantor gave a quick twist, yanking the halter free. With a sharp cry of glee, he took to the air and zoomed straight toward the dragon procession.

"Hooray!" Darek shouted, leaping joyfully into the air. Then he crouched down and clapped his hand over his mouth.

Pola stared at him. "Have you taken leave of your senses?" he asked. "What are you yelling about? The hunting party heard you for sure!"

"I know, I know," Darek said. "I'm sorry. That wasn't me shouting. It was . . . Zantor, sort of."

Pola narrowed his eyes. "Did you get sunstroke up there today?" he asked.

Darek shook his head. "No. At least, I don't think so. Something else is going on. Something is happening in my mind. I don't understand either, but we don't have time to worry about it right now."

Pola sighed and stared at the fleeing dragon. "That's for sure," he said. "As soon as your father sees Zantor, he'll know for sure that we're here. What are we going to do?"

Darek thought about facing his father and the others and swallowed nervously. "You can go home," he said to Pola. "They won't know you

were with me. This was all my idea, anyway. I'll . . . take the blame."

Pola stared at him a long time, then walked over to his yuke and climbed into the saddle.

"See you back home," Darek said quietly.

"No you won't," Pola said. He leaned forward and handed the reins of the other yuke to Darek. Then he smiled. "An adventure's an adventure, all the way to the end," he said. "I'm with you, my friend."

Darek smiled and hoisted himself up into the saddle. He reached out to Pola, and they clasped arms in a Brotherhood shake.

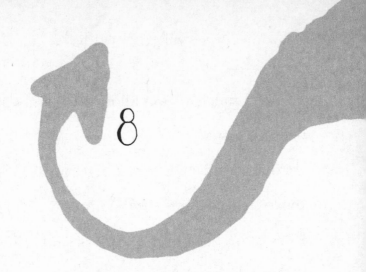

8

DAREK'S FATHER'S EYES WERE STERN.

"I don't care what your reason is!" he boomed. "You disobeyed an order, and you will pay the price when we return home."

"Yes, sir." Darek bowed humbly. "I'm sorry, sir."

"Aargh!" Darek's father stomped off. "Get out of my way. I've more important things to worry about."

Darek went back and stood beside Pola. They were silent for a while, watching the dragon procession. Darek felt awful, standing there, doing nothing, as the dragonlings walked into a trap. Then an idea began to take shape in his mind. If he could get close to the dragonlings, he might be able to free them. They would fly straight back to their mother. Maybe then the men would give up this foolish quest rather than risk a direct confrontation. It was a long shot. But if Darek didn't do something soon, it would be too late. He approached his father once more.

"Father," he said hesitantly. "I . . . think maybe I can help."

"Out of my sight, I told you!" his father bellowed.

Darek took a step back, but then Clep came up and put a hand on Darek's shoulder. "Wait a moment," Clep said. Then he turned to Yanek.

"A word with you, Father?" Clep asked.

Yanek stared at his two sons a long moment. Then he and Clep stepped to one side and put their heads together. Their voices rose and fell. Darek strained to catch snatches of their conversation.

"Way with dragons . . . ," he heard Clep say.

"Disobedient whelp . . . ," his father replied.

"Understands them . . . ," Clep said.

"Taught a lesson . . . ," his father grumbled.

As Darek watched his father and brother argue, his own feelings warred within him. Clep was standing up for him, taking his side. How could he let his brother down and free the dragons now? And what would the elders do to his father if Darek made trouble again?

"Out of time . . . ," he heard Clep say at last. Both Clep and Yanek turned then and looked toward the mountain. The party of dragons, now including Zantor, would soon have to be dealt with.

Yanek swore under his breath and looked over at Darek. "Do you think you can get close to those beasts without spooking them?" he asked.

"Yes, Father."

"Can you get tethers on them?"

Of this Darek wasn't so sure, but one thing he did know. "If anyone can, Father," he said, "I can."

"Well enough, then," Yanek said. "I'll settle my score with you later. Take the tethers and go."

"Yes, sir." Darek looked over at Pola, and Pola smiled back. He raised his arm and clenched his hand into a fist, palm forward. It was a Brotherhood fist. *Lord Eternal go with you,* it meant. Pola understood. He knew Darek had a difficult choice to make, and he was offering his support, no matter what Darek decided. Darek nodded his thanks to his friend. Then he started for the dragons. But what should he do? Free them or capture them?

"Son."

Darek stopped and turned. His father and Clep stood side by side. Both raised their fists as well. They trusted him, Darek realized. He felt a warm pride inside. Then, one by one, the other hunters in the party raised their Brotherhood fists too. Darek swallowed hard. He couldn't let them down. Not now. Besides, what if he freed the dragons and the men did decide to go after them again? The capture might not go so smoothly next time.

He wasn't being a traitor to Zantor and the dragons, Darek told himself as he started up the mountain. He was just doing his best to see that no one, dragon or Zorian, got hurt.

9

DAREK DIDN'T KNOW WHY THE LITTLE dragons seemed so glad to see him. Did they remember him from his earlier visit to their cave, or did they take their cue from Zantor, who greeted him with nuzzles and thrums? Either way, they welcomed him eagerly into their rollicking reunion with Zantor.

When Darek offered them sugar cubes, they gobbled them up and followed after him, begging for more. They were suspicious of the tethers at first, but Darek had a plan. He slipped a tether on and off Zantor, giving him a sugar cube reward each time. Before long, the other three dragons were wearing tethers and munching on sugar cubes too.

Soon all four dragons slept in a contented

little heap in the back of a wagon pulled by Darek and Pola on their yukes. Night had fallen, and they guided the yukes carefully along a path lit only by Zoriak's twin moons. Behind them, in two columns, rode the rest of the hunting party.

Darek was glad things were going so well, but he still couldn't help worrying. It was all too easy. Much too easy. He kept watching over his shoulder for the Great Blue.

"Maybe she doesn't care," Pola said hopefully. "Maybe the dragonlings are old enough to be on their own now. Maybe she's ready to let them go."

"Maybe," Darek said. This didn't seem likely, but he *was* surprised that they had made it all the way back to the Black Mountains without any sign of the angry mother. Maybe Pola was right. Maybe he was worrying for nothing. He settled back in the saddle and allowed himself a small sigh of relief.

And then he heard it.

The shriek, though far off, sent chills up his spine. "She's coming," he whispered.

The hunting party had heard it too.

"Circle up!" Darek heard his father shout.

The two columns behind Darek and Pola split and arched out around them. Soon the boys and the dragonlings were enclosed in a great circle.

"Now what?" Pola asked.

"Battle," Darek said bitterly. "Didn't you know it would come to this?"

The Great Blue shrieked again, closer this time. With cries of alarm the dragonlings awoke. Darek could feel Zantor's fear. He hastily tossed some sugar cubes back into the wagon, trying to keep them all calm.

"GRRRAWWWK! GRRRAWWWK!"

The ground around them shook as the Great Blue thundered out of the sky, swooping down almost on top of her young ones.

"Rrronk! Rrronk!" the dragonlings cried, straining at their tethers.

Darek's and Pola's yukes danced and bucked.

"Control your mounts!" Darek's father shouted. "Prepare for battle. Shields up, bows ready!"

"GRRRAWWWK!" The Great Blue swooped again, this time letting loose a blast of flame. The little ones shrieked, and Darek's yuke reared up on its hind legs. Pola's yuke spooked and reared too. Then, at the same time, both yukes bolted. The wagon lurched after them, bouncing over the rough ground.

"Eeeiiieee! Eeeiiieee!" the little dragonlings

screamed. Their cries seemed to whip the yukes into a frenzy. Darek and Pola fought for control of the reins, but there was no holding the frightened animals back. Their hooves thundered, tearing up the ground and bathing them all in a cloud of dust.

"Get out of the way!" Darek shouted as the wagon bore down on the battle circle. Men and yukes scattered as the wagon broke through. Behind them Darek and Pola could hear the great dragon scream as she charged once more. Sounds of a battle raged as the wagon continued to barrel out of control. It was headed straight for the Black Mountains of Krad! Fear roared in Darek's ears. His own terror, and Zantor's, too, blocked out all thought.

The wagon jounced over the foothills as the

runaway yukes started up the mountain pass. Clouds of black smoke loomed ahead. The acrid smell stung Darek's nose. There was no escape. They were headed straight into the Mountains of No Return!

"Jump!" Darek shrieked to Pola as the first ghostly wisps of smoke began to drift past them. "Jump!"

At the last moment Darek threw his reins aside and jumped. He landed with a thud and rolled over and over, coming to rest at last against a rock. He looked up just in time to see the runaway wagon and the four little dragons disappearing into the black, smoky haze.

And then he saw something else. A figure still sat astride one of the yukes!

"Pola!" Darek shrieked. *"Pola, jump!"*

But Pola didn't jump. Instead he raised his arm high, his hand clenched in a Brotherhood fist.

"An adventure's an adventure!" he shouted.

And then they were gone. . . . Pola, Zantor, all of them. Vanished.

Darek got to his feet and ran a short way into the mist. "Pola! Zantor!" he cried. But there was no answer. No sound. Darek's eyes watered, and his nose stung. He turned and staggered out of the mist again. Tears streamed down his cheeks. He turned once more and stared in stunned disbelief at the spot where the wagon had disappeared. Minutes passed. Maybe even hours. Darek didn't know. He felt empty inside, drained, as if nothing was left of his heart but an aching hole.

Then, just as dawn broke, there was a horrible, agonized cry, and the battle sounds in the distance ceased. Darek turned slowly, and the ache inside him deepened. There, on the ground, surrounded by the hunters, lay the Great Blue. The soft rays of the morning sun peeked over the mountains and glinted off her bent and lifeless wings.

10

DAREK RUBBED HIS HAND ACROSS THE top of Pola's Memory Stone. In time, maybe, he would be able to come here to the Memory Place and think warm thoughts, the way he did when he and Clep visited Yoran's Memory Stone. But now all he felt was pain.

If only Zantor were still here to comfort him, to make him smile with his silly dragon antics. But Zantor was gone too. Gone forever, along with

Pola and the other three dragonlings. The Zorians would never know another Great Blue. Darek sighed deeply. Sadness seemed to fill every corner of his mind and body, leaving no room for anything else. He slowly rose to his feet and started toward home.

"Darek?"

The voice startled him and caught him unaware. He turned, and when he saw who had spoken, his sorrow turned to something darker. Darek had never hated before, but he hated now.

"I . . . I've been waiting for a chance to speak with you," Rowena said.

Darek stared straight ahead, not trusting himself to speak.

"I . . . I want to tell you that I'm sorry," she went on. "That I . . ."

"Sorry!" Darek whirled now and faced her. "You're *sorry?*" He spat the words like fire. "You're *sorry* that my two best friends in the world are dead?"

"They're not . . . dead," Rowena said, her eyes glassy with tears. "They're just . . . gone."

Darek glared at her. "How do you know they're not dead?" he asked. "Besides, what difference does it make? I'll never see Pola or Zantor again. Pola's parents will never see their son again." He turned and gazed off into the sky, off toward the Yellow Mountains of Orr. "And no Zorian from this day forward will ever again see the beauty of a Great Blue," he added softly.

"I know. . . ." Rowena's voice was almost a sob. "I'm sorry," she repeated. "What more can I say?"

Darek spun around angrily. "You're *sorry*, all right," he said in a low snarl. "You're just about the sorriest excuse for a Zorian I've ever laid eyes on." Then he turned and strode away.

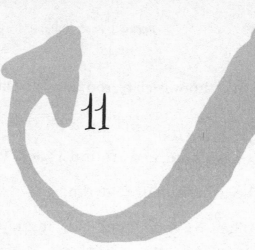

11

DAREK TOSSED AND TURNED. ANOTHER
sleepless night. He sat up and stared off toward the
Black Mountains of Krad. Where were Pola and
Zantor? he wondered. How were they? Were they
dead or alive? Outside he heard the clatter of yuke
hooves and wondered who might be passing by at
this late hour. Then something flew in through the
open window and landed at the foot of his bed.

The yuke hooves clattered away as Darek reached down.

It was a note, tied around a rock. Darek yanked off the twine and unfolded it.

"They are gone, not dead," it said. "I know this. Don't ask me to explain how. But I do know. And where there is life, there is hope. I ride tonight for the Black Mountains, there to undo the wrong I've done."

Darek stared at the note for a long moment until its meaning finally sank in. Rowena was heading out on a quest to find Pola and the dragons.

"Zatz!" he cried. "That fool girl!"

He pulled on his boots and his jerkin, then dashed through the sleeping house and out to the barn. He saddled the fastest yuke in the herd and flung himself onto its back. Out into the night he rode, faster and harder than he'd ever ridden before. Wind filled his mouth and tore at his hair. The yuke's hooves flew over the moon-silvered ground, tearing up league after league. At last the Black Mountains loomed closer. Overhead the sky grew pale with the approach of dawn.

As he bore down on the mountains, Darek spied a figure up ahead. Her loosened hair streamed wildly out behind her. Rowena and her yuke moved as one, smoothly gliding over the landscape. Darek frowned. She sat a good yuke; he had to grant her that. He spurred his yuke harder in an effort to close the gap between them, but his yuke was winded. Overtaking the girl before she reached the pass would not be easy.

"Rowena!" he screamed. *"Rowena, stop!"* But his words only blew back into his own mouth.

Rowena did not stop or even slow when she reached the foothills. On she raced toward the mist-shrouded peaks.

The acrid, dead smell of the mountains made Darek's breath catch in his throat. He was running out of time. He reached back and pulled his yuke's tether rope from behind his saddle. He fiddled with the noose until it was the right size. Then he stood in the stirrups, swung the rope overhead a few times, and let it fly.

"Uumph!" Rowena landed on the ground with a thud. Her frightened yuke clattered off into the foothills.

"You dragon-wit!" she screamed as Darek approached. "What do you think you're doing?"

"Saving your foolish hide," Darek yelled. "Have you taken leave of your senses?"

"What is it to you?" Rowena cried. She got to her feet and slapped angrily at her dust-caked clothes.

"Are you hurt?" Darek asked.

"No, I am not hurt—no thanks to you!" Rowena turned and stomped away.

"Where are you going?" Darek shouted.

"I told you where I'm going."

"Oh, no you're not!"

"Oh, yes I am!"

Darek slid down off his yuke, ran up behind Rowena, and grabbed her arm. "No you're not," he repeated. "You've caused enough trouble already. . . ."

"Me!" Rowena whirled around. "And I suppose you're Sir Innocent, huh? At least *I* have the guts to admit when *I'm* wrong."

Darek stared at her. "What are you talking about?" he asked. "What did I do?"

"What *didn't* you do is more the question!" Rowena said. She pulled free and started up the mountain again. Darek ran after her once more.

"I'm listening, okay?" he said. "How is any of this my fault?"

Rowena glared at him. "If you must know the truth," she said, "I never even wanted a dragon of my own. All I wanted was a chance to spend a little time with Zantor, to play with him now and then. But you were too selfish to allow that. You were too jealous, because you knew he liked me as much as you!"

Darek's mouth dropped open. He tried to think of some sharp words to fling back at her, but he could not.

Rowena stopped walking and faced him squarely. "Did you really think you could keep Zantor all to yourself?" she asked. "You proved to us all how wonderful he was, then you shut us out. Did you really think that was fair?"

Darek tore his eyes from Rowena's and looked down at the ground. Her words stung like the blade of a finely honed knife. And their aim was just as deadly true. He *had* been selfish and jealous. If he'd been willing to share . . .

Darek's shoulders sagged, and his arms fell limply at his sides as the truth became painfully clear. If he had been a little more considerate, Zantor and Pola might still be there.

"You're right," he said softly. "It *is* my fault. Pola . . . Zantor . . . everything."

There was a long silence, and then Rowena put

a hand on his shoulder. "No," she said. "I can't let you take all the blame. I was jealous of you too. And I behaved like a spoiled child. We are both to blame."

Darek looked up, surprised. This was a new side of Rowena, a side he had to respect. "It took guts for you to admit that," he said.

Rowena smiled and added quietly, "You've got guts too."

"Maybe we've been wrong about each other, huh?" Darek said.

Rowena nodded. "Maybe."

It wasn't customary to offer a Brotherhood shake to a girl, but somehow it felt like the right thing to do. Darek reached out his arm. "What do you say we start over?" he asked. "Friends?"

"Friends," Rowena said. She clasped his arm

and gave it a hearty shake. They smiled into each other's eyes for a moment. Then Rowena looked away. "Well," she said, "I'd better get going."

"Going where?" Darek asked.

"There." Rowena pointed into the mist.

"What?" Darek couldn't believe his ears. "You're not still going!"

"I am."

"But . . . it's forbidden," Darek said.

Rowena smiled again. "That's never stopped *you* from doing what you want," she said.

Darek shook his head. Why did everybody keep throwing that back at him?

"The things I did were important . . . ," he started to say.

Rowena raised her eyebrows. "And rescuing Pola and Zantor isn't?"

Darek sighed. "Rowena," he said, "we don't even know if they're alive."

"They *are* alive," Rowena insisted. "I know."

Darek stared at her for a long moment. "Why do you keep saying that?" he asked. *"How* do you know?"

A blush of crimson stained Rowena's cheeks.

"Because," she said, lowering her eyes, "Zantor . . . told me."

"Wh-what?" Darek stammered. A chill crept up his back.

"He . . . speaks to me," Rowena went on, "in my mind."

The chill spread out to Darek's fingers and toes. He sat down on the ground with a thud.

"I know you don't believe me—" Rowena began.

"No," Darek interrupted. He looked up at her and nodded slowly. "I do."

"You do?"

"Yes." Darek licked his lips. "He speaks to me, too."

Rowena's eyes widened. "He does? Really?"

"Yes." Darek nodded again.

"Then you've heard it!" Rowena exclaimed.

"Heard it? Heard what?"

Rowena dropped to her knees beside Darek and stared into his eyes. "Listen!"

For the first time in days, Darek pushed the heavy weight of sadness aside and opened his heart and mind. He listened, quietly, to the thoughts in his head. And then, quite clearly, he heard it! It came faintly at first, then stronger.

"*Rrronk! Rrronk! RRRONK!*"

"It *is* him," Darek whispered.

Rowena nodded.

Images started crowding into Darek's head. Dragons. Lots of dragons. The other Blues were there, and Pola, too!

"They're all together!" he shouted. "They're alive!"

Rowena smiled and nodded again.

"But where?" Darek asked. "Where?"

"Up there, somewhere," Rowena said, pointing into the mist again. Then she turned back to Darek. "And I intend to find them. Are you with me?"

Darek sat a moment longer, letting it all sink in. Then he got to his feet and stared once more at the bleak mist-shrouded crags. Pola's last words rang in his memory: *An adventure's an adventure!*

"All the way to the end," Darek added softly. Then he turned to Rowena and smiled.

"Yes," he said. "I'm with you, my friend."

Dragons of Krad

To my brother Jim, with love

Prologue

WHEN DAREK RESCUED A BABY
dragon and brought it home to his village, he
dreamed of a bright new tomorrow where dragons and Zorians could live together as friends. And
indeed, after a difficult beginning, Darek and his
dragon friend, Zantor, did win the hearts of the villagers.

But Darek didn't count on the jealousy of the
other Zorian children. Rowena, daughter of the

Chief Elder, grew to love Zantor deeply. When Darek refused to allow her to play with Zantor, Rowena begged her father for a dragonling of her own. This wish sparked a dragonquest that ended in tragedy. Darek's best friend, Pola, along with Zantor and three other Great Blue dragonlings were lost when a runaway wagon carried them into the dreaded Black Mountains of Krad.

Filled with grief and rage, Darek confronted Rowena and blamed her for the tragedy. Determined to right the wrongs she had done, Rowena slipped away in the night on a quest to find Pola and the dragons. When Darek discovered that she was headed for the Black Mountains, he followed, bent on stopping her. But Rowena would not be stopped. Instead she helped Darek see that they shared the blame for the tragedy.

Now the two have discovered that they share something else—the ability to communicate with Zantor. While they are arguing, a mind message comes from the dragonling—a cry for help. Putting aside past differences, Darek and Rowena set off on a new quest. Together they venture into the Black Mountains, risking everything to find their friends.

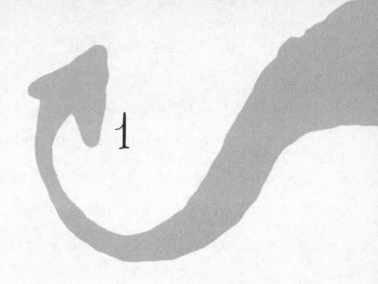

1

DARK MISTS SWIRLED AROUND
Darek as he made his way up a narrow pass into
the Black Mountains of Krad. Rowena, daughter
of the Zorian Chief Elder, followed a few steps
behind. The mist felt damp against Darek's skin,
and the stench of it made him gag. It smelled like
rotted burning flesh, and that worried him.

Darek heard a cough and looked back over his
shoulder.

"Are you all right?" he asked.

"Yes." Rowena nodded. "I'm getting tired, though. My eyes sting, and it's hard to breathe."

"Shall we rest awhile?" Darek asked.

"No. Pola and Zantor may be in danger. We've got to keep going."

Darek nodded. He could hear the mind cries too. His dragon friend, Zantor, was sending messages of distress. Zantor and Darek's best friend, Pola, had disappeared into the Black Mountains more than a week ago. They and three other Great Blue dragonlings had been carried off by a runaway wagon. Darek and Rowena felt responsible. They had been jealous of each other and had quarreled over Zantor. As a result, the Chief Elder had ordered his men to capture another dragonling for Rowena. While on the dragonquest, Pola, Zantor, and the others had been lost.

Rowena coughed again and gasped for air.

"Pull your collar up over your mouth and nose," Darek said. "The cloth will filter some of the smoke."

Strange shapes loomed out of the mist. Black rocks, like cinders, dotted their path. All Darek's senses were alert, keen to the dangers that might assail them at any moment.

"I wonder what our families will think when they wake this morning and find us gone," he said quietly.

Rowena didn't answer right away.

"We must not think of that," she said at last. "We must dream of the day when we return with Pola and the dragons."

Darek wished he could be sure that day would come, but he could not. No one had ever returned from the Black Mountains of Krad. For centuries now, it had been forbidden even to venture into them. What would his parents and his older brother, Clep, think when they realized where he had gone? He could see his mother's tearstained face now.

We will find a way back, Mother, he promised silently.

"Did you hear that?" Rowena suddenly cried out.

Darek stopped and listened. He thought he heard a soft scuffling sound, but when he peered into the mist, all he could make out were strange, twisted rock forms and the stumps of long-dead trees. "I don't see anything," he whispered.

"No," Rowena said. "I guess not." She put her hand to her forehead and moaned softly.

"Ooohh," she said. "My head and stomach ache."

Darek's head hurt too. Could the very mists be poisonous? he wondered.

"We're almost to the peak," he told Rowena. "It will be easier going down the other side. We won't have to breathe as hard."

The ground beneath them leveled off at long last, and they started to descend. Darek began to move with greater caution. If something or someone was waiting below, he wanted to see it before it saw him. His headache was worse, making it harder and harder to think. Behind him, he heard Rowena moan once more.

"Are you sure you're all right?" he asked again.

"Yes," she said, but her voice trembled.

Darek's worry deepened. He had to get her

out of the mountains quickly. "Can you walk any faster?" he asked.

"I—I don't know. I can't even think straight."

Darek turned. Rowena's skin was very pale, and her lips looked blue.

"Lean on me," he said.

Rowena gladly took his arm, and they struggled on together. Darek shook his head. It felt as if the mist were seeping into his mind. Minutes seemed to drag by. Rowena was leaning on him more and more heavily.

"Is it much farther?" she asked weakly.

"No, not much. See, the mist is thinning."

"Good, because I don't feel . . . ooohh." Rowena suddenly pushed Darek aside, clapped a hand over her mouth, and started to run.

Darek stumbled on a cinder and fell. "Rowena,

wait!" he cried. He scrambled to his feet again, but before he could catch her, Rowena disappeared into the mist.

"Rowena!" he called, but there was no reply, only a distant retching sound.

Then, suddenly, there was a scream.

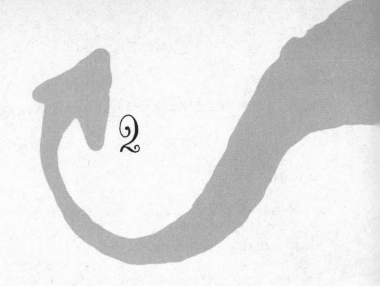

2

DAREK FOUGHT THE URGE TO RUN
in the direction of the scream. Instead he moved
cautiously, stealing from rock to rock. If someone,
or something, had caught Rowena, he had to be
careful. It would do neither of them any good if he
got captured too. The mist had cleared a little, and
he could begin to see something of Krad. It was
a bleak, colorless place, with runty, withered trees
and stubby brown grasses.

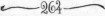

A movement below caught his eye, and he strained to see.

Rowena!

His friend had reached the plateau at the foot of the mountains. There she was surrounded by a number of bent little creatures that hopped about her excitedly. They were chanting over and over in high, flutelike voices.

"A pretty!" they cried. "A pretty! A pretty!"

Rowena hugged her arms around her like a frightened child. "Go away! Go away!" she cried. "Leave me alone!"

Before long, there was another sound— hooves pounding in the distance. Darek looked toward the horizon and saw a group of riders thunder up over the lip of the plateau. The riders were broad and tall, with dark hooded

capes. They were mounted on long-haired white yukes, much like the ones back in Zoriak, only larger. As the riders bore down on Rowena, the little bent creatures around her shrieked and scurried away.

One of the smaller ones was too slow. A whip lashed out from the hand of one of the riders and stung it with a fierce blow on the leg. The creature yelped and scrabbled into the brush. The rider threw his head back and laughed. His hood fell away, and Darek saw a face that was human-like but covered in fur.

A Kraden!

A chill crept up Darek's back. Back in Zoriak, he had heard stories of Kradens—big, hairy men who had supposedly driven the Zorians out of Krad long ago. Darek had always thought they were just old tales. But these Kradens were real—living and breathing! Poor Rowena looked terrified.

"Who are you?" one of the Kradens demanded.

"Rowena," she answered in a trembling voice.

"Why have you come here?" the man asked.

Rowena seemed at a loss to answer.

Darek felt confused too. Why *had* they come there? Had the mist addled his mind? Why couldn't he remember?

Then he heard a sound deep inside his head. *Rrronk!* Yes! Zantor. Zantor and Pola. That was why they had come. He must keep focused on that.

Rowena must have heard the mind cry too. "My friends!" she said suddenly. "They're in trouble. I've come to help them."

"Have you, now?" The men looked at one

another and chuckled. "And how is a slip of a girl like you going to help anyone?"

Rowena drew herself up and tossed her head. "I'm stronger than I look," she announced.

At this, all the men burst out laughing.

"That's good news," one of them said, "because we've plenty of work for you to do."

Rowena crossed her arms. "Work?" she said. "I'll not work for you. I'm the daughter of the Chief Elder."

"Are you, now?" another Kraden asked. "Well, then, we'll have to find you a jewel-handled broom, won't we?"

With another loud laugh, the Kradens swooped forward, and one of them scooped Rowena up, pulling her into his saddle.

"Come, lads," he said. "Let's take *Her Highness*

to visit old Jazee." Then he and the others turned their yukes around and thundered away.

Darek stared after them. Who was old Jazee? he wondered. And what did the man mean when he said there was plenty of work to do? It did not bode well.

Darek decided to try to keep his own presence a secret until he could learn more. Slowly he crept down the mountainside until he reached the place where Rowena had been captured. He noticed a trail of dark droplets among the footprints and remembered the small creatures and the lash of the whip. Suddenly he heard a high, thin cry.

Gleeep. Gleeep.

Darek's head jerked around. The wounded creature was lying beside a nearby rock, nursing its leg. It caught sight of him and scrambled to

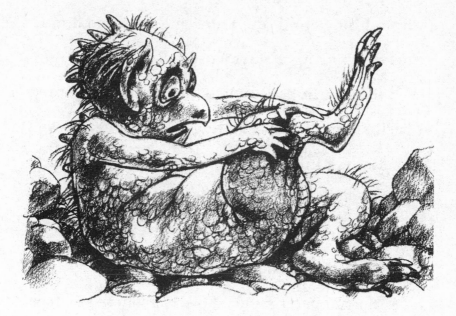

get away, but it was only able to move a few steps
before collapsing again.

"Gellp!" it cried.

Darek frowned. He had no time to help a
wounded . . . whatever. He started to walk away,
but his conscience would not let him. Quickly he
pulled his shirt out of his britches and tore a strip
from the hem. Then he unfastened the waterskin

from his belt and squirted a little into the dirt at his feet, mixing a muddy paste. Taking a handful of the paste, he approached the creature. It shrank back, staring at him with huge yellow-green eyes.

"I won't hurt you," Darek soothed. "I just want to help." He knelt beside the creature and gently straightened its leg.

"Gellp!" it cried again.

"Sorry," Darek said. "This should make you feel better." The creature was the size of a young child, with scaly gray skin. It looked almost like a cross between a dragon and a human. Darek couldn't help feeling kindly toward it. He packed the healing mud over the wound, then gently bandaged the leg.

"There," Darek said, getting to his feet again. "If you stay off it for a day or two, you should be fine."

The creature turned and pointed a knobby finger toward the road. "Your pretty?" it asked.

Darek looked down the road too. There was no sign of Rowena or the men now. "No," he answered. "She's not my pretty. But she's my friend. Do you know where they've taken her?"

"Zahr take pretty," the creature said.

"Zahr?" Darek said. "Who's Zahr?"

The creature gave a little cough. "Zahr, king," it said hoarsely.

Darek stared again at the empty road. "Where did Zahr take pretty?" he asked.

"Prison," the creature said.

Darek whirled around. "Prison! What do you mean, prison?"

The creature cringed. "Go now," it said, scrambling away.

"No, wait." Darek took a breath to calm himself. "Please tell me more about the prison," he pleaded.

The creature coughed again. "Go now," it repeated. And then, almost magically, it disappeared.

"Hey, wait!" Darek called after it. "One more question, please! Have you seen another Zorian, like me, or a small blue dragon?"

"Zahhhr," came the faint, choked reply.

3

DARTING FROM TREE TO SCRUBBY
tree, Darek slowly made his way across the plateau.
The mist was thinner now, and his head seemed
to be clearing. In the distance, he heard fearful
roaring sounds. Cautiously he approached the
lip where he had first seen the Kradens. He got
down on his belly, inched forward, and peered
out across the valley. A large rambling village
stretched in front of him. It had a grim look to it.

A gray, smoke-stained castle stood at its center. This was surrounded by smaller houses and hundreds of squat stone hovels. The mist, though thin, hung over everything. Suddenly Darek heard a roar just below him. He looked down, and his breath caught in his throat.

"Zatz!" he swore softly.

There at the base of the plateau was a huge cage, nearly half the size of the town. Great creatures milled about in it, roaring and belching flame at one another.

Red Fanged dragons!

Darek had never seen a Red Fanged dragon before. The last one in Zoriak had been killed long before he was born. He knew all about them from legends, though. They were not red, as their name might suggest, but pearly white. Quite beautiful,

actually, were it not for the vicious red fangs that gave their mouths the look of dripping blood. It was not just their looks that made them fearsome, though. They were also huge, second only in size to the Great Blues. And they were flesh lovers. Reds dined mostly on other dragons, but in Zoriak they had been known to raid the village from time to time.

Darek shuddered at the thought. He stared down at the cage again. How much meat must it take to satisfy the appetites of so many Red Fanged dragons? he wondered. Portions of charred dragon skeletons lay strewn about the pen, and a steady stream of smoke rose up from it. Red Fanged dragons always flamed their prey alive before eating it. So this was the source of the mist, Darek suddenly realized. Dragonsbreath!

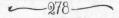

Why would the Kradens keep these beasts? he wondered.

"Well, well!" A loud voice startled Darek. "What have we here?"

Darek looked up and saw a dark hooded figure towering over him. He started to scramble to his knees, but something hard and sharp dug into his back and pressed him to the dirt.

"Not so fast, Zorian!" the voice commanded.

Darek slowly twisted to get a better look at the figure. A thick metal-encrusted boot was planted near his shoulder. Darek's gaze followed it up. A large furry-faced man stared down at him.

"State your name and mission," the man snarled.

Darek tried to keep his voice from trembling. "Darek," he said. "Darek of Zoriak. Some . . . some of my friends fled into these mountains a few days back. I . . . I'm only trying to find them."

The Kraden laughed. "Another one?" he asked. "What sorts of fools are the Zorians raising these days?"

Darek did not answer.

"Well," the Kraden said, "no matter. Fresh blood is always welcome here."

The Kraden lifted the lance from between Darek's shoulders and plunged it into the dust not a finger's breadth from his nose.

"On your feet!" he bellowed.

Darek scrambled to do as he was told. He stood straight and tall. Still, he only came up to the man's middle.

The Kraden glared down at him, pulling on his hairy chin. "How old are you?" he asked.

"A Decanum," Darek said.

The Kraden shook his head and swore. "Too young for the mines," he grumbled. "You any good with dragons?"

"Yes, sir," Darek said, swallowing hard again. "But . . . I don't plan to stay."

At this, the Kraden threw his head back and roared. He laughed until tears rolled down his furry cheeks. Then he slapped his leg and laughed some more.

"Don't plan to stay . . . ," he repeated breathlessly when at last he could speak again. "That's a good one, lad. A good one indeed."

Then his eyes narrowed, and his lips twisted into a sneer. "No one ever leaves Krad," he growled.

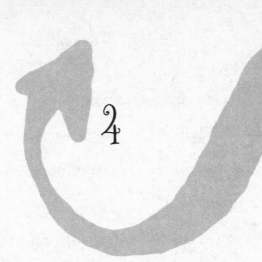

4

CASTLE KRAD WAS AS DARK AND forbidding up close as it had looked from afar. Darek stared at its twisted, smoke-stained battlements.

"Is that where Zahr lives?" he asked.

The Kraden's eyes narrowed.

"Where did you hear the name of Zahr?" he asked.

"A little creature told me," Darek said, "back

on the mountain. He said Zahr had taken my friends."

The Kraden's brows crashed together. "Blasted Zynots," he swore. "What else did they tell you?"

Darek shook his head. "Nothing," he said.

The Kraden eyed him suspiciously. "Well, no matter," he said. "That's all you'll remember soon enough—nothing." He pushed open the heavy door of a low stone house and motioned Darek inside.

It was steamy and dark inside and smelled of medicines and herbs. It took a few moments for Darek's eyes to adjust to the dimness. Then he was able to make out an old cronelike woman bent over the hearth.

"Another customer for you, Jazee," the man said.

The woman looked up in surprise. "Another?" she said. "That's three in a fortnight!"

Darek's ears perked up. Three! He and Rowena were two. The third must have been Pola!

"Aye." The man nodded. "This one thinks he's here on holiday. Told me he's not staying."

The crone cackled. "Jazee will cure him of that," she said. She picked up one of her vials and

poured a few drops of green liquid into a carved stone cup. "Drink up, boy," she said.

Darek pressed his lips tight and turned away.

"Do as Jazee says," the man growled. He grabbed Darek and pulled his mouth open. The crone poured the liquid down Darek's throat. It burned and made him gag. When he looked at the woman again, he felt light-headed and dizzy. He tried to look away, but her eyes held his fast.

"Tell me who you are," she commanded.

"Darek," Darek mumbled. The woman's face wavered and swam before his eyes.

"Darek who?" the crone asked.

Darek searched inside his head for an answer, but his mind was nothing but a vast, empty cave. "I . . . don't know."

The woman smiled. "You are Darek of Krad,"

she told him, "prisoner to the Kingdom of Zahr.
From your past life, you will remember only the
things that are of use to us here. Go now with
Org, and do as you are commanded."

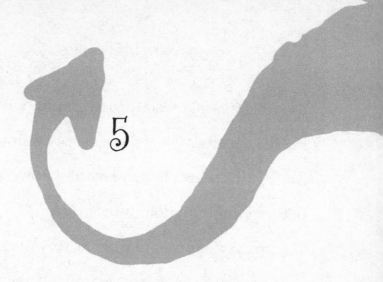

5

DAREK FOLLOWED ORG THROUGH
narrow, twisted, foul-smelling streets. Kraden
children hissed and spat at him. Women leaned
out of the doorways and called him names like
"dragon-wit" and "fang-breath." It was a relief to
reach the pastures at the far side of town at last.
Vast numbers of dragons grazed there, but not the
Red Fangs. They were kept in their cage on the
outskirts of the village. Darek recognized some of

the dragons—Green Horned, Yellow Crested, and Purple Spotted. Others were new to him.

"You'll know all there is to know of dragons before long," Org told him.

Darek was not unhappy at this prospect. The dragons were far more pleasant, it seemed, than the people of Krad. But why were the great creatures content to stay among such men?

"Why don't the dragons just fly away?" he asked Org.

"They can't," Org told him. "We bind their wings when they're young, until their flight muscles wither. You'll see soon enough. Come. Might as well get you started."

Darek followed Org into a long, low building. It was a combination stable and nursery for the dragons, as well as a dormitory for the prisoners who

tended them. A number of prisoners were hard at work mucking out the dragon stalls. They looked up when Darek and Org came in. Darek felt an immediate kinship with them. The prisoners were not large and furry like the Kradens. They looked much like Darek and seemed close to him in age too. The prisoners paused and stared as Darek and Org passed, but the crack of an overseer's whip quickly returned them to their duties.

"Got a new one for you, Daxon," Org said, pushing Darek toward another Kraden.

The man named Daxon seemed pleased. "Three in a fortnight," he said, raising his eyebrows. "To what do we owe this good fortune?"

Org shrugged. "Word must be spreading about the pleasures of life here in Krad."

Daxon roared with laughter over this joke.

Org grabbed Darek by the collar and shoved him in front of Daxon. "Bow," he said, pushing Darek to his knees. "Daxon is master of the stockyards, your master now too. You will call him 'master' when you speak to him, and you will obey his orders without question." Then he let Darek go and turned to face Daxon.

"His name is Darek," he said. "Jazee probed his thoughts. She says he should be a natural with dragons. Rebellious by nature, though, so don't spare the whip."

Daxon laughed. "When have you ever known me to spare the whip, my friend?" He looked down at Darek, pulling at the fur on his chin. "Rebellious, huh?" he said slowly. "Well, we'll just have to see to it that you're too tired to rebel, won't we?" Daxon looked over toward the other prisoners. "Pola!" he shouted. "Come here!"

One of the prisoners dropped his rake and hurried over. Darek couldn't help noticing how thin and tired the boy looked. His hands were all raw and blistered. The prisoner bowed to Daxon.

"Yes, Master?" he said.

"Take this new prisoner, and teach him everything you've learned. Start in the nursery. No supper for either of you until the pens are cleaned, the dragonlings fed, and the newborns wingbound."

Pola's face fell. "Yes, Master," he whispered, bowing again. Then to Darek he said, "Follow me."

Darek rose to follow, but suddenly Daxon's hand flew out and boxed his ear. "Bow!" he thundered.

Darek quickly dipped his head. "Yes, Master," he mumbled.

"That's better," Daxon said. "Never enter or leave my presence without bowing!"

Darek bowed once more, just to be safe, then turned and silently followed Pola.

6

A MILLION QUESTIONS RACED through Darek's mind as he followed Pola along the corridor to the nursery. He hoped he and this prisoner boy would have a chance to talk privately. Maybe Pola could help him understand what was happening to him.

"Here," Pola said. He took a rake down from a hook on the wall and handed it to Darek. Then he pushed a door open and motioned Darek through.

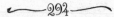

The air inside was warm and damp and filled with the chirpings and callings of young dragons. Darek couldn't help smiling at the colorful creatures tumbling and playing on the nursery floor. He noticed a little cluster of Blues huddled together, sleeping, on the far side of the room. His smile broadened. They were so beautiful, even as babies. But the bandages wound tightly around their silvery wings saddened Darek.

"How long do they have to wear those things?" he asked.

"Half an anum," Pola said tiredly. "Until their wing muscles shrink beyond repair."

"Why don't the Kradens want them to fly?" Darek asked.

"They're easier to manage this way," Pola said.

"Who *are* these Kradens?" Darek began. "And why—"

"Look," Pola interrupted. "We've got a lot of work ahead of us if we want to eat."

Just then, Darek heard a commotion. He looked and saw that one of the little Blues had awakened. It was struggling to make its way through the maze of other dragons toward Darek and Pola.

"*Thrummm!*" Darek could hear it singing as it got closer. "*Thrummm, thrummm, thrummm.*" Darek could have sworn its big green eyes were looking right at him.

Pola frowned. "That dratted Blue," he said. "Too darn friendly for its own good."

The Blue dragon kept making little hops in a sad attempt to fly. But that, of course, was impossible. At last, it hurled itself through the air and

smacked with a thud into Darek's chest. Both of them tumbled to the ground.

"Thrummm," the dragonling sang. *"Thrummm, thrummm, thrummm."* Then *thwip, thwip!* Out flicked its forked tongue, covering Darek with tickly kisses.

Darek twisted and rolled, laughing until his stomach hurt.

"Stop it! Hey!" he begged. "What's wrong with you, you silly thing?" He finally managed to push the beast off and get back to his feet. Still, the creature kept dancing around him, butting him and nuzzling his chest.

"He seems to want something in your jerkin pocket," Pola said.

"There isn't anything in my pocket," Darek said. He put his arms up to fend off another nuzzle.

"He sure seems to think there is," Pola said.

"Well, there isn't," Darek insisted. But he felt his pocket just to be sure.

There *was* something there. Darek reached in and pulled out several hard, white lumps.

"*Thrummm,*" sang the little dragon. It gobbled the lumps before Darek even got a good look at them.

"What were they?" Pola asked.

"I don't know," Darek said. "But *he* sure seemed to know. I wonder how?"

Pola shrugged. "Smell?"

Darek shook his head. "Dragons don't have much sense of smell."

The little dragon nuzzled Darek's pocket once more. "Sorry, pal," Darek said with a laugh. "I don't have any more." He rubbed the budding horns on the dragon's head.

"I wouldn't do that if I were you," Pola warned.

"Do what?" Darek asked.

"Get too friendly with him. It'll just make it harder in the end."

"In the end?" Darek repeated. "What do you mean?"

"When they feed him to the Red Fangs," Pola said.

Darek's breath caught in his throat. "What?" he whispered hoarsely.

"Didn't they tell you?" Pola asked quietly. "That's what they raise them for."

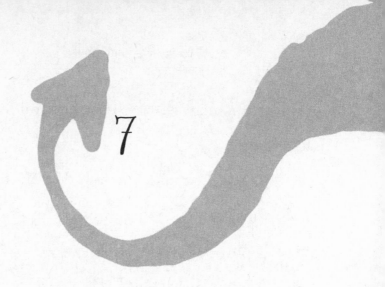

7

DAREK AND POLA SAT STARING AT
the empty table in front of them. Darek's stomach
was hollow and aching, and his blistered hands
stung. He and Pola hadn't finished their chores
fast enough to suit Daxon.

"I'm sorry I wasn't faster," Darek said. "This is
my fault."

Pola waved his words away. "I didn't finish in

time my first day, either," he said. "You'll be faster tomorrow."

And Darek would, he vowed, if it killed him. Pola would not have to go hungry another day on his account.

"Wench! More slog!" Daxon yelled from a nearby table.

A young girl, around Darek's age, made her way among the tables. She was balancing a heavy tray of foaming mugs.

"Faster!" Daxon bellowed.

"I'm moving as fast as I can!" the girl snapped. She reached Daxon and banged a mug down in front of him. Flecks of foam splashed up into his face. Daxon grabbed her wrist and glared into her eyes. She glared back. Darek held his breath, wondering what would happen next.

Daxon began to laugh. "Spirit!" he said, releasing her wrist. "I like a wench with spirit. Too bad you Zorians are so ugly."

The girl whirled and stomped away, and Daxon and his friends had another laugh.

Ugly? Darek thought. He saw nothing ugly about the girl. He thought her quite beautiful, in fact. And he also admired her spirit.

"What is a Zorian?" he asked Pola.

"We are Zorians," Pola said. "At least, that's what the Kradens call us."

"Are all . . ."

"No more questions." Pola put a finger to his lips and nodded toward Daxon, who was eyeing them suspiciously. "We are forbidden to speak of anything but our work."

* * *

Darek's tiny cell of a room was cold and dark. The walls were rough gray stone, and there was one small barred window. He shivered as he lay on his pallet, a threadbare blanket clutched tightly around him. His body was exhausted, but his mind was even more tired. All day, he'd been straining to remember who he was, where he had come from. But the effort had given him nothing more than a pounding headache.

Darek's thoughts were suddenly interrupted by a soft scraping noise. He sat up, clutching his blanket close.

One of the large stones in the wall near the floor was moving!

As Darek watched, the stone slid slowly into the room, and a face appeared. A body followed the face, and then another. Soon four boys and two girls

had crawled into the room. Pola was among them, and so was the girl who had spilled slog on Daxon.

The boy who had been first to appear pressed a finger to his lips in warning. "I am Arnod," he whispered. "We come in friendship."

"What if they find you here?" Darek asked.

Arnod snorted softly. "They'll feed us all to the Red Fangs," he said.

Darek's eyes widened, but Arnod waved his worries away. "They won't find us," he said. "Daxon and his men drink themselves into a stupor every night. They have no knowledge of our meetings."

One of the girls smiled. "They think us simple-minded fools," she added. "It suits our purpose to let them believe that."

Darek nodded his understanding, and the prisoners sat down cross-legged around his pallet. They told him their names, and the one named Arnod leaned forward.

"You and Rowena are new," Arnod said, nodding toward the girl who had spilled the slog. "And Pola arrived just last week. There must be a

connection. What can you tell us of who you are or how you came here?"

Darek sighed and slowly shook his head. "I remember nothing," he whispered.

"Nor I," Rowena added.

The faces of Arnod and the others fell.

"I'm sorry," Darek said.

"It's all right," Arnod said. "It was the same with Pola. It has always been the same. We were hoping you might be from Zoriak. But we aren't even sure such a place exists anymore. . . ."

"Zoriak?" Darek repeated. "What is Zoriak?"

Arnod sighed. "It is a long story. Our legends tell us that this valley was once called Zor. It was peaceful and beautiful then, and the mountains that ringed it were green and full of life. Only Zorians lived here."

"What happened?" Rowena asked.

"The Kradens came, from Beyond. They were bigger and stronger. They conquered most of us and made us prisoners, but a few Zorians escaped over the mountains. In the Long Ago, some of them would come back and try to help us escape too. They talked of a land they had named Zoriak, which means 'New Zor.' They said we could live there in freedom. But few of those escapes succeeded, and then the mountains died. Those who came after that, like you, knew nothing of Zoriak."

"How did the mountains die?" Darek asked.

"The dragonsbreath," Arnod explained. "For some reason, it clings to the mountain peaks, killing everything."

"If the Red Fangs are the cause of the dragons-breath," Rowena said, "why do the Kradens breed them?"

"They love blood sport," Arnod said. "They compete to raise the biggest and fiercest dragons. Then they pit them against one another and wager on the outcomes. The Kradens use them in battle too. King Zahr is at war with his brother, Rebbe, whose kingdom lies south of the Great Plain of Krad."

Darek's eyes widened. "King Zahr makes war against his own brother?"

"Yes." Arnod nodded. "They had a falling-out long ago over a prize Red Fang. They have been at war ever since."

"This Zoriak," said Rowena. "Has anyone ever gone in search of it?"

Arnod shook his head. "No. The Kradens have no interest in the place. Besides, they cannot tolerate the dragonsbreath in the mountains. It is poison to them in such density. Zorians tolerate it better, but it addles their brains."

It was all too much. Darek's head was growing heavy from the talk. He was even starting to hear strange sounds, like dragon whimpers, in his ears. He caught Rowena's eye and saw that she looked as tired and confused as he.

Pola reached out and clapped them each on the arm. "Enough talk for one night, friends," he said. "We will speak of these things again soon. For now, you must sleep."

8

THE NEXT DAY, DAREK WORKED AT
a furious pace. He refused to give in to his hunger
or fatigue, refused to pay heed to his swollen hands
or aching back. There would be dinner tonight,
he was sure. He was keeping right up with Pola,
despite the annoying little Blue. The dragonling
still kept butting him playfully and darting in to
give him quick licks on the cheek.

"Go away!" Darek shouted repeatedly. At times,

he gave the little beast a gentle shove or raised his arm to block its advances.

"*Rrronk,*" the little creature would whimper. Darek had no intention of encouraging it in any way, though. He had enough to worry about without getting attached to a Red Fang's dinner.

"Persistent, isn't he?" Pola remarked.

"Yes." Darek frowned. "Why doesn't he bother you? Why is it just me?"

Pola shrugged. "He used to hang around me, until you arrived. But he was nowhere near as affectionate with me. It's almost like he knows you."

Darek felt a little prickle run up his spine. He stared at the dragon. "Maybe he does," he said softly. "Remember that pocket business yesterday?"

Pola paused in his work and gave Darek a long, thoughtful look. He glanced over his shoulder to see if Daxon or any of his men were around, then moved closer.

"It's curious," he said. "The other prisoners say that the Blues arrived the same day I did. They've been wondering where they came from. There haven't been any Blues here in the stockyard for many years. The Kradens don't usually raise them, because they're so large and fierce. The Red Fangs have a hard time killing them."

A door opened, and Darek turned to see the girl Rowena come in with a broom. She walked by, sweeping.

"*Thrummm!*" Darek sang out. The next thing he knew, he was dancing around the girl, butting her with his head.

"What are you doing?" she cried. She whacked at him with her broom.

"*Thrummm, thrummm,*" Darek sang. And then the little Blue was there, dancing and thrumming, too. Round and round the girl they both frolicked.

"Enough!" a voice boomed.

A whip lashed out and stung Darek with a blow on the back. Stunned, he found himself hoisted up, dangling in front of Daxon's eyes.

"What kind of foolishness is this?" the Master roared.

Darek shook his head hard.

"Um—I—I don't know," he stammered. "Something came over me. I'm sorry."

"You'll be sorry, all right," the Master said, "when you don't eat again tonight! Pola, tether that dragon in the pen. Wench! Back to the kitchen with you!"

Darek looked at the sad little dragon as Pola led it away. For an instant, something seemed to pass between them. It was too fast-moving, too vague to capture, but it felt strangely like a memory.

Darek felt himself blushing when the prisoners filed into his room that night. How could he explain his silly actions to Rowena?

"I'm sorry about today," he began.

"No need." Rowena gave him a strange look. "I understand."

"You do?"

She nodded. "I think so."

"Understand what?" Arnod asked.

Darek turned to him. "I think one of the Blue

dragons might hold the key to who we are," he whispered. "I've got to find a way to spend more time with him."

"But how could a dragon help us?" Arnod asked.

"I don't know," Darek said. "I just think he can."

"Yes." Rowena nodded. "Darek's right. I feel it too."

Arnod shrugged. "It won't be easy to arrange," he said. "And there may not be much time left."

"Time left?" Darek wrinkled his brow. "What do you mean?"

"The Kradens will probably feed him and the other Blues to the Fangs early, before they grow too big and strong."

"Then we have to start soon," Darek said. "Tonight, if possible."

Arnod sat back and chewed his lip thoughtfully. "We have passages all through the complex," he said. "But Daxon posts a watch on the nursery and stables at night. It would be too dangerous to go there."

"There must be somewhere else," Darek said.

"There's the granary, next to the nursery," Arnod said. "We may be able to sneak the Blue in there. It's dangerous, though. Very dangerous. If the creature makes a noise—if you are discovered—the passages, everything will be uncovered. We could all be fed to the Fangs."

Darek shivered, but then he took a deep breath and squared his shoulders. "You speak longingly of freedom," he said, "but you will never taste it unless you make it happen. And you cannot make it happen without taking risks. I, for one, would rather die than spend the rest of my life a prisoner." He looked around the circle of faces. "What about you?"

Pola leaned forward quickly and clapped a hand on Darek's knee. "I'm with you, my friend," he said.

Rowena nodded. "I, too."

Arnod and the others exchanged glances, then one by one they nodded as well. Arnod stretched his right arm out toward the center of the circle, and the others did the same. Darek placed his hand on top.

"To freedom!" he said.

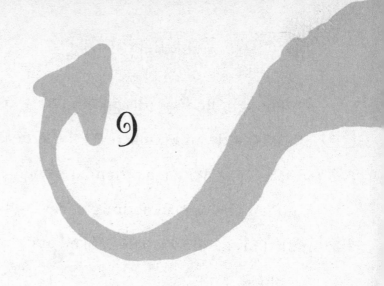

9

"THRUMMM, THRUMMM, THRUMMM,"
the dragonling sang softly.

Darek stroked its head and looked deep into its eyes. "Do you know me, young one?" he asked. "Have we been friends in another place?"

Warm feelings flowed into Darek's mind. Joy, love—emotions strangely out of place in this cold, dark granary. But that was all he seemed to get from the dragon—just feelings.

Though he was disappointed, Darek murmured gently and stroked the little beast's blue-scaled back. When his hand reached the wing bindings, he felt something sticky and wet. He pulled his hand away and looked at it.

Blood.

"Poor thing," he said. "Why didn't you let us know your bindings were cutting you? Here, let me help."

Carefully Darek unwound the bindings until the little creature fluttered its wings.

"*Thrummm, thrummm,*" it cried again. In its joy, it fluttered right up off the floor.

"Shush," Darek said, laughing softly. Then, as he watched the beast flutter around the room, an idea slowly came to him. If he brought the dragonling here every night and let him exercise his wings, he might still be able to fly. And if he could fly, then somehow, someday, Darek might be able to ride him back to where he came from. Back to . . . "Home," Darek whispered, looking deeply into the dragon's eyes again. "Do you want to take me *home*?"

Suddenly an image sprang into Darek's mind, an image that the dragonling seemed to be sending. It was a lovely farmhouse with rolling green pastures around it. There was a barn, too, filled with bales of sweet-smelling zorgrass. Outside, in the paddock, a boy was playing with a little Blue dragon. When the boy called out the beast's name, Darek's breath caught in his throat.

"Zantor," he whispered, still gazing into the dragon's eyes. "That's your name! And that's our home, yours and mine, isn't it?"

The little forked tongue flicked out and planted a kiss on his cheek. *"Thrummm,"* Zantor sang. *"Thrummm, thrummm, thrummm."*

Darek smiled and rubbed the dragon's nubby head. "Pola," he said. "Tell me about Pola."

Images filled Darek's head again, pictures of Darek, Zantor, and Pola. First they were romping through fields, then splashing in a brook. Lastly he saw the three of them lazing in front of a crackling fire.

"So, he's my best friend," Darek said. "No wonder I like him so well. And what of the girl Rowena?"

Warm, loving feelings flooded through Darek. He felt the touch of gentle hands and saw beautiful eyes staring into his. For a moment, he could hardly breathe. Then he laughed softly.

"She's very special to you, isn't she, Zantor?" he whispered.

"*Thrummm,*" Zantor sang.

The long days of toil passed quickly for Darek. He worked harder than any of the other prisoners, and muscles began to bulge on his back and arms. Whenever Daxon sent for him or assigned him a new task, he went out of his way to please. He wanted Daxon to be happy, to enjoy every drop of his evening slog, and to stay far away from the granary at night.

Darek and his friends had begun training Zantor and some of the other dragons to fly with riders on their backs. Little by little, Zantor was giving Darek and Rowena and Pola their memories back. They, in turn, shared what they learned with the others. There were still many gaps, but this much they knew: Zoriak *was* real, a beautiful green place, with sparkling clear air. Freedom waited there, and their families, too, if only they could figure out how to return. Exactly where Zoriak was, they still didn't know. But Darek was confident that Zantor would be able to remember and lead them there.

Darek, Pola, Rowena, Arnod, and the others had fashioned saddles and bridles out of bits of cloth and leather. Working together each night, they soon became friends. The dragons were growing bigger every day. Before long, they would all make their escape.

There was still the dragonsbreath to contend with, of course. But Darek, Pola, and Rowena knew they had come through it once without losing their wits, so there had to be a chance of doing it again. It was only a chance, of course, but it was a chance they were willing to take.

10

DAREK HAD BEEN ASSIGNED TO THE
stalls instead of the nursery all morning. At lunch-
time, he looked up to see Pola running toward
him. He was pale and out of breath.

"What is it?" Darek asked. "What's wrong?"

Pola looked around nervously. "The Blues!"
he whispered. "They took one of them early this
morning!"

"What?" Darek felt the blood draining from his face. "Which one?"

"Leezin, the one Arnod was training. She's . . . she's dead by now, fed to the Red Fangs."

Tears sprang to Darek's eyes. Gentle Leezin— dead?

"They could take the others as soon as tomorrow!" Pola warned.

Darek stared down at the floor, and his feet blurred through his tears. Zantor—fed to the Red Fangs tomorrow! He could not bear to think of it. Then he realized something else. Everything they had worked for, everything they had planned, would all be gone without the dragons. He sucked in a deep breath and looked up again.

"We must leave tonight," he said.

Pola's eyes widened. "Tonight! But the dragons aren't strong enough," he said. "We'll never make it."

"Then we'll die trying," Darek said.

It was decided that only Darek, Pola, and Rowena would go. Their Blues were bigger and stronger than the other dragons and stood a chance of success. Trying to fly the smaller dragons while they were still so young would have been much too dangerous for riders and dragons alike.

Well after dark, Darek, Pola, and Rowena stood in a circle in the granary with the others. They reached their hands into the center.

"We will be back, my friends," Darek said.

"We will be waiting," Arnod replied.

"Train as many dragons as you can," Darek said. "They will be useful when the time comes."

Arnod and the others nodded.

Darek felt tears start behind his eyes. He and his friends were being brave, but in their hearts they knew they might never see one another again. It would be a miracle if the escape succeeded, and whatever the result, it would surely bring the wrath of Zahr down on those who remained behind. But it did no good to dwell on such things. They had no choice.

"The alarms will sound as soon as the doors open," Arnod warned. "Your only hope will be to get a strong head start before they get the Fangs into the air."

"We will," Darek assured him. He mounted Zantor, and Pola and Rowena mounted the two remaining Blues.

"Now!" he commanded Arnod.

Arnod and the others pulled back the granary doors. Immediately the piercing shriek of a siren split the air. Darek shouted the flight command, and the three dragons pushed off with their powerful legs, pumping their small wings mightily. The ground began to fall away beneath them.

"We're going to make it!" Pola shouted.

"Yes!" Rowena cried out. "We're going home!"

Darek wasn't quite as certain. He could feel Zantor's heart pounding against his knees. He and the others were heavy burdens for dragons so young. Below them, Krad was springing to life. Men scurried everywhere. Arrows were shot into the air but fell far short of their marks. Before long, though, Darek heard the horrible screams of Red Fangs. He looked back and saw several beasts and riders in pursuit.

"Home, Zantor, home!" he cried. "Faster!"

Zantor pumped his wings harder, but arrows whizzed around them now. The Red Fangs were fast approaching. Soon they would be within flaming distance. Darek glanced from left to right. Pola and Rowena were still with him, and the mountains were drawing closer. If they could just make it into the thick of the mist, they would be safe. The Kradens could not pursue them there. But Zantor's heart was thumping rapidly now. How much longer could he endure?

Suddenly there was a burst of flame off to Darek's right. A Red Fang was gaining on him. The flame came again, closer. Darek cried out and dropped the reins as his sleeve caught fire.

"You okay?" Pola called.

"Yes!" Darek lurched wildly, trying to beat out the flames. He gripped Zantor's back with just his knees. Rowena flew in close and desperately tried to help him. The mist was thickening. Safety was so close!

"Go on!" Darek called to Rowena as he tried to shrug out of his burning shirt. "Whatever happens, just keep going!"

Then there was a searing pain in his leg. Darek stared mutely at the arrow shaft and the widening circle of red. Another arrow whizzed by, plunging into Zantor's neck. *"Eeeiiieee!"* Zantor screamed. And then they were falling. . . .

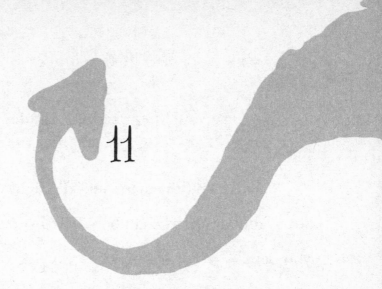

11

"WELL, WELL. GOOD MORNING."

Darek blinked to clear the haze from his eyes. A great fur-covered face stared down at him—a Kraden. He swallowed hard as the truth sank in. He had been captured again. He tried to move but winced in pain. Where was he? he wondered. He blinked again and looked around. He appeared to be in a cave of some sort, lit by torches on the walls.

"Who are you?" he asked the Kraden. "Where am I?"

"I am Azzon," the man said, "the rightful King of Krad. You are in my chambers. The Zynots brought you here."

"Zynots?" Darek mumbled.

"The little creatures who inhabit these mountains," the man explained. "They tell me you did them a kindness in the past. They wished to repay it."

Azzon nodded at Darek's leg. Darek looked down and saw that it had been wrapped in a plaster and bandaged.

"I have no memory of Zynots," he said. "Nor do I think it a kindness to deliver me back into Kraden hands."

"We are not in Kraden hands," a voice said. "Azzon is a friend."

Darek turned to see Rowena ducking through a low door. Pola followed her into the room.

"What are you two doing here?" Darek cried.

"We came back when you fell," Pola said.

"You fools!" Darek shook his head. "I told you to keep going!"

"It is well that they did not," Azzon said, "or they would be witless by now."

"We've already been through the mountains once," Darek argued. "The dragonsbreath did not harm us."

"Your lungs were clean and strong then," Azzon said. "You have lived too long in Krad now. You would not have made it this time."

Darek turned back to Pola and Rowena. "Zantor?" he asked. "What of Zantor?"

Pola and Rowena exchanged troubled glances.

"We don't know," Pola said quietly. "He disappeared after you fell."

Darek was silent, remembering the arrow.

"We freed our dragons," Rowena said, "and sent them after him. They'll find him."

Darek bit his lip, close to tears. Poor Zantor. Even if the other dragons did find him, how could they help if he was hurt or dying?

12

AZZON SAT BACK IN HIS CHAIR AND puffed slowly on a long clay pipe.

"There is not much more to tell," he said. "Kradens have always known of the existence of Zoriak, but it never troubled us. The few Zorians who came over the mountains were easily dealt with. The dragonsbreath potion quickly robbed them of their memories. In time, our Zorian

prisoners began to wonder if the old legends of Zoriak were even true."

"What about the Zynots?" Darek asked. "Who are they?"

Azzon laughed. "Your ancient kin," he said. "They are Zorians who lost their wits and their way in the Long Ago. In time, their bodies changed. Now they are prisoners of the mountain, able to breathe only dragonsbreath." Azzon pulled thoughtfully at the graying fur on his chin. "They are timid and foolish," he said, "but kind and good, too. I owe my life to them."

"Your life?" Rowena's brow wrinkled in disbelief. "How came the King of Krad to owe his life to Zynots?"

Azzon smiled sadly. "As you have seen," he said, "Kradens love blood sport, and I, their king, loved it better than any other. There was never a dragon fight bloody enough for me, a battle fierce enough, until the day my sons, Zahr and Rebbe, turned on each other. It was then, and only then, that I saw what I had done to them. I had raised them like Red Fangs, living to kill. When I tried to stop them from killing each other, they turned their fury on me."

Azzon took a long puff on his pipe and stared blankly at the walls. Darek swallowed hard and glanced at Pola and Rowena.

"I fled into these mountains, expecting to die," Azzon went on softly. "The Zynots found me and brought me here, to this cave beneath the mountains. The dragonsbreath cannot penetrate here. The Zynots have seen to my needs ever since, but it is a lonely life. They cannot tarry long in my world, nor I in theirs."

"Is there no way out?" Darek asked.

"Not for me," Azzon said. Then he leaned forward and rested his arms on his knees. "But perhaps for you. Before we speak of it, though, you must explain something to me."

"What is that?" Darek asked.

Azzon narrowed his eyes. "How did you get your memories back?"

Darek straightened in his seat. He dared not tell Azzon the truth. Who knew if Azzon could be trusted? He scrambled to come up with an answer that would satisfy Azzon without giving away the secret of Zantor's mind messages. What was it Azzon had said earlier? Something about a dragonsbreath potion?

"We didn't get our memories back," Darek

said quickly. "I . . . never really lost mine. I never drank the potion."

Azzon regarded him intently. "How can that be?"

Darek scrambled to think. His first memories of Krad were of a dark house, an old crone, and a guard. "The old woman gave me the potion," he explained, "but her house was dark and steamy. I tilted my head back and let it run out of the side of my mouth and down my neck. Then I pretended my memory was gone."

Azzon continued to stare hard at Darek. "How did you know the potion was meant to rob your memory?" he asked.

"The guard, Org, spoke of it."

After a time, Azzon nodded slowly. Then he rose and reached for a shelf on the wall. He took down a vial of green liquid and three small cups.

Then he turned to face Darek and the others again.

"Be assured," he said. *"I* will not be as careless

as Jazee."

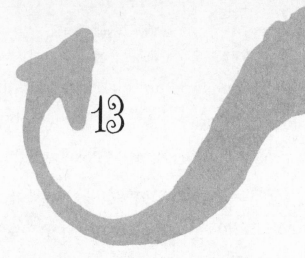

13

"BUT WAIT!" DAREK JUMPED UP. "You said you were a friend! Why are you sending us back?"

"I'm not sending you back," Azzon said. "I'm sending you home."

"Home?" Darek sat down again with a thump.

"Home?" Pola and Rowena echoed.

"Yes." Azzon nodded. "There is a tunnel. An underground passage to Zoriak. I will take you

there tonight. But you must go without your memories."

"But our friends . . . ," Pola started to protest.

"I cannot allow you to remember your friends," Azzon said. "You might try to help them."

"What's wrong with that?" Rowena asked. "Maybe we could help you, too."

Azzon shook his head. "If I wanted to help myself, I could go with you tonight," he said. "But I am old and wise. I know that things are not always as simple as they seem. Your world and mine are not ready to come together."

"Why not?" Darek asked. "Maybe we could make your world better."

"Better how?" Azzon asked. "By trying to destroy my sons? They may be cruel and evil, but they are still my sons. And what of the dragons of

Krad, the mighty Red Fangs? Would you kill them? Then you might as well kill the Zynots, for they will die anyway without the dragonsbreath. Have you the stomach for so much killing?"

Darek swallowed. He had no stomach for killing at all.

"Azzon is right," Rowena said sadly.

Pola nodded.

"But what of our friends?" Darek asked.

"If freedom means as much to your friends as it does to you," Azzon said, "they will find their own way."

14

DAREK, ROWENA, AND POLA STOOD
facing Azzon. The night air was soft and fragrant.
Zoriak's twin moons smiled down on them, wel-
coming them home. Azzon took out his vial.

"Drink," he commanded, pouring them each
a portion of the green liquid. "I have added
something to make you sleep. When you wake in
the morning, you will know your names, and you
will remember one another. But you will recall

nothing that has happened for at least two or three anums. . . ."

"Two or three anums!" Darek cried. "But . . . we won't even remember Zantor!"

"I'm sorry," Azzon said. "I cannot take the risk of allowing you to remember more. You must trust me. It is better this way." Then he smiled sadly and added, "Good life to you, my friends."

Darek, Pola, and Rowena slowly lifted their cups. "And to you, Azzon," they said softly. Then they tilted their heads and drank. Darek thought one last time about Arnod and the others.

"Farewell, my friends," he whispered. "Lord Eternal be with you." Then he thought about Zantor, and tears stung his eyes. "And with you, little friend," he whispered, "wherever you are."

✳ ✳ ✳

Darek opened his eyes and blinked. He was in a gently sloping field of zorgrass.

"What?" he whispered. "What am I doing here?" He rolled over and blinked again. "Pola? Rowena?" he said. "What are we all doing here?"

Pola and Rowena sat up and looked around.

"We're in the foothills of the Yellow Mountains!" Pola said.

"How did we get *here?*" Rowena asked.

"I don't know." Darek shook his head. "I do know one thing, though. Our parents are going to kill us."

"Uh-oh." Rowena pointed up at the sky. "You mean, if *they* don't kill us first!"

Three young Blue dragons were winging their way over the Yellow Mountains.

"Stay calm," Darek said. "Maybe they won't see us."

"They see us, all right!" Pola shouted. "Here they come!"

They all jumped to their feet, and Rowena and Pola started to run. But for some reason, Darek didn't. Instead he stood and watched the dragons dip lower, lower, until they landed right in front of him.

One of them, a male, stared at him with pain-filled eyes. *"Rrronk!"* he cried.

"Why, you're hurt!" Darek said. A broken arrow shaft protruded from the dragon's neck.

Darek approached carefully.

"Here," he said, grabbing the shaft. "Let me help." He pulled, and the arrow came out clean. The young dragon seemed tired but grateful. He laid his head gently on Darek's shoulder.

"Thrummm," he sang softly. *"Thrummm, thrummm, thrummm."*

"Why . . . they're friendly." Rowena cried out.

Darek turned to see her and Pola watching in amazement.

"Is that one all right?" Pola asked, approaching cautiously.

"I think so." Darek reached up and gently stroked the dragon's neck. "Poor thing. I wonder who shot him? This arrow isn't Zorian."

The little dragon pulled back. He tilted his head and looked deeply into Darek's eyes. For an instant, something seemed to pass between them, something too fast-moving, too vague to capture.

Something that felt strangely like a memory.

Jackie French Koller has been a storyteller since the sixth grade, when she amused her friends by spinning tales on the playground. She has also edited a children's newspaper, taught writing in public schools, and studied art. Ms. Koller lives in Groton, Massachusetts, with her husband and children.

FOLLOW THE TRAIL AND SOLVE MYSTERIES WITH FRANK AND JOE!

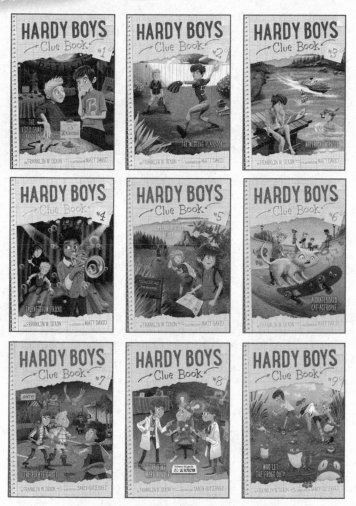

HardyBoysSeries.com

Nancy Drew
✷ CLUE BOOK ✷

Test your detective skills with Nancy and her best friends, Bess and George!

NancyDrew.com

EBOOK EDITIONS ALSO AVAILABLE
From Aladdin ✷ simonandschuster.com/kids